SWIFT'S IRISH WRITINGS

Swift's Irish Writings

Selected Prose and Poetry

Edited by
Carole Fabricant
and
Robert Mahony

palgrave
macmillan

First published in 2010 by
PALGRAVE MACMILLAN®
in the United States—a division of St. Martin's Press LLC,
175 Fifth Avenue, New York, NY 10010.

Where this book is distributed in the UK, Europe and the rest of the world,
this is by Palgrave Macmillan, a division of Macmillan Publishers Limited,
registered in England, company number 785998, of Houndmills,
Basingstoke, Hampshire RG21 6XS.

Palgrave Macmillan is the global academic imprint of the above companies
and has companies and representatives throughout the world.

Palgrave® and Macmillan® are registered trademarks in the United States,
the United Kingdom, Europe and other countries.

ISBN: 978–0–312–22888–0

Library of Congress Cataloging-in-Publication Data

Swift, Jonathan, 1667–1745.
    Swift's Irish writings : selected prose and poetry / edited by Carole
Fabricant, Robert Mahony.
        p. cm.
    This edition presents Jonathan Swift's most important Irish writings in
both prose and verse, together with introductions and annotations.
        ISBN 978–0–312–22888–0 (hardback)
        1. Ireland—Literary collections. 2. Swift, Jonathan, 1667–1745—
Knowledge—Ireland. I. Fabricant, Carole. II. Mahony, Robert. III. Title.

PR3722.F33 2010
828'.509—dc22   2009047074

A catalogue record of the book is available from the British Library.

Design by Newgen Imaging Systems (P) Ltd., Chennai, India.

First edition: June 2010

10 9 8 7 6 5 4 3 2 1

Printed in the United States of America.

CONTENTS

Part 2   Poems

NOTE ON THE TEXT

Most of the texts in this volume are based on the George Faulkner four-volume edition of Swift's *Works* published in Dublin in 1735: specifically volume II, "His Poetical Writings," and volume IV, "His Papers relating to *Ireland*." Unless otherwise noted, the copy-text for a particular work is this edition. Where another copy-text has been used, it is identified in the headnote to the work in question.

The texts herein basically reproduce the original eighteenth-century editions, retaining their spelling, punctuation, and use of italics and capitalization. Modernizing such features has been eschewed in order to avoid producing a flattened-out, homogenized text that seems to exist in an historical limbo. These original textual features reveal much about the writing and printing practices in the eighteenth century, and in certain instances reflect aspects of Swift's personal style: his use of typography (especially italics and capitalization) to emphasize points in his argument and of particular spellings and word forms to suggest colloquial or dialectal speech, to underscore puns, and so on. On rare occasions, however, very minor alterations of the original printing (especially regarding punctuation) have been made to ensure a fully readable and understandable text.

The volume has been divided into two sections, the first presenting his prose writings; the second, his poetry. Within each section the works have been organized chronologically, according to the date of composition. In those instances where this is not known for certain, a conjectural date, based on both internal textual evidence and historical data, is provided and indicated with a question mark on the contents page.

During Swift's lifetime the beginning of the year was computed from March 25 instead of January 1. All dates indicated in this volume adhere to current practice; hence a work of Swift's that according to the title page was published, say, on February 10, 1723 is recorded here as February 10, 1724.

Chronology

1667   November 30, Jonathan Swift is born in Hoey's Court, near Dublin Castle, to Abigail Swift (née Erick), widow of Jonathan Swift, Swift's father and namesake, who had died a few months earlier.

1673   Begins his education at Kilkenny College.

1682   April, admitted to Trinity College, Dublin, where his undergraduate years are marked by a number of minor breaches of college discipline.

1686   Graduates from Trinity "ex speciali gratia," by special grace—probably suggesting not so much academic insufficiency as his being allowed to dispense with one or more of the normal qualifications for graduation, perhaps because of family connections.

1689   James II, who had fled to France in late 1688, returns from exile to Ireland, calls a parliament, and rules the country with partiality toward Catholics. Many Protestants leave for England or Scotland, Swift among them, who travels to visit his mother, now permanently resettled in Leicester, and then takes up employment as secretary to Sir William Temple in Moor Park, Temple's estate in Surrey. While there he meets Esther Johnson, a ward of Temple's and thirteen years his junior, who becomes his lifelong friend and the subject of poems addressed to "Stella."

1692   Takes the M.A. degree at Oxford as a step toward ordination as a minister.

1695   January 13, ordained a priest of the Church of Ireland in Dublin, and at the end of this month is made prebendary of Kilroot, near Carrickfergus, Co. Antrim, an area where Presbyterians greatly outnumber Anglicans. He hates the place, and by the end of the year returns to Temple at Moor Park.

1699   January 27, Temple dies at Moor Park; Swift lingers as his literary executor and secures appointment in August as chaplain to the Earl of Berkeley, one of the Lords Justices chosen to rule Ireland during the absence of the Lord Lieutenant.

1700   February 20, given the parish of Laracor, near Trim, Co. Meath, as Vicar. Later that year he is installed as prebendary of Laracor in St. Patrick's Cathedral, Dublin.

1701   Accompanies Lord Berkeley to England in April; Esther Johnson moves to Dublin in August, and Swift returns to Dublin in September.

1702   February 16, receives the Doctorate in Divinity from Trinity
         College, Dublin. Visits England frequently during the decade,
         on official or private business.

1704   10 May, *A Tale of a Tub* and *Battel of the Books* published in
         London.

1707–09 In England for his lengthiest visit since his Moor Park days, to
         represent the interests of the Irish clergy, and especially to seek
         remission of the "First Fruits" (a tax paid by the Church of Ireland
         to the Crown), but finds the Whig government in London unco-
         operative. He writes and publishes *The Bickerstaff Papers.*

1710   April 24, death of Swift's mother. Queen Anne dismisses her Whig
         ministers in August, replacing them with a Tory ministry led by
         Robert Harley and Henry St. John. The Tories win by a landslide
         in the general election in October. Swift returns to London to
         represent the Irish clergy and quickly finds common purpose with
         the Tory ministers, who befriend him and convince him to write
         The Examiner on their behalf. He becomes involved in London's
         literary scene and publishes satiric pieces in *The Tatler.*

1711   February 27, publication of *Miscellanies in Prose and Verse*; final
         number of *The Examiner* appears, 14 June; publication of Swift's
         Conduct of the Allies, very influential in promoting the peace
         treaty ending the War of the Spanish Succession, November 27.

1713   June 13, consecrated Dean of St. Patrick's Cathedral, Dublin;
         Swift had hoped to be rewarded for his efforts on behalf of the
         Tory government with a bishopric in England, but his notoriety
         as (assumed) author of *A Tale of a Tub* made it too difficult for
         the ministry even to persuade the Queen to name him to a bish-
         op's see in Ireland. The Deanship of St. Patrick's is nominated
         not by the monarch but by the Lord Lieutenant of Ireland,
         James Butler, 2nd Duke of Ormonde, who is friendly to Swift.
         After his installation, Swift quickly returns to England. He
         meets regularly with other members of the Scriblerus Club
         (Alexander Pope, John Gay, Dr. Arbuthnot) to satirize abuses in
         learning.

1714   August 1, Queen Anne dies and the Tory ministry collapses;
         with the new reign of George I the Whigs are again (and remain
         until 1760) ascendant. Swift hurries to Ireland to take up his
         post as Dean of St. Patrick's after swearing formal allegiance to
         the new king, and thereafter returns to England only twice, for
         extended visits. In November Esther Vanhomrigh (pr. "van-um-
         mery"), whom Swift dubbed "Vanessa" when they became
         friends in London, takes up residence in Celbridge, outside
         Dublin. Their relationship, which had perhaps become romantic
         in England, deteriorates in Ireland.

1715   May, Swift makes the first of many extended visits to Gaulstown,
         Co. Westmeath, the seat of the Rochfort family.

1720   May, publication of *A Proposal for the Universal Use of Irish Manufacture*, timed to coincide with the birthday of George I; the government regards its argument for Irish economic self-reliance as seditious and the printer is prosecuted, but the grand jury refuses to find him guilty or even incriminate the pamphlet. Swift spends much of the summer in Loughgall, Co. Armagh, at the home of his friend, Robert Cope.

1721   Mid-June to October, makes long visit to the Rochforts at Gaulstown.

1722   Makes a lengthy summer journey through the northern counties, leaving Dublin at the end of May, spending some time at his friend Thomas Sheridan's house at Quilca, Co. Cavan and returning in mid-October to Dublin.

1723   June 2, Vanessa dies. Swift leaves Dublin on June 3 for a southern and western tour of Ireland, first heading southwest toward Cork, then west and north toward Galway, and then returning to Dublin in September. At Christmastime, he travels to Quilca with Stella and her friend Rebecca Dingley.

1724   March, appearance of the first of the *Drapier's Letters* against the patent granted to William Wood to mint small copper coinage for Ireland. Four more *Letters* appear at intervals throughout the year, and Wood's patent is finally surrendered in August 1725. Swift's exaltation as national folk hero and "Hibernian Patriot" dates from this time. Throughout the following decade he will write numerous tracts and broadsides attacking Britain's colonialist policies vis-à-vis Ireland.

1726   March, begins a visit to England lasting until August, staying primarily at the Twickenham estate of Alexander Pope and preparing *Gulliver's Travels* for publication in London (it appears 28 October).

1727   April, begins his final visit to England, mostly with Pope in Twickenham, until September; delayed by weather in Holyhead, in Wales, while travelling back to Ireland, details of which trip are recorded in his *Holyhead Journal*.

1728   January 28, Stella dies and is buried in St. Patrick's Cathedral. Early in June, Swift makes the first of three successive visits to the seat of Sir Arthur Acheson near Market Hill, Co. Armagh, which provide the setting and material for over a dozen poems.

1729   June to October, visits the Achesons in Market Hill; for a while, Swift considers buying property nearby, but thinks better of it. October, publication of *A Modest Proposal*, following almost two years of famine conditions in Ireland.

1731   June, visits Market Hill for the last time. November, likely composition of *Verses on the Death of Dr. Swift* (published 1739).

1734–35   The printer George Faulkner proposes, and then Swift oversees, a collected edition of his works in verse and prose in four volumes. In later years Faulkner continues to add volumes to the set.

1735 November to Christmas, visits Sheridan in Co. Cavan. This is his final extended visit outside Dublin.

1740 May, makes his last will.

1742 August, given to the care of guardians because he is "of unsound mind and memory," and unable any longer to look after his own affairs.

1745 October 19, dies in the Deanery of St. Patrick's and is buried in the Cathedral alongside Stella, under the famous epitaph he composed for himself.

INTRODUCTION

This volume brings together a wide range of Jonathan Swift's writings on Ireland, including works never before anthologized, hence until now available only to specialists in the field in eighteenth-century and standard editions. A collection such as this addresses the need created by our changing perception of Swift in recent years, from a canonical English Neoclassical writer, an Augustan satirist sharing the stage with John Dryden and Alexander Pope, to an Anglo-Irish writer whose perspective and literary output were profoundly influenced by his inextricable ties to his native Ireland and by his status as a colonial subject. As a result of this new perception, Swift has become an increasingly important figure in certain growing fields of academic inquiry such as Irish Studies, Global Studies, and Postcolonial Studies.

This edition contains only works whose explicit and primary focus is on some aspect of Irish politics, society, or daily life. These, however, are not the only texts that reveal the impact of Ireland on Swift's thought and writings. On the contrary, evidence of this impact may be seen to varying degrees in virtually all of his works, including *A Tale of a Tub* and *Gulliver's Travels*. Recent criticism has gone beyond the latter's specific, long-recognized references to Ireland to consider the whole of the *Travels* as an example, both generically and ideologically, of the early Anglo-Irish novel;[1] and attention has of late been directed to the *Tale*'s significant Irish dimension.[2] Thus the pieces in this volume not only illuminate Swift's specific engagement with Irish affairs but also shed light on his entire corpus of writings, inviting the reader to view even his most "classic" canonical works in a new and contextually richer framework, as artistic expressions of a life that was rooted in the rhythms and idioms of Ireland.

That Swift's was an Irish life is indisputable on a very literal level. Born in Hoey's Court off Werburgh Street in Dublin in 1667, Swift was raised and educated in his native country, going off to Kilkenny School sixty miles southwest of the capital at age six, and matriculating at Trinity College, Dublin when he was fifteen. He did not leave Ireland until the age of twenty-one, when, having obtained his B.A., he fled to England to escape the

---

[1] See Aileen Douglas, "The Novel before 1800," in *The Cambridge Companion to the Irish Novel*, ed. John Wilson Foster (Cambridge: Cambridge University Press, 2006), 25–28; and Terry Eagleton, *Heathcliff and the Great Hunger: Studies in Irish Culture* (London: Verso, 1995), 145–225 ("Form and Ideology in the Anglo-Irish Novel").

[2] See Andrew Carpenter, "'A Tale of a Tub' as an Irish Text," *Swift Studies* 20 (2005): 30–40; and David Deeming, "The 'Tale,' Temple, and Swift's Irish Aesthetic," in *Representations of Swift*, ed. Brian A. Connery (Newark: University of Delaware Press, 2002), 25–40.

turmoil of the war then being waged in Ireland between the forces of James II and William of Orange. He spent a good part of the following years in England, first as amanuensis to Sir William Temple at Moor Park in Surrey, and later as an emissary of the Church of Ireland, sent to obtain remission of certain ecclesiastical fees paid to the Crown (known as "the First Fruits"), although he returned to Ireland on several occasions during this period, most significantly to be ordained a priest in Dublin (1695), after which he took up his first church living in Kilroot, near Belfast, and subsequently was presented to the vicarage of Laracor, near Dublin (1700). The heyday of his sojourn in England was the period 1710–14, when he worked for the Tory ministry under Robert Harley (1st Earl of Oxford), writing pro-government essays for the periodical *The Examiner* while taking advantage of London's lively cultural life by participating in several literary clubs (most famously, the Scriblerus Club) and collaborating in exercises of wit with the likes of John Gay, Dr. Arbuthnot, and Pope. The collapse of the Tory government and the death of Queen Anne in the summer of 1714 necessitated Swift's return to Dublin, where he took up his post as Dean of St. Patrick's Cathedral, an office he occupied for the next thirty-one years until his death. During that time (until the irreversible decay of his mental faculties in 1742) he conscientiously carried out his clerical duties while pursuing a hectic, often controversial, career of political activism, leaving Ireland during that period only twice, to visit England in 1726 and 1727. By the time Swift died on October 19, 1745, he had been an inhabitant of Ireland for more than sixty years.

But the claim that Swift's was a distinctively Irish life does not rest merely on the fact that he was born in Ireland and spent most of his life there. Swift did not simply reside in Dublin; he imaginatively appropriated its environs and made them his own, giving them pride of place in many of his writings (both prose and poetry) and transforming the city into a worthy subject for political and literary consideration, even when (as was so often the case) the picture he drew of it was far from attractive. An inveterate walker, he daily wandered through the streets of the Liberties (the area just west of the old city walls), getting to know the weavers of the nearby Coombes (whose interests he espoused in several prose tracts and poems) and the beggars entreating passersby in the vicinity of the cathedral. He also had a chance to interact with other humble inhabitants of the area when, eschewing the private carriages to which men of his rank were accustomed, he used a common Irish stage coach as a means of public conveyance.[3] Moreover, as an enthusiastic horseman, Swift explored parts of Ireland far beyond the English Pale, riding through far-flung regions of Ulster in the spring of 1722 (going "where I do not know, nor what Cabbins or Bogs are in my Way" [C 2:433]) and traversing

---

[3] See *The Correspondence of Jonathan Swift*, 5 vols., ed. Harold Williams (2nd ed.; Oxford: Clarendon Press, 1958), 2:393; hereafter abbreviated as *C* followed by page number in the text. F. Elrington Ball conjectures that this coach "was probably of most primitive construction" and notes that this is the earliest instance he knows of where a man of Swift's rank made use of such a humble form of transport; see *The Correspondence of Jonathan Swift*, 6 vols., ed. Ball (London: Bell, 1910–14), 3:85, n.3.

remote Gaelic-speaking areas during his three-month journey to Cork and
other regions of southwest Ireland in the summer of 1723. Witnessing firsthand the way the rural poor lived, he could later speak with authority of their
deprivations in his political tracts, as when he described "The Families of
Farmers, who pay great Rents, living in Filth and Nastiness upon Butter-milk
and Potatoes, without a Shoe or Stocking to their Feet; or a House so convenient as an *English* Hog-sty, to receive them" (*A Short View of the State of
Ireland*). Supplemented by periodic visits to the houses of friends located in
counties as far afield as Westmeath, Cavan, and Armagh, Swift's travels
throughout Ireland contributed to anything but a "short" (except in the sense
of "close-up") view of the country and underscored his determination to fully
inhabit the land to which he had been consigned by birth and fate.

Swift's was a colonial as well as an Irish life: a point no less essential for
understanding his work even though somewhat more contentious. The critical controversies surrounding this issue have coalesced around two questions: Whether Ireland was in fact a colony of England in the eighteenth
century; and if so, whether Swift belonged to the class of colonizers or colonized: a question that foregrounds Swift's hyphenated identity as an Anglo-
Irishman, treated as subordinate by the English but occupying a position of
dominance over the native Catholic population. Debates related to the first
question were fuelled by those historians often referred to as "revisionists,"
who challenged the orthodoxies of Irish nationalist historiography, arguing,
for example, for the need to situate the British-Irish relationship within a
broader European framework, and suggesting models other than colonialism (e.g., the political structure of the *Ancien Régime*) to characterize this
relationship.[4] Objections to viewing Ireland as a colony were often based on
the fact that Ireland did not conform to supposedly "typical" colonial examples such as India and the Caribbean. As one historian has argued, Ireland
"was neither a physically distant nor a racially separate possession. It was a
neighbouring island, whose inhabitants were European in physical appearance, culture, and religion. And it is this which makes the colonial label less
than satisfactory."[5] But as various postcolonial theorists have pointed out,
there is no such thing as a "pure" or prototypical colony, measured against
which all others are found wanting (or judged to be something else).
Colonialism can take many different forms, and as a historical process it is
capable of changing over time. Depending on whether it functions through
administrative rule from afar or via plantations or settler communities nearer
at hand, it assumes different political manifestations while in all cases
predicated on a system of domination and exploitation (through extraction
of natural resources, restrictions on trade, etc.).

We can perhaps most fruitfully think about eighteenth-century Ireland
within a transatlantic (hence ultimately global) rather than a strictly

[4] See Ciaran Brady, ed., *Interpreting Irish History: The Debate on Historical Revisionism* (Dublin and Portland, OR: Irish Academic Press, 1994).
[5] S.J. Connolly, *Religion, Law and Power: The Making of Protestant Ireland 1660–1760* (Oxford: Clarendon Press, 1995 [1992]), 111.

Anglo-Irish or narrowly European framework, since it was to the west that Britain looked to further its imperial designs and that its flows of capital moved. As Joe Cleary observes in making a case for Ireland's connections to the West Indies and the American colonies during this period, "All of these colonial sites were commercially orientated towards the emerging Atlantic economy," even though they were barred from trading with one another by colonial mercantilist policies that forced their trade "to be channelled through the British and Spanish imperial centres."[6] Swift's Irish tracts, with their repeated attacks on the Navigation and Woollen Acts and their wry allusions to England's "just Claim to the Balance of Trade on their Side with the whole World" (*Answer to the Craftsman*),[7] demonstrate that Swift understood all too well the nature of Britain's mercantile policies and her imperial ambitions at the expense of Ireland, just as the tracts' occasional references to Irish emigration to the Americas recognize the economic forces that simultaneously subjugated and connected Britain's colonies on both sides of the Atlantic.

Swift may have acknowledged the fact of Ireland's colonial status but he never accepted the idea of it. On the contrary, in many of his tracts he fiercely rejected the notion that Ireland was a colony, most notably in *Drapier's Letter IV*, where he invokes the act of 1541 giving Henry VIII the title of "King of Ireland" and making Ireland a "sovereign Kingdom" in order to affirm Ireland's equality with England under the Crown. He shared this belief with most of his fellow Anglo-Irishmen, who considered themselves in no way inferior to their brethren across the channel, with whom they assumed ethnic and cultural ties. Some revisionists have used this fact as another argument against viewing Ireland as a colony, in effect taking Irish Protestants' view of themselves as a measure of their actual status. This was not a mistake Swift ever made. His firm belief that Ireland was no more a "depending Kingdom" than England went hand in hand with his clear-sighted realization that Ireland was indeed being treated as such—even worse, being literally transformed into one through a series of repressive laws passed in London. This was the conundrum facing Swift that he could neither tolerate nor resolve: Ireland was at one and the same time a nation entitled to the full rights and privileges accorded a kingdom under the British Crown, and an inferior colony with drastically circumscribed powers, whose only *raison d'être* was to enhance the wealth and power of the "mother country." What was the ontological status of this Ireland that was both a place and a "no-place" (though the very opposite of a "utopia" in the usual sense of the word)? How was one to characterize the irreducible contradiction at its core? Swift's answer was to portray a country so strange and unlike any other that it defied definition, resisting all known descriptive categories as

[6] Cleary, "'Misplaced Ideas'? Colonialism, Location, and Dislocation in Irish Studies," in *Ireland and Postcolonial Theory*, ed. Clare Carroll and Patricia King (Notre Dame: University of Notre Dame Press, 2003), 32–33.

[7] *The Prose Works of Jonathan Swift*, 14 vols., ed. Herbert Davis (Oxford: Blackwell, 1939–74), 12:177. All references to prose works of Swift that are not included in this volume are to this edition, and are hereafter indicated by a *P* followed by page number in the text.

well as common comparisons with other (particularly European) nations—a place marked by deformity ("where each of the inhabitants had but one eye, one leg, and one hand") and where universal principles ceased to operate (see *Maxims Controlled in Ireland*). Even in those implied or oblique analogies with other colonized or enslaved peoples (the Indians of colonial America and the Africans), the Irish are shown to be in an unenviable category of their own; thus the situation of the Irish in being denied basic freedoms (of trade, manufacture, etc.) "is an Absurdity, that a *wild Indian* would be ashamed of" (*An Answer to a Paper, called a Memorial*). The simultaneous confirmation and denial of Ireland's colonial status that runs throughout Swift's tracts generates an inherently ironic rhetoric—a rhetoric of alternating excess and silence, of double meanings and wry comments punctuated by logical gaps and abrupt breaks ("But my Heart is too heavy to continue this Irony longer..." [*A Short View of the State of Ireland*]).

Granted Swift's opposition to Britain's interventions in Irish political and economic affairs, the question remains: Which group(s) in Irish society was he speaking for, or whose interests was he representing, in his vehement protests against the attitudes and policies of the British authorities? Many would have it that Swift's oppositional stance was a limited one, restricted to defending the rights of the small set of Anglicans of English ancestry (constituting perhaps 15 percent of the total Irish population) who dominated the (albeit severely hobbled) Irish Parliament and governed the operations of the Church of Ireland—in short, that Swift was only concerned with asserting the rights of the elite group that Edmund Burke would later revile as "the Protestant Ascendancy."[8] These critics see Swift the political activist as the voice of what is often referred to as "colonial nationalism" in Ireland—a form of pro-Irish sentiment that had little to do with the nationalist movements later in the century but that instead merely expressed the outrage of those who took for granted their own superiority and therefore deeply resented being treated as inferiors.[9] Other critics view Swift's denunciations of British policies in more expansive terms, as expressions of an Irish (proto-)nationalism not confined to the narrow interests of a small minority at a circumscribed point in time, but rather, reflective of a broader critique of colonial domination, abuse of power, or political and economic injustice. D.G. Boyce, for example, argues that "it is misleading...to refer to Protestants' sentiment as 'colonial nationalism', as if it were in some way to be distinguished from the mainstream of the Irish nationalist tradition....What is commonly called 'colonial nationalism' is really an important strand in the complicated skein of Irish nationalism."[10]

---

[8] See in particular Burke's letter to Richard Burke, *post* February 19, 1792, in *The Writings and Speeches of Edmund Burke*, ed. Paul Langford (Oxford: Clarendon Press, 1981–c.2000), 9:642–44.

[9] See, e.g., J.G. Simms, *Colonial Nationalism, 1698–1776: Molyneux's "The Case of Ireland...Stated* (Cork: Mercier Press, 1976). This term is also used by R.F. Foster in *Modern Ireland 1600–1972* (New York and London: Penguin, 1989); see in particular ch. 8, "The Ascendancy Mind" (167–94).

[10] Boyce, *Nationalism in Ireland*, 3rd Edition (London and New York: Routledge, 1995 [1982]), 107. Joep Leerssen more or less agrees with this assessment as it applies to Swift while

It is not difficult to find evidence of Swift's influence on subsequent Irish nationalists from Henry Grattan (who invoked the "Spirit of Swift" in a published revision of his famous parliamentary speech on behalf of Irish independence) to James Connolly, who deemed *A Modest Proposal* "the most vehement and bitter indictment of the society of [its] day" and used passages from it to support his condemnation of the capitalist-colonialist system responsible for Ireland's chronic famine.[11] What these later nationalists would have found particularly congenial in Swift's work was his conception and promotion of an Irish "patriotism" that placed the highest premium on loyalty to one's native country and that was clearly differentiated from all other demands on one's loyalty (such as those of the British Crown). In his clerical capacity Swift used the pulpit to instill this idea in his parishioners, impressing upon them the "duty of loving our country" while hastening to explain that "by the love of our country, I do not mean loyalty to our King, for that is a duty of another nature." Warning that "all offences against our own country . . . are ungrateful and unnatural," he chose matricide as the most fitting emblem for violations of this patriotic duty (Sermon, *Doing Good*). As the Drapier he echoed this sentiment to explain why "a Tradesman hid in Privacy and Silence should *cry out* when the Life and Being of his Political *Mother* are attempted before his Face" (*Letter V*). His ironic admonition in *A Modest Proposal* (repeated in nonironic contexts elsewhere in his writings) to be "*a little cautious not to sell our Country and Consciences for nothing*" expresses a theme—of betrayal and venality within a nationalist context—that was to become central to Irish political and imaginative literature in the generations to come.

Several factors help explain Swift's ability to produce writings that went beyond the confines of "colonial nationalism" to speak for larger segments of the Irish population. A major one was the fact that it was not the Catholics but the Dissenters who bore the brunt of Swift's antagonism and in his view posed the greatest threat to the institutions of Irish society. Religious fanaticism and fundamentalism, not the supposedly insidious machinations of the papacy and its followers, were the objects of his apprehension and aversion. While he hardly held the Catholic religion in high esteem and never advocated for an extension of Catholics' rights, he forcefully challenged the anti-Catholic paranoia so prevalent at the time by attacking those who portrayed the Catholics as a disgruntled and restive group composed largely of Jacobites (supporters of the Pretender, the exiled Stuart claimant to the throne), ready to rebel against Protestant rule

---

viewing the "Patriot" movement in eighteenth-century Ireland as generally reflective of a broader tradition of liberal and philanthropic values centered on the idea of "citizenship"; see *Mere Irish and Fíor-Ghael: Studies in the Idea of Irish Nationality, Its Development and Literary Expression prior to the Nineteenth Century* (1986; Notre Dame: University of Notre Dame Press in assoc. with Field Day, 1997), 296–315; and "Anglo-Irish Patriotism and Its European Context: Notes towards a Reassessment," *Eighteenth-Century Ireland* 3 (1988): 7–24.

[11] See excerpt from "Speech in the Irish Parliament, 16 April 1782," in *The Field Day Anthology of Irish Writing*, 3 vols., ed. Seamus Deane, et al. (Derry: Field Day Publications; distributed by Norton, 1991), 1:919; and Connolly, *Labour in Irish History* (Dublin: New Books Publications, 1983), 14.

the moment an occasion presented itself. The proponents of this view appear in Swift's tracts as a disreputable band of demagogues and opportunists, a "Race of small Politicians" who spread reports of "chimerical Invasions" by the Pretender "in order to do a seasonable Jobb" (*The Presbyterians Plea of Merit* [*P* 12:272]). Swift tells an imagined English M.P. that the alleged formidability of the *"Popish* Interest" in Ireland is "nothing but Misrepresentation and Mistake," assuring him that, like women and children, the Catholics are "out of all Capacity of doing any Mischief." To vividly underscore his point, he subverts the then common characterization of Catholicism as a savage beast readying to rend apart the Protestant church by describing it as "a *Lyon* at [our] Feet, bound fast with three or four Chains, his Teeth drawn out, and his Claws pared to the Quick" (*A Letter from a Member of the House of Commons in Ireland…Concerning the Test Act*). This is a message he communicated to his Irish audience as well, including members of his own congregation when, in his sermon *On Brotherly Love*, he asserted that the Catholics have been "put out of all visible Possibility of hurting us" (*P* 9:172).

On several occasions Swift goes even beyond this primarily negative defense of the Catholics to stress their long-demonstrated fidelity to the British Crown and obedience to government authority. He recounts, for example, that during his trip through the southern parts of Ireland in 1723, he spoke with many Catholic priests in the parishes he passed through and "found them every where abounding in Professions of Loyalty to the late King *George*" at the same time that he learned of the hardships they suffered under previous English administrations (*The Presbyterians Plea of Merit* [*P* 12:273]). Adopting the persona of a Catholic in *Reasons Humbly Offered to the Parliament of Ireland, for Repealing the Sacramental Test*, he emphasizes the "innumerable Oppressions" suffered by the Catholics at the hands of successive waves of English settlers (referred to as "Invaders") and insists that, in contrast to the Dissenters, "The *Catholicks* were always Defenders of Monarchy." Thus, while Swift never explicitly called for repeal of the Penal Laws restricting the rights of Irish Catholics, his frequently expressed view of their political character and diminished status in Irish society at the very least made a powerful case for the gratuitousness, if not indeed injustice, of enacting any further laws (as was periodically proposed) to broaden the restrictions placed on them. His generally benign view of the native Catholics allowed him to imagine their inclusion in the "Whole People of Ireland" whose interests he defended as the Drapier—who, one might note, concludes his *Fourth Letter* with a plea to "to be left to possess our *Brogues* and *Potatoes in Peace*," thus symbolically evoking items most closely associated with Catholics, not Protestants, and suggesting bonds of cross-sectarian identification and solidarity that could only fully blossom later in the century.

Another factor behind Swift's ability to speak in his writings for a broader range of interests than those signified by the label "colonial nationalism" is that of class. Although technically belonging to the Protestant elite in Ireland and distantly related to distinguished members within it, Swift was born into somewhat constricted circumstances—his father having died before he was born and his mother having limited resources of her own—so that throughout his formative years he was dependent on the generosity of others (especially, a wealthy uncle) for his educational and related needs. His status in the Temple household was hardly a privileged one—indeed, although he performed many indispensable tasks for his employer, his tenure at Moor Park was largely that of a glorified servant or secretary—and the necessity to support himself made him turn to the church for hoped-for career advancement and for a desirable preferment that never materialized. The position he ultimately obtained, that of Dean of St. Patrick's Cathedral in Dublin, was a relatively modest one, capable of supporting a comfortable but far from affluent existence, and limited in the power it could exert within the Church of Ireland. Swift's experience with financial need and dependency no doubt influenced his ability, rare for someone in his position at the time, to view matters through the eyes of the have-nots in society, and helps explain the relationships he forged with the humble denizens of the Liberties surrounding St. Patrick's—those whom, as the Drapier, he calls "my faithful Friends the common People" (*Letter V*) and who, in the guise of the "Jolly boys of St. Kevans, St. Patrick's, Donore,/And Smithfield," he depicts as co-conspirators in a plan to exact street justice from a bully lawman (*The Yahoo's Overthrow*, 1–2). The latter poem underscores the literary ramifications of Swift's felt kinship with the lower classes, which produced numerous broadsides and other pieces representing a popular satiric tradition, permeated with the rhythms of Dublin street slang and rich in dialectal expression. The Drapier's reference to "my *Brethren*, the Makers of *Songs* and *Ballads*" (*Letter V*) was therefore as applicable to Swift himself as it was to his tradesman-persona. In later life Swift would often reaffirm this bond, telling one correspondent that Ireland is a country "where I have no friends but Citizens and the rabble" (*C* 4:409) and explaining to another, "I am only a favourite of my old friends the rabble; and I return their love, because I know none else who deserve it" (*C* 4:537).

To be sure, such statements require qualification. The contradictions inherent in Swift's hyphenated identity as an Anglo-Irishman and in his position as an official within a ruling-class institution precluded any simple, uncomplicated identification with the lower classes. Thus Swift devotes a significant portion of his sermon, *Causes of the Wretched Condition of Ireland*, to castigating the behavior of servants, and he has no compunctions about attacking an opponent by emphasizing his inferior familial connections—Sir Thomas Prendergast is ridiculed as the "Worthy Offspring of a Shoeboy" (*A Character...of the Legion Club*, l. 68); the politician Richard Tighe is mocked for descending from a baker (*Tom Mullinex and Dick*, l. 12); and Lord Joshua Allen is reviled for behavior that befits the offspring of a line of "Butchers" (*Traulus, The Second Part*, 23–42).[12] Nevertheless, the fact remains that Swift's relations with the lower classes were never as hostile or contentious as his relations with members of the upper class in Irish Protestant society. (Indeed, the satiric targets just mentioned all occupied positions of social or political authority, and it is that which is the primary object of the author's disgust.) At various

---

[12] See *The Poems of Jonathan Swift*, 3 vols., ed. Harold Williams (2nd ed.; Oxford: Clarendon Press, 1958).

points in his life Swift found himself in sometimes fierce conflict with prominent figures in the Irish Parliament, top officials of the judiciary, wealthy landowners, and (not least) the bishops of his own church, whom he frequently
castigated for their indifference to the miserable conditions in Ireland and
their abusive treatment of the lower clergy: "Our Bishops puft up with Wealth
and with Pride,/To Hell on the Backs of the Clergy wou'd ride…" (*On the
Irish Bishops*, 17–18). Continuing disputes with a rich landowner who lived
near him in Laracor elicited an angry letter from Swift that noted, "This odd
way of dealing among you folks of great estates in Land and money, although
I have been used to, I cannot well reconcile myself with" (*C* 3:366). Experiences
such as this one shaped his generic portrayal of the country squire who "grows
rich by Avarice, Injustice, Oppression" and who is "a Tyrant in the
Neighbourhood over Slaves and Beggars, whom he calleth his Tenants" (*The
Intelligencer, No. IX* [*P* 12:53]). Swift's use here of the highly charged term
"Slaves" in a specifically class-based context underscores his understanding of
the larger political implications of the relationship between rich and poor.

These implications are explored at greater length in *The Intelligencer, No.
XIX*, where Swift speaks on behalf of the working poor in the north of
Ireland, through the persona of an enlightened country gentleman: "But the
Sufferings of me, and those of my Rank, are Trifles in Comparison of what
the meaner Sort [peddlers, shopkeepers, farmers, handicraftsmen, day labor-
ers, etc.] undergo;…those poor Men for want of good Payment, are forced
to take up their *Oat-meal*, and other Necessaries of Life, at almost double
Value; and, consequently, are not able to discharge half their Score; especially under the Scarceness of *Corn*, for two Years past; and the melancholy
Disappointment of the present *Crop*" (*The Intelligencer, No. XIX*). This
sympathetic awareness of the life of "the meaner Sort" helps to explain why,
in the fictive or satiric worlds that Swift creates, he tends to move downward,
not upward, on the socioeconomic ladder, inhabiting the realms and speaking through the personae of servants, maids, footmen, tradesmen, and the
like. This sense of connection with the "lower orders" was evident in his life
as well as in his writings. Thus, despite his reputed harshness toward servants, he was disconsolate over the death of his own servant, Alexander
McGee—"I have lost one of my best friends," he confided to a
correspondent—and he "bestowed a gentleman's funeral on McGee's body,"
erecting a tablet commemorating his virtues in St. Patrick's Cathedral.[13]

The point here is not to romanticize or sentimentalize Swift's relationship
to the underclass. Indeed, it is precisely our tendency to conceive of such a
relationship in overly sentimental terms that makes it difficult for us to appreciate Swift's attitude and behavior in this regard. If we are looking for evidence of his "great love for his fellow man" or undying compassion for the
sufferings of others, we will be disappointed in our quest and unable to
understand—in fact, literally unable to *see*—Swift's connections to those less

---

[13] See Irvin Ehrenpreis, *Swift: The Man, His Works, and the Age*, 3 vols. (Cambridge, MA:
Harvard University Press, 1962–1983), 3:323.

fortunate than himself. Swift's dissatisfaction with prevailing conditions ran very deep, and in the anger he directed at broad sections of Irish society—bishops, landlords, judges, courtiers, members of parliament—the poor were certainly not exempt. The highest authorities in the land could not escape the infection Swift saw all around him, and neither could the lowest segments of the populace. In that sense high and low were on equal footing for Swift, subject to the same moral diseases and similarly prone to act in ways both contrary to their own interests and destructive of the polity as a whole. The biblical parable that opens the *Fourth Drapier's Letter*, of Esau selling his birthright for a mess of pottage, is intended to apply equally to the poorest Irish peasant and the wealthiest squire; all belong to that category of beings who, because of sustained political oppression, "lose by Degrees the very Notions of *Liberty*" and fall victim to "that *Poverty* and *Lowness of Spirit*, to which a *Kingdom* may be subject, as well as a *particular Person*."

Swift showed that he understood very well not only the institutional and empirical manifestations of this oppression but also how it operates psychologically to perpetuate itself throughout all ranks of society. As he put it in the *Proposal for the Universal Use of Irish Manufacture*, "I know not how it comes to pass, (and yet, perhaps, I know well enough) that *Slaves* have a natural Disposition to be *Tyrants*; and that when my *Betters* give me a Kick, I am apt to revenge it with six upon my *Footman*; although, perhaps, he may be an honest and diligent Fellow." Given his regular use of the term "Slaves" to refer to all Irishmen vis-à-vis the British, this example helps explain not only the petty injustices of the "middling" class turning in frustration on their servants (and presumably the latter in turn passing along the unwarranted blows to ones even lower down on the social scale), but also the abuse of the impoverished native population at the hands of an Irish Protestant establishment that has itself become (especially after the Declaratory Act of 1720) "enslaved." For Swift the nature of oppression is to insinuate and amplify itself throughout every level of society, and the results are invariably ugly, whether they register in those at the top levels of society or those at the bottom of the heap.

Swift understood that oppression hits the poor particularly hard, not only because it causes them the greatest amount of material hardship but also because it has the power to corrupt and deform their character to an especially egregious extent since they must bear the full brunt of its devastating force. If it did not have this power then it wouldn't be oppression, it would be something much more limited in its scope and much less insidiously destructive in its effect. Similar to most of his contemporaries, Swift was quite capable of making a distinction between the "deserving" and the "undeserving" poor, and there were times when he did so with an uncompromising, even repellent harshness (as in his *Proposal for Giving Badges to the Beggars of Dublin*). But more often this distinction is in effect rendered moot by the sheer power and intensity of his detailed descriptions of the pitiable circumstances in which the poor lived—extreme conditions that stymied the individual will and subordinated all members of the group to collective forces beyond their control: "I confess myself to be touched with a very sensible pleasure, when I hear of a mortality in any country-parish or village, where the wretches are forced to pay for a filthy cabin and two ridges of potatoes treble the worth, brought up to steal or beg, for want of work, to whom death would be the best thing to be wished for, on account both of themselves and the public" (*Maxims Controlled in Ireland*). Here the sheer enormity of the miseries facing the poor turns the distressed reflections of the Dean into the mordant commentary of the Modest Proposer within the space of a single sentence. By creating thieves and beggars (here more or less equated) while effectively doing away with any alternatives, these extreme conditions do not allow us the luxury of fine moral discriminations between the "good" poor and the "bad" poor.

At the same time (and here is where Swift diverges most dramatically from romantic idealists and sentimentalists) these conditions produce human beings who are not the least bit attractive in either appearance or way of life: beings who are dirty, ignorant, diseased, desperate, incapable of taking care of themselves, brought up to survive through dishonesty and servility, themselves exploited and ready to exploit others (or worse) for their daily bread. There is nothing "politically correct" about the way the native Irish or the poor are portrayed in Swift's writings—but given the conditions they describe, how could it be otherwise? It requires little effort to sympathize with the poor when they are envisioned as a good-hearted and noble-minded group heroically struggling against near-impossible odds. It is quite a bit harder—but no less necessary—to be sympathetic toward them when they are portrayed as distasteful beings wallowing in their own excrement, lashing out in uncomprehending anger at those least culpable for their plight. Swift, never one to worry about piercing the bubble that protects his readers' comfort zone, gives us this more difficult task to perform—one that many fall short of achieving by failing to recognize that it is not necessary to idealize the oppressed in order to be a serious foe of oppression, nor to romanticize the poor in order to be an opponent of economic exploitation. Swift sets up the perfect sting operation: Those readers who fail to see that the hungry deserve to be advocated for because they are hungry, and not because they are attractive or noble-spirited or closer to godliness, are as lacking in humanity as the Modest Proposer no matter how acutely they understand the irony of his stance. So it is that the native Irish are portrayed in *A Modest Proposal* in decidedly less than positive terms. And so it is too that they are shown to be victims of a predatory class of landowners and a cannibalistic country eager to suck the blood out of its colonized subjects. The noble poor, like the benevolent aristocracy, are revealed here as mere figments of the imagination. In Swift's writings both classes are corrupted, made ugly and contemptible, by the extreme political and economic imbalances that define the system of which they are equally a part.

The absence of any concept of the noble poor in Swift's writings is due not only to his disdain for comforting shibboleths and his fundamentally bleak view of human nature, but also to his unwavering focus on local and specific situations, to his status first and foremost as an *occasional* writer, which precluded flights into the airy realm of abstractions and generalizations.[14] Not that he was incapable of articulating universal principles when the circumstances demanded—one thinks, for example, of his assertion in the *Fourth Drapier's Letter*, "For in *Reason*, all *Government* without the Consent of the *Governed*, is the *very Definition of Slavery*"—but even in this instance the general is only arrived at through an amalgam of specific historical examples, and characteristically it gives way immediately to a concrete, precisely focused image: "But in *Fact, Eleven Men well armed, will certainly subdue one single Man in his Shirt.*" Not surprising, then, that the most memorable affirmation of human liberty we come away with from the *Letter to Molesworth* is not the invocation of the "universally agreed Maxim, that *Freedom consists in a people being governed by Laws made with their own Consent,*" but rather, the image of the Drapier riding his nag around the grounds of Lord Molesworth's estate and (along with the nag) becoming intoxicated with the "Air of Freedom breathing round [him]."

It follows that no meaningful characterization of Swift as thinker or writer can afford to stray very far from existential realities. Nor indeed can it ignore the concrete particulars of his life, conveyed with the understanding that respect for such particulars need not produce a naïve or uncritical positivism. For those inclined to view Swift within the terms of postcolonial theory, concepts such as ambivalence, colonial mimickry, and hybridity are clearly useful, but limited in their applicability to the extent that they too often support a generalizing discourse that overrides crucial distinctions regarding nationality, race, and ethnicity. Those more inclined toward Marxist theory will find Sartre's existential and individual mediations of ideology more valuable than Althusser's ideological abstractions.[15] But whatever conceptual framework we might be inclined to use for Swift, what is needed is one that allows us to theorize from the bottom up (so to speak) rather than the top down: one that enables us to appreciate the radical uniqueness of Swift's perspective and writings while helping us to understand how his insertion in a matrix of events at a specific time and place in history determined the parameters within which he could think and write, producing inescapable ideological ties to his contemporaries. In this sense our view of Swift may be seen to mirror Swift's view of Ireland, as a country marked by exceptionalism while yet bearing unmistakable resemblances to other colonies in the emerging British Empire. Here as in other respects, the Irish Swift stands as a concrete (and especially illuminating) embodiment of the contradictions of his age, class, and nation.

---

[14] See Edward W. Said's argument to this effect in his essay, "Swift as Intellectual," in *The World, the Text, and the Critic* (Cambridge, MA: Harvard University Press, 1983), 72–89 (esp. 79–83).

[15] Compare, e.g., Jean-Paul Sartre, *Search for a Method*, trans. Hazel E. Barnes (New York: Vintage, 1968), esp. ch. II, "The Problem of Mediations" (35–84); and Louis Althusser, *Lenin and Philosophy and Other Essays*, ed. Ben Brewster (New York and London: Monthly Review Press, 1971), esp. Pt. II, "Ideology and Ideological State Apparatuses" (127–85). But see Althusser's more grounded essay "On the Young Marx" (in *For Marx*, trans. Ben Brewster [London: Verso, 1979], 49–86), which argues for the need to uncover "the concrete man and the real history that produced" Marx's thought (71). Interestingly, Althusser's characterization of Marx's temperament in terms of "an intransigent insistence on reality, and a prodigious feeling for the concrete" (71) functions as an equally apt description of Swift's temperamental affinities.

PART 1

PROSE WORKS

THE STORY OF THE INJURED LADY,

Written by HERSELF;

In a LETTER to her *Friend*, with his ANSWER

Though not published until 1746, this pamphlet was written in 1707, shortly after ratification of the Act of Union between England and Scotland. Showing the influence of William Molyneux's The Case of Ireland... Stated *(1698), it is Swift's earliest sustained protest against England's treatment of Ireland as a colony. Both Ireland's pitiable plight and what Swift saw as England's ill-advised "marriage" with Scotland are dramatized through the allegory of a dysfunctional* ménage-a-trois *consisting of a "Gentleman in the Neighbourhood" (England) and his "two Mistresses" (Scotland and Ireland). The Friend's Answer urges the Lady to take concrete steps to combat her oppression rather than merely play the role of passive victim, thus underscoring the need of the Irish to help themselves through organized political action. Copy-text:* Works, *ed. Faulkner, 1746.*

* * *

SIR,

BEING ruined by the Inconstancy and Unkindness of a Lover, I hope, a true and plain Relation of my Misfortunes may be of Use and Warning to credulous Maids, never to put too much Trust in deceitful Men.

A Gentleman in the Neighbourhood had two Mistresses, another and myself; and he pretended honourable Love to us both. Our three Houses stood pretty near one another; his was parted from mine by a River, and from my Rival's by an old broken Wall. But before I enter into the Particulars of this Gentleman's hard Usage of me, I will give a very just impartial Character of my Rival and myself.

As to her Person she is tall and lean, and very ill-shaped; she hath bad Features, and a worse Complexion; she hath a stinking Breath, and twenty ill Smells about her besides; which are yet more unsufferable by her natural Sluttishness; for she is always lousy, and never without the Itch. As to her other Qualities, she hath no Reputation either for Virtue, Honesty, Truth, or Manners; and it is no Wonder, considering what her Education hath been.

Scolding and Cursing are her common Conversation. To sum up all; she is poor and beggarly, and gets a sorry Maintenance by pilfering wherever she comes. As for this Gentleman who is now so fond of her, she still beareth him an invincible Hatred; revileth him to his Face, and raileth at him in all Companies. Her House is frequented by a Company of Rogues and Thieves, and Pickpockets, whom she encourageth to rob his Hen-roosts, steal his Corn and Cattle, and do him all manner of Mischief. She hath been known to come at the Head of these Rascals, and beat her Lover until he was sore from Head to Foot, and then force him to pay for the Trouble she was at. Once, attended with a Crew of Raggamuffins, she broke into his House, turned all Things topsy-turvy, and then set it on Fire.[1] At the same Time she told so many Lies among his Servants, that it set them all by the Ears, and his poor Steward was knocked on the Head;[2] for which I think, and so doth all the Country, that she ought to be answerable. To conclude her Character; she is of a different Religion, being a Presbyterian of the most rank and virulent Kind, and consequently having an inveterate Hatred to the Church; yet, I am sure, I have been always told, that in Marriage there ought to be an Union of Minds as well as of Persons.

I will now give my own Character, and shall do it in few Words, and with Modesty and Truth.

I was reckoned to be as handsome as any in our Neighbourhood, until I became pale and thin with Grief and ill Usage. I am still fair enough, and have, I think, no very ill Feature about me. They that see me now will hardly allow me ever to have had any great Share of Beauty; for besides being so much altered, I go always mobbed[3] and in an Undress, as well out of Neglect, as indeed for want of Cloaths to appear in. I might add to all this, that I was born to a good Estate, although it now turneth to little Account under the Oppressions I endure, and hath been the true Cause of all my Misfortunes.

Some Years ago, this Gentleman taking a Fancy either to my Person or Fortune, made his Addresses to me; which, being then young and foolish, I too readily admitted; he seemed to use me with so much Tenderness, and his Conversation was so very engaging, that all my Constancy and Virtue were too soon overcome; and, to dwell no longer upon a Theme that causeth such bitter Reflections, I must confess with Shame, that I was undone by the common Arts practised upon all easy credulous Virgins, half by Force, and half by Consent, after solemn Vows and Protestations of Marriage. When he had once got Possession, he soon began to play the usual Part of a too fortunate Lover, affecting on all Occasions to shew his Authority, and to

---

[1] Evokes memories of the Scottish cross-border invasions during the English Civil Wars (1642–51) and in general taps into the stereotype of the Scottish Highlanders as wild and rebellious.

[2] Refers to the beheading of King Charles I (January 30, 1649).

[3] In flimsy or careless attire; in a state of partial undress.

act like a Conqueror.[4] First, he found Fault with the Government of my Family, which I grant, was none of the best, consisting of ignorant illiterate Creatures; for at that Time, I knew but little of the World. In compliance to him, therefore, I agreed to fall into his Ways and Methods of Living; I consented that his Steward should govern my House, and have Liberty to employ an Under Steward, who should receive his Directions.[5] My Lover proceeded further, turning away several old Servants and Tenants, and supplying me with others from his own House. These grew so domineering and unreasonable, that there was no Quiet, and I heard of nothing but perpetual Quarrels, which although I could not possibly help, yet my Lover laid all the Blame and Punishment upon me; and upon every Falling-out, still turned away more of my People, and supplied me in their Stead with a Number of Fellows and Dependents of his own, whom he had no other Way to provide for. Overcome by Love, and to avoid Noise and Contention, I yielded to all his Usurpations, and finding it in vain to resist, I thought it my best Policy to make my Court to my new Servants, and draw them to my Interests; I fed them from my own Table with the best I had, put my new Tenants on the choice Parts of my Land, and treated them all so kindly, that they began to love me as well as their Master. In process of Time, all my old Servants were gone, and I had not a Creature about me, nor above one or two Tenants but what were of his chusing; yet I had the good Luck by gentle Usage to bring over the greatest Part of them to my Side. When my Lover observed this, he began to alter his Language; and, to those who enquired about me, he would answer, that I was an old Dependent upon his Family, whom he had placed on some Concerns of his own; and he began to use me accordingly, neglecting by Degrees all common Civility in his Behaviour. I shall never forget the Speech he made me one Morning, which he delivered with all the Gravity in the World. He put me in Mind of the vast Obligations I lay under to him, in sending me so many of his People for my own Good, and to teach me Manners: That it had cost him ten Times more than I was worth, to maintain me: That it had been much better for him if I had been damned, or burnt, or sunk to the Bottom of the Sea: That it was but reasonable I should strain myself as far as I was able, to reimburse him some of his Charges: That from henceforward he expected his Word should be a Law to me in all Things: That I must maintain a Parish-watch against Thieves and Robbers,[6] and give Salaries to an Overseer, a Constable, and Others, all of

---

[4] Unlike King Henry II, who, according to Molyneux, came to Ireland in 1172 not as a conqueror but in peace, treating the Irish as subjects having the same basic liberties the English enjoyed.

[5] The Lord-Lieutenant of Ireland.

[6] Mandated by the "Act for the better suppressing Tories, Robbers, and Rapparees; and for preventing Robberies, Burglaries, and other heinous Crimes" (1695), which provided for stricter enforcement of laws protecting (mainly English and Protestant) property and severer penalties against chiefly "papist" offenders. "Rapparees" were Irish rebels who fought on the Jacobite side during the late 1680s and 1690s; the term came to be synonymous with bandits and highwaymen.

his own chusing, whom he would send from Time to Time to be Spies upon
me: That, to enable me the better in supporting these Expences, my Tenants
shall be obliged to carry all their Goods cross the River to his Town-market,
and pay Toll on both Sides, and then sell them at half Value. But because
we were a nasty Sort of People, and that he could not endure to touch any
Thing we had a Hand in, and likewise, because he wanted Work to employ
his own Folks, therefore we must send all our Goods to his Market just in
their Naturals; the Milk immediately from the Cow without making it into
Cheese or Butter; the Corn in the Ear; the Grass as it is mowed; the Wool as
it cometh from the Sheeps Back; and bring the Fruit upon the Branch, that
he might not be obliged to eat it after our filthy Hands: That, if a Tenant
carried but a Piece of Bread and Cheese to eat by the Way, or an Inch of
Worsted to mend his Stockings, he should forfeit his whole Parcel:[7] And
because a Company of Rogues usually plied on the River between us, who
often robbed my Tenants of their Goods and Boats, he ordered a Waterman
of his to guard them, whose Manner was to be out of the Way until the poor
Wretches were plundered; then to overtake the Thieves, and seize all as lawful Prize to his Master and himself. It would be endless to repeat an hundred
other Hardships he hath put upon me; but it is a general Rule, that whenever
he imagines the smallest Advantage will redound to one of his Foot-boys by
any new Oppression of me and my whole Family and Estate, he never dispu-
teth it a Moment. All this hath rendered me so very insignificant and contemptible at Home, that some Servants to whom I pay the greatest Wages,
and many Tenants who have the most beneficial Leases, are gone over to
live with him; yet I am bound to continue their Wages, and pay their Rents;
by which Means one Third Part of my whole Income is spent on his Estate,
and above another Third by his Tolls and Markets; and my poor Tenants are
so sunk and impoverished, that, instead of maintaining me suitable to my
Quality, they can hardly find me Cloaths to keep me warm, or provide the
common Necessaries of Life for themselves.[8]

Matters being in this Posture between me and my Lover; I received
Intelligence that he had been for some Time making very pressing Overtures
of Marriage to my Rival, until there happened some Misunderstandings
between them; she gave him ill Words, and threatened to break off all
Commerce with him. He, on the other Side, having either acquired Courage
by his Triumphs over me, or supposing her as tame a Fool as I, thought at
first to carry it with a high Hand;[9] but hearing at the same Time, that she

---

[7] Refers to the legislative acts passed by England to restrict Irish trade. The Woollen Act of
1699 banned Ireland's export of manufactured woolen goods and limited its export of raw
wool to England.

[8] Describes the economic devastation caused by absentee landlords, whom Swift repeatedly
condemned for draining Ireland's resources and enriching England at Ireland's expense.

[9] The English Alien Act of 1705 threatened Scotland with harsh treatment and a ban on its
trade with England if it refused to accept the Hanoverian succession and to enter into negotiations for the union.

had Thoughts of making some private Proposals to join with me against him, and doubting with very good Reason that I would readily accept them, he seemed very much discontented. This I thought was a proper Occasion to shew some great Example of Generosity and Love; and so, without further Consideration, I sent him Word, that hearing there was like to be a Quarrel between him and my Rival; notwithstanding all that had passed, and without binding him to any Conditions in my own Favour, I would stand by him against her and all the World, while I had a Penny in my Purse, or a Petticoat to pawn.[10] This Message was subscribed by all my chief Tenants; and proved so powerful, that my Rival immediately grew more tractable upon it. The Result of which was, that there is now a Treaty of Marriage concluded between them, the Wedding Cloaths are bought, and nothing remaineth but to perform the Ceremony, which is put off for some Days, because they design it to be a publick Wedding. And to reward my Love, Constancy, and Generosity, he hath bestowed on me the Office of being Sempstress to his Grooms and Footmen, which I am forced to accept or starve. Yet, in the Midst of this my Situation, I cannot but have some Pity for this deluded Man, to cast himself away on an infamous Creature, who, whatever she pretendeth, I can prove, would at this very Minute rather be a Whore to a certain Great Man, that shall be nameless,[11] if she might have her Will. For my Part, I think, and so doth all the Country too, that the Man is possessed; at least none of us are able to imagine what he can possibly see in her, unless she hath bewitched him, or given him some Powder.[12]

I am sure, I never sought his Alliance, and you can bear me Witness, that I might have had other Matches; nay, if I were lightly disposed, I could still perhaps have Offers, that some, who hold their Heads higher, would be glad to accept. But alas, I never had any such wicked Thought; all I now desire is, only to enjoy a little Quiet, to be free from the Persecutions of this unreasonable Man, and that he will let me manage my own little Fortune to the best Advantage; for which I will undertake to pay him a considerable Pension every Year, much more considerable than what he now gets by his Oppressions; for he must needs find himself a Loser at last, when he hath drained me and my Tenants so dry, that we shall not have a Penny for him or ourselves. There is one Imposition of his, I had almost forgot, which I think unsufferable, and will appeal to you, or any reasonable Person, whether it be so or not. I told you before, that by an old Compact we agreed to have the same Steward, at which Time I consented likewise to regulate my Family and Estate by the same Method with him, which he then shewed me writ

---

[10] Unlike Scotland, the Irish House of Lords declared its allegiance to Queen Anne and its acceptance of the Hanoverian succession.

[11] James Francis Edward Stuart, also known as the "Old Pretender"; the exiled Catholic claimant to the throne.

[12] Perhaps a wry reference to the superstitious and arcane practices (of "second sight," etc.) often associated with the Scottish Presbyterians.

down in Form, and I approved of.[13] Now, the Turn he thinks fit to give this Compact of ours is very extraordinary; for he pretends that whatever Orders he shall think fit to prescribe for the future in his Family, he may, if he will, compel mine to observe them, without asking my Advice or hearing my Reasons. So that I must not make a Lease without his Consent, or give any Directions for the well-governing of my Family, but what he countermands whenever he pleaseth. This leaveth me at such Confusion and Uncertainty, that my Servants know not when to obey me, and my Tenants, although many of them be very well inclined, seem quite at a Loss.

But, I am too tedious upon this melancholy Subject, which however, I hope, you will forgive, since the Happiness of my whole Life dependeth upon it. I desire you will think a while, and give your best Advice what Measures I shall take with Prudence, Justice, Courage, and Honour, to protect my Liberty and Fortune against the Hardships and Severities I lie under from that unkind, inconstant Man.

The ANSWER to the *Injured Lady*

MADAM,

I have received your Ladyship's Letter, and carefully considered every Part of it, and shall give you my Opinion how you ought to proceed for your own Security. But first, I must beg Leave to tell your Ladyship, that you were guilty of an unpardonable Weakness the other Day, in making that Offer to your Lover, of standing by him in any Quarrel he might have with your Rival; you know very well, that she began to apprehend he had Designs of using her as he had done you; and common Prudence might have directed you rather to have entered into some Measures with her for joining against him, until he might at least be brought to some reasonable Terms: But your invincible Hatred to that Lady hath carried your Resentments so high, as to be the Cause of your Ruin; yet, if you please to consider, this Aversion of yours began a good while before she became your Rival, and was taken up by you and your Family in a Sort of Compliment to your Lover, who formerly had a great Abhorrence for her. It is true, since that Time you have suffered very much by her Encroachments upon your Estate,[14] but she never pretended to govern or direct you; and now you have drawn a new Enemy upon yourself; for I think you may count upon all the ill Offices she can possibly do you by her Credit with her Husband; whereas, if instead of openly declaring against her without any Provocation, you had but sat still a while, and said nothing, that Gentleman would have lessened his Severity to you out of perfect Fear. This Weakness of yours, you call Generosity; but I doubt there was more in the Matter: In short, Madam, I have good Reasons to think you

---

[13] Refers to the letters that Irish religious and political leaders gave to Henry II upon his arrival in Ireland, swearing fealty to the king and his heirs.

[14] Through the migration and settlement of large numbers of Scotsmen in Ulster, in the north of Ireland.

were betrayed to it by the pernicious Counsels of some about you: For, to my certain Knowledge, several of your Tenants and Servants, to whom you have been very kind, are as arrant Rascals as any in the Country. I cannot but observe what a mighty Difference there is in one Particular between your Ladyship and your Rival. Having yielded up your Person, you thought nothing else worth defending, and therefore you will not now insist upon those very Conditions for which you yielded at first. But your Ladyship cannot be ignorant, that some Years since your Rival did the same Thing, and upon no Conditions at all; nay, this Gentleman kept her as a Miss, and yet made her pay for her very Diet and Lodging.[15] But, it being at a Time when he had no Steward, and his Family out of Order, she stole away, and hath now got the Trick, very well known among Women of the Town, to grant a Man the Favour over Night, and the next Day have the Impudence to deny it to his Face. But, it is too late to reproach you with any former Oversights, which cannot now be rectified. I know the Matters of Fact as you relate them are true and fairly represented. My Advice therefore is this. Get your Tenants together as soon as you conveniently can, and make them agree to the following Resolutions.

First. That your Family and Tenants have no Dependence upon the said Gentleman, further than by the old Agreement, which obligeth you to have the same Steward, and to regulate your Household by such Methods as you shall both agree to.

Secondly. That you will not carry your Goods to the Market of his Town, unless you please, nor be hindered from carrying them any where else.

Thirdly. That the Servants you pay Wages to shall live at Home, or forfeit their Places.

Fourthly. That whatever Lease you make to a Tenant, it shall not be in his Power to break it.

If he will agree to these Articles, I advise you to contribute as largely as you can to all Charges of Parish and County.

I can assure you, several of that Gentleman's ablest Tenants and Servants are against his severe Usage of you, and would be glad of an Occasion to convince the rest of their Error, if you will not be wanting to yourself.

If the Gentleman refuses these just and reasonable Offers, pray let me know it, and, perhaps I may think of something else that will be more effectual.

I am,

MADAM,

Your Ladyship's, &c.

---

[15] Refers to the military occupation of Scotland under Oliver Cromwell following his defeat of the king's Scottish forces in 1651.

A LETTER FROM A MEMBER OF THE HOUSE OF COMMONS IN *IRELAND* TO A MEMBER OF THE HOUSE OF COMMONS IN *ENGLAND*, CONCERNING THE SACRAMENTAL TEST

This pamphlet, written and anonymously printed in late December of 1708, was Swift's response to the growing pressure being exerted by certain Whigs—in particular Alan Brodrick, Speaker of the Irish House of Commons (subsequently 1st Viscount Midleton and Lord Chancellor of Ireland)—to bring about repeal of Ireland's Sacramental Test Act, passed four years earlier, which required that holders of public office take Communion according to the rites of the Anglican Church. More specifically, Swift's pamphlet was designed to counter a rabidly anti-Catholic, implicitly pro-Dissenter sermon preached in London by Dr. Ralph Lambert (later Dean of Derry and Bishop of Meath) that provided ammunition for the anti-Test forces. A strong supporter of the Test Act, Swift here uses the persona of an Irish parliamentarian to reject the notion that Irish Catholics represent a danger to the government and to cast doubts on the actions and motives of Dissenters, whom he portrays not as victims of persecution (their recurring complaint) but as persecutors themselves. This Letter *is also significant for its depiction of Ireland as a nation capable of determining its own affairs without outside (i.e., English) intervention, making the* Letter *one of the earliest of Swift's proto-nationalist writings.*

* * *

Dublin, Dec. 4, 1708.

    SIR,

I received your Letter, wherein you tell me of the strange Representations made of us on your Side of the Water. The Instance you are pleased to mention, is that of the Presbyterian *Missionary*, who, according to your Phrase, hath been lately *persecuted* in *Drogheda* for his Religion:[1] But it is easy to observe, how mighty industrious some People have been for three or four Years past, to hand about Stories of the Hardships, the Merits, the Number, and the Power of the *Presbyterians* in *Ireland,* to raise formidable Ideas of the Dangers of *Popery* there, and to transmit all for *England,* improved by great Additions, and with special Care to have them inserted, with Comments, in those infamous weekly Papers that infest your Coffee-Houses. So, when the Clause enacting a *Sacramental Test* was put in Execution, it was given out in *England,* that half the Justices of Peace through this Kingdom had laid down their Commissions; whereas upon Examination, the whole Number was found to amount only to a Dozen or Thirteen, and those generally of the lowest Rate in Fortune and Understanding, and some of them superannuated. So, when the Earl of *Pembroke* was in *Ireland,*[2] and the Parliament sitting, a formal Story was very gravely carried to his Excellency by some zealous Members, of a Priest newly arrived from Abroad, to the *North-West* Parts of *Ireland,* who had publickly preached to his People, to fall a murthering the Protestants; which Abuse, although invented to serve an End they were then upon, and are still driving at, it was presently handed over, and printed with shrewd Remarks by your worthy Scriblers. In like Manner, the Account of that Person who was lately expelled our University for reflecting on the memory of King *William,* what a Dust it raised, and how foully it was related, is fresh enough in Memory.[3] Neither would People be convinced till the University was at the Pains of publishing a *Latin* Paper to justify themselves. And, to mention no more, this Story of the *Persecution* at *Drogheda,* how it hath been spread and aggravated, what Consequences drawn from it, and what Reproaches fixed on those who have least deserved them, we are already informed. Now, if the End of all this Proceeding were a Secret and Mystery, I should not pretend to give it an Interpretation. But sufficient Care hath been taken to explain it. First, by Addresses artificially (if not illegally) procured, to shew the miserable State of the Dissenters in *Ireland,* by reason of the *Sacramental Test,* and to desire the Queen's intercession that it might be repealed. Then it is manifest that our Speaker, when he was last Year in *England,* sollicited, in Person, several Members of both Houses, to have it repealed by an Act there, though it be a Matter purely national, that cannot possibly interfere with the Trade and Interest of *England,* and although he himself appeared formerly the most zealous of all Men against the Injustice of binding a Nation by Laws,

---

[1] A Presbyterian minister was briefly imprisoned for actively proselytizing in Drogheda (a port town on the east coast of Ireland, approximately 35 miles north of Dublin) but was freed through the intervention of Lord-Lieutenant Wharton.

[2] In 1707, serving as Lord-Lieutenant of Ireland.

[3] Refers to the expulsion of Edward Forbes by the Provost and Senior Fellows of Trinity College, Dublin, for stating at the summer commencement supper in 1708 that the Queen's right to the throne was no better than that of her predecessor since both rested on the same foundation—an incident that resulted in the mandating of a declaration of loyalty to the Queen by all Trinity College members.

to which they do not consent.[4] And lastly, those weekly Libellers, whenever they get a Tale by the End relating to *Ireland*, without once troubling their Thoughts about the Truth, always end it with an Application against the *Sacramental Test*, and the absolute Necessity there is of repealing it in both Kingdoms. I know it may be reckoned a Weakness to say any thing of such Trifles as are below a serious Man's Notice; much less would I disparage the Understanding of any Party, to think they would choose the Vilest and most Ignorant among mankind, to employ them for Asserters of a Cause. I shall only say, that the scandalous Liberty those Wretches take, would hardly be allowed, if it were not mingled with Opinions that *some Men* would be glad to advance. Besides, how insipid so ever those Papers are, they seem to be levelled to the Understandings of a great Number. They are grown a necessary Part in Coffee-house Furniture, and some Time or other may happen to be read by Customers of all Ranks, for Curiosity or Amusement; because they lie always in the Way. One of these Authors (the Fellow that was *pilloried*, I have forgot his Name) is indeed so grave, sententious, dogmatical a Rogue, that there is no enduring him;[5] the *Observator* is much the brisker of the two; and, I think, farther gone of late in Lies and Impudence than his *Presbyterian* Brother.[6]

I now come to answer the other Part of your Letter, and shall give you my Opinion freely about repealing the *Sacramental Test*; only, whereas you desire my Thoughts as a Friend, and not as I am a Member of Parliament, I must assure you they are exactly the same in both Capacities.

I must begin by telling you, we are generally surprised at your wonderful Kindness to us on this Occasion, in being so very industrious to teach us to see our Interests, in a Point where we are so unable to see it our selves. This hath given us some Suspicion; and although, in my own Particular, I am hugely bent to believe, that whenever you concern your selves in our Affairs, it is certainly *for our Good*; yet I have the Misfortune to be something singular in this Belief, and therefore I never attempt to justify it, but content my self to possess my own Opinion in private, for fear of encountring Men of more Wit, or Words than I have to spare.

We at this Distance, who see nothing of the Spring of Actions, are forced, by mere Conjecture, to assign two Reasons for your desiring us to repeal the *Sacramental Test*. One is, because you are said to imagine it will be a Step towards the like *good Work* in *England*: The other more immediate, that it

---

[4] A view later echoed by the Drapier, who addressed his *Sixth Letter* to Brodrick, by then Lord Midleton.

[5] The reference is to Daniel Defoe (1660–1731), Dissenter and editor of the long-running newspaper, *The Review* (1704–13), whose Whiggish and Low Church positions invariably clashed with Swift's. Defoe was placed in the pillory in 1703 for his satire on "High-Flying" Tories, *The Shortest Way with the Dissenters*.

[6] *The Observator* was an anti-Jacobite periodical started in 1702 by John Tutchin (d. 1707), a zealous Whig of Puritan background whose attacks on various public figures (including Queen Anne and Members of Parliament) resulted in a government prosecution against him for seditious libel.

will open a Way for rewarding *several Persons*, who have well deserved upon a *great Occasion*, but who are now unqualified through that Impediment.

I do not frequently quote Poets, especially *English*, but I remember there is in some of Mr. *Cowley*'s Love Verses, a Strain that I thought extraordinary at Fifteen, and have often since imagined it to be spoken by *Ireland*.

> *Forbid it Heaven my Life should be*
> *Weigh'd with her least Conveniency.*[7]

In short, whatever Advantage you propose to your selves by repealing the *Sacramental Test*, speak it out plainly, it is the best Argument you can use, for we value your Interest much more than our own. If your little Finger be sore, and you think a Poultice made of our *Vitals* will give it any Ease, speak the Word, and it shall be done; the Interest of our whole Kingdom is, at any Time, ready to strike to that of your poorest *Fishing Towns*; it is hard you will not accept our Services, unless we believe, at the same Time, that you are only consulting our Profit, and giving us Marks of your Love. If there be a Fire at some Distance, and I immediately blow up my House before there be Occasion, because you are a Man of Quality, and apprehend some Danger to a *Corner of your Stable*; yet why should you require me to attend next Morning at your Levee, with my humble Thanks for the Favour you have done me?

If we might be allowed to judge for our selves, we had Abundance of Benefit by the *Sacramental Test*, and foresee a Number of Mischiefs would be the Consequence of repealing it; and we conceive the Objections made against it by the *Dissenters*, are of no Manner of Force. They tell us of their Merits in the late War in *Ireland*,[8] and how chearfully they engaged for the Safety of the Nation; that if they had thought they had been fighting only other Peoples Quarrels, perhaps it might have cooled their Zeal; and that, for the Future, they shall sit down quietly, and let us do our Work our selves; nay, that it is necessary they should do so, since they cannot take up Arms under the Penalty of High Treason.

Now, supposing them to have done their Duty, as I believe they did, and not to trouble them about the *Fly on the Wheel*; I thought *Liberty, Property,* and *Religion* had been the three Subjects of the Quarrel: And have not all those been amply secured to them? Had they, at that Time, a *mental Reservation for Power and Employments*? And must these two Articles be added henceforward in our National Quarrels? It is grown a mighty Conceit, among some Men, to melt down the Phrase of a *Church Established by law*,

---

[7] These lines are from the verse "Love undiscovered," from Abraham Cowley's volume of love poems, *The Mistress* (1647). Swift's earliest poems were odes loosely modeled on Cowley's Pindarics.

[8] The Williamite Wars of 1689–91 between the forces of the newly enthroned Protestant William III and the ousted Roman Catholic James II, which ended in the latter's defeat and exile.

into that of the *Religion of the Magistrate*; of which Appellation it is easier to find the Reason than the Sense: If, by the *Magistrate*, they mean the *Prince*, the Established Church was the same it is now. If, by the same Word they mean the Legislature, we desire no more. Be that as it will, we of this Kingdom believe the Church of *Ireland* to be the National Church, and the only one established by Law, and are willing, by the same Law, to give a *Toleration* to Dissenters. But if once we repeal our *Sacramental Test*, and grant a *Toleration*, or suspend the Execution of the Penal Laws, I do not see how we can be said to have any Established Church remaining; or rather why there will not be as many Established Churches as there are sects of Dissenters. No, say they, yours will still be the National Church, because your Bishops and Clergy are maintained by the Publick; but, *That*, I suppose, will be of no long Duration, and it would be very unjust it should; because, to speak in *Tindal*'s phrase, it is not reasonable that Revenues should be annexed to one Opinion more than another, when all are equally lawful; and it is the same Author's Maxim, That no free-born Subject ought to pay for maintaining Speculations he does not believe.[9] *But why should any Man, upon Account of Opinions he cannot help, be deprived of the Opportunity of serving his Queen and Country?* Their Zeal is commendable, and when Employments go a begging for want of Hands, they shall be sure to have the Refusal; only, upon Condition, they will not pretend to them upon Maxims which equally include *Atheists, Turks, Jews, Infidels, and Hereticks*; or, which is still more dangerous, even *Papists* themselves; the former you allow, the other you deny, because these last own a foreign Power, and therefore must be shut out. But there is no great Weight in this; for their Religion can suit with free States, with limited or absolute Monarchies, as well as a better; and the *Pope*'s Power in *France* is but a Shadow; so that, upon this Foot, there need be no great Danger to the Constitution, by admitting *Papists* to Employments. I will help you to enough of them, who shall be ready to allow the *Pope* as little Power here as you please; and the bare Opinion of his being Vicar of Christ, is but a *speculative Point*, for which no Man, it seems, ought to be deprived the Capacity of serving his Country.

But, if you please, I will tell you the great Objection we have against repealing this same *Sacramental Test*. It is, that we are verily perswaded the Consequence will be an entire Alteration of Religion among us in a no great Compass of Years. And, pray observe, how we reason here in *Ireland* upon this Matter.

We observe the *Scots*, in our Northern Parts, to be an industrious People, extreamly devoted to their Religion, and full of an *undisturbed* Affection towards each other. Numbers of that *noble Nation*, invited by the Fertilities of the Soil, are glad to exchange their barren Hills of *Loughabar*, by a Voyage of

---

[9] The views cited here are from *The Rights of the Christian Church* (1706) written by the English Deist Matthew Tindal (1657–1733): a highly controversial work that defended a form of natural religion and argued for the supremacy of the State over the Church. Swift attacked the work in a satirical tract that remained unfinished and unpublished in his lifetime.

three Hours, for our fruitful Vales of *Down* and *Antrim*, so productive of that
Grain, which, at little Trouble and less Expence, finds Diet and Lodging for
themselves and their Cattle.[10] These people by their extream Parsimony, wonderful *Dexterity in Dealing*, and firm Adherence to one another, soon grow
into Wealth from the *smallest Beginnings*, never are rooted out where they once
fix, and increase daily by new Supplies. Besides, when they are the superior
Number in any Tract of Ground, they are not *over patient of Mixture*; but such,
whom they cannot *assimilate*, soon find it their Interest to remove. I have done
all in my Power, on some Land of my own, to preserve two or three *English*
Fellows in their Neighbourhood, but found it impossible, although one of
them thought he had sufficiently made his Court by turning *Presbyterian*. Add
to all this, that they bring along with them from *Scotland*, a most formidable
Notion of our Church, which they look upon, at least, three Degrees worse
than *Popery*; and it is natural it should be so, since they come over full fraught
with that Spirit which taught them to abolish Episcopacy at home.[11]

Then we proceed farther, and observe, that the Gentlemen of Employments
here, make a very considerable Number in the House of Commons, and have
no *other Merit* but that of doing their Duty in their several Stations; therefore, when the *Test* is repealed, it will be highly reasonable they should give
Place to those who have much *greater Services* to plead. The Commissions
of the Revenue are soon disposed of, and the Collectors and other Officers
throughout this Kingdom, are generally appointed by the Commissioners,
which give them a mighty Influence in every County. As much may be
said of the great Offices in the Law; and when this Door is open to let
Dissenters into the Commissions of the Peace, to make them High-Sheriffs,
Mayors of Corporations, and Officers of the Army and Militia; I do not see
how it can be otherwise, considering their Industry and our Supineness,
but that they may, in a very few Years, grow to a Majority in the House
of Commons, and consequently make themselves the National Religion,
and have a fair Pretence to demand the Revenues of the Church for their
Teachers. I know it will be objected, that if all this should happen as I
describe, yet the *Presbyterian* religion could never be made the National by
Act of Parliament, because our Bishops are so great a Number in the House
of Lords; and without a Majority there, the Church could not be abolished.
But I have *two very good Expedients* for that, which I shall leave you to guess,
and, I dare swear, our Speaker here has often thought on, especially having

---

[10] Lochabar is a rugged region in the Scottish West Highlands; Down and Antrim are counties situated along the eastern coast of what is now Northern Ireland. Only a short distance
separates the two countries between these points, which thus became a popular route for
Scotsmen emigrating to Ireland.

[11] Post-Restoration efforts to enforce episcopal church government in Scotland had come
to a tumultuous end upon the ascension of William III to the throne (1688). Mob attacks
("rabblings") against episcopal ministers culminated in an Act (June 7, 1690) restoring
Presbyterianism as the national religion. Swift would have had firsthand knowledge of the
Scottish Kirk, and its antagonism toward episcopacy, from his first church living in Kilroot,
near Belfast, in the heart of the northern Presbyterian settlement.

endeavoured at *one of them* so lately. That this Design is not so foreign from *some Peoples* Thoughts, I must let you know what an honest *Bell-weather* of our House (you have him now in *England*, I wish you could keep him there) had the Impudence, some Years ago, in Parliament Time, to shake my Lord Bishop of *Killaloo* by his Lawn Sleeve, and tell him in a threatening Manner, *That he hoped to live to see the Day, when there should not be one of his Order in the Kingdom*.[12]

These last Lines, perhaps, you think a Digression; therefore to return, I have told you the Consequences we fully reckon upon, from repealing the *Sacramental Test*, which although the greatest Number of such as are for doing it, are actually in no Manner of Pain about, and many of them care not three Pence whether there be any *Church* or no; yet, because they pretend to argue from Conscience as well as Policy and Interest, I thought it proper to understand and answer them accordingly.

Now, Sir, in Answer to your Question, Whether if any Attempt should be made here for repealing the *Sacramental Test*, it would be likely to succeed? The number of profest *Dissenters* in this Parliament was, as I remember, something under a Dozen, and I cannot call to mind above Thirty others who were expected to fall in with them. This is certain, that the *Presbyterian* Party having with great Industry mustered up their Forces, did endeavour one Day, upon Occasion of a Hint in my Lord *Pembroke*'s Speech, to introduce a Debate about repealing the *Test Clause*, when there appeared, at least, four to one Odds against them; and the ablest of those, who were reckoned the most stanch[13] and thorough-paced *Whigs* upon all other Occasions, fell off with an Abhorence at the first Mention of this.

I must desire you to take Notice, that the Terms of *Whig* and *Tory*, do not properly express the different Interests in our Parliament.

Whoever bears a true Veneration for the Glorious Memory of King *William*, as our great Deliverer from *Popery* and *Slavery*; whoever is firmly loyal to our present Queen, with an utter Abhorrence and Detestation of the *Pretender*; whoever approves the Succession to the Crown in the House of *Hanover*,[14] and is for preserving the Doctrine and Discipline of the Church of *England*, with an *Indulgence* for scrupulous Consciences; such a Man, we think, acts upon right Principles, and may be justly allowed a *Whig*; and, I believe, there are not six Members in our House of Commons, who may not fairly come under this Description. So that the Parties among us are made up, on one side, of *moderate Whigs*, and, on the other, of *Presbyterians* and their *Abettors*; by which last I mean, such who can equally go to a *Church*,

---

[12] The confrontation described here was between Brodrick and Thomas Lindsay, then Bishop of Killaloe; later Archbishop of Armagh and Primate of All Ireland.

[13] Staunch.

[14] According to the Act of Settlement (1701), if Queen Anne died without issue the British throne was to pass to the heirs of the Electress Sophia of Hanover (granddaughter of James I) in order to ensure a Protestant succession and prevent the return of the Catholic Stuarts.

or a *Conventicle*;[15] or such who are indifferent to all Religion in general; or, lastly, such who affect to bear a personal Rancor toward the Clergy. These last, are a Set of Men not of our own Growth; their Principles, at least, have been *imported* of late Years; yet this whole Party, put together, will not, I am confident, amount to above fifty Men in Parliament, which can hardly be worked up into a Majority of three Hundred.

As to the House of Lords, the Difficulty there is conceived, at least, as great as in ours. So many of our Temporal Peers live in *England*, that the Bishops are generally pretty near a *Par* of the House, and we reckon they will be all to a Man against repealing the *Test*; and yet their Lordships are generally thought as good *Whigs* upon our Principles as any in the Kingdom. There are, indeed, a few Lay Lords who appear to have no great devotion for *Episcopacy*; and perhaps one or two more, with whom *certain powerful Motives* might be used for removing any Difficulty whatsoever; but these are in no sort of a Number to carry any point against the Conjunction of the rest, with the whole Bench of Bishops.

Besides, the intire Body of our Clergy is utterly against repealing the *Test*, although they are entirely devoted to her Majesty, and hardly One in a Hundred who are not very good *Whigs*, in our Acceptation of the Word. And I must let you know, that we of *Ireland*, are not yet come up to *other Folks Refinement*:[16] For we generally love and esteem our Clergy, and think they deserve it; nay, we are apt to lay some Weight upon their Opinions, and would not willingly disoblige them, at least unless it were upon some greater Point of Interest than this. And their Judgment, in the present Affair, is the more to be regarded, because they are the last Persons who will be affected by it: This makes us think them impartial, and that their Concern is only for Religion and the Interest of the Kingdom. Because, the Act which repeals the *Test*, will only qualify a *Layman* for an Employment, but not a *Presbyterian* or *Anabaptist* preacher for a Church Living.[17] Now I must take Leave to inform you, that several Members of our House, and my self among the rest, knowing, some Time ago, what was upon the Anvil, went to all the Clergy we knew of any Distinction, and desired their Judgment in the Matter, wherein we found a most wonderful Agreement; there being but *one Divine*, that we could hear of, in the whole Kingdom, who appeared of a contrary Sentiment; wherein he afterwards stood alone in the *Convocation*, very little to his *Credit*, although, as he hoped, very much to his Interest.[18]

---

[15] A clandestine or illegal religious assembly, specifically (during this period) of Nonconformists.

[16] A favorite word of Swift's, almost always used pejoratively; here suggesting excessive sophistication or overly subtle reasoning.

[17] An Anabaptist ("re-baptizer") was a member of a radical reformist sect that denied the scriptural authority of infant baptism and rejected the doctrine of justification by faith, advocating freedom of conscience, good works, and communally owned property.

[18] The reference is to Ralph Lambert, whose "Interest" was served by being named chaplain to the staunchly Whig and anti-Test Act politician Thomas Wharton, then Lord-Lieutenant of Ireland.

I will now consider, a little, the Arguments offered to shew the Advantages, or rather Necessity of repealing the *Test* in *Ireland*. We are told, the *Popish* Interest is here so formidable; that all Hands should be joined to keep it under; that the only Names of Distinctions among us, ought to be those of *Protestant* and *Papist*; and that this Expedient is the only Means to *unite* all Protestants upon one common Bottom. All which is nothing but Misrepresentation and Mistake.

If we were under any real Fear of the *Papists* in this Kingdom, it would be hard to think us so stupid, as not to be equally apprehensive with *others*, since we are likely to be the greatest, and more immediate Sufferers; but on the contrary, we look upon them to be altogether as inconsiderable as the Women and Children. Their Lands are almost entirely taken from them, and they are rendered uncapable of purchasing any more; and for the little that remains, Provision is made by the late Act against Popery, that it will daily crumble away:[19] To prevent which, some of the most considerable among them are already turned Protestants, and so, in all Probability, will many more. Then, the Popish Priests are all registered, and without Permission (which I hope will not be granted) they can have no Successors; so that the Protestant Clergy will find it perhaps no difficult Matter to bring great Numbers over to the Church; and in the mean Time, the common People without Leaders, without Discipline, or natural Courage, being little better than *Hewers of Wood, and Drawers of Water*,[20] are out of all Capacity of doing any Mischief, if they were ever so well inclined. Neither are they, at all, likely to join in any considerable Numbers with an Invader, having found so ill Success when they were much more numerous and powerful; when they had a Prince of their own Religion to head them, had been trained for some Years under a *Popish Deputy*, and received such mighty Aids from the *French King*.[21]

As to that Argument used for repealing the *Test*; that it will unite all Protestants against the *common Enemy*; I wonder by what Figure those Gentlemen speak, who are pleased to advance it: Suppose in order to encrease the Friendship between you and me, a Law should pass that I must have Half your Estate; do you think that would much advance the Union between us? Or, suppose I share my Fortune equally between my own *Children*, and a *Stranger*, whom I take into my Protection; will that be a Method to unite them? It is an odd way of uniting Parties, to deprive a *Majority* of Part of their antient Right, by conferring it on a *Faction* who had never any Right

---

[19] Refers to The Act to Prevent the Further Growth of Popery (1704), which extended the penal laws first enacted in 1695 by severely limiting the rights of Irish Catholics to own, inherit, and bequeath landed property.

[20] See Joshua 9:21–27; a biblical reference frequently cited by Swift.

[21] Describes the situation during the reign of the Catholic James II (1685–88). His appointment of Richard Talbot, 1st Earl of Tyrconnell, as commander in chief of the Irish Army and Lord-Deputy of Ireland resulted in the elevation of Catholics to high-ranking positions in the country's military.

at all, and therefore cannot be said to suffer any Loss or Injury, if it be refused them. Neither is it very clear, how far some People may stretch the Term of *common Enemy*. How many are there of those that call themselves Protestants, who look upon our Worship to be idolatrous as well as that of the *Papists*, and with great Charity put *Prelacy* and *Popery* together, as Terms convertible?

And, therefore, there is one small Doubt I would be willingly satis-fied in, before I agree to the repealing of the *Test*; that is, whether these same Protestants, when they have, by their Dexterity, made themselves the National Religion, and disposed the Church Revenues among their *Pastors* or *Themselves*, will be so kind to allow us *Dissenters*, I do not say a Share in Employments, but a bare *Toleration* by law? The Reason of my Doubt is, because I have been so very idle as to read above fifty Pamphlets, written by as many *Presbyterian* Divines, loudly disclaiming this Idol *Toleration*; some of them calling it (I know not how properly) a *Rag of Popery*, and all agreeing, it was to *establish Iniquity by a Law*. Now, I would be glad to know when and where *their Successors* have renounced this Doctrine, and before what Witnesses. Because, methinks, I should be loath to see my poor titular Bishop *in partibus*,[22] seized on by Mistake in the Dark for a Jesuit, or be forced my self to keep my Chaplain disguised like my Butler, and steal to Prayers in a back Room, as my Grandfather used in those Times when the Church of *England* was *malignant*.[23]

But this is ripping up old Quarrels long forgot; *Popery* is now the *common Enemy*, against which we must all unite; I have been tired in History with the perpetual Folly of those States, who called in Foreigners to assist them against a *common Enemy*: But the Mischief was, these *Allies* would never be brought to allow that the *common Enemy* was quite subdued. And they had Reason; for it proved at last, that one Part of the *common Enemy* was those who called them in; and so the *Allies* became at length the Masters.

It is agreed, among Naturalists, that a *Lyon* is a larger, a stronger, and more dangerous Enemy than a *Cat*; yet if a Man were to have his Choice, either a *Lyon* at his Foot, bound fast with three or four Chains, his Teeth drawn out, and his Claws pared to the Quick, or an angry *Cat* in full Liberty at his Throat; he would take no long Time to determine.

I have been sometimes admiring the wonderful Significancy of that Word *Persecution*, and what various Interpretations it hath acquired even within my Memory. When I was a Boy, I often heard the *Presbyterians* complain,

---

[22] Shortened form of "in partibus infidelium," which means "in the lands of unbelievers."

[23] The "church malignant" was a term regularly applied by seventeenth-century Puritans to the "Church of Rome," or the "followers of Antichrist." Swift is making the point that, from a Dissenting Protestant perspective, Catholicism and Anglicanism are equally anathema. The "Grandfather" referred to here is Thomas Swift (d. 1658), vicar of Goodrich, in Herefordshire, who, according to Swift's autobiographical fragment, was "distinguished by his courage, as well as his loyalty to K. Charles the 1st, and the Sufferings he underwent for that Prince, more than any person of his condition in England."

that they were not permitted to serve God in their own Way; they said, they did not repine at our Employments, but thought that all Men, who live peaceably, ought to have Liberty of Conscience, and Leave to assemble. That Impediment being removed at the Revolution, they soon learned to swallow the *Sacramental Test*, and began to take very large Steps, wherein all who offered to oppose them, were called Men of a *persecuting Spirit*. During the Time the Bill against Occasional Conformity[24] was on Foot, *Persecution* was every Day rung in our Ears, and now at last the *Sacramental Test* it self has the same Name. Where then is this Matter likely to end, when the obtaining of one Request is only used as a Step to demand another? A Lover is ever complaining of *Cruelty*, while any thing is denied him; and when the Lady ceases to be *cruel*, she is from the next Moment at his Mercy: So *Persecution*, it seems, is every Thing that will not leave it in Men's Power to *persecute others*.

There is one Argument offered against a *Sacramental Test*, by a Sort of Men who are content to be stiled of the Church of *England*, who, perhaps, attend its Service in the Morning, and go with their Wives to a *Conventicle* in the Afternoon, confessing they hear very good Doctrine in both. These Men are much offended, that so holy an Institution as that of the Lord's Supper, should be made subservient to such mercenary Purposes, as the getting of an Employment. Now, it seems, the Law, concluding all Men to be Members of that Church where they receive the Sacrament; and supposing all Men to live like Christians (especially those who are to have Employments) did imagine they received the Sacrament, in Course, about four Times a Year, and therefore only desired it might appear by Certificate to the Publick, that such who took an Office, were Members of the Church established, by doing their ordinary Duty. However, *lest we should offend them*, we have often desired they would deal candidly with us; for if the Matter stuck only there, we would propose it in Parliament, that every Man who takes an Employment, should, instead of receiving the Sacrament, be obliged to swear, that he is a member of the Church of *Ireland* by Law established, with *Episcopacy, and so forth*; and as they do now in *Scotland, to be true to the Kirk*. But when we drive them thus far, they always retire to the main Body of the Argument, urge the Hardship that Men should be deprived the Liberty of serving their Queen and Country, on Account of their Conscience: And, in short, have Recourse to the common Stile of their half Brethren. Now, whether this be a sincere Way of arguing, I will appeal to any other Judgment but theirs.

There is another Topick of Clamour somewhat parallel to the foregoing; it seems, by the *Test Clause*, the *Military* Officers are obliged to receive the Sacrament as well as the *Civil*. And it is a Matter of some Patience, to hear the *Dissenters* declaiming upon this Occasion: They cry they are

---

[24] Designed to end the practice of Dissenters' occasionally taking communion in the Established Church in order to qualify for public office while continuing to worship regularly in their own chapels or meeting-houses; the bill was passed by the Commons but defeated by opposition in the House of Lords in 1703.

disarmed, they are used like *Papists*; when an Enemy appears at Home, or from Abroad, they must sit still, and see their Throats cut, or be hanged for High Treason if they offer to defend themselves. Miserable Condition! Woeful Dilemma! It is happy for us all, that the Pretender was not apprised of this *passive Presbyterian* Principle, else he would have infallibly landed in our *Northern Parts*, and found them all sat down in their Formalities, as the *Gauls* did the *Roman* Senators, ready to die with Honour in their Callings.[25] Sometimes, to appease their Indignation, we venture to give them Hopes, that in such a Case, the Government will perhaps connive, and hardly be so severe to hang them for defending it against the Letter of the Law; to which they readily answer, that they will not lie at our Mercy, but let us fight our Battles our selves. Sometimes we offer to get an Act, by which, upon all *Popish* Insurrections at Home, or *Popish* Invasions from Abroad, the Government shall be impowered to grant Commissions to all Protestants whatsoever, without that *persecuting* Circumstance of obliging them to *say their Prayers* when they receive the Sacrament; but they abhor all Thoughts of *occasional* Commissions, they will not do our Drudgery, and we reap the Benefit: It is not worth their while to fight *pro Aris & focis*;[26] and they had rather lose their Estates, Liberties, Religion and Lives, than the Pleasure of *governing*.

But to bring this Discourse towards a Conclusion. If the Dissenters will be satisfied with such a *Toleration* by Law, as hath been granted them in *England*, I believe the Majority of both Houses will fall readily in with it; farther it will be hard to perswade this House of Commons, and, perhaps, much harder the next. For, to say the Truth, we make a mighty Difference here between suffering *Thistles* to grow among us, and wearing them for *Posies*. We are fully convinced in our Consciences, that *We* shall always *tolerate them*, but not quite so fully, that *They* will always *tolerate us*, when it comes to their Turn; and *We* are the Majority, and *We* are in Possession.

He who argues in Defence of a Law in Force, not antiquated or obsolete, but lately enacted, is certainly on the safer Side, and may be allowed to point out the Dangers he conceives to foresee in the Abrogation of it.

For if the Consequences of repealing this Clause, should, at some time or other, enable the *Presbyterians* to work themselves up into the National Church; instead of *uniting* Protestants, it would sow eternal Divisions among them. First, their own Sects, which now lie dormant, would be soon at Cuffs *again* with each other about Power and Preferment; and the *Dissenting Episcopals*, perhaps, discontented to such a Degree, as, upon some *fair unhappy* Occasion, would be able to shake the firmest Loyalty, which none can deny theirs to be.

---

[25] See Livy, *History of Rome*, 5.41 on the Gauls' sack of Rome in 390 B.C.E.

[26] Literally, "for altars and firesides"; more figuratively, used as a motto to express attachment to what is most cherished and venerable, as "For Hearth and Home" or "For God and Country."

Neither is it very difficult to conjecture, from some late Proceedings, at what a Rate this *Faction* is like to drive wherever it gets the *Whip* and the *Seat*. They have already set up Courts of Spiritual Judicature, in open Contempt of the Law: They send *Missionaries* every where, without being invited, in order to *convert* the Church of *England* Folks to *Christianity*. They are as vigilant as *I know who*, to attend Persons on their Death-Beds, and for Purposes much alike. And what Practices such Principles as these (with many others that might be invidious to mention) may spawn, when they are *laid out to the Sun*, you may determine at Leisure.

Lastly, whether we are so entirely sure of their Loyalty upon the present Foot of Government as you may imagine, their Detractors make a Question, which, however, does, I think, by no Means affect the Body of *Dissenters*; but the Instance produced, is of some among their leading Teachers in the *North*, who having refused the *Abjuration Oath*,[27] yet continue their Preaching, and have Abundance of Followers. The Particulars are out of my Head, but the Fact is notorious enough, and, I believe, hath been published; I think it a Pity it has not been *remedied*.

Thus I have fairly given you, Sir, my own Opinion, as well as that of a great Majority in both Houses here, relating to this weighty Affair, upon which, I am Confident, you may securely reckon. I will leave you to make what Use of it you please.

---

[27] An oath enacted in 1701 that required all clergy and public officeholders to reject the Stuarts' claim to the British throne and pledge loyalty to the (Protestant) monarch.

A PROPOSAL for the UNIVERSAL USE of IRISH Manufacture, &c.

UTTERLY REJECTING AND RENOUNCING EVERY THING WEARABLE THAT COMES FROM ENGLAND.

Written in the Year 1720

This pamphlet represents Swift's full emergence into political activism on the Irish stage after several years of relative silence following his return from England in 1714 to take up his post as Dean of St. Patrick's. Directed mainly against the restrictions against Irish trade enforced by laws such as the Woollen Act of 1699, and boldly calling for a boycott of English goods to develop Ireland's economic self-reliance, the tract's appearance was deliberately timed to coincide with the celebrations in Dublin for the 60th birthday of King George I (on May 28, 1720) and aimed to tap into the widespread resentment throughout the country over the recently passed Declaratory Act, which emasculated the powers of the Irish Parliament by declaring Britain's full authority to make laws "to bind the kingdom and people of Ireland." An inflammatory passage in the pamphlet's first printing (deleted in subsequent editions) provoked a government prosecution against its printer, Edward Waters, and made the main prosecutor, Chief Justice William Whitshed, a recurring target of Swift's satiric vitriol from that moment onward.

* * *

IT is the peculiar Felicity and Prudence of the People in this Kingdom, that whatever Commodities, or Productions, lie under the greatest Discouragements from *England,* those are what they are sure to be most industrious in cultivating and spreading. *Agriculture,* which hath been the principal Care of all wise Nations, and for the Encouragement whereof there are so many Statute-Laws in *England,* we countenance so well, that the Landlords are every where, *by penal Clauses,* absolutely prohibiting their Tenants from Plowing; not satisfied to confine them within certain Limitations, as it is the Practice of the *English;* one Effect of which, is already seen in the prodigious Dearness of

Corn, and the Importation of it from *London,* as the cheaper Market: And, because People are the *Riches of a Country,* and that our *Neighbours* have done, and are doing all that in them lie, to make our Wool a Drug to us, and a Monopoly to them; therefore, the politick Gentlemen of *Ireland* have depopulated vast Tracts of the best Land, for the feeding of Sheep.[1]

I could fill a Volume as large as the *History of the wise Men of Goatham* with a Catalogue only of some *wonderful* Laws and Customs we have observed within thirty Years past. It is true, indeed, our beneficial Traffick of Wool with *France,* hath been our only Support for several Years past; furnishing us all the little Money we have to pay our Rents, and go to Market.[2] But our Merchants assure me, *This Trade hath received a great Damp by the present fluctuating Condition of the Coin in* France; *and that most of their Wine is paid for in Specie, without carrying thither any Commodity from hence.*

However, since we are so universally bent upon enlarging our *Flocks,* it may be worth inquiring, what we shall do with our Wool, in case *Barnstable*[3] should be over-stocked, and our *French* Commerce should fail?

I should wish the Parliament had thought fit to have suspended their Regulation of *Church* Matters, and Enlargements of the *Prerogative,* until a more convenient Time, because they did not appear very pressing, (at least to the Persons *principally concerned)* and, instead of those great Refinements in *Politicks* and *Divinity,* had *amused* Themselves and their Committees, a little, with the *State of the Nation.*[4] For Example: What if the House of Commons had thought fit to make a Resolution, *Nemine Contradicente,*[5] against wearing any Cloath or Stuff in their Families, which were not of the Growth and Manufacture of this Kingdom? What if they had extended it so far, as utterly to exclude all Silks, Velvets, Calicoes, and the whole *Lexicon* of Female Fopperies; and declared, that whoever acted otherwise, should be deemed and reputed *an Enemy to the Nation?* What if they had sent up such a Resolution to be agreed to by the House of Lords; and by their own Practice and Encouragement, spread the Execution of it in their several Countries? What if we should agree to make *burying in Woollen* a *Fashion,* as our

---

[1] This paragraph encapsulates what Swift saw as the main problems with land management in Ireland, especially the greed and the ignorance about good agricultural practices on the part of large landowners (and their surrogates, the "middle men"); the tyranny exerted by landlords over small tenant farmers through rent-gouging and short-term leases; and the conversion of tillage into pasture lands to produce more sheep for the profitable exportation of Irish wool to England by (what Swift terms elsewhere) "that abominable Race of Graziers."

[2] The restrictions that England placed on Irish trade produced a clandestine (and robust) trade in wool with France.

[3] Barnstaple, a seaport in Devonshire, on the southwest coast of England, which was a major market for imported Irish wool.

[4] Refers to Parliament's overriding focus on two main issues during the preceding months: proposed legislation to extend the rights of Dissenters, and the conflict between the British and the Irish House of Lords (in the famous Annesley Case) over which body had final jurisdiction in Irish cases, which was resolved in England's favor through passage of the Declaratory Act.

[5] No one contradicting; without a dissenting vote.

Neighbours have made it a *Law*?[6] What if the Ladies would be content with *Irish* Stuffs for the Furniture of their Houses, for Gowns and Petticoats to themselves and their Daughters? Upon the whole, and to crown all the rest, let a firm Resolution be taken, by *Male* and *Female,* never to appear with one single *Shred* that comes from *England; and let all the People say, AMEN.*

I HOPE, and believe, nothing could please his Majesty better than to hear that his loyal Subjects, of both Sexes, in this Kingdom, celebrated his *Birth-Day* (now approaching) *universally* clad in their own Manufacture. Is there Vertue enough left in this deluded People to save them from the Brink of Ruin? If the Mens Opinions may be taken, the Ladies will look as handsome in Stuffs as Brocades,[7] and, since all will be equal, there may be room enough to employ their Wit and Fancy in chusing and matching of Patterns and Colours. I heard the late Archbishop of *Tuam*[8] mention a pleasant Observation of some Body's; *that* Ireland *would never be happy 'till a Law were made for* burning *every Thing that came from* England, *except their* People *and their* Coals: I must confess, that as to the former, I should not be sorry if they would stay at home; and for the latter, I hope, in a little Time we shall have no Occasion for them.[9]

Non tanti mitra est, non tanti Judicis ostrum.[10]

BUT I should rejoice to see a *Stay-Lace*[11] from *England* be thought *scandalous,* and become a Topick for *Censure* at *Visits* and *Tea Tables.*

IF the unthinking Shopkeepers in this Town, had not been *utterly* destitute of common Sense, they would have made some *Proposal to the Parliament,* with a *Petition* to the Purpose I have mentioned; promising to improve the *Cloaths and Stuffs of the Nation, into all possible Degrees of Fineness and Colours, and engaging not to play the Knave, according to their Custom, by exacting and imposing upon the Nobility and Gentry, either as to the Prices or the Goodness.* For I remember, in *London,* upon a general Mourning, the *rascally Mercers* and *Woollen Drapers,* would, in Four and Twenty Hours, raise their *Cloaths* and *Silks* to above a double Price; and if the Mourning continued long, then come whingeing[12] with *Petitions* to the *Court, that they were ready to starve, and their Fineries lay upon their Hands.*

---

[6]The Burial in Woollen Act was passed in 1678 to help the depressed English woolen industry; it required that everyone (except plague victims) be buried in pure English woolen garments.

[7]That is, in domestically manufactured woolen fabrics as in imported, richly wrought fabric with a raised pattern of gold or silver.

[8]John Vesey (1638–1716), who also served as vice-chancellor of the University of Dublin and as a Lord Justice of Ireland.

[9]This statement replaces the (far more inflammatory) sentence that appeared in the first printing of the pamphlet: "Nor am I *even yet* for lessening the number of those Exceptions."

[10]"A mitre is not worth so much, nor the purple robes of a judge."

[11]A string that draws together the opposite edges of a corset by being passed through eyelet holes and pulled tight.

[12]Whining.

I COULD wish our Shopkeepers would immediately think on this *Proposal*, addressing it to all Persons of Quality, and others; but first be sure to get some Body who can write Sense, to put it into Form.

I THINK it needless to exhort the *Clergy* to follow this good Example, because, *in a little Time, those among them who are so unfortunate to have had their Birth and Education in this Country, will think themselves abundantly happy when they can afford* Irish *Crape, and an* Athlone *Hat;* and as to the others, I *shall not presume* to direct them. I have, indeed, seen the present Archbishop of *Dublin* clad from Head to Foot in our own Manufacture; and yet, under the Rose[13] be it spoken, *his Grace deserves as good a Gown, as if he had not been born among us.*[14]

I HAVE not Courage enough to offer *one Syllable* on this Subject to *their Honours* of the Army: Neither have I sufficiently considered the great Importance of *Scarlet* and *Gold Lace.*

THE Fable, in *Ovid*, of *Arachne* and *Pallas*, is to this Purpose.[15] The Goddess had heard of one *Arachne* a young Virgin, very famous for *Spinning* and *Weaving:* They both met upon a Tryal of Skill; and *Pallas* finding herself almost equalled in her own Art, stung with Rage and Envy, knockt her *Rival* down, turned her into a *Spyder,* enjoining her to *spin* and *weave* for ever, *out of her own Bowels,* and *in a very narrow Compass.* I confess, that from a Boy, I always pitied poor *Arachne,* and could never heartily love the Goddess, on Account of so *cruel and unjust a Sentence;* which, however, is *fully executed* upon *Us* by *England,* with further Additions of *Rigor* and *Severity.* For the greatest Part of *our Bowels and Vitals* is extracted, without allowing us the Liberty of *spinning* and *weaving* them.

THE Scripture tells us, that *Oppression makes a wise Man mad;*[16] therefore, consequently speaking, the Reason why some Men are not *mad,* is because they are not *wise:* However, it were to be wished that *Oppression* would, in Time, teach a little *wisdom* to *Fools.*

I WAS much delighted with a Person, who hath a great Estate in this Kingdom,[17] upon his Complaints to me, *how grievously* POOR England *suffers by Impositions from* Ireland. *That we convey our own Wool to* France, *in Spight of all the* Harpies *at the Custom-House.*[18] *That Mr.* Shutleworth, *and others on the* Cheshire *Coasts, are such Fools to sell us their* Bark *at a good Price, for tanning our own Hydes into Leather; with other Enormities of the like Weight and Kind.* To which I will venture to add more: *That the* Mayorality *of this City is always executed by an* Inhabitant, *and often by a* Native, *which*

---

[13] Secretly; in strictest confidence; nowadays usually expressed in its Latin form, *sub rosa.*

[14] William King (1650–1729), Archbishop of Dublin, whose patriotic exertions on behalf of the "Irish interest" endeared him to Swift after some initial conflict between the two men.

[15] Ovid, *Metamorphoses*, vi. Fable I.

[16] Ecclesiastes 7:7.

[17] Arthur Annesley, 5th Earl of Anglesey, whose "great Estate" was Camolin Park in co. Wexford. Annesley took bitter exception to this passage and broke off ties with Swift over it.

[18] The officials employed to enforce the trade restrictions against Ireland—here portrayed as the filthy, predatory monsters (half-female, half-bird) from classical myth.

might as *well be done by a* Deputy, *with a moderate Salary, whereby POOR* England *loseth, at least, one thousand Pounds a Year upon the Ballance. That the Governing of this Kingdom costs the Lord Lieutenant three Thousand six Hundred Pounds a Year, so much* net *Loss to POOR* England. *That the People of* Ireland *presume to dig for Coals* in their own Grounds; *and the Farmers in the County of* Wicklow *send their Turf to the very Market of* Dublin, *to the great Discouragement of the Coal Trade at* Mostyn *and* White-haven.[19] *That the Revenues of the* Post-Office *here, so righteously belonging to the* English *Treasury, as arising chiefly from our own Commerce with each other, should be remitted to* London, *clogged with that grievous Burthen of Exchange, and the Pensions paid out of the* Irish *Revenues to* English *Favourites, should lie under the same Disadvantage, to the great Loss of the Grantees. When a* Divine *is sent over to a* Bishoprick *here, with the Hopes of Five and Twenty Hundred Pounds a Year; upon his Arrival he finds, alas! a dreadful Discount of Ten or Twelve* per Cent. *A* Judge, *or a* Commissioner *of the Revenue, has the same Cause of Complaint.*[20] Lastly, *The Ballad upon* Cotter *is vehemently suspected to be* Irish *Manufacture; and yet is allowed to be sung in our open Streets, under the very* Nose *of the* Government.[21]

THESE are a *few* among the many Hardships we put upon that *POOR* Kingdom of *England;* for which, I am confident, every *honest* Man wisheth a *Remedy:* And, I hear, there is a Project *on Foot* for transporting our best Wheaten *Straw,* by Sea and Land Carriage, to *Dunstable;* and *obliging us by a Law,* to take off yearly so many *Tun of Straw-Hats,* for the Use of our Women; which will be a *great Encouragement* to the Manufacture of that industrious Town.

I WOULD be glad to learn among the Divines, whether a Law *to bind Men without their own Consent,* be obligatory *in foro Conscientiæ;*[22] because, I find *Scripture, Sanderson* and *Suarez,* are wholly silent in the Matter.[23] The Oracle of *Reason,* the great *Law of Nature,* and general Opinion of *Civilians,*[24] wherever they treat of *limitted Governments,* are, indeed, decisive enough.

---

[19] Mostyn is a port on the northeast coast of Wales; Whitehaven, in Cumberland, was considered second only to Newcastle as a coal-shipping port.

[20] These problems resulted from Ireland's lack of a fixed and stable exchange rate with England, made worse by Ireland's inability to mint its own currency or use British sterling, which made Ireland dependent on foreign coins that tended to have a different value in each of the two countries.

[21] The subject of numerous popular ballads, James Cotter, member of a well-to-do Catholic family from Cork, was considered a Jacobite and political trouble-maker; he was hanged for rape in 1720.

[22] "In the forum of conscience."

[23] Robert Sanderson (1587–1663), Bishop of Lincoln, wrote extensively on theological matters and produced several works dealing specifically with questions of conscience. Francisco Suarez (1548–1617) was a Spanish Jesuit and political philosopher who criticized the theory of Divine Right and posited the original equality of all men. This paragraph is Swift's first explicit articulation in print of certain of John Locke's political ideas, which he was to expand upon in *The Drapier's Letters.*

[24] Those who study, write about, or are authorities on the civil law.

IT is wonderful to observe the Biass among our People in favour of *Things, Persons,* and *Wares* of all Kinds that come from *England*. The *Printer* tells his *Hawkers,* that *he has got an excellent new Song just brought from* London. I have somewhat of a Tendency that way my self; and upon hearing a *Coxcomb*[25] from thence displaying himself, with great Volubility, upon the *Park,* the *Play-House,* the *Opera,* the *Gaming Ordinaries,*[26] it was apt to beget in me a Kind of Veneration for his Parts and Accomplishments. It is not many Years, since I remember a *Person*[27] who, by his Style and Literature, seems to have been *Corrector* of a Hedge-Press, in some *Blind-Alley* about *Little-Britain,* proceed *gradually* to be an *Author,* at least a *Translator* of a lower Rate, although somewhat of a larger Bulk, than any that now *flourishes* in *Grub-street;*[28] and, upon the Strength of this Foundation, came over *here; erect* himself up into an *Orator* and *Politician,* and lead a *Kingdom* after him. This, I am told, was the *very Motive* that prevailed on the Author of a Play called, *Love in a Hollow-Tree,* to do us the *Honour* of a Visit; presuming, with very good Reason, *that he was a Writer of a superior Class.*[29] I know *another,* who, for thirty Years past, hath been the *common Standard of Stupidity in England,* where he was never heard a Minute in any *Assembly,* or by any *Party,* with *common Christian Treatment;* yet, upon his Arrival hither, could put on a *Face of Importance and Authority,* talked more than Six, without either *Gracefulness, Propriety,* or *Meaning;* and, at the same Time, be admired and followed as the Pattern of *Eloquence* and *Wisdom.*

NOTHING hath humbled me so much, or shewn a greater Disposition to a *contemptuous* Treatment of *Ireland* in some chief *Governors;* than that high Style of several Speeches from the *Throne,* delivered, as usual, after the *Royal Assent,* in *some Periods* of the two last *Reigns.* Such Exaggerations of the prodigious *Condescensions* in the Prince, to pass *those good Laws,* would have but an odd Sound at *Westminster:* Neither do I apprehend, how any *good Law* can pass, wherein the *King's* Interest is not as much concerned as that of the *People.* I remember, after a Speech on the like Occasion, delivered by my Lord *Wharton,* (I think it was his last) he desired Mr. *Addison* to

---

[25] A foolish, ostentatiously conceited person; a fop; a mere pretender to knowledge or accomplishments.

[26] Public eating houses that also specialized in gambling.

[27] Presumed to be Martin Bladen (1680–1746), soldier, politician, and steadfast Whig; his translation is identified in a Faulkner note as "Supposed to be *Caesar's* Commentaries, dedicated to the D[uke] of Marlborough." It appeared in 1712.

[28] A "hedge-press" was a press that was clandestine or of poor quality (usually both). "*Little-Britain*" was a street in London known for its cheap clothing stalls and second-hand book shops; Grub Street was home to a large number of professional (largely occasional) writers who were denigrated by Tory satirists as scribblers and hacks; cf. Swift's *A Tale of a Tub* and Pope's *The Dunciad.*

[29] William Luckyn (1683–1756), 1st Viscount Grimston, published *The Lawyer's Fortune, or Love in a Hollow Tree* in 1705 but later removed it from circulation after it became the object of widespread ridicule. He is satirized for having achieved "the low Sublime" in Swift's *On Poetry: A Rhapsody* (1733).

ask my Opinion of it:[30] My Answer was, *That his Excellency had very honestly forfeited his Head, on Account of one Paragraph; wherein he asserted, by plain Consequence*, a dispensing Power *in the Queen*.[31] His Lordship owned *it was true*, but *swore* the Words were *put into his Mouth* by direct Orders from Court. From whence it is clear, that some *Ministers* in those Times, were apt, from their *high* Elevation, to look *down* upon this Kingdom, as if it had been one of their *Colonies* of *Out-casts* in *America*.[32] And I observed a little of the same Turn of Spirit in *some great Men*, from whom I expected better; although, to do them Justice, it proved no Point of Difficulty to make them *correct their Idea*, whereof the *whole Nation* quickly found the Benefit. ——But that is *forgotten*. How the Style hath since run, I am wholly a Stranger; having never seen a Speech since the last of the Queen.

I WOULD now expostulate a little with our Country Landlords; who, by unmeasurable *screwing* and *racking* their Tenants all over the Kingdom,[33] have already reduced the miserable *People* to a *worse Condition* than the *Peasants* in *France*, or the *Vassals* in *Germany* and *Poland;* so that the whole *Species* of what we call *Substantial Farmers*, will, in a very few Years, be utterly at an End. It was pleasant to observe these Gentlemen, *labouring* with all their *Might*, for preventing the *Bishops* from letting their Revenues at a moderate half Value, (whereby the whole *Order* would, in an Age, have been reduced to manifest Beggary) at the very Instant, when they were every where *canting* their own Lands upon short Leases,[34] and sacrificing their *oldest Tenants for a Penny an Acre advance*. I know not how it comes to pass, (and yet, perhaps, I know well enough) that *Slaves* have a natural Disposition to be *Tyrants;* and that when my *Betters* give me a Kick, I am apt to revenge it with six upon my *Footman;* although, perhaps, he may be an honest and diligent Fellow. I have heard *great* Divines affirm, that *nothing is so likely to call down an universal Judgment from Heaven upon a Nation, as universal Oppression;* and whether this be not already verified in Part, *their Worships* the Landlords are *now* at full Leisure to consider. Whoever travels this Country, and observes the *Face* of Nature, or the *Faces*, and Habits, and Dwellings of

---

[30] Thomas Wharton (1648–1715), 1st Earl of Wharton, was a prominent Whig politician who served as Lord-Lieutenant of Ireland and led the opposition to the Sacramental Test Act; he was frequently attacked by Swift. Joseph Addison (1672–1719) was a Whig politician and writer who coedited the famous periodical, *The Spectator*, and who maintained a friendship with Swift. He served as Secretary to Wharton when the latter was Lord-Lieutenant of Ireland.

[31] The putative power of the Crown to override statutes—in this case, ones enacted by the Irish Parliament.

[32] Convicted criminals in England were often "transported" to colonies such as Virginia and Maryland to serve out their terms in hard labor.

[33] That is, extorting money from tenants or charging exorbitant rents, at times equal to the full value of the land.

[34] Dividing up their land into small parcels and then putting them out to lease, usually for highly inflated rents.

the *Natives,* will hardly think himself in a Land where either *Law, Religion,* or *common Humanity* is professed.

I CANNOT forbear saying one Word upon a *Thing* they call a *Bank,* which, I hear, is projecting in this Town.[35] I never saw the *Proposals,* nor understand any one Particular of their Scheme: What I wish for, at present, is only a sufficient Provision of *Hemp,* and *Caps,* and *Bells,*[36] to distribute according to the several Degrees of *Honesty* and *Prudence* in *some Persons.* I *hear* only of a monstrous Sum already named; and, if OTHERS do not soon hear of it too, and *hear* it with a *Vengeance,* then am I a Gentleman of less Sagacity than my self, and very few besides, take me to be. And the Jest will be still the better, if it be true, as judicious Persons have assured me, that one Half of this Money will be *real* and the other Half altogether imaginary. The Matter will be likewise much mended, if the Merchants continue to carry off our Gold, and our Goldsmiths to melt down our heavy Silver.

---

[35] Refers to the proposal in 1720 to establish a National Bank of Ireland, which obtained royal approval but was defeated by the Irish Parliament. Swift's staunch opposition to the proposal stemmed from his hostility toward the institutions of the new economy based on credit and speculation.

[36] Refers to the rope used for hanging criminals, and the insignia of the fool or jester.

THE LAST SPEECH AND DYING WORDS
OF EBENEZOR ELLISTON,

Who was Executed the Second Day of May 1722
Published at his Desire, for the Common Good

In this parody of the confession and repentance speeches of criminals sold on the day of their hanging, Swift uses the occasion of an actual execution in the spring of 1722 to shine the spotlight on a serious problem—the growing incidence of crime in the city of Dublin—while deftly exploiting the subgenre's satiric potential.[1] Like other of his writings (e.g., A Full Account of…the Execution of William Wood, *and the poems* Clever Tom Clinch going to be hanged *and* The Yahoo's Overthrow*), this broadside reflects Swift's imaginative engagement with the public and popular rituals surrounding crime and punishment in his day.*

* * *

I AM now going to suffer the just Punishment for my Crimes prescribed by the Law of God and my Country. I know it is the constant Custom, that those who come to this Place should have Speeches made for them, and cryed about in their own Hearing, as they are carried to Execution; and truly they are such Speeches that although our Fraternity be an ignorant illiterate People, they would make a Man ashamed to have such Nonsense and false *English* charged upon him even when he is going to the Gallows: They contain a pretended Account of our Birth and Family; of the Fact for which we are to die; of our sincere Repentance; and a Declaration of our Religion. I cannot expect to avoid the same Treatment with my Predecessors. However, having had an Education one or two Degrees better than those of my Rank

---

[1]N.B. *About the Time that this Speech was written, the Town was much pestered with Street-Robbers; who, in a barbarous Manner would seize on Gentlemen, and take them into remote Corners, and after they had robbed them, would leave them bound and gagged. It is remarkable, that this Speech had so good an Effect, that there have been very few Robberies of that kind committed since* (Faulkner's note).

and Profession;[2] I have been considering ever since my Commitment, what it might be proper for me to deliver upon this Occasion.

AND First, I cannot say from the Bottom of my Heart, that I am truly sorry for the Offence I have given to God and the World; but I am very much so, for the bad Success of my Villainies in bringing me to this untimely End. For it is plainly evident, that after having some time ago obtained a Pardon from the Crown, I again took up my old Trade; my evil Habits were so rooted in me, and I was grown so unfit for any other kind of Employment. And therefore although in Compliance with my Friends, I resolve to go to the Gallows after the usual Manner, Kneeling, with a Book in my Hand, and my Eyes lift up; yet I shall feel no more Devotion in my Heart than I have observed in some of my Comrades, who have been drunk among common Whores the very Night before their Execution. I can say further from my own Knowledge, that two of my Fraternity after they had been hanged, and wonderfully came to Life, and made their Escapes, as it sometimes happens; proved afterwards the wickedest Rogues I ever knew, and so continued until they were hanged again for good and all;[3] and yet they had the Impudence at both Times they went to the gallows, to smite their Breasts, and lift up their Eyes to Heaven all the Way.

SECONDLY, From the Knowledge I have of my own wicked Dispositions and that of my Comrades, I give it as my Opinion, that nothing can be more unfortunate to the Publick, than the Mercy of the Government in ever pardoning or transporting us; unless when we betray one another, as we never fail to do, if we are sure to be well paid;[4] and then a Pardon may do good; by the same Rule, *That it is better to have but one Fox in a Farm than three or four.* But we generally make a Shift to return after being transported,[5] and are ten times greater Rogues than before, and much more cunning. Besides, I know it by Experience, that some Hopes we have of finding Mercy, when we are tryed, or after we are condemned, is always a great Encouragement to us.

THIRDLY, Nothing is more dangerous to idle young Fellows, than the Company of those odious common Whores we frequent, and of which this Town is full: These Wretches put us upon all Mischief to feed their Lusts and Extravagancies: They are ten times more bloody and cruel than Men; their Advice is always not to spare if we are pursued; they get drunk with us, and are common to us all; and yet, if they can get any Thing by it, are sure to be our Betrayers.

---

[2]Elliston's parents were devout Dissenters who gave him a solid education and put him apprentice to a silkweaver.

[3]Perhaps playing on the memory of a hoax Swift and a few friends perpetrated on the eve of All Fool's Day, 1713, when they circulated a story, several days after the execution of one Richard Noble, that the condemned man was "but half-hanged, and was brought to life by His Friends, but was since seised again, and is now in a Messenger's hands at the Black Swan in Holborn"; related in the *Journal to Stella.*

[4]Refers to the professional informers known as "Thief-Takers," the most famous of whom was Jonathan Wild, alternately admired and reviled as "Thief-Taker General of Great Britain and Ireland" until his execution in 1725.

[5]That is, after being sentenced to a period of indentured servitude in the American colonies in lieu of hanging or imprisonment in England.

NOW, as I am a dying Man, something I have done which may be of good Use to the Publick. I have left with an honest Man (and indeed the only honest Man I was ever acquainted with) the Names of all my wicked Brethren, the present Places of their Abode, with a short Account of the chief Crimes they have committed; in many of which I have been their Accomplice, and heard the rest from their own Mouths: I have likewise set down the Names of those we call our Setters,[6] of the wicked Houses we frequent, and of those who receive and buy our stolen Goods. I have solemnly charged this honest Man, and have received his Promise upon Oath, that whenever he hears of any Rogue to be tryed for Robbing, or House-breaking, he will look into his List, and if he finds the Name there of the Thief concerned, to send the whole Paper to the Government. Of this I here give my Companions fair and publick Warning, and hope they will take it.

IN the Paper abovementioned, which I left with my Friend, I have also set down the Names of several Gentlemen who have been robbed in *Dublin* Streets for three Years past: I have told the Circumstances of those Robberies; and shewn plainly that nothing but the Want of common Courage was the Cause of their Misfortunes. I have therefore desired my Friend, that whenever any Gentlemen happens to be robbed in the Streets, he will get that Relation printed and published with the first Letters of those Gentlemens Names, who by their own Want of Bravery are likely to be the Cause of all the Mischief of that Kind, which may happen for the future.

I CANNOT leave the World without a short Description of that Kind of Life, which I have led for some Years past; and is exactly the same with the rest of our wicked Brethren.

ALTHOUGH we are generally so corrupted from our Childhood, as to have no Sense of Goodness; yet something heavy always hangs about us, I know not what it is, that we are never easy till we are half drunk among our Whores and Companions; nor sleep sound, unless we drink longer than we can stand. If we go abroad in the Day, a wise Man would easily find us to be Rogues by our Faces; we have such a suspicious, fearful, and constrained Countenance; often turning back, and slinking through narrow Lanes and Allies. I have never failed of knowing a Brother Thief by his Looks, though I never saw him before. Every Man among us keeps his particular Whore, who is however common to us all, when we have a mind to change. When we have got a Booty, if it be in Money, we divide it equally among our Companions, and soon squander it away on our Vices in those Houses that receive us; for the Master and Mistress, and the very Tapster, go snacks;[7] and besides make us pay treble Reckonings. If our Plunder be Plate, Watches, Rings, Snuff-boxes, and the like; we have Customers in all Quarters of the Town to take them off. I have seen a Tankard worth Fifteen Pounds sold to a Fellow in —— Street for Twenty Shillings; and a Gold Watch for Thirty. I have set down his Name,

---

[6] Individuals employed by robbers to spy on their intended victims and sometimes to act as lures or decoys for them.

[7] Share and share alike.

and that of several others in the Paper already mentioned. We have Setters watching in Corners, and by dead Walls, to give us Notice when a Gentleman goes by; especially if he be any thing in Drink. I believe in my Conscience, that if an Account were made of a Thousand Pounds in stolen Goods; considering the low Rates we sell them at, the Bribes we must give for Concealment, the Extortions of Ale-house Reckonings, and other necessary Charges, there would not remain Fifty Pounds clear to be divided among the Robbers. And out of this we must find Cloaths for our Whores, besides treating them from Morning to Night; who, in Requital, reward us with nothing but Treachery and the Pox. For when our Money is gone, they are every Moment threatning to inform against us, if we will not go out to look for more. If any Thing in this World be like Hell, as I have heard it described by our Clergy; the truest Picture of it must be in the Back-Room of one of our Ale-houses at Midnight; where a Crew of Robbers and their Whores are met together after a Booty, and are beginning to grow drunk; from which Time, until they are past their Senses, is such a continued horrible Noise of Cursing, Blasphemy, Lewdness, Scurrility, and brutish Behaviour; such Roaring and Confusion, such a Clatter of Mugs and Pots at each other's Heads; that *Bedlam*, in Comparison, is a sober and orderly Place:[8] At last they all tumble from their Stools and Benches, and sleep away the rest of the Night; and generally the Landlord or his Wife, or some other Whore who has a stronger Head than the rest, picks their Pockets before they wake. The Misfortune is, that we can never be easy till we are drunk; and our Drunkenness constantly exposes us to be more easily betrayed and taken.

THIS is a short Picture of the Life I have led; which is more miserable than that of the poorest Labourer who works for four Pence a Day; and yet Custom is so strong, that I am confident, if I could make my Escape at the Foot of the Gallows, I should be following the same Course this very Evening. So that upon the whole, we ought to be looked upon as the common Enemies of Mankind; whose Interest it is to root us out like Wolves, and other mischievous Vermin, against which no fair Play is required.

IF I have done Service to Men in what I have said, I shall hope I have done Service to God; and that will be better than a silly Speech made for me full of Whining and Canting,[9] which I utterly despise, and have never been used to; yet such a one I expect to have my Ears tormented with, as I am passing along the Streets.

GOOD People fare ye well; bad as I am, I leave many worse behind me. I hope you shall see me die like a Man, the Death of a Dog.

E.E.

---

[8]The Hospital of St. Mary of Bethlehem ("Bedlam"), rebuilt in 1676 near London Wall, was an asylum for the mentally deranged. See Swift's *Character...of the Legion Club.*

[9]Speaking in a sing-song tone; affectedly using religious or pietistic phrases for hypocritical purposes.

The Drapier's Letters (1724)

Letter I

A Letter To the *Shop-Keepers, Tradesmen, Farmers,* and *Common-People* of *IRELAND*

The Drapier's Letters *were Swift's contribution to the widespread protest that arose after William Wood, an English entrepreneur and projector who owned copper and iron works throughout Britain, obtained a patent from the Crown in July 1722 to mint more than £100,000 of copper half-pence for Ireland over a fourteen-year period. Opposition to this scheme, which came from all segments of Irish society, was fueled by the absence of safeguards to ensure the value of the coins, the belief that Wood got his patent through government bribery and corruption, and the simmering resentment over Ireland's inability to mint its own money as a result of Britain's colonial restrictions on the country's economy. Swift's persona, "M.B. Drapier," a middle-class tradesman and cloth dealer (whose initials perhaps stand for "Marcus Brutus"), entered a battle that was already heated, but he rapidly took center stage and became a lightning rod for the controversy: a figure both denounced by the authorities and treated with adulation by the Irish populace, who elevated him to the status of folk hero and "Hibernian Patriot" after Wood's patent was withdrawn by the British govern-ment. Swift addressed each of his* Letters—*seven in all, though only the first five were printed at the time*—*to a different individual or group within Irish soci-ety, varying the style and language according to each one's intellectual capacity and interests. The first* Letter, *circulated in March 1724, is appealing to the humblest and least educated of his countrymen.*

* * *

Brethren, Friends, Countrymen, and *Fellow-Subjects.*

WHAT I intend now to say to you, is, next to your Duty to God, and the Care of your Salvation, of the greatest Concern to your selves, and your Children; your *Bread* and *Cloathing,* and every common Necessary of Life entirely depend upon it. Therefore I do most earnestly exhort you as *Men,* as *Christians,* as *Parents,* and as *Lovers of your Country,* to read this Paper with the utmost Attention, or get it read to you by others; which that you may do at the less Expence, I have ordered the Printer to sell it at the lowest Rate.[1]

IT is a great Fault among you, that when a Person writes with no other Intention than *to do you Good, you will not be at the Pains to read his Advices:* One Copy of this Paper may serve a Dozen of you, which will be less than a Farthing[2] apiece. It is your Folly, that you have no common or general Interest in your View, not even the Wisest among you; neither do you know or enquire, or care who are your Friends, or who are your Enemies.

ABOUT four Years ago, a little Book was written to advise all People to wear the *Manufactures of this our own Dear Country:* It had no other Design, said nothing against the *King* or *Parliament,* or *any* Person whatsoever, yet the POOR PRINTER was prosecuted two Years, with the utmost Violence; and even some WEAVERS themselves, for whose Sake it was written, being upon the JURY, FOUND HIM GUILTY.[3] This would be enough to discourage any Man from endeavouring to do you Good, when you will either neglect him, or fly in his Face for his Pains; and when he must expect only *Danger to himself* and to be fined and imprisoned, perhaps to his Ruin.

HOWEVER, I cannot but warn you once more of the manifest Destruction before your Eyes, if you do not behave your selves as you ought.

I WILL therefore first tell you the *plain Story of the Fact;* and then I will lay before you, how you ought to act in common Prudence, and according to the *Laws of your Country.*

THE *Fact is thus;* It having been many Years since COPPER HALF-PENCE or FARTHINGS were last Coined in this *Kingdom,* they have been for some Time very scarce, and many *Counterfeits* passed about under the Name of RAPS: Several Applications were made to *England,* that we might have Liberty to *Coin New Ones,* as in former Times we did; but they did not succeed.[4] At last one Mr. WOOD, a *mean ordinary Man, a Hard-Ware Dealer,* procured a *Patent* under His MAJESTY'S BROAD SEAL, to coin 108000 *l.* in *Copper* for this *Kingdom;* which Patent however did not oblige any one here to take them, unless they pleased.[5] Now you must know, that the HALF-PENCE and FARTHINGS in *England* pass for very little more than they are worth: And if you should beat them to Pieces, and sell them to the *Brazier,*[6] you would not lose much above a Penny in a Shilling. But Mr. WOOD made his HALF-PENCE

---

[1] Swift himself bore the printer's costs, enabling the letter to be sold cheaply, in quantities of three dozen for two shillings; 2,000 copies were distributed throughout the country in March 1724.

[2] A coin worth a quarter of a penny.

[3] Refers to the publication in 1720 of Swift's *Proposal for the Universal Use of Irish Manufacture,* and the ensuing prosecution and imprisonment of its printer, Edward Waters.

[4] Although there were instances in the sixteenth and seventeenth centuries when coins had been minted in Dublin, in more recent times the matter was handled via patents given to private individuals in England, usually for a handsome consideration.

[5] The patent explicitly stated that the half-pence were "to pass and be received as current money by such as shall be willing to receive the same."

[6] Someone who makes articles out of brass.

of such *Base Metal,* and so much smaller than the *English* ones, that the *Brazier* would hardly give you above a *Penny* of good Money for a *Shilling* of his; so that this sum of 108000 *l.* in good Gold and Silver, must be given for TRASH that will not be worth above *Eight* or *Nine Thousand Pounds* real Value. But this is not the Worst; for Mr. WOOD, when he pleases, may by Stealth send over *another* 108000 *l.* and buy *all our Goods for Eleven Parts in Twelve,* under the Value. For Example, if a *Hatter* sells a Dozen *of Hats* for *Five Shillings* a-piece, which amounts to *Three Pounds,* and receives the Payment in Mr. WOOD's Coin, he really receives only the Value of *Five Shillings.*

PERHAPS you will wonder how such an *ordinary Fellow* as this Mr. WOOD could have so much Interest as to get His MAJESTY's Broad Seal for so great a Sum of bad Money, to be sent to this poor Country; and that all the *Nobility* and *Gentry* here could not obtain the same Favour, and let us make our own HALF-PENCE, as we used to do. Now I will make that Matter very plain. We are at a great Distance from the *King's Court,* and have no body there to solicit for us, although a great Number of *Lords* and *Squires,* whose Estates are here, and are our Countrymen, spend all their *Lives* and *Fortunes* there. But this same Mr. WOOD was able to attend constantly for his own Interest; he is an ENGLISHMAN and had GREAT FRIENDS, and it seems knew very well *where to give Money,* to those that would speak to OTHERS that could speak to the KING, and would tell a FAIR STORY.[7] And HIS MAJESTY, and perhaps the great Lord or Lords who advised him, might think it was for our *Country's Good;* and so, as the Lawyers express it, the KING was deceived in his Grant;[8] which often happens in *all Reigns.* And I am sure if His MAJESTY knew that such a Patent, if it should take Effect according to the Desire of Mr. WOOD, would utterly ruin this Kingdom, which hath given such great Proofs of its *Loyalty*; he would immediately recall it, and perhaps shew his Displeasure to SOME BODY OR OTHER: *But a Word to the Wise is enough.* Most of you must have heard with what Anger our *Honourable House of Commons* received an Account of this WOOD's PATENT. There were several *Fine Speeches* made upon it, and plain Proofs, that it was all a WICKED CHEAT from the *Bottom to the Top;* and several *smart Votes* were printed, which that same WOOD had the Assurance to answer likewise in *Print,* and in so confident a Way, as if he were *a better Man than our whole Parliament* put together.[9]

---

[7] Refers to Wood's connections with the London Court and, more specifically, his reported payment of £10,000 to George I's mistress, the Duchess of Kendal (Duchess of Munster in the Irish peerage), to acquire possession of the patent that was given to her by the king.

[8] A concept in English common law that presumes the king's innocence of malicious intent or wrong-doing, blaming instead the schemes or misrepresentations of his agents for whatever harmful actions were taken in his name.

[9] "Humble Addresses" to the King by both Houses of the Irish Parliament accused Wood of "a most Notorious Fraud and Deceit in Coining the said *Half-Pence*" and petitioned the Crown for relief from the latter's "Fatal Effects." Wood responded with disdainful and accusatory statements printed in several London newspapers.

THIS WOOD, as soon as his *Patent* was passed, or soon after, sends over a great many *Barrels of those* HALF-PENCE, to *Cork* and other *Sea-Port Towns,* and to get them off, offered an *Hundred Pounds* in his *Coin* for *Seventy* or *Eighty* in *Silver:* But the *Collectors* of the KING's Customs very honestly refused to take them, and so did almost every body else. And since the Parliament hath condemned them, and desired the KING that they might be stopped, all the *Kingdom* do abominate them.

BUT WOOD is still working *under hand* to force his HALF-PENCE upon us; and if he can by help of his *Friends* in *England* prevail so far as to get an Order that the *Commissioners* and *Collectors* of the *King's* Money shall receive them, and that the *Army* is to be paid with them, then he thinks *his Work shall be done*. And this is the Difficulty you will be under in such a *Case:* For the common Soldier when he goes to the *Market* or *Ale-house,* will offer this Money, and if it be refused, perhaps he will *swagger* and *hector,* and *threaten* to *beat* the *Butcher* or *Ale-wife,*[10] or take the Goods by Force, and throw them the bad HALF-PENCE. In this and the like Cases, the *Shop-keeper,* or *Victualler,*[11] or *any other Tradesman* has no more to do, than to demand ten times the Price of his Goods, if it is to be paid in WOOD's Money; for Example, Twenty Pence of that Money for a *Quart* of *Ale,* and so in all things else, and not part with his Goods till he gets the *Money.*

FOR suppose you go to an *Ale-house* with that base Money, and the *Landlord* gives you a Quart for Four of these HALF-PENCE, what must the *Victualler* do? His *Brewer* will not be paid in that Coin, or if the *Brewer* should be such a Fool, the *Farmers* will not take it from them for their *Bere,*[12] because they are bound by their Leases to pay their Rents in Good and Lawful Money of *England,* which this is not, nor of *Ireland* neither, and the *Squire their Landlord* will never be so bewitched to take such *Trash* for his Land; so that it must certainly stop somewhere or other, and wherever it stops it is the same Thing, and we are all undone.

THE common Weight of these HALF-PENCE is between four and five to an *Ounce;* suppose five, then three Shillings and four Pence will weigh a Pound, and consequently *Twenty Shillings* will weigh *Six Pounds Butter Weight.*[13] Now there are many hundred *Farmers* who pay Two hundred Pounds a Year Rent: Therefore when one of these *Farmers* comes with his Half-Year's Rent, which is One hundred Pound, it will be at least Six hundred Pound weight, which is Three Horses Load.

IF a *Squire* has a mind to come to Town to buy Cloaths and Wine and Spices for himself and Family, or perhaps to pass the Winter here; he must bring with him five or six Horses loaden with *Sacks* as the *Farmers* bring their Corn; and when his Lady comes in her Coach to our Shops, it must be

---

[10] A woman who keeps an alehouse.

[11] A purveyor of food and drink; an inn-keeper.

[12] "A sort of Barley in *Ireland*" (Faulkner's note).

[13] Formerly 18 or more ounces to the pound; hence its figurative meaning, "for good measure."

followed by a Car loaded with Mr. WOOD's Money. And I hope we shall have the Grace to take it for no more than it is worth.

THEY say SQUIRE CONOLLY has *Sixteen Thousand Pounds a Year;* now if he sends for his *Rent* to Town, *as it is likely he does,* he must have *Two Hundred and Fifty Horses* to bring up his *Half Year's Rent,* and two or three great *Cellars* in his House for Stowage.[14] But what the Bankers will do I cannot tell. For I am assured, that some great Bankers keep by them *Forty Thousand Pounds* in ready Cash to answer all Payments, which Sum in Mr. WOOD's Money, would require Twelve Hundred Horses to carry it.

FOR my own Part, I am already resolved what to do; I have a pretty good Shop of *Irish Stuffs*[15] and *Silks,* and instead of taking Mr. WOOD's bad Copper, I intend to Truck with my Neighbours the *Butchers,* and *Bakers,* and *Brewers,* and the rest, *Goods for Goods,* and the little *Gold* and *Silver* I have, I will keep by me like my *Heart's Blood* till better Times, or until I am just ready to starve, and then I will buy Mr. WOOD's Money, as my Father did the Brass Money in King *James's* Time;[16] who could buy *Ten Pound* of it with a *Guinea,* and I hope to get as much for a *Pistole,* and so purchase *Bread* from those who will be such Fools as to sell it me.[17]

These *Half-pence,* if they once pass, will soon be *Counterfeit,* because it may be cheaply done, the *Stuff* is so *Base.* The *Dutch* likewise will probably do the same thing, and send them over to us to pay for our *Goods;* and Mr. WOOD will never be at rest, but coin on: So that in some Years we shall have at least five Times 108000 *l.* of this *Lumber.* Now the current Money of this Kingdom is not reckoned to be above Four Hundred Thousand Pounds in all; and while there is a *Silver* Six-Pence left, these *Blood-suckers* will never be quiet.

WHEN once the *Kingdom* is reduced to such a Condition, I will tell you what must be the End: The *Gentlemen of Estates* will all turn off their *Tenants* for want of Payment; because, as I told you before, the *Tenants* are obliged by their Leases to pay *Sterling,* which is Lawful Current Money of *England;* then they will turn their own *Farmers, as too many of them do already,* run all into *Sheep* where they can, keeping only such other *Cattle* as are necessary;[18] then they will be their own *Merchants,* and send their *Wool* and *Butter,* and *Hides,* and *Linnen* beyond Sea for ready *Money,* and *Wine,* and *Spices,* and

---

[14]William Conolly (d. 1729) was a prominent Whig politician, Speaker of the Irish House of Commons, reputed to be the wealthiest man in Ireland. The "House" referred to is Castletown House, the sumptuous Palladian mansion he was then building in Celbridge, near Dublin.

[15]Woolen fabrics; manufactured materials.

[16]Refers to the base coinage with which James II paid his troops during his Irish campaign in 1689–90.

[17]A guinea was an English coin first issued in 1663 and initially valued at 20 shillings, but revalued as the equivalent of 21 shillings in 1717. A pistole was an old Spanish gold piece worth between 16 and 18 shillings.

[18]Refers to the widespread use of agricultural lands for pasturing sheep, a practice frequently attacked by Swift; cf. note 1 to *A Proposal for the Universal Use of Irish Manufacture.* The word "turn" here means "evict."

Silks. They will keep only a few miserable *Cottagers.*[19] The *Farmers* must *Rob* or *Beg,* or leave their *Country.* The *Shop-keepers* in this and every other Town, must *Break* and *Starve:* For it is the *Landed-man* that maintains the *Merchant,* and *Shop-keeper,* and *Handicrafts-Man.*

BUT when the *Squire* turns *Farmer* and *Merchant* himself, all the good Money he gets from abroad, he will hoard up to send for *England,* and keep some poor *Taylor* or *Weaver,* and the like, in his own House, who will be glad to get Bread at any Rate.

I SHOULD never have done, if I were to tell you all the Miseries that we shall undergo, if we be so *Foolish* and *Wicked* as to take this *Cursed Coin.* It would be very hard, if all *Ireland* should be put into *One Scale,* and *this sorry Fellow* WOOD *into the other:* That Mr. WOOD should weigh down *this whole Kingdom,* by which *England* gets above a Million of good Money every Year clear into their *Pockets:* And that is more than the *English* do by *all the World besides.*

BUT your *great Comfort is,* that, as his Majesty's *Patent* doth not oblige you to take this *Money,* so the *Laws* have not given the *Crown* a Power of forcing the *Subjects* to take what *Money* the *King* pleases: For then by the same Reason we might be bound to take *Pebble-stones,* or *Cockle-shells,* or *stamped Leather* for *Current Coin,*[20] if ever we should happen to live under an ill *Prince;* who might likewise by the same Power make a *Guinea* pass for Ten Pounds, a *Shilling* for Twenty Shillings, and so on; by which he would in a short Time get all the *Silver* and *Gold* of the *Kingdom* into his own Hands, and leave us nothing but *Brass* or *Leather,* or what he pleased. Neither is any thing reckoned more *Cruel* or *Oppressive* in the *French Government,* than their common Practice of calling in all their Money after they have sunk it very low, and then coining it a-new at a much higher Value; which however is not the Thousandth Part so wicked as this *abominable Project* of Mr. *Wood.* For the *French* give their Subjects *Silver* for *Silver,* and *Gold* for *Gold;* but this *Fellow* will not so much as give us good *Brass* or *Copper* for our *Gold* and *Silver,* nor even a Twelfth Part of their Worth.

HAVING said this much, I will now go on to tell you the Judgments of some great *Lawyers* in this Matter; whom I fee'd[21] on purpose for your Sakes, and got their *Opinions* under their *Hands,* that I might be sure I went upon good Grounds.

A *Famous* Law-Book *called the* Mirrour of Justice,[22] *discoursing of the Charters (or Laws) ordained by our* Ancient Kings, *declares the* Law *to be*

---

[19] Peasants who live in a cottage belonging to a farm, sometimes with a small piece of land attached, for which they must provide labor on the farm; also known as "cottiers."

[20] Swift might have in mind here the situation in the American colonies, where items such as tobacco and shells were used as currency. North Carolina had recently declared seventeen different items legal tender.

[21] Hired; engaged for a sum of money.

[22] *The Mirrour of Justices* (originally *La Somme appelle Mirroir des Justices*), a compilation of common-law cases (published in 1646) that was put together by Andrew Horne, legal writer and chamberlain of London during the reign of Edward I (1272–1307).

as follows: It was ordained that no King *of this Realm should* Change, *or* Impair *the* Money, *or make any other* Money *than of* Gold *or* Silver *without the Assent of all the Counties, that is,* as my Lord *Coke* says, *without the Assent of* Parliament.[23]

THIS Book is very Ancient, and of great Authority for the Time in which it was wrote, and with that Character is often quoted by that great Lawyer my Lord *Coke.* By the Laws of *England,* the several Metals are divided into *Lawful* or *true Metal* and *unlawful* or *false Metal;* the Former comprehends *Silver* or *Gold,* the Latter all *Baser Metals:* That the Former is only to pass in Payments, appears by an Act of *Parliament* made the Twentieth Year of *Edward* the *First,* called the *Statute concerning the passing of Pence;*[24] which I give you here as I got it translated into *English;* For some of our *Laws* at that time were, as I am told, writ in *Latin: Whoever in Buying or Selling presumeth to refuse an Half-penny or Farthing of Lawful Money, bearing the Stamp which it ought to have, let him be seized on as a Contemner of the King's Majesty, and cast into Prison.*

BY this *Statute,* no Person is to be reckoned a *Contemner* of the *King's Majesty,* and for that Crime to be *committed to Prison;* but he who refuseth to accept the King's Coin made *of Lawful Metal:* by which as I observed before, *Silver* and *Gold* only are intended.

THAT this is the true *Construction* of the *Act,* appears not only from the plain Meaning of the Words, but from my Lord *Coke's* Observation upon it. By this Act (says he) it appears, that no Subject can be forced to take in *Buying* or *Selling* or other *Payments,* any Money made but of lawful Metal; that is, of *Silver* or *Gold.*

THE Law of *England* gives the King all Mines of *Gold* and *Silver,* but not the Mines of other *Metals;* the Reason of which *Prerogative* or *Power,* as it is given by my Lord *Coke,* is because Money can be made of *Gold and Silver;* but not of other Metals.[25]

PURSUANT to this Opinion, *Half-pence* and *Farthings* were anciently made of *Silver,* which is evident from the Act *of Parliament* of *Henry* the IVth. Chap. 4.[26] whereby it is enacted as follows: *Item, for the great Scarcity that is at present within the Realm of* England *of Half-pence and Farthings of* Silver; it is *ordained and established, that the Third Part of all the* Money *of* Silver Plate *which shall be brought to the* Bullion, *shall be made in* Half-pence *and* Farthings. This shews that by the Words *Half penny* and *Farthing* of Lawful

[23] Sir Edward Coke (1552–1634) was a noted jurist opposed to the abuses of the royal prerogative by James I and Charles I, who wrote a four-part compendium, *Institutes of the Laws of England,* the second part of which (specifically, 2 *Inst.* 576 and 2 *Inst.* 577) is the source of Swift's citations in this and the following paragraphs.

[24] To establish the Crown as the absolute arbiter of what constitutes "lawful tender" and thus eliminate the corrupt practices of private minters, Edward I appointed a commission in 1293 to help standardize the currency and proclaimed that no subject should be forced to accept coins made of any metal other than silver or gold.

[25] This is a significant point given Wood's extensive holdings in copper and steel mines.

[26] The correct reference is 4 Henry IV. c. 10.

Money in that Statute concerning the *passing of* Pence, is meant a small Coin
in *Half-pence* and *Farthings* of *Silver*.

THIS is further manifest from the Statute of the Ninth Year of *Edward*
the IIId. Chap. 3. which enacts, *That no sterling* Half-penny *or* Farthing *be
Molten for to make Vessels, or any other thing by the Gold-smiths, nor others,
upon Forfeiture of the* Money *so molten (or melted.)*

By another Act in this *King's* Reign, *Black Money* was not to be current in
England.[27] And by an Act made in the Eleventh Year of his Reign, Chap. 5.
Galley Half-pence were not to pass:[28] What kind of *Coin* these were I do not
know; but I presume they were made of *Base Metal*. And these Acts were no
New *Laws*, but further Declarations of the old *Laws* relating to the *Coin*.

THUS the *Law* stands in Relation to *Coin*. Nor is there any Example to
the contrary, except one in *Davis's Reports;*[29] who tells us, that in the time
of *Tyrone's* Rebellion,[30] *Queen Elizabeth* ordered *Money* of *mixt Metal* to
be coined in the Tower of *London*, and sent over hither for Payment of the
Army; obliging all People to receive it; and Commanding, that all *Silver
Money* should be taken only as *Bullion*, that is, for as much as it weighed.
Davis tells us several Particulars in this Matter too long here to trouble you
with, and that the *Privy Council* of this *Kingdom* obliged a *Merchant* in
England to receive this *mixt Money* for Goods transmitted hither.

BUT this Proceeding is rejected by all the best Lawyers, as contrary to
Law, the *Privy Council* here having no such legal Power. And besides it is
to be considered, that the *Queen* was then under great Difficulties by a
Rebellion in this *Kingdom* assisted from *Spain*. And, whatever is done in
great Exigences and dangerous Times, should never be an Example to proceed by in Seasons of *Peace* and *Quietness*.

I WILL now, my dear Friends, to save you the Trouble, set before you in
short, what the *Law* obliges you to do; and what it does not oblige you to.

FIRST, you are obliged to take all Money in Payments which is coined by
the *King*, and is of the *English* Standard or Weight; provided it be of *Gold*
or *Silver*.

SECONDLY, you are not obliged to take any Money which is not of *Gold*
or *Silver;* not only the *Half-pence* or *Farthings* of *England*, but of any
other Country. And it is meerly for Convenience, or Ease, that you are
content to take them; because the Custom of coining *Silver Half-pence*

---

[27] The outlawing of "black money," or coins made of copper as opposed to silver ("white money"), occurred in Henry IV's reign, not Edward III's.

[28] The outlawing of galley half-pence, or cheap silver coins thought to have been introduced into England by Genoese sailors, was mandated by 9 Henry IV. c. 4. Continued illicit circulation of the coin resulted in a further parliamentary ban during the reign of Henry V (3 Henry V. c. 1).

[29] The report of law cases in Ireland published in 1615 by Sir John Davies, who served as attorney general of Ireland.

[30] An insurrection in the 1590s against English rule in Ireland, led by Hugh O'Neill, Earl of Tyrone, in alliance with King Philip III of Spain. It ended in 1603 with the defeat of the Irish chieftains.

and *Farthings* hath long been left off; I suppose, on Account of their being subject to be lost.

THIRDLY, Much less are we obliged to take those *Vile Half-pence* of that same *Wood,* by which you must lose almost Eleven-Pence in every Shilling.

THEREFORE, my Friends, stand to it One and All: Refuse this *Filthy Trash.* It is no Treason to rebel against Mr. *Wood.* His *Majesty* in his Patent obliges no body to take these *Half-pence:* Our *Gracious Prince* hath no such ill Advisers about him; or if he had, yet you see the Laws have not left it in the *King*'s Power, to force us to take any Coin but what is Lawful, of right Standard, *Gold* and *Silver.* Therefore you have nothing to fear.

AND let me in the next Place apply my self particularly to you who are the poorer Sort of *Tradesmen:* Perhaps you may think you will not be so great Losers as the Rich, if these *Half-pence* should pass; because you seldom see any *Silver,* and your Customers come to your Shops or Stalls with nothing but *Brass;* which you likewise find hard to be got. But you may take my Word, whenever this Money gains Footing among you, you will be utterly undone. If you carry these *Half-pence* to a Shop for *Tobacco* or *Brandy,* or any other Thing you want; the Shop-keeper will advance his Goods accordingly, or else he must break[31] and leave the *Key under the Door.* Do you think I will sell you a Yard of Ten-penny Stuff for Twenty of Mr. *Wood*'s *Half-pence?* No, not under Two Hundred at least; neither will I be at the Trouble of counting, but weigh them in a Lump. I will tell you one Thing further; that if Mr. *Wood*'s Project should take, it will ruin even our Beggars: For when I give a Beggar a Half-penny, it will quench his Thirst, or go a good Way to fill his Belly; but the Twelfth Part of a Half-penny will do him no more Service than if I should give him three Pins out of my Sleeve.

IN short; these *Half-pence* are like the *accursed Thing,* which, as the *Scripture* tells us, the *Children of Israel* were forbidden to touch.[32] They will run about like the *Plague* and destroy every one who lays his Hands upon them. I have heard *Scholars* talk of a Man who told the King that he had invented a Way to torment People by putting them into a *Bull* of Brass with Fire under it: But the *Prince* put the *Projector* first into his own *Brazen Bull* to make the Experiment.[33] This very much resembles the Project of Mr. *Wood;* and the like of this may possibly be Mr. *Wood*'s Fate; that the *Brass* he contrived to torment this *Kingdom* with, may prove his own Torment, and his Destruction at last.

N. B. The Author of this Paper is informed by Persons who have made it their Business to be exact in their Observations on the true Value of these

---

[31] Become bankrupt; fail financially.

[32] Joshua 6:18.

[33] Refers to the proverbial cruelty of the Sicilian tyrant Phalaris (sixth century B.C.E.), who was known for roasting his enemies in a brazen bull; he inflicted the same punishment on the Athenian who first presented the bull to him.

Half-pence; that any Person may expect to get a Quart of Two-penny Ale for Thirty Six of them.

I DESIRE that all Families may keep this Paper carefully by them to refresh their Memories whenever they shall have farther Notice of Mr. *Wood*'s Half-pence, or any other the like Imposture.

Letter II

A LETTER to Mr. *Harding* the Printer, upon Occasion of a *Paragraph* in his News-Paper of *August* 1st, 1724, relating to Mr. *Wood's* Half-Pence

This epistle, addressed to the printer of The Drapier's Letters, *John Harding, was published on August 6, 1724, shortly after news appeared in several Dublin papers that the inquiry and assay of Wood's coinage, ordered by a Committee of the Council in London, had found in Wood's favor and would soon be made public in an official report (printed copies of which became available on August 18). Along with attacking the assay itself, Swift uses this* Letter *to counter Wood's proposed compromise that no more than £40,000 of copper would be minted "unless the exigences of trade require[d] more," which Swift saw as an insidious attempt to placate the opposition without actually answering any of their objections. The "News-Letter" referred to is the weekly periodical that Harding put out, which printed both news items from London and anti-Wood articles from Dublin.*

* * *

IN your News-Letter of the First Instant, there is a Paragraph, dated from *London, July* 25th, relating to *Wood's* Halfpence; whereby it is plain, what I foretold in my *Letter to the Shop-keepers, &c.* that this vile Fellow would never be at Rest; and that the Danger of our Ruin approaches nearer; And therefore the Kingdom requires *New* and *Fresh Warning.* However I take that Paragraph to be in a great Measure, an Imposition upon the Publick; at least I hope so, because I am informed that *Wood* is generally his own News-Writer. I cannot but observe from that Paragraph, that this Publick Enemy of ours, not satisfied to Ruin us with his Trash, takes every Occasion to treat this Kingdom with the utmost Contempt. He represents *Several of our Merchants and Traders upon Examination before a Committee of Council agreeing, that there was the utmost Necessity of Copper-Money here, before his Patent; so that several Gentlemen have been forced to Tally with their Workmen, and give them Bits of Cards, sealed and subscribed with their Names.* What then? If a Physician prescribe to a Patient a *Dram* of Physick, shall a Rascal Apothecary cram him with a *Pound,* and mix it up with *Poyson?* And is not a Landlord's Hand and Seal to his own Labourers a better Security for Five or Ten Shillings, than *Wood's* Brass Ten Times below the Real Value, can be to the Kingdom, for an Hundred and Eight Thousand Pounds?

BUT who are these *Merchants and Traders of Ireland* that make this Report of *the utmost Necessity we are under for Copper Money?* They are only a few Betrayers of their Country, Confederates with *Wood,* from whom they are to purchase a great Quantity of his Coin, perhaps at half the Price that we are to take it, and vend it among us to the Ruin of the Publick, and their own private Advantage. Are not these excellent Witnesses, upon whose Integrity the Fate of a Kingdom must depend; who are Evidences in their own Cause, and Sharers in this Work of Iniquity?

IF we could have deserved the Liberty of coining for our selves, as we formerly did, (and why we have not is *every Body's Wonder as well as mine*) Ten Thousand Pounds might have been coined here in *Dublin* of only one Fifth below the intrinsick Value, and this Sum, with the Stock of Half-pence we then had, would have been sufficient: But *Wood,* by his Emissaries, Enemies to God and this Kingdom, hath taken Care to buy up as many of our old Half-pence as he could; and from thence the present Want of Change arises; to remove which, by Mr. *Wood's* Remedy, would be, to cure a Scratch on the Finger by cutting off the Arm. But supposing there were not one Farthing of Change in the whole Nation, I will maintain, that Five and Twenty Thousand Pounds would be a Sum fully sufficient to answer all our Occasions. I am no inconsiderable Shop-keeper in this Town, I have discoursed with several of my own, and other Trades; with many Gentlemen both of City and Country; and also, with great Numbers of Farmers, Cottagers, and Labourers; who all agree that Two Shillings in Change for every Family, would be more than necessary in all Dealings. Now by the largest Computation (even before that grievous Discouragement of *Agriculture,* which hath so much lessened our Numbers) the Souls in this Kingdom are computed to be One Million and a half;[1] which, allowing Six to a Family, makes Two Hundred and Fifty Thousand Families, and consequently, Two Shillings to each Family will amount only to Five and Twenty thousand Pounds: Whereas this *Honest Liberal Hard-ware-Man Wood,* would impose upon us above *Four Times* that Sum.

YOUR Paragraph relates further; that Sir *Isaac Newton* reported an *Assay* taken at the *Tower,* of *Wood's* Metal;[2] by which it appears, that *Wood had in*

---

[1] In 1730 the population was estimated at 2,000,000 by the Surveyor-General of Ireland, Arthur Dobbs; recent historians have tended to suggest a higher figure.

[2] The noted mathematician and astronomer Sir Isaac Newton (1642–1727), in his capacity as Master of the Mint, was in charge of ascertaining the worth of new currency—its conformity to set standards of size, weight, and composition—through assays that took place at the Royal Mint in the Tower of London. Known as the Trial of the Pyx, this public testing of coinage based on random samples was first established in 1282 by King Edward I.

all respects performed his Contract. His Contract! With whom? Was it with the Parliament or People of *Ireland?* Are not they to be the Purchasers? But they detest, abhor, and reject it, as Corrupt, Fraudulent, mingled with Dirt and Trash. Upon which he grows angry, goes to Law, and will impose his Goods upon us by Force.

BUT your News-Letter says, that an *Assay* was made of the Coin. How impudent and insupportable is this? Wood takes Care to coin a Dozen or two Half-pence of good Metal, sends them to the *Tower* and they are approved, and these must answer all that he hath already Coined, or shall Coin for the future. It is true, indeed, that a Gentleman often sends to my Shop for a *Pattern* of *Stuff;* I cut it fairly off, and if he likes it, he comes or sends and compares the *Pattern* with the whole Piece, and probably we come to a Bargain. But if I were to buy an hundred Sheep, and the Grazier should bring me one single Weather,[3] fat and well fleeced by way of *Pattern,* and expect the same Price round for the whole hundred, without suffering me to see them before he was paid, or giving me good Security to restore my Money for those that were *Lean,* or *Shorn,* or *Scabby;* I would be none of his Customer. I have heard of a Man who had a Mind to sell his House, and therefore carried a Piece of *Brick* in his Pocket, which he shewed as a *Pattern* to encourage Purchasers: And this is directly the Case in Point with Mr. *Wood's Assay.*

THE next Part of the Paragraph contains Mr. *Wood's* voluntary Proposals *for preventing any future Objections or Apprehensions.*

HIS First Proposal is; That *whereas he hath already coined seventeen thousand Pounds, and has Copper prepared to make it up forty thousand Pounds, he will be content to Coin no more, unless the EXIGENCES OF TRADE REQUIRE IT, although his Patent empowers him to coin a far greater Quantity.*

To which if I were to answer it should be thus: Let Mr. *Wood* and his Crew of *Founders* and *Tinkers*[4] coin on till there is not an old Kettle left in the Kingdom: Let them coin old Leather, Tobacco-pipe Clay, or the Dirt in the Streets, and call their Trumpery[5] by what Name they please from a Guinea to a Farthing; we are not under any Concern to know how he and his Tribe or Accomplices think fit to employ themselves. But I hope, and trust, that we are all to a Man fully determined to have nothing to do with him or his Ware.

THE King has given him a Patent to coin Half-pence, but hath not obliged us to take them: And I have already shewn in my *Letter to the Shop-keepers, &c.* that the Law hath not left it in the Power of the *Prerogative* to compel the Subject to take any Money, beside Gold and Silver, of the Right Sterling and Standard.

---

[3] "Wether," or a castrated ram.

[4] Casters of metal, and menders of pots and pans. The term "tinker" had a particularly pejorative connotation (esp. in Scottish and northern Irish dialect), signifying a gypsy or itinerant beggar, and often implying a thief.

[5] Deceit; trickery.

Wood further proposes, (if I understand him right, for his Expressions are dubious) that *he will not coin above Forty Thousand Pounds unless* THE EXIGENCES OF TRADE REQUIRE IT: First, I observe, that this Sum of *Forty Thousand Pounds* is almost double to what I proved to be sufficient for the whole Kingdom, although we had not one of our old Half-pence left. Again I ask, who is to be Judge when the EXIGENCES OF TRADE REQUIRE IT? Without doubt, he means himself; for as to us of this poor Kingdom, who must be utterly ruined if his Project should succeed, we were never *Once* consulted till the Matter was over; and he will judge of our EXIGENCES by his own: Neither will these be ever at an End, till he and his Accomplices will think they have enough: And it now appears that he will not be content with all our Gold and Silver, but intends to buy up our Goods and Manufactures with the same Coin.

I SHALL not enter into Examination of the Prices for which he now proposes to sell his Half-pence, or what he calls his Copper, by the Pound; I have said enough of it in my former Letter, and it hath likewise been considered by others. It is certain, that by his own first Computation, we were to pay Three Shillings for what was intrinsically worth but One, although it had been of the true Weight and Standard for which he pretended to have contracted; but there is so great a Difference both in Weight and Badness in several of his Coins, that some of them have been Nine in Ten below the intrinsick Value, and most of them Six or Seven.

HIS last Proposal being of a peculiar Strain and Nature, deserves to be very particularly considered, both on Account of the Matter and the Style. It is as follows.

Lastly, in Consideration of the direful Apprehensions which prevail in Ireland, *that Mr.* Wood *will by such Coinage drain them of their Gold and Silver; he proposes to take their Manufactures in Exchange; and that no Person be* OBLIGED *to receive more than Five-pence Half-penny at one Payment.*

FIRST, Observe this little impudent *Hard-ware-Man* turning into ridicule *the Direful Apprehensions of a whole Kingdom,* priding himself as the Cause of them, and daring to prescribe what no King *of England* ever attempted, how far a whole Nation shall be obliged to take his Brass Coin. And he has Reason to insult; for sure there was never an Example in History, of a great Kingdom kept in Awe for above a Year, in daily Dread of utter Destruction; not by a powerful Invader at the Head of Twenty thousand Men; not by a Plague or a Famine; not by a tyrannical Prince (for we never had one more Gracious) or a corrupt Administration; but by one single, diminutive, insignificant Mechanick.[6]

BUT to go on. To remove our DIREFUL APPREHENSIONS *that he will drain us of our Gold and Silver by his Coinage,* this little Arbitrary *Mock-Monarch* most Graciously offers to *take our Manufactures in Exchange.* Are our *Irish*

---

[6]One employed in a manual occupation; also a contemptuous term for a low or vulgar fellow.

Understandings indeed so low in his Opinion? Is not this the very Misery we complain of? That his cursed Project will put us under the Necessity of selling our Goods for what is equal to *Nothing*. How would such a Proposal sound from *France* or *Spain,* or any other Country with which we traffick, if they should offer to deal with us only upon this Condition, that we should take their Money at Ten Times higher than the intrinsick Value? Does Mr. *Wood* think, for Instance, that we will sell him a Stone[7] of Wool for a Parcel of his *Counters* not worth *Six-pence,* when we can send it to *England* and receive as many Shillings in Gold and Silver? Surely there was never heard such a Compound of Impudence, Villany, and Folly.

HIS Proposals conclude with perfect *High-Treason*. He promises, that no Person shall be OBLIGED to receive more than Five-pence Half-penny of his Coin in one Payment: By which it is plain, that he pretends to OBLIGE every Subject in this Kingdom to take so much in every Payment, if it be offered: Whereas his Patent *Obliges* no Man; nor can the Prerogative, by Law, claim such a Power; as I have often observed: So that here Mr. Wood takes upon him the *Entire Legislature,* and an absolute Dominion over the Properties of the whole Nation.

GOOD GOD! Who are this Wretch's *Advisers?* Who are his *Supporters, Abettors, Encouragers,* or *Sharers?* Mr. *Wood* will OBLIGE me to take Five-pence Half-penny of his Brass in every Payment. And I will shoot Mr. *Wood* and his Deputies through the Head, like *High-way Men* or *House-breakers,* if they dare to force one Farthing of their Coin on me in the Payment of an Hundred Pounds. It is no Loss of Honour to submit to the *Lion:* But who, with the Figure of a *Man,* can think with Patience of being devoured alive by a *Rat?* He has laid a Tax upon the People of *Ireland* of Seventeen Shillings at least in the Pound: A Tax, I say, not only upon Lands, but Interest-Money, Goods, Manufactures, the Hire of Handicraftsmen, Labourers and Servants. Shop-keepers, look to your selves. *Wood* will *oblige* and force you to take Five-pence Half-penny of his Trash in every Payment; and many of you receive Twenty, Thirty, Forty Payments in one Day; or else you can hardly find Bread: And pray consider, how much that will amount to in a Year: Twenty times Five-pence Half-penny is Nine Shillings and Two Pence; which is above an Hundred and Sixty Pounds a Year: Whereby you will be Losers of at least One Hundred and Forty Pounds by taking your Payments in his Money. If any of you be content to deal with Mr. *Wood* on such Conditions, they may: But for my own particular; *Let his Money perish with him.* If the famous Mr. *Hambden* rather chose to go to Prison, than pay a few Shillings to King *Charles* I. without Authority of Parliament;[8] I will rather chuse to

---

[7] A measure of weight, varying with different commodities from 8 to 24 pounds; today used almost entirely as equivalent to 14 pounds.

[8] Refers to the noted parliamentarian John Hamden's refusal to pay the Ship Money tax, a levy traditionally collected in English coastal towns to support the navy, which King Charles I expanded (according to Hamden, illegally) to inland areas in 1636. Hamden was brought before the Exchequer Court the following year and narrowly lost his case.

be *Hanged* than have all my Substance Taxed at Seventeen Shillings in the Pound, at the Arbitrary Will and Pleasure of the venerable Mr. *Wood*.

THE Paragraph concludes thus. N. B. (that is to-say *Nota Bene,* or *Mark well) No Evidence appeared from* Ireland *or elsewhere, to prove the Mischiefs complained of; or any Abuses whatsoever committed in the Execution of the said Grant.*

THE Impudence of this Remark exceeds all that went before. First, the House of Commons in *Ireland;* which represents the whole People of the Kingdom: And, Secondly, the Privy Council Addressed His Majesty against these Half-pence. What could be done more to express the universal Sense of the Nation? If his Copper were Diamonds, and the Kingdom were entirely against it; would not That be sufficient to reject it? Must a Committee of the whole House of Commons, and our whole Privy Council go over to Argue *Pro* and *Con* with Mr. *Wood?* To what End did the King give his Patent for Coining Half-pence in *Ireland?* Was it not, because it was represented to His Sacred Majesty, that such a Coinage would be of Advantage to the Good of this Kingdom, and of all His Subjects here? It is to the Patentee's Peril if his Representation be false; and the Execution of his Patent be Fraudulent and Corrupt. Is he so Wicked and Foolish to think that his Patent was given him to Ruin a Million and a Half of People, that he might be a Gainer of Three or Fourscore Thousand Pounds to himself? Before he was at the Charge of passing a Patent; much more of Raking up so much Filthy Dross, and Stamping it with His Majesty's *Image and Superscription;* should he not first in common Sense, in common Equity, and common Manners, have consulted the principal Party concerned; that is to say, the People of the Kingdom, the House of Lords or Commons, or the Privy Council? If any Foreigner should ask us, *Whose Image and Superscription* there is on *Wood's* Coin? We should be ashamed to tell him it was *Cæsar's.* In that great Want of Copper Half-pence, which he alledges we were, Our City set up *our Cæsar's* Statue in excellent Copper, at an Expence that is equal in Value to Thirty Thousand Pounds of his Coin: And we will not receive his *Image* in worse Metal.[9]

I OBSERVE many of our People putting a Melancholly Case on this Subject. It is true, say they, we are all undone if *Wood's* Half-pence must pass; but what shall we do, if his Majesty puts out a *Proclamation* commanding us to take them? This hath been often dinned in my Ears. But, I desire my Countrymen to be assured that there is nothing in it. The King never issues out a *Proclamation* but to enjoin what the *Law* permits him. He will not issue out a *Proclamation* against *Law:* Or if such a Thing should happen by a Mistake, we are no more obliged to obey it, than to run our Heads into the Fire. Besides, his Majesty will never command us by a *Proclamation,* what he does not offer to command us in the Patent it self. There he leaves

---

[9]Refers to the equestrian statue of King George I that was erected on Essex Bridge in Dublin and unveiled on August 1, 1722.

it to our Discretion; so that our Destruction must be intirely owing to our selves. Therefore, let no Man be afraid of a *Proclamation,* which will never be granted; and if it should, yet upon this Occasion, will be of no Force. The King's Revenues here, are near four Hundred Thousand Pounds a Year. Can you think his Ministers will advise him to take them in *Wood*'s Brass, which will reduce the Value to Fifty Thousand Pounds. *England* gets a Million *sterl.*[10] by this Nation; which, if this Project goes on, will be almost reduced to nothing: And do you think those who live in *England* upon *Irish* Estates, will be content to take an Eighth or a Tenth Part, by being paid in *Wood*'s Dross.

IF *Wood* and his *Confederates,* were not convinced of our Stupidity, they never would have attempted so audacious an Enterprize. He now sees a Spirit hath been raised against him, and he only watches till it begins to flag; he goes about *watching* when to *devour* us. He hopes we shall be weary of contending with him; and at last out of Ignorance, or Fear, or of being perfectly tired with Opposition, we shall be forced to yield. And, therefore, I confess, it is my chief Endeavour to keep up your Spirits and Resentments. If I tell you there is a Precipice under you, and that if you go forwards you will certainly break your Necks: If I point to it before your Eyes, must I be at the Trouble of repeating it every Morning? Are our People's *Hearts waxed gross?* Are *their Ears dull of hearing,* and have *they closed their Eyes?*[11] I fear there are some few *Vipers* among us, who, for Ten or Twenty Pounds Gain, would sell their Souls and their Country; although at last, it would end in their own Ruin as well as ours. Be not like *the deaf Adder, who refuses to hear the Voice of the Charmer, charm he never so wisely.*[12]

ALTHOUGH my Letter be directed to you, Mr. *Harding,* yet I intend it for all my Countrymen. I have no Interest in this Affair, but what is common to the Publick: I can live better than many others: I have some Gold and Silver by me, and a Shop well furnished; and shall be able to make a Shift, when many of my Betters are starving. But I am grieved to see the Coldness and Indifference of many People with whom I discourse. Some are afraid of a *Proclamation;* others shrug up their Shoulders, and cry, What would you have us to do? Some give out, there is no Danger at all: Others are comforted that it will be a common Calamity, and they shall fare no worse than their Neighbours. Will a Man, who hears Midnight-Robbers at his Door, get out of Bed, and raise his Family for a common Defence? And shall a whole Kingdom lie in a Lethargy, while Mr. *Wood* comes at the Head of his *Confederates* to rob them of all they have, to ruin us and our Posterity for ever? If a Highwayman meets you on the Road, you give him your Money to save your Life; but, God be thanked, Mr. *Wood* cannot touch a Hair of your Heads. You have all the Laws of God and Man on your Side. When he, or his Accomplices, offer you his Dross, it is but saying *No,* and you are safe. If

[10] That is, sterling; the British pound made up of silver pence (hence "genuine" money).
[11] Matthew 13:15; Acts 28:27.
[12] Psalm 58:3–5.

a mad Man should come to my Shop with a Handful of Dirt raked out of the Kennel,[13] and offer it in Payment for Ten Yards of Stuff, I would pity or laugh at him; or, if his Behaviour deserved it, kick him out of my Doors. And, if Mr. *Wood* comes to demand any Gold or Silver, or Commodities for which I have paid my Gold and Silver, in Exchange for his Trash, can he deserve or expect better Treatment?

WHEN the *evil Day* is come, (if it must come) let us mark and observe those who presume to offer these Half-pence in Payment. Let their Names and Trades, and Places of Abode, be made publick, that every one may be aware of them, as Betrayers of their Country, and Confederates with Mr. *Wood*. Let them be watched at Markets and Fairs. And let the first honest Discoverer give the Word about, that *Wood*'s Half-pence have been offered; and caution the poor innocent People not to receive them.

PERHAPS I have been too tedious; but there would never be an End, if I attempted to say all that this melancholly Subject will bear. I will conclude with humbly offering one Proposal; which if it were put in Practice, would blow up this destructive Project at once. Let some skilful judicious Pen draw up an ADVERTISEMENT to the following Purpose. That,

Whereas one William Wood, *Hard-ware-man, now or lately sojourning in the City of* London, *hath, by many Misrepresentations procured a Patent for coining an Hundred and Eight Thousand Pounds in Copper Half-pence for this Kingdom; which is a Sum five times greater than our Occasions require. And whereas it is notorious that the said* Wood *hath coined his Half-pence of such base Metal, and false Weight, that they are, at least, six Parts in seven below the real Value. And, whereas we have Reason to apprehend, that the said* Wood *may, at any time hereafter, clandestinely coin as many more Half-Pence as he pleases. And, whereas the said Patent neither doth, nor can oblige his Majesty's Subjects, to receive the said Half-Pence in any Payment, but leaves it to their voluntary Choice; because, by Law the Subject cannot be obliged to take any Money, except* Gold *or* Silver. *And, whereas, contrary to the Letter and Meaning of the said Patent, the said* Wood *hath declared, that every Person shall be obliged to take Five-pence Half-penny of his Coin in every Payment. And, whereas the House of* Commons, *and Privy-Council, have severally addressed his most sacred Majesty, representing the ill Consequences which the said Coinage may have upon this Kingdom. And lastly, whereas it is universally agreed, that the whole Nation, to a Man, (except Mr.* Wood *and his Confederates) are in the utmost Apprehensions of the ruinous Consequences, that must follow from the said Coinage. Therefore we, whose Names are underwritten, being Persons of considerable Estates in this Kingdom, and Residers therein, do unanimously resolve, and declare, that we will never receive one Farthing, or Half-Penny of the said* Wood*'s coining; and that we will direct all our Tenants to refuse the said Coin from any Person whatsoever; of which, that they may not be ignorant,*

[13] Gutter.

we have sent them a Copy *of this* Advertisement, *to be read to them by our Stewards, Receivers,* &c.

I COULD wish, that a Paper of this Nature might be drawn up, and signed by two or three Hundred principal Gentlemen of this Kingdom; and printed Copies thereof sent to their several Tenants: I am deceived, if any Thing could sooner defeat this execrable Design of *Wood* and his *Accomplices:* This would immediately give the Alarm, and set the Kingdom on their Guard: This would give Courage to the meanest Tenant and Cottager. *How long, O Lord, righteous and true.*——[14]

I MUST tell you in particular, Mr. *Harding,* that you are much to blame. Several Hundred Persons have enquired at your House, for my *Letter to the Shop-keepers,* &c. and you had none to sell them. Pray keep your self provided with that Letter, and with this; you have got very well by the former; but I did not then write for your Sake, any more than I do now. Pray advertise both in every News-Paper; and let it not be your Fault or mine, if our Countrymen will not take Warning. I desire you, likewise, to sell them as cheap as you can.

I am your Servant,

Aug. 4, 1724.   M. B.

---

[14] Revelation 6:10.

Letter IV

To the Whole People of *IRELAND*

Printed and distributed to coincide with the arrival in Ireland of the new Lord-Lieutenant, John Carteret, on October 22, 1724, this Letter uses ideas derived from John Locke's political writings and from William Molyneux's The Case of Ireland...Stated *(1698) to assert Ireland's equality with England and to reject its alleged status as a "dependent" kingdom. Judged seditious by the authorities, it provoked a government proclamation calling the pamphlet "Wicked and Malicious," one "tending to alienate the Affections of [the King's] Good Subjects of England and Ireland from each other." The fact that no one stepped forward to claim the sizable reward offered for discovery of the Drapier (see headnote in Faulkner edition, below) is an indication of how popular and widely admired the figure of the Drapier had become.*

N. B. *This was the Letter against which the Lord Lieutenant* (Carteret) *and Council, issued a Proclamation, offering three Hundred Pounds to discover the Author; and for which,* Harding *the Printer was tried before one* Whitshed, *then Chief Justice:*[1] *But the noble Jury would not find*[2] *the Bill; nor would any Person discover the Author* (Faulkner headnote).

* * *

My dear Countrymen,

HAVING already written three *Letters,* upon so disagreeable a Subject as Mr. *Wood* and his *Half-pence;* I conceived my Task was at an End:[3] But, I find that Cordials must be frequently applied to weak Constitutions, *Political* as well as *Natural.* A People long used to Hardships, lose by Degrees the very Notions of *Liberty;* they look upon themselves as Creatures at Mercy; and that all Impositions laid on them by a stronger Hand, are, in the Phrase of

---

[1]William Whitshed, who was already in Swift's crosshairs for having prosecuted the printer of *A Proposal for the Universal Use of Irish Manufacture.* See Swift's poem, *Whitshed's Motto on his Coach.*

[2]Ascertain the validity of; bring in a verdict on.

[3]The Drapier's *Third Letter,* entitled *Some Observations Upon a Paper...,* was addressed "To the Nobility and Gentry of Ireland"; it had been published on September 5, 1724.

the *Report, legal* and *obligatory*.[4] Hence proceed that *Poverty* and *Lowness of Spirit,* to which a *Kingdom* may be subject, as well as a *particular Person.* And when *Esau* came fainting from the Field, at the Point to die, it is no Wonder that he sold his *Birth-Right for a Mess of Pottage*.[5]

I THOUGHT I had sufficiently shewn to all who could want Instruction, by what Methods they might safely proceed, whenever this *Coin* should be offered to them: And, I believe, there hath not been, for many Ages, an Example of any Kingdom so firmly united in a Point of great Importance, as this of ours is at present, against that detestable Fraud. But, however, it so happens, that some weak People begin to be alarmed a-new, by Rumours industriously spread. *Wood* prescribes to the News-Mongers in *London,* what they are to write. In one of their Papers published here by some obscure Printer, (and certainly with a bad Design) we are told, that the *Papists in* Ireland *have entered into an Association against his Coin;* although it be notoriously known, that they never once offered to stir in the Matter: So that the two Houses of Parliament, the Privy-Council, the great Number of Corporations, the Lord-Mayor and Aldermen of *Dublin,* the Grand-Juries, and principal Gentlemen of several Counties, are stigmatized in a Lump, under the Name of *Papists.*

THIS Impostor and his Crew, do likewise give out, that, by refusing to receive his Dross for Sterling, we *dispute the King's Prerogative; are grown ripe for Rebellion, and ready to shake off the Dependency of* Ireland *upon the Crown of* England. To Countenance which Reports, he hath published a Paragraph in another News-Paper, to let us know, that *the Lord Lieutenant is ordered to come over immediately to settle his Half-pence.*

I INTREAT you, my dear Countrymen, not to be under the least Concern upon these and the like Rumours; which are no more than the last Howls of a Dog dissected alive, as I hope he hath sufficiently been. These Calumnies are the only Reserve that is left him. For surely, our continued and (almost) unexampled Loyalty, will never be called in Question, for not suffering our selves to be robbed of all that we have, by one obscure *Ironmonger*.[6]

As to disputing the King's *Prerogative,* give me Leave to explain to those who are ignorant, what the Meaning of that Word *Prerogative* is.

THE Kings of these Realms enjoy several Powers, wherein the Laws have not interposed: So, they can make War and Peace without the Consent of Parliament; and this is a very great *Prerogative.* But if the Parliament doth not approve of the War, the King must bear the Charge of it out of his own Purse; and this is as great a Check on the Crown. So the King hath a *Prerogative* to coin Money, without Consent of Parliament: But he cannot compel the Subject to take that Money, except it be Sterling, Gold or Silver; because, herein he is limited by Law. Some Princes have, indeed, extended their *Prerogative* further than the Law allowed them: Wherein, however, the

---

[4]The official report issued by the Committee of the English Privy Council on August 6, 1724, which reaffirmed the worth and legality of Wood's half-pence.

[5]Genesis 25:29–34.

[6]See Swift's poem, *On Wood the Iron-Monger.*

Lawyers of succeeding Ages, as fond as they are of *Precedents,* have never dared to justify them. But, to say the Truth, it is only of late Times that *Prerogative* hath been fixed and ascertained. For, whoever reads the Histories of *England,* will find that some former Kings, and those none of the worst, have, upon several Occasions, ventured to controul[7] the Laws, with very little Ceremony or Scruple, even later than the Days of Queen *Elizabeth.* In her Reign, that pernicious Counsel of sending *base Money* hither,[8] very narrowly failed of losing the Kingdom; being complained of by the Lord Deputy, the Council, and the whole Body of the *English* here: So that soon after her Death, it was recalled by her Successor, and lawful Money paid in Exchange.

HAVING thus given you some Notion of what is meant by the King's *Prerogative,* as far as a *Tradesman* can be thought capable of explaining it, I will only add the Opinion of the great Lord *Bacon;* that, *as God governs the World by the settled Laws of Nature, which he hath made, and never transcends those Laws, but upon high important Occasions: So, among earthly Princes, those are the Wisest and the Best, who govern by the known Laws of the Country, and seldomest make Use of their* Prerogative.[9]

NOW, here you may see that the vile Accusation of *Wood* and his Accomplices, charging us with *disputing the King's Prerogative,* by refusing his Brass, can have no Place; because compelling the Subject to take any Coin, which is not Sterling, is no Part of the King's *Prerogative;* and I am very confident, if it were so, we should be the last of his People to dispute it; as well from that inviolable Loyalty we have always paid to his Majesty, as from the Treatment we might in such a Case justly expect from some, who seem to think, we have neither *common Sense,* nor *common Senses.* But, God be thanked, the best of them are only our *Fellow-Subjects,* and not our *Masters.* One great Merit I am sure we have, which those of *English* Birth can have no Pretence to; that our Ancestors reduced this Kingdom to the Obedience of ENGLAND; for which we have been rewarded with a worse Climate, the Privilege of being governed by Laws to which we do not consent; a ruined Trade, a House of *Peers* without *Jurisdiction;* almost an Incapacity for all Employments, and the Dread of *Wood's* Half-pence.

BUT we are so far from disputing the King's *Prerogative* in coining, that we own he hath Power to give a Patent to any Man, for setting his Royal Image and Superscription upon whatever Materials he pleases; and Liberty to the Patentee to offer them in any Country from *England* to *Japan;* only attended with one small Limitation, that *no body alive is obliged to take them.*

---

[7] Contradict; overrule.

[8] To pay the army during Tyrone's Rebellion; see *Drapier's Letter I*, note 30.

[9] Cf. Sir Francis Bacon's *A Briefe Discourse of the Happy Union of the Kingdoms of England and Scotland* (1603): "There is a great affinity and consent between the rules of nature, and the true rules of policy: the one being nothing else but an order in the government of the world; and the other an order in the government of an estate." Swift is here creatively tweaking Bacon's strongly royalist sentiment in order to emphasize the limits rather than the broad scope of kingly prerogative.

UPON these Considerations, I was ever against all Recourse to *England* for a Remedy against the present impending Evil; especially, when I observed, that the Addresses of both Houses, after long Expectance, produced nothing but a REPORT altogether in Favour of *Wood;* upon which, I made some Observations in a former Letter; and might at least have made as many more: For, it is a Paper of as singular a Nature as I ever beheld.

BUT I mistake; for before this *Report* was made, his Majesty's *most gracious Answer* to the House of Lords was sent over, and printed; wherein there are these Words, *granting the Patent for coining Half-pence and Farthings,* AGREEABLE TO THE PRACTICE OF HIS ROYAL PREDECESSORS, *&c.* That King *Charles* II, and King *James* II, (AND THEY ONLY) did grant Patents for this Purpose, is indisputable, and I have shewn it at large.[10] Their Patents were passed under the great Seal of *Ireland,* by References to *Ireland;* the Copper to be coined in *Ireland,* the Patentee was bound, on Demand, to receive his Coin back in *Ireland,* and pay Silver and Gold in Return. *Wood's* Patent was made under the great Seal of *England,* the Brass coined in *England,* not the least Reference made to *Ireland;* the Sum immense, and the Patentee under no Obligation to receive it again, and give good Money for it: This I only mention, because, in my private Thoughts, I have sometimes made a Query, whether the *Penner* of those Words in his Majesty's *most gracious Answer,* AGREEABLE TO THE PRACTICE OF HIS ROYAL PREDECESSORS, had maturely considered the several Circumstances; which, in my poor Opinion, seem to make a Difference.

LET me now say something concerning the other great Cause of some People's Fear; as *Wood* has taught the *London* News-Writer to express it: That *his Excellency the Lord Lieutenant is coming over to settle* Wood's *Half-pence.*

WE know very well, that the Lords Lieutenants, for several Years past, have not thought this Kingdom *worthy the Honour of their Residence,* longer than was absolutely necessary for the King's Business; which consequently *wanted no Speed in the Dispatch.*[11] And therefore, it naturally fell into most Mens Thoughts, that a new Governor coming at an *unusual* Time, must portend some *unusual* Business to be done; especially, if the common Report be true; that the Parliament prorogued to I know not when, is, by a new Summons (revoking that Prorogation) to assemble soon after his Arrival:[12] For which

---

[10] In the *Third Drapier's Letter,* which alludes to the patent obtained by Sir William Armstrong and Colonel George Legg from Charles II in 1680, granting them the right to issue copper halfpence in Ireland for twenty-one years. The patent was subsequently sold to John Knox and then resold to Colonel Roger Moore, who was "forced to leave off coining" in 1694 because of "the great Crouds of People continually offering to return his Coinage upon him" in exchange for gold or silver, as per the terms of the patent. Moore's later attempt to resume coining in Ireland ended similarly.

[11] That is, was done quickly.

[12] Refers to the adjournment of Parliament because of the half-pence crisis and the summons to reconvene soon after Carteret's arrival. This reconvening did not take place until almost a year later, by which time Wood's patent had been surrendered.

extraordinary Proceeding, the Lawyers on t'other Side the Water, have, by great good Fortune, found two *Precedents.*

ALL this being granted, it can never enter into my Head, that so *little a Creature as Wood* could find Credit enough with the King and his Ministers, to have the Lord Lieutenant of *Ireland* sent hither in a Hurry, upon his Errand.

FOR, let us take the whole Matter nakedly, as it lies before us, without the Refinements of some People, with which we have nothing to do. Here is a Patent granted under the great Seal of *England,* upon false Suggestions, to one *William Wood,* for coining Copper Half-pence for *Ireland:* The Parliament here, upon Apprehensions of the worst Consequences from the said Patent, address the King to have it recalled: This is refused, and a Committee of the Privy-Council *report* to his Majesty, that *Wood* has performed the Conditions of his Patent. He then is left to do the best he can with his Half-pence; no Man being obliged to receive them; the People here, being likewise left to themselves, unite as one Man; resolving they will have nothing to do with his Ware. By this plain Account of the Fact, it is manifest, that the King and his Ministry are wholly out of the Case; and the Matter is left to be disputed between him and us. Will any Man therefore attempt to persuade me, that a Lord Lieutenant is to be dispatched over in great Haste, before the ordinary Time, and a Parliament summoned, by anticipating a Prorogation; merely to put an Hundred Thousand Pounds into the Pocket of a *Sharper,*[13] by the Ruin of a most loyal Kingdom?

BUT supposing all this to be true. By what Arguments could a Lord Lieutenant prevail on the same Parliament, which addressed with so much Zeal and Earnestness against this Evil; to pass it into a Law? I am sure their Opinion of *Wood* and his Project is not mended since their last Prorogation: And supposing those *Methods* should be used, which, *Detractors* tell us, have been sometimes put in Practice for *gaining Votes;* it is well known, that in this Kingdom there are few Employments to be given; and if there were more; it is *as well known* to whose Share they must fall.[14]

BUT, because great Numbers of you are altogether ignorant in the Affairs of your Country, I will tell you some Reasons, why there are so few Employments to be disposed of in this Kingdom. All considerable Offices for Life here, are possessed by those, to whom the Reversions were granted; and these have been generally Followers of the Chief Governors, or Persons who had Interest in the Court of *England.*[15] So the Lord *Berkely* of *Stratton,* holds that great Office of *Master of the Rolls;* the Lord *Palmerstown* is *First Remembrancer,* worth near 2000 *l. per Ann.* One *Dodington,* Secretary to the Earl of *Pembroke,* begged the Reversion of *Clerk of the Pells,* worth 2500 *l.* a

---

[13] A swindler or cheat.

[14] That is, Englishmen rather than the Anglo-Irish who were born and reside in Ireland; hence the latter's votes cannot be swayed by promises of career advancement.

[15] Refers to lucrative sinecures in Ireland held by those well-connected in the English Court and perpetuated through "reversions," or the right of succession to an office after the death or retirement of the officeholder.

Year, which he now enjoys by the Death of the Lord *Newtown*. Mr. *Southwell* is Secretary of State, and the Earl of *Burlington* Lord High Treasurer of *Ireland* by Inheritance.[16] These are only a few among many others, which I have been told of, but cannot remember. Nay the Reversion of several Employments during Pleasure are granted the same Way. This among many others, is a Circumstance whereby the Kingdom of *Ireland* is distinguished from all other Nations upon Earth; and makes it so difficult an Affair to get into a Civil Employ, that Mr. *Addison* was forced to purchase an old obscure Place, called *Keeper of the Records in* Bermingham's *Tower,* of Ten Pounds a Year, and to get a Salary of 400 *l.* annexed to it, though all the Records there are not worth Half a Crown, either for Curiosity or Use.[17] And we lately saw a *Favourite Secretary,* descend to be *Master of the Revels,*[18] which by his *Credit and Extortion* he hath made *Pretty Considerable.* I say nothing of the Under-Treasurership worth about 9000 *l.* a Year; nor the Commissioners of the Revenue,[19] Four of whom generally live in *England:* For I think none of these are granted in Reversion. But the Jest is, that I have known upon Occasion, some of these absent Officers as *Keen* against the Interest of *Ireland,* as if they had never been indebted to Her for a *Single Groat.*[20]

I CONFESS, I have been sometimes tempted to wish that this Project of *Wood* might succeed; because I reflected with some Pleasure what a *Jolly Crew* it would bring over among us of *Lords* and *Squires,* and *Pensioners* of *Both Sexes,* and Officers *Civil* and *Military;* where we should live together as merry and sociable as Beggars; only with this one Abatement, that we should neither have *Meat* to feed, nor *Manufactures* to Cloath us; unless we could be content to *Prance* about in *Coats of Mail;* or eat Brass as Ostritches do Iron.

I RETURN from this Digression, to that which gave me the Occasion of making it: And I believe you are now convinced, that if the Parliament of *Ireland* were as *Temptable* as any *other* Assembly, *within a Mile* of Christendom (which God forbid) yet the *Managers* must of Necessity fail for want of *Tools* to work with. But I will yet go one Step further, by Supposing that a

---

[16] Lord Berkely was a descendant of 1st Baron John Berkeley, Lord-Lieutenant of Ireland (1670–72); Henry Temple, Baron Palmerstown, was a nephew of Sir William Temple and Chief Remembrancer of Ireland; George Bubb Dodington, Whig politician and patron of letters, owned Irish estates inherited from his uncle and served as Lord of the Treasury under Walpole and later as an advisor to the Prince of Wales; Edward Southwell, who worked closely with Archbishop King, acquired extensive property in Co. Down through marriage and became M.P. for Kinsale; Richard Boyle, 3rd Earl of Burlington and 4th Earl of Cork, was perhaps the richest of Ireland's absentee landlords and the subject of Pope's *Epistle to Burlington.*

[17] The Whig politician and writer Joseph Addison served as Secretary to Sir Thomas Wharton during the latter's tenure as Lord-Lieutenant of Ireland (1708–10). Bermingham's Tower was the place in Dublin Castle where official records were kept.

[18] "Mr. *Hopkins,* Secretary to the Duke of *Grafton*" (Faulkner's note). A Master of the Revels was a person who organized entertainments in the royal household or the Inns of Court.

[19] A seven-member board that possessed considerable power since it controlled a large patronage system of government functionaries. All members served as Commissioners of Customs, while five also acted as Commissioners of Excise.

[20] An English coin equal to four pence; also a figurative term for an insignificant amount.

Hundred new Employments were erected on Purpose to gratify *Compliers:* Yet still an insuperable Difficulty would remain. For it happens, I know not how, that *Money* is neither *Whig* nor *Tory,* neither of *Town* nor *Country Party;* and it is not improbable, that a Gentleman would rather chuse to live upon his *own Estate,* which brings him *Gold* and *Silver,* than with the Addition of an *Employment;* when his *Rents* and *Sallary* must both be paid in *Wood's* Brass, at above Eighty *per Cent.* Discount.

FOR these, and many other Reasons, I am confident you need not be under the least Apprehensions, from the sudden Expectation of the *Lord Lieutenant,* while we continue in our present hearty Disposition; to alter which, there is no suitable Temptation can possibly be offered: And if, as I have often asserted from the best Authority, the *Law* hath not left a *Power* in the *Crown* to force any Money, except Sterling, upon the Subject; much less can the Crown *devolve* such a *Power* upon *another.*

THIS I speak with the utmost Respect to the *Person* and *Dignity* of his Excellency the Lord *Carteret;* whose Character was lately given me, by a Gentleman that hath known him from his first Appearance in the World: That Gentleman describes him as a young Man of great Accomplishments, excellent Learning, Regular in his Life, and of much Spirit and Vivacity. He hath since, as I have heard, been employed abroad; was principal Secretary of State; and is now about the 37th Year of his Age appointed Lord Lieutenant of *Ireland.* From such a Governour this Kingdom may reasonably hope for as much Prosperity, as *under so many Discouragements* it can be capable of receiving.[21]

IT is true indeed, that within the Memory of Man, there have been Governors of so much Dexterity, as to carry Points of terrible Consequence to this Kingdom, by their Power with *those who were in Office;* and by their Arts in managing or deluding others with *Oaths, Affability,* and even with *Dinners.* If *Wood's* Brass had, in those Times, been upon the *Anvil,* it is obvious enough to conceive what Methods would have been taken. *Depending* Persons would have been told in plain Terms, that it was a *Service expected from them, under Pain of the publick Business being put into more complying Hands.* Others would be allured by *Promises.* To the *Country Gentlemen,* besides *good Words, Burgundy* and *Closeting;*[22] it might, perhaps, have been hinted, how *kindly it would be taken to comply with a Royal Patent, although it were not compulsory.* That if any Inconveniences ensued, it might be made up with other *Graces or Favours hereafter:* That *Gentlemen ought to consider, whether it were prudent or safe to disgust* England: They would be desired to *think of some good Bills for encouraging of Trade, and setting the Poor to work: Some further Acts against Popery,*

---

[21] See Swift's *Vindication of His Excellency John, Lord Carteret* (1730) for a more extended tribute to the Baron, whom he first got to know as a twenty-year-old in London, in 1710. Carteret was actually 34, not 37, at the time of this writing.

[22] The practice of making political deals behind closed doors or exerting undue influence through secret meetings.

and for uniting Protestants.[23] There would be solemn Engagements, that we should *never be troubled with above Forty Thousand Pounds in his Coin, and all of the best and weightiest Sort, for which we should only give our Manufactures in Exchange, and keep our Gold and Silver at home.* Perhaps, *a seasonable Report of some Invasion would have been spread in the most proper Juncture;* which is a great Smoother of Rubs in publick Proceedings: And we should have been told, that *this was no Time to create Differences, when the Kingdom was in Danger.*[24]

THESE, I say, and the like Methods, would, in corrupt Times, have been taken to let in this Deluge of Brass among us: and, I am confident, would even then have not succeeded; much less under the Administration of so excellent a Person as the Lord *Carteret;* and in a Country, where the People of all Ranks, Parties, and Denominations, are convinced to a Man, that the utter undoing of themselves and their Posterity for ever, will be dated from the Admission of that execrable Coin: That if it once enters, it can be no more confined to a small or moderate Quantity, than the *Plague* can be confined to a few Families; and that no *Equivalent* can be given by any earthly Power, any more than a dead Carcass can be recovered to Life by a Cordial.

THERE is one comfortable Circumstance in this universal Opposition to Mr. *Wood,* that the People sent over hither from *England,* to *fill up our Vacancies, Ecclesiastical, Civil and Military,* are all on our Side: *Money,* the great *Divider* of the World, hath, by a strange Revolution, been the great *Uniter* of a most *divided* People. Who would leave a Hundred Pounds a Year in *England,* (*a country of Freedom*) to be paid a Thousand in *Ireland* out of *Wood*'s Exchequer? The *Gentleman They* have lately made *Primate,* would never quit his Seat in an *English* House of Lords, and his Preferments at *Oxford* and *Bristol,* worth Twelve Hundred Pounds a Year, for four Times the Denomination here, but not half the Value:[25] Therefore, I expect to hear he will be as good an *Irishman,* at least, upon *this one Article,* as any of his Brethren; or even of *Us,* who have had the *Misfortune* to be born in this Island. For those who, in the common Phrase, do not *come hither to learn the Language,* would never change a better Country for a worse, to receive *Brass* instead of *Gold.*

ANOTHER Slander spread by *Wood* and his Emissaries is, that, by opposing him, we discover an Inclination to *shake off our Dependance upon the Crown of* England. Pray observe, how important a Person is this same *William Wood;*

[23] The first of the Penal Laws in Ireland restricting Catholic rights was passed in 1695; several others followed shortly thereafter. Swift took a dim view of "uniting Protestants," especially in its function as a slogan used by Dissenters to justify repealing the Test Act.

[24] Refers to reports of a supposedly imminent Jacobite rebellion. Swift repeatedly attacked "the political Spreaders of those chimerical Invasions," viewing them as motivated by narrow partisan interests to magnify the threat posed by Catholics (which Swift deemed nonexistent) in order to silence opposition and exploit Protestant paranoia.

[25] Refers to Hugh Boulter, who had been appointed Archbishop of Armagh and Primate of All Ireland several months before the composition of this *Letter.* He was a staunch Whig and champion of the "English interest" in Ireland, hence an object of Swift's intense dislike; see Swift's poem *Ay and No, A Tale from Dublin.*

and how the publick Weal[26] of two Kingdoms, is involved in his private Interest. First, all those who refuse to take his Coin *are Papists;* for he tells us, that *none but Papists are associated against him.* Secondly, they *dispute the King's Prerogative.* Thirdly, they *are ripe for Rebellion.* And Fourthly, they are going to *shake off their Dependance upon the Crown of* England; that is to say, *they are going to chuse another King:* For there can be no other Meaning in this Expression, however some may pretend to strain it.

AND this gives me an Opportunity of explaining, to those who are ignorant, another Point, which hath often *swelled in my Breast.* Those who come over hither to us from *England,* and some *weak* People among ourselves, whenever, in Discourse, we make mention of *Liberty* and *Property,* shake their Heads, and tell us, *that Ireland is a depending Kingdom;* as if they would seem, by this Phrase, to intend, that the People of *Ireland* is in some State of Slavery or Dependance, different from those of *England:* Whereas, a *depending Kingdom* is a *modern Term of Art;* unknown, as I have heard, to all antient *Civilians,*[27] and *Writers upon Government;* and *Ireland* is, on the contrary, called in some Statutes an *Imperial Crown,* as held only from God; which is as high a Style, as any Kingdom is capable of receiving. Therefore by this Expression, a *depending Kingdom,* there is no more understood, than that by a Statute made here, in the 33d Year of *Henry* VIII, *The King and his Successors, are to be Kings Imperial of this Realm, as united and knit to the Imperial Crown of* England.[28] I have looked over all the *English* and *Irish* Statutes, without finding any Law that makes *Ireland depend* upon *England;* any more than *England* doth upon *Ireland.* We have, indeed, obliged ourselves to have *the same King with them;* and consequently they are obliged to have the *same King with us.* For the Law was made by *our own Parliament;* and our Ancestors then were not such *Fools (whatever they were in the preceding Reign)* to bring themselves under I know not what *Dependance,* which is now talked of, without any Ground of *Law, Reason,* or *common Sense.*

LET whoever think otherwise, I *M. B. Drapier,* desire to be excepted. For I declare, next under God, I *depend* only on the King my Sovereign, and on the Laws of my own Country, And I am so far from *depending* upon the People of *England,* that, if they should ever *rebel* against my Sovereign, (which GOD forbid) I would be ready at the first Command from his Majesty to take Arms against them; as some of my Countrymen did against *theirs* at *Preston.*[29] And, if such a Rebellion should prove so successful as to fix the

---

[26] Well-being; prosperity.

[27] Those who study or write about the civil law.

[28] Refers to the statute enacted in 1541 by the Parliament in Dublin, whereby Henry VIII exchanged his inherited title of "Lord of Ireland" for the new title "King of Ireland," which could be construed as placing Ireland on an equal plane with England, as two kingdoms sharing the same monarch. This entire paragraph is intended as a direct repudiation of the Declaratory Act of 1720, "binding" Ireland to England.

[29] Refers to the loyalist troops under General Carpenter, Irish soldiers among them, who defeated the Jacobite force led by Thomas Forster at Preston, thus ending the Jacobite Rebellion of 1715.

Pretender[30] on the Throne of *England;* I would venture to transgress that *Statute* so far, as to lose every Drop of my Blood, to hinder him from being *King* of *Ireland*.

IT is true, indeed, that within the Memory of Man, the Parliaments of *England* have *sometimes* assumed the Power of binding this Kingdom, by Laws enacted there; wherein they were, at first, openly opposed (as far as *Truth, Reason,* and *Justice* are capable of *opposing*) by the famous Mr. *Molineaux,* an *English* Gentleman born here; as well as by several of the greatest Patriots, and *best Whigs* in *England;* but the *Love and Torrent* of Power prevailed. Indeed, the Arguments on both Sides were invincible. For in *Reason,* all *Government* without the Consent of the *Governed,* is the *very Definition of Slavery:* But in *Fact, Eleven Men well armed, will certainly subdue one single Man in his Shirt.* But I have done. For those who have used *Power* to cramp *Liberty,* have gone so far as to resent even the *Liberty* of *Complaining;* although a Man upon the Rack, was never known to be refused the Liberty of *roaring* as loud as he thought fit.

AND, as we are apt to *sink* too *much* under *unreasonable* Fears, so we are too soon inclined to be *raised* by groundless Hopes, (according to the Nature of all *consumptive* Bodies like ours.) Thus, it hath been given about for several Days past, that *Somebody in England,* empowered a second *Somebody* to write to a third *Somebody* here, to assure us, that we *should no more be troubled with those Half-pence.* And this is reported to have been done by the *same Person,* who was said to have sworn some Months ago, that he woud *ram them down our Throats* (though I doubt they would *stick in our Stomachs*).[31] But which ever of these Reports is true or false, it is no Concern of ours. For, *in this Point,* we have nothing to do with *English Ministers:* And I should be sorry to leave it in their Power to *redress* this Grievance, or to *enforce* it: For the *Report of the Committee* hath given me a *Surfeit.*[32] The Remedy is wholly in your own Hands; and therefore I have digressed a little, in order to refresh and continue that *Spirit* so seasonably raised amongst you; and to let you see, that by the Laws of GOD, of NATURE, of NATIONS, and of your own Country, you ARE and OUGHT to be as FREE a People as your Brethren in *England.*

IF the Pamphlets published at *London* by *Wood* and his *Journeymen,*[33] in Defence of his Cause, were Re-printed here, and that our Countrymen could be persuaded to read them, they would convince you of his wicked Design, more than all I shall ever be able to say. In short, I make him a perfect *Saint,* in Comparison of what he appears to be, from the Writings of those whom he *Hires* to justify his *Project.* But he is so far *Master of the Field (let others guess the Reason)* that no *London* Printer dare publish any Paper written in

---

[30] James Francis Edward Stuart, the Catholic claimant to the throne then living in exile in France.

[31] Refers to the reported threat made by the British Prime Minister, Robert Walpole.

[32] Disgust; nausea.

[33] Hirelings; those who drudge for another.

Favour of *Ireland:* And here no Body hath yet been so *bold,* as to publish any Thing in *Favour* of *him.*

THERE was a few Days ago a Pamphlet sent me of near 50 Pages, written in Favour of Mr. *Wood* and his Coinage; printed in *London.*[34] It is not worth answering, because probably it will never be published here: But it gave me an Occasion, to reflect upon an Unhappiness we lie under, that the People of *England* are utterly ignorant of our Case; Which, however, is no Wonder; since it is a Point they do not in the least concern themselves about; farther than, perhaps, as a Subject of Discourse in a Coffee-House, when they have nothing else to talk of. For I have Reason to believe, that no Minister ever gave himself the Trouble of reading any Papers written in our Defence; because I suppose *their Opinions are already determined,* and are formed wholly upon the Reports of *Wood* and his Accomplices; else it would be impossible, that any Man could have the Impudence, to write such a Pamphlet, as I have mentioned.

OUR *Neighbours, whose Understandings are just upon a Level with Ours* (which perhaps are none of the *Brightest)* have a strong Contempt for most Nations, but especially for *Ireland:* They look upon us as a Sort of *Savage Irish,* whom our Ancestors conquered several Hundred Years ago: And if I should describe the *Britons* to you, as they were in *Cæsar's* Time, when they *painted their Bodies, or cloathed themselves with the Skins of Beasts,* I should act full as reasonably as they do. However, they are so far to be excused, in relation to the present Subject, that, hearing only *one Side of the Cause,* and having neither Opportunity nor Curiosity to examine the *other,* they *believe a Lye,* merely for their Ease; and conclude, because Mr. *Wood* pretends to have *Power,* he hath also *Reason* on his Side.

THEREFORE, to let you see how this Case is represented in *England* by *Wood* and his Adherents, I have thought it proper to extract out of that Pamphlet, a few of those notorious Falshoods, in Point of *Fact* and *Reasoning,* contained therein; the Knowledge whereof, will confirm my Countrymen in their *Own* Right Sentiments, when they will see by comparing both, how much their *Enemies are in the Wrong.*

FIRST, The Writer positively asserts, *That* Wood*'s Half-pence were current among us for several Months, with the universal Approbation of all People, without one single Gain-sayer; and we all to a Man thought our selves Happy in having them.*

SECONDLY, He affirms, *That we were drawn into a Dislike of them, only by some Cunning Evil-designing Men among us, who opposed this Patent of* Wood, *to get another for themselves.*

THIRDLY, That *those who most declared at first against* WOOD'*s Patent, were the very Men who intended to get another for their own Advantage.*

FOURTHLY, That *our Parliament and Privy-Council, the Lord Mayor and Aldermen of* Dublin, *the Grand-Juries and Merchants, and in short the whole*

---

[34] Entitled, *Some Farther Account of the Original Disputes in Ireland, about Farthings and Half-pence. In a Discourse with a Quaker of Dublin.*

Kingdom, nay, the very Dogs (as he expresseth it) *were fond of those Half-pence, till they were inflamed by those few designing Persons aforesaid.*

FIFTHLY, He says directly, That *all those who opposed the Half-pence, were Papists, and Enemies to King* George.

THUS far I am confident the most ignorant among you can safely swear from your own Knowledge, that the Author is a most notorious Lyar in every Article; the direct contrary being so manifest to the whole Kingdom, that if Occasion required, we might get it confirmed *under Five hundred thousand Hands.*

SIXTHLY, He would persuade us, That *if we sell Five Shillings worth of our Goods or Manufactures for Two Shillings and Four-pence worth of Copper, although the Copper were melted down, and that we could get Five Shillings in Gold or Silver for the said Goods; yet to take the said Two Shillings and Four-pence in Copper, would be greatly for our Advantage.*

AND Lastly, He makes us a very fair Offer, as empowered by *Wood,* That *if we will take off Two hundred thousand Pounds in his Half-pence for our Goods, and likewise pay him Three per Cent. Interest for Thirty Years, for an hundred and Twenty thousand Pounds* (at which he computes the Coinage above the *intrinsick Value of the Copper) for the Loan of his Coin, he will after that Time give us good Money for what Half-pence will be then left.*

LET me place this Offer in as clear a Light as I can, to shew the unsupportable Villainy and Impudence of that incorrigible Wretch. First (says he) *I will send Two hundred thousand Pounds of my Coin into your Country: The Copper I compute to be in real Value Eighty thousand Pounds, and I charge you with an hundred and twenty thousand Pounds for the Coinage; so that you see, I lend you an Hundred and twenty thousand Pounds for Thirty Years; for which you shall pay me Three per Cent. That is to say, Three thousand Six hundred Pounds, per Ann. which in Thirty Years will amount to an Hundred and eight thousand Pounds. And when these Thirty Years are expired, return me my Copper, and I will give you Good Money for it.*

THIS is the Proposal made to us by *Wood* in that Pamphlet, written by one of his *Commissioners:* And the Author is supposed to be the same Infamous *Coleby* one of his *Under-Swearers* at the *Committee of Council,* who was tryed for *Robbing the Treasury here,* where he was an Under-Clerk.[35]

BY this Proposal he will first receive Two hundred thousand Pounds, in Goods or Sterling, for as much Copper as he values at Eighty thousand Pounds; but in Reality not worth Thirty thousand Pounds. Secondly, He will receive for Interest an Hundred and Eight thousand Pounds: And when our Children come Thirty Years hence, to return his Half-pence upon his Executors (for before that Time he will be probably gone *to his own Place*) those Executors will very reasonably reject them as Raps and Counterfeits; which they will be, and Millions of them of his own Coinage.

---

[35] In his *Third Letter,* the Drapier says of Coleby that "although he was acquitted for want of legal Proof, yet every Person in the Court believed him to be guilty." An *"Under-swearer"* is one who supports another by oath.

METHINKS, I am fond of such a *Dealer* as this, who mends every Day upon our Hands, like a *Dutch* Reckoning;[36] where, if you dispute the Unreasonableness and Exorbitance of the Bill, the Landlord shall bring it up every Time with new Additions.

ALTHOUGH these and the like Pamphlets, published by *Wood* in *London,* be altogether unknown here, where no body could read them, without as much *Indignation* as *Contempt* would allow; yet I thought it proper to give you a Specimen how the *Man* employs his Time; where he Rides alone without any Creature to contradict him; while OUR FEW FRIENDS there wonder at our Silence: And the *English* in general, if they think of this Matter at all, impute our Refusal to *Wilfulness* or *Disaffection,* just as *Wood* and his *Hirelings* are pleased to represent.

BUT although our Arguments are not suffered to be printed in *England,* yet the Consequence will be of little Moment. Let *Wood* endeavour to *persuade* the People *There,* that we ought to *Receive* his Coin; and let Me *Convince* our People *Here,* that they ought to *Reject* it under Pain of our utter Undoing. And then let him do his *Best* and his *Worst.*

BEFORE I conclude, I must beg Leave, in all Humility to tell Mr. *Wood,* that he is guilty of great *Indiscretion,* by causing so Honourable a Name as that of Mr. *Walpole* to be mentioned so often, and in such a Manner, upon his Occasion. A short Paper, printed at *Bristol,* and re-printed here, reports Mr. *Wood* to say, that he *wonders at the Impudence and Insolence of the* Irish, *in refusing his Coin,* and *what he will do when Mr.* Walpole *comes* to *Town.* Where, by the Way, he is mistaken; for it is the *True English People* of *Ireland,* who refuse it; although we take it for granted, that the *Irish* will do so too, whenever they are asked.[37] In another printed Paper of his contriving, it is roundly expressed, that Mr. *Walpole will cram his Brass down our Throats.* Sometimes it is given out, that we must *either take these Half-pence or eat our Brogues.*[38] And, in another News-Letter but of Yesterday, we read, that the same great Man *hath sworn to make us swallow his Coin in Fire-Balls.*[39]

THIS brings to my Mind the known Story of a *Scotch* Man, who receiving Sentence of Death, with all the Circumstances of *Hanging, Beheading, Quartering, Embowelling,* and the like; cried out, *What need all this* COOKERY? And I think we have Reason to ask the same Question: For if we believe *Wood,* here is a *Dinner* getting ready for us, and you see the *Bill of Fare;* and I am sorry the *Drink* was forgot, which might easily be supplied with *Melted Lead* and *Flaming Pitch.*

---

[36]A verbal or lump-sum account devoid of itemized particulars and thus open to falsification.

[37]The distinction being made here is between Protestants and Catholics; the point of this passage is to counter the widespread rumors that the resistance to Wood's half-pence was part of a "papist" plot to undermine Protestant rule in Ireland.

[38]Rude shoes made of untanned leather, commonly worn by the lower classes in rural Ireland. Perhaps also punning on the term signifying the distinctively Irish mode of speech, hence suggesting that the Irish will be made to "eat their words."

[39]Round projectiles filled with explosives or other combustible materials.

WHAT vile Words are these to put into the Mouth of a great Counsellor, in high Trust with his Majesty, and looked upon as a prime Minister? If Mr. *Wood* hath no better a Manner of representing his Patrons; when I come to be a *Great Man*, he shall never be suffered to attend at my *Levee*.[40] This is not the Style of a Great Minister; it savours too much of the *Kettle* and the *Furnace*; and came entirely out of *Wood's Forge*.

As for the Threat of making us *eat our Brogues*, we need not be in Pain; for if his Coin should pass, that *Unpolite Covering for the Feet*, would no longer be a *National Reproach*; because, then we should have neither *Shoe* nor *Brogue* left in the Kingdom. But here the Falshood of Mr. *Wood* is fairly detected; for I am confident Mr. *Walpole* never heard of a *Brogue* in his whole Life.

As to *Swallowing these Half-pence in Fire-balls*, it is a Story equally improbable. For, to execute this *Operation*, the whole Stock of Mr. *Wood's* Coin and Metal must be melted down, and molded into hollow *Balls* with *Wild-fire*, no bigger than a *reasonable* Throat can be able to swallow. Now, the Metal he hath prepared, and already coined, will amount to at least Fifty Millions of Half-pence to be *Swallowed* by a Million and a Half of People; so that allowing Two Half-pence to each *Ball*, there will be about Seventeen *Balls* of *Wild-fire* a-piece, to be swallowed by every Person in the Kingdom: And to administer this Dose, there cannot be conveniently fewer than Fifty thousand *Operators*, allowing one *Operator* to every Thirty;[41] which, considering the *Squeamishness* of some Stomachs, and the *Peevishness* of *Young Children*, is but reasonable. Now, under Correction of better Judgments, I think the Trouble and Charge of such an Experiment, would exceed the Profit; and therefore I take this *Report* to be *spurious;* or, at least, only a new *Scheme* of Mr. *Wood* himself; which, to make it pass the better in *Ireland*, he would Father upon a *Minister of State*.

BUT I will now demonstrate, beyond all Contradiction, that Mr. *Walpole* is against this Project of Mr. *Wood;* and is an entire Friend to *Ireland*; only by this one invincible Argument, That he has the Universal Opinion of being a wise Man, an able Minister, and in all his Proceedings, pursuing the *True Interest* of the *King his Master:* And that, as his *Integrity* is above all *Corruption*, so is his *Fortune* above all *Temptation*. I reckon therefore, we are perfectly safe from that *Corner;* and shall never be under the Necessity of Contending with so *Formidable a Power;* but be left to possess our *Brogues* and *Potatoes* in *Peace*, as *Remote from Thunder as we are from Jupiter*.[42]

I am, My dear Countrymen, your Loving Fellow-Subject, Fellow-Sufferer, and Humble Servant,

M. B.

Oct. 13, 1724.

---

[40]Walpole was regularly characterized in derision as "a Great Man" in Opposition satire. A "levee" is a morning reception or assembly held by a person of high rank or political distinction.

[41]The insinuation here is that the army would have to be called out to force Wood's half-pence on the Irish populace.

[42] "*Procul à Jove, procul à fulmine*" (Faulkner's note). An ancient adage meaning that there is safety in remaining distant from the seats of power.

Letter V

To the Right Honourable the Lord Viscount *Molesworth*, at his House at *Brackdenstown*, near *Swords*

Appearing in print on December 31, 1724, this Letter is addressed to Robert Molesworth (1656–1725), a prominent Whig statesman and political writer, and an M.P. in both the British and Irish parliaments, whose country seat two miles north of Dublin served as a well-known meeting place for liberal and unorthodox thinkers, including William Molyneux, the churchman Edward Synge, and the Dissenting philosopher Francis Hutcheson. In earlier days Molesworth was attacked by Swift for his anti-clericalism, but he later won Swift's respect through his strong support of the "Irish interest." According to a prefatory set of "Directions to the Printer," the Letter "contains only a short Account of my self, and an humble Apology for my former Pamphlets, especially the last; *with little mention of Mr. Wood, or his Half-pence...." The more relaxed and personal tone suggested here is a reflection of Swift's sense that the worst of the coinage crisis was over, underscored by the Drapier's judicial triumph a month earlier in relation to his paper,* Seasonable Advice *(see notes 32 and 36, below). Nevertheless, this Letter takes its place alongside the earlier ones as a serious political statement in its espousal of liberty as the ultimate political goal, and if anything, is even more subversive than the others in its author's identification with thinkers and writers who represent a radical Whig, even Republican tradition.*

*   *   *

My LORD,

I REFLECT too late on the Maxim of common Observers, that those who meddle in Matters out of their Calling, will have reason to repent; which is now verified in me: For, by engaging in the Trade of a Writer, I have drawn upon my self the Displeasure of the Government, signified by a *Proclamation*; promising a Reward of Three Hundred Pounds, to the first *faithful* Subject who shall be able, and inclined to *inform* against me. To which I may add, the *laudable Zeal and Industry* of my Lord Chief Justice *Whitshed*, in his

Endeavours to discover so dangerous a Person.[1] Therefore, whether I repent or no, I have certainly Cause to do so; and the common Observation still stands good.

IT will sometimes happen, I know not how, in the Course of human Affairs, that a Man shall be made liable to *legal* Animadversions,[2] where he hath nothing to answer for, either to *God* or his *Country*; and condemned at *Westminster-Hall*,[3] for what he will never be charged with at the *Day of Judgment.*

AFTER strictly examining my own Heart, and consulting some Divines of great Reputation, I cannot accuse my self of any *Malice*, or *Wickedness against the Publick*; of any *Designs to sow Sedition*; of *reflecting on the King and his Ministers*; or of endeavouring *to alienate the Affections of the People of this Kingdom from those of* England.[4] All I can charge my self with, is a weak Attempt to serve a Nation in Danger of Destruction, by a most wicked and malicious Projector;[5] without waiting until I were called to its Assistance: Which Attempt, however it may perhaps give me the Title of *Pragmatical*[6] and *Overweening*, will never lie a Burthen upon my Conscience. God knows, whether I may not, with all my Caution, have already run my self into a second Danger, by offering thus much in my own Vindication. For I have heard of a *Judge*, who, upon the Criminal's *Appeal* to the *dreadful Day of Judgment*, told him, he had incurred a *Premunire*, for *appealing to a foreign Jurisdiction*:[7] And of another in *Wales*, who severely checked the Prisoner for offering the same Plea; taxing him with reflecting on the Court by such a Comparison; because *Comparisons were odious.*

BUT, in Order to make some Excuse for being more speculative than others of my Condition; I desire your Lordship's Pardon, while I am doing a very foolish Thing; which is to give you some little Account of my self.

I WAS bred in a Free-School, where I acquired some little Knowledge in the *Latin Tongue.* I served my Apprenticeship in *London*, and there set up for my self with good Success; until by the *Death of some Friends, and the Misfortunes of others*, I returned into this Kingdom;[8] and began to employ my Thoughts in cultivating the *Woollen-Manufacture* through all its Branches;

---

[1] See *Drapier's Letter IV*, note 1.

[2] Criticism; censure; the act of taking judicial cognizance of offenses and inflicting punishment.

[3] The seat of parliament in London.

[4] Refers to the articles in the indictment made against the Drapier in connection with *Letter IV*.

[5] That is, William Wood. The word "projector" was a highly pejorative term in Swift's lexicon, associated with the impractical and/or fraudulent schemes of economic speculators, mad scientists, etc.

[6] Opinionated; self-important; guilty of impertinent meddling.

[7] A penalty or liability, derived from the legal term *praemunire facias*, designating a writ against any person accused of prosecuting in a foreign court a suit cognizable by the law of England.

[8] A thinly veiled reference to the period in which Swift worked for the Tory ministry in London (1710–14) until the "Death" of Queen Anne and the political "Misfortunes" of Oxford and Bolingbroke forced his return to Ireland.

wherein I met with great Discouragement, and powerful Opposers; whose Objections appeared to me very strange and singular. They argued, that the People of *England* would be offended, if our Manufactures were brought to equal theirs. And even some of the *Weaving*-Trade were my Enemies; which I could not but look upon as *absurd* and *unnatural*. I remember your Lordship, at that Time, did me the Honour to come into my Shop, where I shewed you a Piece of *black and white Stuff,* just sent from the *Dyer*;[9] which you were pleased to approve of, and be my Customer for it.

HOWEVER, I was so mortified, that I resolved, for the future, to sit quietly in my Shop, and deal in *common Goods,* like the rest of my Brethren; untill it happened some Months ago, considering with my self, that the *lower and poorer Sort of People* wanted a *plain, strong, coarse Stuff, to defend them against cold* Easterly *Winds; which then blew very fierce and blasting for a long Time together*; I contrived one on purpose, which sold very well all over the Kingdom, and preserved many Thousands from *Agues.* I then made a *second* and a *third* Kind of *Stuffs* for the *Gentry,* with the same Success;[10] insomuch, that an *Ague* hath hardly been heard of for some Time.

THIS incited me so far, that I ventured upon a fourth Piece, made of the best *Irish* Wool I could get; and I thought it grave and rich enough to be worn by the best *Lord* or *Judge* of the Land.[11] But of late, some *great Folks* complain, as I hear, that when they had it on, they felt a *Shuddering in their Limbs,* and have thrown it off in a Rage; cursing to Hell the poor *Drapier,* who invented it: So that I am determined, never to *work for Persons of Quality* again; except for your *Lordship* and a *very few more.*

I ASSURE your Lordship, upon the Word of an honest Citizen, that I am not richer, by the Value of one of Mr. *Wood's* Half-pence, with the Sale of all the several *Stuffs* I have contrived: For, I give the whole Profit to the *Dyers* and *Pressers.* And, therefore, I hope you will please to believe, that no other Motive, besides the Love of my Country, could engage me to busy my Head and Hands, to the Loss of my Time; and the Gain of nothing but *Vexation* and *ill Will.*

I HAVE now in Hand one *Piece of Stuff* to be woven on purpose for your Lordship; although I might be ashamed to offer it to you, after I have confessed, that it will be made only from the *Shreds and Remnants of the Wool employed in the Former.*[12] However I shall *work* it up as well as I can; and at worst, you need only give it among your Tenants.

I AM very sensible how ill your Lordship is like to be entertained with the Pedantry of a *Drapier,* in the Terms of his own Trade. How will the Matter be mended, when you find me entring again, although very

---

[9] "*By this is meant, a preceding Discourse in this Volume, entitled,* A Proposal for the universal Use of *Irish* Manufactures" (Faulkner's note). Molesworth was one of the people from whom Swift sought help in freeing the *Proposal*'s printer, Edward Waters, from jail and prosecution.

[10] *Alluding to the* Drapier's *three first letters* (Faulkner's note).

[11] *Meaning the fourth Letter, against which the Proclamation was issued* (Faulkner's note).

[12] *Meaning the present Letter* (Faulkner's note).

sparingly, into an Affair of State? For such is now grown the Controversy with Mr. *Wood*, if some *great Lawyers* are to be credited. And as it often happens at Play, that Men begin with *Farthings*, and go on to *Gold*, till some of them lose their Estates and die in Jayl: So it may possibly fall out in my Case, that by *playing* too long with Mr. *Wood's* Half-pence, I may be drawn in to pay a *Fine*, double to the Reward for *Betraying* me; be sent to Prison, and *not be delivered thence until I shall have payed the uttermost Farthing.*

THERE are, My Lord, three Sorts of Persons with whom I am resolved never to dispute: A *High-way-man* with a Pistol at my Breast; a *Troop* of *Dragoons*[13] who come to plunder my House; and a *Man of the Law* who can make a Merit of accusing me. In each of these Cases, *which are almost the same*, the best Method is to *keep out of the Way*; and the next Best is to *deliver your Money, surrender your House*, and *confess nothing.*

I AM told, that the two Points in my last Letter, from which an Occasion of Offence hath been taken, are where I mention His Majesty's Answer to the Address of the House of Lords upon Mr. *Wood's* Patent; and where I discourse upon *Ireland's* being a *Dependant Kingdom.* As to the former, I can only say, that I have treated it with the utmost Respect and Caution; and I thought it necessary to shew, where *Wood's* Patent differed in many essential Parts, from all others that ever had been granted; because the contrary had, for want of due Information, been so strongly and so largely asserted. As to the other, of *Ireland's Dependancy*, I confess to have often heard it mentioned but was never able to understand what it meant. This gave me the Curiosity to inquire among several Eminent Lawyers, who professed they knew nothing of the Matter.[14] I then turned over all the Statutes of both Kingdoms without the least Information, further than an *Irish* Act that I quoted of the 33d of *Henry* VIII. uniting *Ireland* to *England* under one King.[15] I cannot say, I was *sorry* to be disappointed in my Search; because it is certain, I could be *contented* to *depend* only upon *God* and my *Prince*, and the *Laws of my own Country, after the Manner of other Nations.* But since my *Betters* are of a *different Opinion*, and desire *further Dependencies*, I shall outwardly submit; yet still insisting in my own Heart, upon the *Exception* I made of *M. B. Drapier*: Indeed that Hint was borrowed from an idle Story I had heard in *England*, which perhaps may be common and beaten; but because it *insinuates neither Treason nor Sedition*, I will just barely relate it.

SOME Hundred Years ago, when the Peers were so great that the Commons were looked upon as little better than their *Dependents*; a Bill was brought in for making some new Additions to the Power and Privileges

---

[13] A species of cavalry soldier or mounted infantry.

[14] The chief of these was Robert Lindsay, a graduate of Trinity College, Dublin who became the legal advisor to the Chapter of St. Patrick's Cathedral in 1722.

[15] In 1541; see *Letter IV*, note 28.

of the Peerage. After it was read, one Mr. *Drue*, a Member of the House,[16] stood up, and said, he very much approved the Bill, and would give his Vote to have it pass; but however, for some Reasons best known to himself, he desired that a Clause might be inserted for *excepting the Family of the* Drues. The Oddness of the Proposition taught others to reflect a little; and the Bill was thrown out.

WHETHER I were mistaken, or WENT TOO FAR in examining the *Dependency*, must be left to the impartial Judgment of the World, as well as to the Courts of Judicature; although indeed not in so *effectual* and *decisive a Manner*. But to affirm, as I hear some do, in order to countenance a fearful and servile Spirit, that this Point did not *belong to my Subject*, is a False and Foolish Objection. There were several scandalous Reports industriously spread by *Wood* and his Accomplices, to discourage all Opposition against his infamous Project. They gave it out that we were prepared for a *Rebellion*; that we disputed the King's *Prerogative*; and were shaking off our *Dependency*. The first went so far, and obtained so much Belief against the most visible Demonstrations to the contrary, that a great Person of this Kingdom, now in *England*, sent over such an Account of it to his Friends, as would make any good Subject both grieve and tremble.[17] I thought it therefore necessary to treat that Calumny as it deserved. Then I proved by an invincible Argument, that we could have no Intention to dispute His Majesty's *Prerogative*; because the *Prerogative* was not concerned in the Question; the Civilians and Lawyers of all Nations agreeing, that *Copper is not Money*. And lastly, to clear us from the Imputation of shaking off our *Dependency*; I shewed wherein I thought, and shall ever think, this *Dependency* consisted; and cited the Statute above-mentioned made in *Ireland*, by which it is enacted, that *whoever is King of* England, *shall be King of* Ireland; and that the Two Kingdoms shall be *for ever knit together under one King*. This, as I conceived, did wholly acquit us of intending to break our *Dependency*; because, it was altogether out of our Power: For surely no King of *England* will ever consent to the Repeal of that Statute.

BUT upon this Article I am charged with a heavier Accusation. It is said I WENT TOO FAR, when I declared, that *if ever the* Pretender *should come to be fixed upon the Throne of* England (*which God forbid*) *I would so far venture to transgress this Statute, that I would lose the last Drop of my Blood, before I would submit to him as King of* Ireland.

THIS I hear on all Sides, is the strongest and weightiest Objection against me; and which hath given the most Offence; that I should be so bold to declare against a direct Statute; and that my Motive, how strong soever, could make me reject a King whom *England* should receive. Now, if in

---

[16] Probably an allusion to Edward Drew (c. 1542–98), who acquired a reputation for wise and witty counsel as Queen's Serjeant, in which office he regularly provided legal references and interpretation to the Privy Council.

[17] No doubt referring to Charles Fitzroy, 2nd Duke of Grafton, during his rather stormy and ineffectual tenure as Lord-Lieutenant of Ireland until his dismissal in the spring of 1724.

defending myself from this Accusation, I should freely confess, that I WENT TOO FAR; that the Expression was very indiscreet, although occasioned by my Zeal for His present Majesty, and His Protestant Line, in the House of *Hanover*; that I shall be careful never to offend again in the like kind: And that I hope this free Acknowledgement and Sorrow for my Error, will be some Attonement, and a little soften the Hearts of my powerful Adversaries: I say, if I should offer such a Defence as this, I do not doubt, but some People would wrest it to an ill Meaning, by a spiteful Interpretation. And therefore, since I cannot think of any other Answer, which that Paragraph can admit, I will leave it to the Mercy of every candid Reader; but still without recanting my own Opinion.

I WILL now venture to tell your Lordship a Secret, wherein I fear you are too deeply concerned. You will therefore please to know, that this Habit of Writing and Discoursing, wherein I unfortunately differ from *almost* the whole Kingdom, and am apt to grate the Ears of more than I could wish; was acquired during my Apprenticeship in *London*, and a long Residence there after I had set up for my self. Upon my Return and Settlement here, I thought I had only *changed one Country of Freedom for another*. I had been long conversing with the Writings of your Lordship, Mr. *Locke*, Mr. *Molineaux*, Colonel *Sidney*, and other dangerous Authors, who talk of *Liberty as a Blessing, to which the whole Race of Mankind hath an original Title; whereof nothing but unlawful Force can divest them*.[18] I knew a good deal of the several *Gothick* institutions in *Europe*; and by what Incidents and Events they came to be destroyed:[19] And I ever thought it the most uncontrolled[20] and universally agreed Maxim, that *Freedom consists in a People being governed by Laws made with their own Consent; and Slavery in the Contrary*. I have been likewise told, and believe it to be true; that *Liberty* and *Property* are Words of known Use and Signification in this Kingdom; and that the very Lawyers pretend to understand, and have them often in their Mouths. These were the Errors which have misled me; and to which alone I must impute the severe Treatment I have received. But I shall in Time *grow wiser*, and learn to consider my *Driver*, the *Road I am in*, and *with whom I am Yoked*. This I will venture to say; that the boldest and most obnoxious Words I ever delivered, would in *England* have only exposed me as a stupid Fool, who went to prove

---

[18] Swift has in mind here Locke's *Two Treatises of Government* (1690) and Molesworth's *An Account of Denmark* (1693), which lamented that country's turn to absolutism after its constitutional revolution of 1660; its Preface characterized liberty and health as "the greatest natural blessings of mankind." The inclusion of Algernon Sidney in this list is particularly daring given that Sidney (1622–83) was a leading figure in the radical Whig tradition who espoused a form of classical republicanism and was executed for his alleged involvement in a plot to assassinate Charles II. His *Discourses concerning Government* (pub. 1698) promoted liberty as the highest virtue and advocated the people's right to rebel against tyranny.

[19] "Gothick" in this context is meant to evoke associations with the "ancient constitution," or the body of common law and the mixed form of government predating the Norman Conquest, on which the concept of English liberty is based.

[20] Indisputable.

that *the Sun shone in a clear Summer's Day*: And I have Witnesses ready to depose, that your Lordship hath said and writ fifty Times worse; and, what is still an Aggravation, with infinitely more Wit and Learning, and stronger Arguments: So that as Politicks run, I do not know a Person of more exceptionable Principles than your self: And if ever I shall be discovered, I think you will be bound in Honour to pay my Fine, and support me in Prison; or else I may chance to *Inform* against you by Way of *Reprizal*.

IN the mean time, I beg your Lordship to receive my Confession; that if there be any such Thing as a *Dependency* of *Ireland* upon *England*, otherwise than as I have explained it, either by the *Law* of *God*, of *Nature*, of *Reason*, of *Nations*, or of the *Land* (which I shall die rather than grant) then was the *Proclamation* against me, the most *Merciful* that ever was put out; and instead of accusing me as *Malicious, Wicked,* and *Seditious;* it might have been directly as guilty of *High Treason*.

ALL I desire is, that the Cause of my Country against Mr. *Wood* may not suffer by any Inadvertency of mine: Whether *Ireland* depend upon *England*, or only upon *God*, the *King*, and the *Law*; I hope no Man will assert that it *depends* upon Mr. *Wood*. I should be heartily sorry, that this *Commendable* Resentment against me should accidentally (and *I hope*, what was never intended) strike a Damp upon that Spirit in all Ranks and Corporations of Men against the desperate and ruinous Design of Mr. *Wood*. Let my Countrymen blot out those Parts in my last Letter which they dislike; and let no *Rust* remain on my *Sword*, to cure the Wounds I have given to our most mortal Enemy. When Sir *Charles Sidley* was taking the Oaths, where several Things were to be *Renounced;* he said, he loved *Renouncing*; asked if any more were to be *Renounced;* for he was ready to *Renounce* as much as they pleased.[21] Although I am not so thorough a *Renouncer;* yet let me have but *Good City Security* against this pestilent Coinage, and I shall be ready not only to *Renounce* every Syllable in all my Four Letters, but deliver them cheerfully with my own *Hands* into *those* of the common *Hangman*, to be burnt with no better Company than the *Coiner's Effigies*;[22] if any Part of it hath escaped out of the *Secular*[23] *Hands* of my faithful Friends the common People.

BUT, whatever the Sentiments of *some People* may be, I think it is agreed that many of those who *Subscribed* against me, are on the Side of a vast

---

[21] Sir Charles Sedley (1639–1701) was a Restoration courtier and wit, author of amorous lyrics and dramatic comedies, and an M.P. who ended his career as Speaker of the House of Commons. The "oaths" referred to were those imposed after the Glorious Revolution on members of parliament and other high officeholders, promising fidelity to the new monarchs, William and Mary, and rejecting the claims of the Pretender. Sedley had personal reasons for "renouncing" the latter: against his wishes James had taken Sedley's daughter Catharine as his mistress and amidst scandal had made her a countess.

[22] During this period books judged to be seditious or blasphemous were burned by the hangman.

[23] Of or belonging to the "common" or "unlearned" people.

Majority in the Kingdom, who opposed Mr. *Wood*.[24] And it was with great Satisfaction, that I observed some *Right Honourable Names* very *amicably* joined with my own at the Bottom of a *strong Declaration,* against him, and his Coin.[25] But if the Admission of it among us be *already determined;* the *worthy* Person who is to *betray* me, ought in Prudence to do it with all convenient Speed; or else it may be difficult to find Three Hundred Pounds in *Sterling* for the Discharge of his *Hire;* when the Publick shall have lost Five Hundred Thousand; if there be so much in the Nation; besides Four Fifths of its Annual Income for ever.

I AM told by Lawyers; that in all Quarrels between Man and Man, it is of much Weight which of them gave the first Provocation, or struck the first Blow. It is manifest that Mr. *Wood* hath done both: And therefore I should humbly propose to have him first *Hanged,* and his *Dross* thrown into the Sea: After which the *Drapier* will be ready to stand his Tryal. *It must needs be that Offences come; but Wo unto him by whom the Offence cometh.*[26] If Mr. *Wood* had held his *Hand;* every body else would have held their *Tongues:* And then, there would have been little Need of *Pamphlets, Juries,* or *Proclamations* upon this Occasion. The Provocation must Needs have been great, which could stir up an obscure, indolent *Drapier,* to become an *Author.* One would almost think the very *Stones* in the Street would *rise* up in such a Cause: And I am not sure, they will not *do so* against Mr. *Wood,* if ever he comes within their Reach. It is a known Story of the Dumb Boy, whose Tongue forced a Passage for Speech by the Horror of seeing a Dagger at his Father's Throat. This may lessen the Wonder, that a Tradesman hid in Privacy and Silence should *cry out* when the Life and Being of his Political *Mother* are attempted before his Face; and by so infamous a Hand.

BUT in the mean Time, Mr. *Wood* the *Destroyer* of a Kingdom, walks about in Triumph (unless it be true, that he is in Jayl for Debt) while he who endeavoured to *assert the Liberty of his Country,* is forced to *hide his Head* for occasionally dealing in a Matter of *Controversy.* However, I am not the first who hath been condemned to Death for *gaining a great Victory* over a powerful Enemy, by disobeying for *once* the strict Orders of Military Discipline.[27]

---

[24] Refers to the fact that many of the same Privy Council members who signed the Proclamation against the Drapier had five months earlier (on May 20, 1724) signed an "Address to the King" warning that Wood's half-pence would bring about the nation's ruin.

[25] Perhaps a reference to *A Declaration of the Grand Jury and the rest of the inhabitants of the Liberty of St Patrick's Dublin,* which John Harding published on August 20, 1724.

[26] Matthew 18:7.

[27] See 1 Samuel 14:13–45. The reference is to Jonathan, who despite leading a successful attack against the Philistines was condemned to death for violating Saul's stricture against eating on the day of battle. He was saved by the people, who cried, "Shall Jonathan die, who hath wrought this great salvation in Israel? God forbid: as the Lord liveth, there shall not one hair of his head fall to the ground." Significantly, this same cry was taken up by the common people of Dublin in response to the official Proclamation against the Drapier.

I AM now resolved to follow (after the usual Proceeding of Mankind, because it is too late) the Advice given me by a certain *Dean*.[28] He shewed the Mistake I was in, of trusting to the general good Will of the People; that I had succeeded hitherto, better than could be expected; but that some unfortunate *Circumstantial Lapse,* would probably bring me within the Reach of *Power:* That my good Intentions would be no Security against *those who watched every Motion of my Pen, in the Bitterness of my Soul.*[29] He produced an Instance of a Person as innocent, as disinterested and as well meaning as my self; who had written a very seasonable and inoffensive Treatise, exhorting the People of this Kingdom to wear their own Manufactures; for which, however, the Printer was prosecuted with the utmost Virulence; the *Jury sent back Nine Times;* and the Man given up to the Mercy of the Court.[30] The *Dean* further observed, That I was in a Manner left alone to stand the *Battle;* while others, who had Ten thousand Times better Talents than a *Drapier,* were so prudent to lie still; and perhaps thought it no unpleasant Amusement to look on with Safety, while another was giving them *Diversion* at the Hazard of his Liberty and Fortune; and thought they made a sufficient Recompence by a little Applause: Whereupon he concluded with a short Story of a *Jew* at *Madrid;* who being condemned to the Fire on Account of his Religion; a Crowd of School-boys following him to the Stake, and apprehending they might lose their *Sport,* if he should happen to recant; would often *clap him on the Back,* and cry, *Sta firme Moyese (Moses, continue stedfast.)*

I ALLOW this Gentleman's Advice to have been very good, and his Observations just; and in one Respect my Condition is worse than that of the *Jew;* for *no Recantation will save me.* However, it should seem by *some late Proceedings,* that my State is not altogether deplorable. This I can impute to nothing but the Steddiness of *two impartial Grand Juries;*[31] which hath confirmed in me an Opinion I have long entertained; That, as Philosophers say, *Virtue is seated in the Middle;* so in another Sense, the little *Virtue* left in the World is chiefly to be found among the *middle* Rank of Mankind; who are neither *allured* out of her Paths by *Ambition,* nor *driven* by *Poverty.*

SINCE the *Proclamation,* occasioned by my last Letter, and a *due* Preparation for proceeding against me in a Court of Justice, there have been two printed Papers clandestinely spread about; whereof no Man is able to trace the Original, further than by *Conjecture;* which, with its usual Charity, lays them to my Account. The former is entituled, *Seasonable Advice,* and appears to have been intended for Information of the Grand-Jury; upon the

---

[28] "*The* Author, *it is supposed, means himself*" (Faulkner's note).

[29] For biblical echoes, see Job 10:1, 21–25; Isaiah 38:15; and 1 Samuel 1:10.

[30] Another reference to Chief Justice Whitshed's overzealous prosecution of Swift's printer in 1720.

[31] Refers to the Grand Jury discharged by Chief Justice Whitshed for refusing to make a presentment of libel against Swift's pamphlet, *Seasonable Advice;* and the new Grand Jury that was convened in its place a week later, which did likewise.

Supposition of a Bill to be prepared against that Letter.[32] The other is an Extract from a printed Book of Parliamentary Proceedings, in the Year 1680; containing an angry Resolution of the House of Commons in *England*, against *dissolving Grand-Juries*.[33] As to the former, your Lordship will find it to be the Work of a more artful Hand, than that of a common *Drapier*. It hath been censured for endeavouring to influence the Minds of a Jury, which ought to be wholly free and unbyassed; and for that Reason, *it is manifest*, that no *Judge* was ever known, either *upon* or *off* the Bench, either by *himself*, or his *Dependents*, to use the *least Insinuation*, that might possibly affect the Passions, or Interests, of any one single *Jury-man*, much less of a whole *Jury*; whereof every Man *must be convinced*, who will just give himself the Trouble to dip into the common printed Tryals; so as, it is amazing to think, what a Number of *upright Judges* there have been in both Kingdoms, for above *Sixty Years past;* which, considering how long they held their Offices *during Pleasure*,[34] as they *still do among us*, I account next to a *Miracle*.

As to the other Paper, I must confess it is a sharp Censure of an *English* House of Commons, against *dissolving Grand-Juries*, by any Judge before the End of the Term, Assizes, or Sessions, while Matters are under their Consideration, and not presented; as arbitrary, illegal, destructive to pub-lick Justice, a manifest Violation of his Oath, and as a Means to subvert the Fundamental Laws of the Kingdom.

HOWEVER, the Publisher seems to have been mistaken in what he aimed at. For, whatever *Dependence* there may be of *Ireland* upon *England;* I hope he would not insinuate, that the Proceedings of a *Lord Chief Justice* in *Ireland*, must *depend* upon a *Resolution* of an *English* House of Commons. Besides, that *Resolution* although it were levelled against a particular Lord Chief Justice, Sir *William Scroggs*, yet the Occasion was directly contrary. For, *Scroggs dissolved the Grand-Jury* of *London,* for fear they *should* present; but our's in *Dublin* was *dissolved*, because they would *not* present; which *wonderfully alters the Case*.[35] And, therefore, a *second Grand-Jury* supplied that Defect, by making a Presentment that hath *pleased the whole Kingdom*.[36] However, I think it is agreed by all Parties, that both the one and the other

---

[32] Swift wrote and circulated *Seasonable Advice* shortly after the arrest of his printer, Harding, on November 7, for the publication of *Drapier's Letter IV.* The anonymous paper proclaimed both Harding's and the Drapier's innocence, and reminded jurors that the charge against Harding was inseparable from the attempt to derail the opposition against Wood's half-pence.

[33] Also by Swift; entitled *An Extract*, it presented debates in the English House of Commons in 1680 to prove the illegality of Chief Justice Whitshed's actions.

[34] That is, "during Pleasure (of the Crown)"; subject to the Crown's favor or approval.

[35] As Lord Chief Justice of England, Sir William Scroggs (c. 1623–83) discharged the Grand Jury (on June 26, 1680) that was considering the Earl of Shaftesbury's attempt to indict the Duke of York as a popish recusant and thereby prevent the latter's succession to the throne. The discharge was declared illegal by the House of Commons and resulted in Scrogg's impeachment.

[36] While declining to make a presentment of libel against Swift's *Seasonable Advice*, the second Grand Jury returned a presentment instead against those who were using deception to

Jury behaved themselves in such a Manner, as ought to be remembered to
their Honour, while there shall be any Regard left among us, for *Virtue* or
publick Spirit.

I AM confident, your Lordship will be of my Sentiments in one Thing; that
some short plain authentick Tract might be published, for the Information
both of *Petty* and *Grand Juries,* how far their Power reacheth, and where it
is limited; and that a printed Copy of such a Treatise might be deposited in
every Court, to be consulted by the Jury-men, before they consider of their
Verdict; by which, Abundance of Inconveniencies would be avoided; whereof
innumerable Instances might be produced from former Times, because I will
say nothing of the present.

I HAVE read somewhere of an *Eastern* King, who put a *Judge* to Death for
an iniquitous Sentence; and ordered his *Hide to be stuffed into a Cushion,*
and placed upon the Tribunal for the Son to sit on; who was preferred to his
Father's Office.[37] I fancy, such a *Memorial* might not have been unuseful to a
Son of Sir *William Scroggs*, and that both he and his Successors would often
wriggle in their Seats, as long as the *Cushion* lasted: I wish the Relater had
told us what Number of such *Cushions* there might be in that Country.

I CANNOT but observe to your Lordship, how nice and dangerous a Point
it is grown, for a private Person to inform the People; even in an Affair,
where the publick Interest and Safety are so highly concerned, as that of
Mr. *Wood;* and this in a Country, where *Loyalty is woven into the very Hearts
of the People,* seems a little extraordinary. Sir *William Scroggs* was the first
who introduced that *commendable Acuteness into the Courts of Judicature;*
but how far this Practice hath been imitated by his Successors, or *strained
upon Occasion*, is out of my Knowledge. When Pamphlets, *unpleasing to the
Ministry*, were presented as Libels, he would order the offensive Paragraphs
to be read before him; and said, it was strange, that the Judges and Lawyers
of the *King's-Bench* should be duller than all the People of *England*: And
he was often so very happy in applying the initial Letters of Names, and
expounding *dubious Hints,* (the two common Expedients among Writers of
that Class, for escaping the Law) that he discovered much *more* than ever the
Authors intended; as many of them, or their Printers, found to their Cost. If
such Methods are to be followed in examining, what I have already written,
or may write hereafter, upon the Subject of Mr. *Wood,* I defy any Man of
fifty Times my Understanding and Caution, to avoid being *entrapped*; unless
he will be content to write what none will read, by repeating over the old
Arguments and Computations; whereof the World is already grown weary.
So that my good Friend *Harding* lies under this *Dilemma;* either to let my

---

impose the half-pence on Ireland; moreover, they extolled the efforts of "PATRIOTS" who
had worked to expose Wood's "Fraudulent" scheme.

[37] Refers to the punishment that Cambyses II, King of ancient Persia (529–521 B.C.E),
inflicted on the royal judge Sisamnes; as recounted in Herodotus, *Histories*, 5.25.2.

learned Works hang for ever a-drying upon his Lines; or venture to publish them at the Hazard of being laid by the Heels.[38]

I NEED not tell your Lordship where the Difficulty lies: It is true, that the King and the Laws *permit* us to refuse this Coin of Mr. *Wood;* but, at the same Time, it is equally true, that the King and the Laws *permit* us to receive it. Now, it is *barely possible,* that the Ministers in *England* may not suppose the Consequences of uttering[39] that Brass among us, to be so ruinous as we apprehend; because, perhaps, if they understood it in that Light, they would, in common Humanity, use their Credit with his Majesty for saving *a most Loyal Kingdom from Destruction.* But, as long as it shall please those great Persons to think that Coin will not be *so very* pernicious to us, we lie under the Disadvantage of being censured as *obstinate,* in not complying with a Royal Patent. Therefore, nothing remains, but to make Use of that *Liberty,* which the *King* and the *Laws* have left us; by continuing to refuse this Coin; and by frequent Remembrances to keep up that Spirit raised against it; which otherwise may be apt to flag, and perhaps in Time to sink altogether. For, any publick Order against receiving or uttering Mr. *Wood's* Half-pence, is not *reasonably* to be expected in this Kingdom, without Directions from *England;* which I think no body presumes, or is so sanguine to hope.

BUT to confess the Truth, my Lord, I begin to grow weary of my Office as a Writer; and could heartily wish it were devolved upon my *Brethren,* the Makers of *Songs* and *Ballads;* who, perhaps, are the best qualified at present, to gather up the Gleanings of this Controversy.[40] As to my self, it hath been my Misfortune to begin, and pursue it upon a wrong Foundation. For, having detected the Frauds and Falshoods of this vile Impostor *Wood* in every Part, I foolishly *disdained* to have Recourse *to whining, lamenting,* and *crying for Mercy;* but rather chose to *appeal* to *Law* and *Liberty,* and *the common Rights of Mankind,* without considering the *Climate* I was in.

SINCE your last Residence in *Ireland,* I frequently have taken my Nag to ride about your Grounds; where I fancied my self to feel an Air of *Freedom* breathing round me; and I am glad the low Condition of a Tradesman, did not qualify me to wait on you at your House; for then, I am afraid, my Writings would not have escaped *severer Censures.* But I have lately sold my Nag, and honestly told his greatest Fault, which was that of snuffing up the Air about *Brackdenstown;* whereby he became such a Lover of *Liberty,* that I could scarce hold him in. I have likewise buried, at the Bottom of a strong Chest, your Lordship's Writings, under a Heap of others that treat of

---

[38] In other words, either to let Swift's works languish unpublished on his printing press, or else risk being put in irons or arrested and placed in confinement. The term "laid by the heels" can also function figuratively, to mean "disgraced" or "overthrown."

[39] Putting into circulation.

[40] A reference to the many popular ballads written in support of the Drapier's campaign against Wood's half-pence, a number of them composed at a club formed at the Sign of the Drapier's Head in Truck Street. Swift himself contributed to this output with about a dozen broadsides of his own; see, e.g., *Prometheus.*

Liberty; and spread over a *Layer* or two of *Hobbs, Filmer, Bodin,* and many more Authors of that Stamp,[41] to be readiest at Hand, whenever I shall be disposed to take up a *new Set* of Principles in Government. In the mean time, I design quietly to look to my Shop, and keep as far out of your Lordship's Influence as possible; and if you ever see any more of my Writings on this Subject, I promise you shall find them as innocent, as insipid, and without a Sting, as what I have now offered you. But, if your Lordship will please to give me an easy Lease of some Part of your Estate in *Yorkshire,*[42] thither I will carry my Chest; and turning it upside down, resume my Political Reading where I left it off; feed on plain homely Fare, and live and die a FREE honest *English* Farmer: But not without Regret, for leaving my Countrymen under the Dread of the brazen Talons of Mr. *Wood;* my most loyal and innocent Country-men; to whom I owe so much for their good Opinion of me, and my poor Endeavours to serve them. I am, with the greatest Respect,

> *My Lord,*
> *Your Lordship's*
> *Most Obedient,*
> *And most Humble Servant,*
>
>   M. B.

From my Shop in
  St. *Francis-street,*
  Dec. 14, 1724.

---

[41] That is, political theorists who espoused an absolutist form of government, hence quint-essential enemies of liberty. Thomas Hobbes (1588–1679), author of *Leviathan* (1651), advocated complete submission to a centralized authority in order to ensure the individual's self-preservation. Sir Robert Filmer (c. 1588–1653) was the author of *Patriarcha,* which drew a parallel between familial and political structures, defending strong hierarchical authority in both. Jean Bodin (1530–96) is best known for his *Six Livres de la République* (1576), which views society as an association of families structured along patriarchal lines and ruled by a sovereign who possesses unlimited law-making powers.

[42] Lands purchased from the Wharton family, at Eddington, in Yorkshire, England.

DOING GOOD:

A SERMON,

On the Occasion of WOOD'S PROJECT

Written in the Year MDCCXXIV

One of only eleven sermons by Swift that have survived (with another of doubtful attribution), this sermon may be considered a companion piece to The Drapier's Letters—*according to Herbert Davis, it was written sometime between August 4 and October 26, 1724. It is significant both for the light it sheds on the inextricable links Swift saw between his dual roles as dean and political activist, and for its promotion of Irish patriotism as the highest civic virtue and as an almost sacred duty for all inhabitants of Ireland. Copy-text:* Works, *ed. Faulkner, 1765.*

* * *

GALATIANS, vi. 10.

As we have therefore opportunity, let us do Good unto all men.

NATURE directs every one of us, and God permits us, to consult our own private Good before the private Good of any other person whatsoever. We are, indeed, commanded to love our Neighbour as ourselves, but not as well as ourselves. The love we have for ourselves is to be the pattern of that love we ought to have towards our neighbour: But, as the copy doth not equal the original, so my neighbour cannot think it hard, if I prefer myself, who am the original, before him, who is only the copy. Thus, if any matter equally concern the life, the reputation, the profit of my neighbour, and my own; the law of nature, which is the law of God, obligeth me to take care of myself first, and afterwards of him. And this I need not be at much pains in persuading you to; for the want of self-love, with regard to things of this world, is not among the faults of mankind. But then, on the other side, if, by a small hurt and loss to myself, I can procure a great good to my neighbour, in that case his interest is to be preferred. For example, if I can be sure of saving his life, without great danger to my own; if I can preserve him from being undone, without ruining myself, or recover his reputation without blasting mine; all this I am obliged to do: And, if I sincerely perform it, I do then obey the command of God, in loving my neighbour as myself.

But, beside this love we owe to every man in his particular capacity under the title of our neighbour, there is yet a duty of a more large, extensive nature, incumbent on us; which is, our love to our neighbour in his public capacity, as he is a member of that great body, the commonwealth, under the same government with ourselves; and this is usually called love of the public, and is a duty to which we are more strictly obliged than even that of loving ourselves; because therein ourselves are also contained, as well as all our neighbours, in one great body. This love of the public, or of the commonwealth, or love of our country, was in antient times properly known by the name of *Virtue*, because it was the greatest of all virtues, and was supposed to contain all virtues in it: And many great examples of this virtue are left us on record, scarcely to be believed, or even conceived, in such a base, corrupted, wicked age as this we live in.[1] In those times it was common for men to sacrifice their lives for the good of their country, although they had neither hope or belief of future rewards; whereas, in our days, very few make the least scruple of sacrificing a whole nation, as well as their own souls, for a little present gain; which often hath been known to end in their own ruin in this world, as it certainly must in that to come.

Have we not seen men, for the sake of some petty employment, give up the very natural rights and liberties of their country, and of mankind, in the ruin of which themselves must at last be involved? Are not these corruptions gotten among the meanest of our people, who, for a piece of money, will give their votes at a venture, for the disposal of their own lives and fortunes, without considering whether it be to those who are most likely to betray or defend them?

But, if I were to produce only one instance of a hundred wherein we fail in this duty of loving our country, it would be an endless labour; and therefore I shall not attempt it.

But here I would not be misunderstood: By the love of our country, I do not mean loyalty to our King, for that is a duty of another nature; and a man may be very loyal, in the common sense of the word, without one grain of public-good at his heart. Witness this very kingdom we live in. I verily believe, that, since the beginning of the world, no nation upon earth ever shewed (all circumstances considered) such high constant marks of loyalty in all their actions and behaviour as we have done: And at the same time, no people ever appeared more utterly void of what is called a Public Spirit. When I say the people, I mean the bulk or mass of the people, for I have nothing to do with those in power.

Therefore, I shall think my time not ill spent, if I can persuade most or all of you who hear me, to shew the love you have for your country, by endeavouring, in your several stations, to do all the public good you are able. For I

---

[1] Swift's notion of "antient virtue" was epitomized in the figure of Brutus, in whose countenance Gulliver sees reflected "the most consummate Virtue" and "the truest Love of his Country" (*Gulliver's Travels*, Pt. III).

am certainly persuaded, that all our misfortunes arise from no other original cause than that general disregard among us to the public welfare.

I therefore undertake to shew you three things.

First, That there are few people so weak or mean, who have it not sometimes in their power to be useful to the public.

Secondly, That it is often in the power of the meanest among mankind to do mischief to the public.

And, lastly, That all wilful injuries done to the public, are very great and aggravated sins in the sight of God.

First, There are few people so weak or mean, who have it not sometimes in their power to be useful to the public.

Solomon tells us of a poor wise man who saved a city by his counsel.[2] It hath often happened that a private soldier, by some unexpected brave attempt, hath been instrumental in obtaining a great victory. How many obscure men have been authors of very useful inventions, whereof the world now reaps the benefit? The very example of honesty and industry in a poor tradesman, will sometimes spread through a neighbourhood, when others see how successful he is; and thus so many useful members are gained, for which the whole body of the public is the better. Whoever is blessed with a true public spirit, God will certainly put it into his way to make use of that blessing, for the ends it was given him, by some means or other: And therefore it hath been observed in most ages, that the greatest actions, for the benefit of the commonwealth, have been performed by the wisdom or courage, the contrivance or industry, of particular men, and not of numbers; and that the safety of a kingdom hath often been owing to those hands from whence it was least expected.

But, secondly, it is often in the power of the meanest among mankind to do mischief to the public: And hence arise most of those miseries with which the states and kingdoms of the earth are infested. How many great princes have been murdered by the meanest ruffians? The weakest hand can open a floodgate to drown a country, which a thousand of the strongest cannot stop. Those who have thrown off all regard for public good, will often have it in their way to do public evil, and will not fail to exercise that power whenever they can. The greatest blow given of late to this kingdom, was by the dishonesty of a few manufacturers; who, by imposing bad ware at foreign markets, in almost the only traffic permitted to us, did half ruin that trade; by which this poor unhappy kingdom now suffers in the midst of sufferings.[3] I speak not here of persons in high stations, who ought to be free from all reflection, and are supposed always to intend the welfare of the community: But we now find by experience, that the meanest instrument may, by the concurrence of accidents, have it in his power to bring a whole kingdom to

---

[2] Ecclesiastes 9:14–15.

[3] During the recent plague in France (which began in Marseilles in 1720), Irish merchants contracted to supply Spain with linen cloth, but because of poor quality and price-gouging most of the wares were returned and the trade destroyed.

the very brink of destruction, and is, at this present, endeavouring to finish his work; and hath agents among ourselves, who are contented to see their own country undone, to be small sharers in that iniquitous gain, which at last must end in their own ruin as well as ours. I confess, it was chiefly the consideration of that great danger we are in, which engaged me to discourse to you on this subject; to exhort you to a love of your country, and a public spirit, when all you have is at stake; to prefer the interest of your prince and your fellow subjects before that of one destructive impostor, and a few of his adherents.[4]

Perhaps it may be thought by some, that this way of discoursing is not so proper from the pulpit. But surely, when an open attempt is made, and far carried on, to make a great kingdom one large poor-house, to deprive us of all means to exercise hospitality or charity, to turn our cities and churches into ruins, to make the country a desert for wild beasts and robbers, to destroy all arts and sciences, all trades and manufactures, and the very tillage of the ground, only to enrich one obscure, ill-designing projector, and his followers; it is time for the pastor to cry out, that the wolf is getting into his flock, to warn them to stand together, and all to consult the common safety. And God be praised for his infinite goodness, in raising such a spirit of union among us, at least in this point, in the midst of all our former divisions; which union, if it continue, will, in all probability, defeat the pernicious design of this pestilent enemy to the nation.

But, from hence, it clearly follows, how necessary the love of our country, or a public spirit, is in every particular man, since the wicked have so many opportunities of doing public mischief. Every man is upon his own guard for his private advantage; but, where the public is concerned, he is apt to be negligent, considering himself only as one among two or three millions, among whom the loss is equally shared, and thus, he thinks, he can be no great sufferer. Meanwhile the trader, the farmer, and the shopkeeper, complain of the hardness and deadness of the times, and wonder whence it comes; while it is, in a great measure, owing to their own folly, for want of that love of their country, and public spirit and firm union among themselves, which are so necessary to the prosperity of every nation.

Another method, by which the meanest wicked man may have it in his power to injure the public, is false accusation, whereof this kingdom hath afforded too many examples: Neither is it long since no man, whose opinions were thought to differ from those in fashion, could safely converse beyond his nearest friends, for fear of being sworn against, as a traitor, by those who made a traffic of perjury and subornation; by which the very peace of the nation was disturbed, and men fled from each other as they would from a lion or a bear got loose. And, it is very remarkable, that the pernicious project now in hand to reduce us to beggary, was forwarded by one of these false accusers, who had been convicted of endeavouring, by perjury and

---

[4]William Wood and his supporters.

subornation, to take away the lives of several innocent persons here among us; and, indeed, there could not be a more proper instrument for such a work.[5]

Another method, by which the meanest people may do injury to the public, is the spreading of lies and false rumours, thus raising a distrust among the people of a nation, causing them to mistake their true interest, and their enemies for their friends: And this hath been likewise too successful a practice among us, where we have known the whole kingdom misled by the grossest lies, raised upon occasion to serve some particular turn. As it hath also happened in the case I lately mentioned, where one obscure man, by representing our wants where they were least, and concealing them where they were greatest, had almost succeeded in a project of utterly ruining this whole kingdom; and may still succeed, if God doth not continue that public spirit, which he hath almost miraculously kindled in us upon this occasion.

Thus we see the public is many times, as it were, at the mercy of the meanest instrument, who can be wicked enough to watch opportunities of doing it mischief, upon the principles of avarice or malice; which, I am afraid, are deeply rooted in too many breasts, and against which there can be no defence, but a firm resolution in all honest men, to be closely united and active in shewing their love to their country, by preferring the public interest to their present private advantage. If a passenger, in a great storm at sea, should hide his goods, that they might not be thrown over board to lighten the ship, what would be the consequence? The ship is cast away, and he loseth his life and goods together.

We have heard of men, who, through greediness of gain, have brought infected goods into a nation, which bred a plague, whereof the owners and their families perished first.[6] Let those among us consider this and tremble, whose houses are privately stored with those materials of beggary and desolation, lately brought over to be scattered like a pestilence among their countrymen, which may probably first seize upon themselves and their families, until their houses shall be made a dunghill.

I shall mention one practice more, by which the meanest instruments often succeed in doing public mischief, and this is by deceiving us with plausible arguments, to make us believe, that the most ruinous project they can offer is intended for our good, as it happened in the case so often mentioned. For the poor ignorant people, allured by the appearing convenience in their

---

[5] Referring to John Browne of the Neale (Co. Mayo), condemned as a betrayer of his country in *Drapier's Letter III* (though his name was excised from later printings).

[6] The 1720 French plague began after merchants in Marseilles pressured the authorities to lift the quarantine on an infected ship so that they could take possession of its cargo of silks and other treasures. The recurrence of the plague there a year later spread fear among the inhabitants of other countries, including Ireland. A letter of Swift's dated January 30, 1722 notes, "We are now preparing for the plague, which everybody expects before May;...Our great tradesmen break, and go off by dozens."

small dealings, did not discover the serpent in the brass, but were ready, like the Israelites, to offer incense to it;[7] neither could the wisdom of the nation convince them, until some, of good intentions, made the cheat so plain to their sight, that those who run may read.[8] And thus the design was to treat us, in every point, as the Philistines treated Samson, (I mean when he was betrayed by Dalilah) first to put out our eyes, and then bind us with fetters of brass.[9]

I proceed to the last thing I proposed, which was to shew you that all wilful injuries done to the public, are very great and aggravated sins in the sight of God.

First, It is apparent from Scripture, and most agreeable to reason, that the safety and welfare of nations are under the most peculiar care of God's providence. Thus he promised Abraham to save Sodom, if only ten righteous men could be found in it. Thus the reason which God gave to Jonas for not destroying Nineveh was, because there were six score thousand men in that city.[10]

All government is from God, who is the God of order, and therefore whoever attempts to breed confusion or disturbance among a people, doth his utmost to take the government of the world out of God's hands, and to put it into the hands of the Devil, who is the author of confusion. By which it is plain, that no crime, how heinous soever, committed against particular persons, can equal the guilt of him who doth injury to the public.

Secondly, All offenders against their country lie under this grievous difficulty, that it is next to impossible to obtain a pardon, or make restitution. The bulk of mankind are very quick at resenting injuries, and very slow in forgiving them: And how shall one man be able to obtain the pardon of millions, or repair the injuries he hath done to millions? How shall those, who, by a most destructive fraud, got the whole wealth of our neighbouring kingdom into their hands, be ever able to make a recompence? How will the authors and promoters of that villainous project, for the ruin of this poor country, be able to account with us for the injuries they have already done, although they should no farther succeed? The deplorable case of such wretches, must entirely be left to the unfathomable mercies of God: For those who know the least in religion are not ignorant that, without our utmost endeavours to make restitution to the person injured, and to obtain his pardon, added to a sincere repentance, there is no hope of salvation given in the Gospel.

Lastly, all offences against our own country have this aggravation, that they are ungrateful and unnatural. It is to our country we owe those laws which protect us in our lives, our liberties, our properties, and our religion. Our country produced us into the world, and continues to nourish us so, that it is usually called our mother; and there have been examples of great

---

[7] See Numbers 21:8–9 and 2 Kings 18:4.
[8] That is, even those who only glimpse in passing can see what is there.
[9] Judges 16:21.
[10] See Genesis 18:32 and Jonah 4:11.

magistrates, who have put their own children to death for endeavouring to betray their country, as if they had attempted the life of their natural parent.[11]

Thus I have briefly shewn you how terrible a sin it is to be an enemy to our country, in order to incite you to the contrary virtue, which at this juncture is so highly necessary, when every man's endeavour will be of use. We have hitherto been just able to support ourselves under many hardships; but now the axe is laid to the root of the tree, and nothing but a firm union among us can prevent our utter undoing. This we are obliged to, in duty to our gracious King, as well as to ourselves. Let us therefore preserve that public spirit, which God hath raised in us for our own temporal interest. For, if this wicked project should succeed, which it cannot do but by our own folly; if we sell ourselves for nought; the merchant, the shop-keeper, the artificer, must fly to the desert with their miserable families, there to starve or live upon rapine, or at least exchange their country for one more hospitable than that where they were born.

Thus much I thought it my duty to say to you, who are under my care, to warn you against those temporal evils, which may draw the worst of spiritual evils after them; such as heart-burnings,[12] murmurings, discontents, and all manner of wickedness, which a desperate condition of life may tempt men to.

I am sensible, that what I have now said will not go very far, being confined to this assembly; but I hope it may stir up others of my brethren to exhort their several congregations, after a more effectual manner, to shew their love for their country on this important occasion. And this, I am sure, cannot be called meddling in affairs of state.[13]

I pray God protect his most gracious Majesty, and this kingdom, long under his government, and defend us from all ruinous projectors, deceivers, suborners, perjurers, false accusers, and oppressors; from the virulence of party and faction; and unite us in loyalty to our King, love to our country, and charity to each other. And this we beg for Jesus Christ his sake; To whom, &c.

---

[11] The most famous example is Lucius Junius Brutus, founder of the Roman Republic (509 B.C.E.), who, as first consul of Rome, condemned his two sons to death for conspiring to restore the banished Tarquin to the throne; see Virgil, *The Aeneid*, Bk. 6 and Livy, *History of Rome* 2.5. Dryden's translation of Virgil declares that Brutus took this action for "love of honour, and his country's good." Swift would perhaps have been thinking here also of the action taken by Lucius's descendant, Marcus Brutus, who 'loved Caesar but loved Rome more.'

[12] Heated or embittered states of mind; secretly nursed resentments.

[13] An ironic reference to George I's decree of December 11, 1714 that preachers should not "meddle in any affairs of state." Swift noted to a correspondent three weeks later that seeing this directive in print "has given me an inclination to preach what is forbid."

A Short VIEW of THE STATE of *IRELAND*

First printed in March 1728, this tract on the most general level attacks what Swift saw as a falsely rosy picture of conditions in Ireland, circulated by those who focused on only the most affluent areas of Dublin and environs while cultivating a self-willed blindness to the country's larger social and economic woes. On a more specific level, the tract is a direct response to John Browne's Seasonable Remarks on Trade, *published several weeks earlier, which depicted Ireland as a flourishing country that could serve as a source of enrichment for England. The pamphlet was subsequently reprinted as Number XV of Swift's and Sheridan's short-lived periodical* The Intelligencer, *and (partially) reprinted in England in the Opposition newspaper,* Mist's Weekly Journal.

* * *

I AM assured, that it hath, for some Time, been practised as a Method of making Men's Court, when they are asked about the Rate of Lands, the Abilities of Tenants, the State of Trade and Manufacture in this Kingdom, and how their Rents are paid; to answer, that in their Neighbourhood, all Things are in a flourishing Condition, the Rent and Purchase of Land every Day encreasing. And if a Gentleman happen to be a little more sincere in his Representations; besides being looked on as not well affected, he is sure to have a Dozen Contradictors at his Elbow. I think it is no Manner of Secret why these Questions are so *cordially* asked, or so *obligingly* answered.

BUT since, with regard to the Affairs of this Kingdom, I have been using all Endeavours to subdue my Indignation; to which, indeed, I am not provoked by any personal Interest, being not the Owner of one Spot of Ground in the whole *Island*,[1] I shall only enumerate by Rules generally known, and never contradicted, what are the true Causes of any Countries flourishing and growing rich; and then examine what Effects arise from those Causes in the Kingdom of *Ireland*.

---

[1]A rhetorically effective statement but one requiring qualification since Swift's income depended (among other things) on rents obtained from the leasing of church lands.

THE first Cause of a Kingdom's thriving, is the Fruitfulness of the Soil, to produce the Necessaries and Conveniences of Life; not only sufficient for the Inhabitants, but for Exportation into other Countries.

THE Second, is the Industry of the People, in working up all their native Commodities, to the last Degree of Manufacture.

THE Third, is the Conveniency of safe Ports and Havens, to carry out their own Goods, as much manufactured, and bring in those of others, as little manufactured, as the Nature of mutual Commerce will allow.

THE Fourth is, that the Natives should, as much as possible, export and import their Goods in Vessels of their own Timber, made in their own Country.

THE Fifth, is the Priviledge of a free Trade in all foreign Countries, which will permit them; except to those who are in War with their own Prince or State.

THE Sixth, is, by being governed only by Laws made with their own Consent; for otherwise they are not a free People.[2] And therefore, all Appeals for Justice, or Applications for Favour or Preferment, to another Country, are so many grievous Impoverishments.

THE Seventh is, by Improvement of Land, Encouragement of Agriculture, and thereby encreasing the Number of their People; without which, any Country, however blessed by Nature, must continue poor.

THE Eighth, is the Residence of the Prince, or chief Administrator of the Civil Power.

THE Ninth, is the Concourse of Foreigners for Education, Curiosity, or Pleasure; or as to a general Mart of Trade.

THE Tenth, is by disposing all Offices of Honour, Profit, or Trust, only to the Natives, or at least with very few Exceptions; where Strangers have long inhabited the Country, and are supposed to understand, and regard the Interest of it as their own.

THE Eleventh, is when the Rents of Lands, and Profits of Employments, are spent in the Country which produced them, and not in another; the former of which will certainly happen, where the Love of our native Country prevails.

THE Twelfth, is by the publick Revenues being all spent and employed at home; except on the Occasions of a foreign War.

THE Thirteenth is, where the People are not obliged, unless they find it for their own Interest or Conveniency, to receive any Monies, except of their own Coinage by a publick Mint, after the Manner of all civilized Nations.

THE Fourteenth, is a Disposition of the People of a Country to wear their own Manufactures, and import as few Incitements to Luxury, either in Cloaths, Furniture, Food, or Drink, as they possibly can live conveniently without.[3]

---

[2] An idea derived from Locke's *Second Treatise of Government* (1690); also expressed in *A Proposal for the Universal Use of Irish Manufacture* and *Drapier's Letters IV* and *V.*

[3] See *A Proposal for the Universal Use of Irish Manufacture.*

THERE are many other Causes of a Nation's thriving, which I cannot at present recollect; but without Advantage from at least some of these, after turning my Thoughts a long Time, I am not able to discover from whence our Wealth proceeds, and therefore would gladly be better informed. In the mean Time, I will here examine what Share falls to *Ireland* of these Causes, or of the Effects and Consequences.

IT is not my Intention to complain, but barely to relate Facts; and the Matter is not of small Importance. For it is allowed, that a Man who lives in a solitary House, far from Help, is not wise in endeavouring to acquire, in the Neighbourhood, the Reputation of being rich; because those who come for Gold, will go off with Pewter and Brass, rather than return empty: And in the common Practice of the World, those who possess most Wealth, make the least Parade; which they leave to others, who have nothing else to bear them out, in shewing their Faces on the *Exchange*.[4]

As to the first Cause of a Nation's Riches, being the Fertility of the Soil, as well as Temperature of Climate, we have no Reason to complain; for, although the Quantity of unprofitable Land in this Kingdom, reckoning Bogg, and Rock, and barren Mountain be double in Proportion to what it is in *England*; yet the native Productions which both Kingdoms deal in, are very near on Equality in Point of Goodness; and might, with the same Encouragement, be as well manufactured. I except Mines and Minerals; in some of which, however, we are only defective in Point of Skill and Industry.

IN the Second, which is the Industry of the People; our Misfortune is not altogether owing to our own Fault, but to a Million of Discouragements.

THE Conveniency of Ports and Havens, which Nature hath bestowed so liberally on this Kingdom, is of no more Use to us, than a beautiful Prospect to a Man shut up in a Dungeon.

As to Shipping of its own, *Ireland* is so utterly unprovided, that of all the excellent Timber cut down within these Fifty or Sixty Years, it can hardly be said, that the Nation hath received the Benefit of one valuable House to dwell in, or one Ship to trade with.

IRELAND is the only Kingdom I ever heard or read of, either in ancient or modem Story, which was denied the Liberty of exporting their native Commodities and Manufactures, wherever they pleased; except to Countries at War with their own Prince or State: Yet this Privilege, by the Superiority of meer Power, is refused us, in the most momentous Parts of Commerce; besides an Act of Navigation, to which we never consented, pinned down upon us, and rigorously executed;[5] and a Thousand other unexampled

---

[4] A building where merchants gather to transact business. In Swift's Dublin, the Exchange (or "Royal Exchange") was located in a building called the Tholsel, in Skinner's Row (now Christchurch Place).

[5] Swift is here lamenting the consequences of the Woollen Act of 1699 and the Navigation Acts of 1663 and 1671, which prevented Ireland from freely trading with colonies abroad by requiring that such trade take place only from English ports and via English ships.

Circumstances, as grievous, as they are invidious to mention. To go on to the rest.

It is too well known, that we are forced to obey some Laws we never consented to; which is a Condition I must not call by its true uncontroverted Name,[6] for fear of Lord Chief Justice *Whitshed's* Ghost, with his *Libertas & natale Solum,* written as a Motto on his Coach, as it stood at the Door of the Court, while he was perjuring himself to betray both.[7] Thus, we are in the Condition of Patients, who have Physick sent them by Doctors at a Distance, Strangers to their Constitution, and the Nature of their Disease: And thus, we are forced to pay five Hundred *per Cent.* to decide our Properties;[8] in all which, we have likewise the Honour to be distinguished from the whole Race of Mankind.

As to Improvement of Land; those few who attempt that, or Planting, through Covetousness, or Want of Skill, generally leave Things worse than they were; neither succeeding in Trees nor Hedges; and by running into the Fancy of Grazing, after the Manner of the *Scythians,* are every Day depopulating the Country.[9]

We are so far from having a King to reside among us, that even the Viceroy[10] is generally absent four Fifths of his Time in the Government.

No strangers from other Countries, make this a Part of their Travels; where they can expect to see nothing, but Scenes of Misery and Desolation.

Those, who have the Misfortune to be born here, have the least Title to any considerable Employment; to which they are seldom preferred, but upon a political Consideration.

One third Part of the Rents of *Ireland,* is spent in *England;* which, with the Profit of Employments, Pensions, Appeals, Journeys of Pleasure or Health, Education at the *Inns* of Court, and both Universities,[11] Remittances at Pleasure, the Pay of all Superior Officers in the Army, and other Incidents, will amount to a full half of the Income of the whole Kingdom, all clear Profit to *England.*

We are denied the Liberty of Coining Gold, Silver, or even Copper. In the Isle of *Man,* they coin their own *Silver;* every petty Prince, Vassal to the

---

[6]That is, slavery.

[7]William Whitshed, attacked elsewhere (and repeatedly) for his judicial harassment of Swift's printers and for prosecuting the case against the Drapier, had died about seven months earlier. His motto ("Liberty and my native Country") is also mocked in Swift's poem, *Whitshed's Motto on his Coach.*

[8]In appeals to the House of Lords; the Declaratory Act (1720) made the British Parliament the court of last resort for all Irish cases.

[9]A common complaint of Swift's; see note 1 to *A Proposal for the Universal Use of Irish Manufacture.* The Scythians, an ancient nomadic people from areas of European and Asiatic Russia, were often likened to the Irish as a way of suggesting the latter's primitiveness or barbarism.

[10]The Lord-Lieutenant of Ireland.

[11]The centers of legal training in London, and Oxford and Cambridge Universities. Those planning to practice law in Ireland had to attend the Inns of Court—adding to the unidirectional flow of money from Ireland to England.

Emperor, can coin what Money he pleaseth.[12] And in this, as in most of the Articles already mentioned, we are an Exception to all other States or Monarchies that were ever known in the World.

As to the last, or Fourteenth Article, we take special Care to act diametrically contrary to it in the whole Course of our Lives. Both Sexes, but especially the Women, despise and abhor to wear any of their own Manufactures, even those which are better made than in other Countries; particularly a Sort of Silk Plad, through which the Workmen are forced to run a Sort of Gold Thread that it may pass for *Indian.*[13] Even Ale and Potatoes are imported from *England,* as well as Corn: And our foreign Trade is little more than Importation of *French* Wine; for which I am told we pay ready Money.

Now, if all this be true, upon which I could easily enlarge; I would be glad to know by what secret Method it is, that we grow a rich and flourishing People, without *Liberty, Trade, Manufactures, Inhabitants, Money,* or the *Privilege of Coining;* without *Industry, Labour,* or *Improvement of Lands,* and with more than half the Rent and Profits of the whole *Kingdom,* annually exported; for which we receive not a single Farthing: And to make up all this, nothing worth mentioning, except the Linnen of the *North,* a Trade casual, corrupted, and at Mercy;[14] and some Butter from *Cork.* If we do flourish, it must be against every Law of Nature and Reason; like the Thorn at *Glassenbury,* that blossoms in the Midst of Winter.[15]

LET the worthy *Commissioners* who come from *England,*[16] ride round the Kingdom, and observe the Face of Nature, or the Faces of the Natives; the Improvement of the Land; the thriving numerous Plantations; the noble Woods; the Abundance and Vicinity of Country-Seats; the commodious Farmers Houses and Barns; the Towns and Villages, where every Body is busy, and thriving with all Kind of Manufactures; the Shops full of Goods, wrought to Perfection, and filled with Customers; the comfortable Diet and Dress, and Dwellings of the People; the vast Numbers of Ships in our Harbours and Docks, and Ship-wrights in our Seaport-Towns; the Roads crouded with Carriers, laden with rich Manufactures; the perpetual Concourse to and fro of pompous Equipages.[17]

---

[12] The Isle of Man, at this time ruled by the 10th Earl of Derby, was permitted to mint its own copper farthings and half-pence. Ireland's inability to mint its own coins fuelled Swift's opposition to Wood's half-pence (see *The Drapier's Letters*).

[13] Irish poplin was a high-quality material (coveted by the Princess of Wales herself) about which Swift remarked in a letter to Henrietta Howard, "our Workmen here are grown so expert, that in this kind of Stuff they are said to excel that which comes from the Indies."

[14] The making of linen was the major industry of the Scottish Presbyterians who had settled in Ulster, and for many years accounted for the relative prosperity of the North of Ireland.

[15] According to legend, when Joseph of Arimathea (a figure who appears both in the Christian Gospels and in Arthurian tales), came into Glastonbury, in Somerset, he fixed his staff in the ground on Christmas Day and it took root, blossoming into leaves and flowers (in some versions, into an ash tree). It is said that this miraculous bloom has reappeared every winter thereafter on the same spot.

[16] See *Drapier's Letter IV,* note 19.

[17] Elegant horse-drawn carriages with attendant servants.

WITH what Envy, and Admiration, would those Gentlemen return from so delightful a Progress? What glorious Reports would they make, when they went back to *England?*

BUT my Heart is too heavy to continue this Irony longer; for it is manifest, that whatever Stranger took such a journey, would be apt to think himself travelling in *Lapland,* or *Ysland,*[18] rather than in a Country so favoured by Nature as ours, both in Fruitfulness of Soil, and Temperature of Climate. The miserable Dress, and Dyet, and Dwelling of the People. The general Desolation in most Parts of the Kingdom. The old Seats of the Nobility and Gentry all in Ruins, and no new ones in their Stead. The Families of Farmers, who pay great Rents, living in Filth and Nastiness upon Butter-milk and Potatoes, without a Shoe or Stocking to their Feet; or a House so convenient as an *English* Hogsty, to receive them. These, indeed, may be comfortable Sights to an *English* Spectator; who comes for a short Time, only *to learn the language,* and returns back to his own Country, whither he finds all our Wealth transmitted.

Nostrâ miseriâ magnus es.[19]

THERE is not one Argument used to prove the Riches of *Ireland,* which is not a logical Demonstration of its Poverty. The Rise of our Rents is squeezed out of the very Blood, and Vitals, and Cloaths and Dwellings of the Tenants; who live worse than *English* Beggars. The Lowness of Interest, in all other Countries a Sign of Wealth, is in us a Proof of Misery; there being no Trade to employ any Borrower. Hence, alone, comes the Dearness of Land, since the Savers have no other Way to lay out their Money. Hence the Dearness of Necessaries for Life; because the Tenants cannot afford to pay such extravagant Rates for Land, (which they must take, or go a-begging) without raising the Price of Cattle, and of Corn, although themselves should live upon Chaff. Hence our encrease of Buildings in this City; because Workmen have nothing to do, but employ one another; and one Half of them are infallibly undone. Hence the daily Encrease of *Bankers*; who may be a necessary Evil in a trading Country, but so ruinous in ours; who, for their private Advantage, have sent away all our Silver, and one Third of our Gold;[20] so that within three Years past, the running Cash of the Nation, which was about five Hundred Thousand Pounds, is now less than two; and must daily diminish, unless we have Liberty to coin, as well as that important Kingdom the Isle of *Man;* and the meanest Prince in the *German* Empire, as I before observed.

I HAVE sometimes thought, that this Paradox of the Kingdom growing rich, is chiefly owing to those worthy Gentlemen the BANKERS; who, except

---

[18] Iceland, then under the rule of the Crown of Denmark; it was largely isolated from the rest of the world by a private trade monopoly in Copenhagen that banned foreign trade.

[19] "By our misery you are great." Cicero, *Letters to Atticus,* II, 19.3.

[20] Silver coins were greatly undervalued in Ireland in comparison with gold ones, which resulted in large amounts of silver being conveyed out of the country and brought to England where they could be exchanged for gold coins that would then turn a profit back in Ireland.

some Custom-house Officers, Birds of Passage,[21] oppressive thrifty 'Squires, and a few others who shall be nameless, are the only thriving People among us: And I have often wished, that a Law were enacted to hang up half a Dozen *Bankers* every Year; and thereby interpose at least some short Delay, to the further Ruin of *Ireland*.[22]

YE are idle, ye are idle, answered *Pharoah* to the *Israelites,* when they complained to *his Majesty,* that they were forced to make Bricks without Straw.[23]

ENGLAND enjoys every one of those Advantages for enriching a Nation, which I have above enumerated; and, into the Bargain, a good Million returned to them every Year, without Labour or Hazard, or one Farthing Value received on our Side. But how long we shall be able to continue the Payment, I am not under the least Concern. One Thing I know, that *when the Hen is starved to Death, there will be no more Golden Eggs.*

I THINK it a little unhospitable, and others may call it a subtil Piece of Malice; that, because there may be a Dozen Families in this Town, able to entertain their *English* Friends in a generous Manner at their Tables; their Guests, upon their Return to *England,* shall report, that we wallow in Riches and Luxury.

YET, I confess, I have known an Hospital, where all the Household-Officers grew rich; while the Poor, for whose Sake it was built, were almost starving for want of Food and Raiment.[24]

To conclude. If *Ireland* be a rich and flourishing Kingdom; its Wealth and Prosperity must be owing to certain Causes, that are yet concealed from the whole Race of Mankind; and the Effects are equally invisible. We need not wonder at Strangers, when they deliver such Paradoxes; but a Native and Inhabitant of this Kingdom, who gives the same Verdict, must be either ignorant to Stupidity; or a Man-pleaser,[25] at the Expence of all Honour, Conscience, and Truth.

---

[21] Swift's term for those Englishmen who come to Ireland and "thrive and fatten here, and fly off when their *Credits* and *Employments* are at an End" (*Drapier's Letter VII*).

[22] For Swift's deep-seated dislike of bankers, emblems of a new economic order in which "*Power,* which…used to follow *Land,* is now gone over to *Money,*" see *The Examiner, No. 13* (1710) and the poem, *The Run Upon the Bankers* (1720).

[23] Exodus 5:17. The implicit analogy suggested here between King George II and the Pharaoh was not likely to endear Swift to the English authorities.

[24] Possibly a reference to the Dublin Workhouse and Foundling Hospital (established in 1702 and reconstituted exclusively as the latter in 1728), of which Swift served as a governor.

[25] A term with highly pejorative connotations in Scriptural usage; see Ephesians 6:5–7 and Galatians 1:10.

THE INTELLIGENCER

NUMBER XIX

Written in the Year 1728

The Intelligencer, *which takes its name from a word meaning "newsgatherer"
or "spy," was a weekly periodical launched by Swift and Thomas Sheridan on
May 11, 1728; it was discontinued after nineteen issues. Its stated aim was "to*
Inform, *or* Divert, *or* Correct, *or* Vex *the Town," as well as to serve a loftier
purpose by recording "every distinguished Action, either of* Justice, Prudence,
Generosity, Charity, Friendship, *or* Publick Spirit*" that came to its editors'
attention.* Number XIX, *heralding its patriotic intent by addressing itself to
the Drapier, examines the economic miseries of Ireland through a persona modeled on Sir Arthur Acheson, an Irish M.P. and landowner in Co. Armagh who
hosted Swift for weeks at a time at his residence, Market Hill (see* My Lady's
Lamentation and Complaint against the Dean *and other "Market Hill"
poems). Along with focusing on the woes suffered by all social classes due to the
scarcity of money in the country, this fictive letter reminds readers of the censorship and political persecution directed against those daring to protest against
the status quo.*

* * *

N.B. *In the following Discourse the* Author *personates a Country Gentleman
in the North of* Ireland. *And this Letter is supposed as directed to the* Drapier.

Having on the 12th *of* October *last, received a LETTER, signed* Andrew
Dealer, *and* Patrick Pennyless; *I believe the following* PAPER, *just come to my
Hands, will be a sufficient Answer to it.*

Sic vos, non vobis, vellera fertis oves.[1]

SIR,

I AM a Country Gentleman, and a Member of *Parliament,* with an Estate
of about 1400*l.* a Year; which, as a *Northern* Landlord, I receive from above
two Hundred Tenants: And my Lands having been let near twenty Years
ago, the Rents, until very lately, were esteemed to be not above half Value;

---

[1] "Thus do ye, sheep, grow fleece for others, not yourselves." Aelius Donatus, *Life of Virgil.*

yet by the intolerable Scarcity of *Silver*,[2] I lye under the greatest Difficulties in receiving them; as well as in paying my Labourers; or buying any Thing necessary for my Family from *Tradesmen*, who are not able to be long out of their *Money*. But the Sufferings of me, and those of my Rank, are Trifles in Comparison of what the meaner Sort undergo; such as the *Buyers* and *Sellers*, at *Fairs* and *Markets*; the *Shopkeepers* in every *Town*; the *Farmers* in general; all those who travel with *Fish, Poultry, Pedlary-ware*, and other Conveniences to sell: But more especially *Handycrafts-men*, who work for us by the Day; and common Labourers whom I have already mentioned. Both these Kinds of People I am forced to employ until their Wages amount to a *Double Pistole*, or a *Moidore*,[3] (for we hardly have any *Gold* of lower Value left us) to divide it among themselves as they can: And this is generally done at an *Ale-house*, or *Brandy-shop*; where, besides the Cost of getting *Drunk*, (which is usually the Case) they must pay *Ten Pence* or a *Shilling*, for changing their *Piece* into *Silver*, to some *Huckstering Fellow*, who follows that *Trade*. But, what is infinitely worse, those poor Men for want of due Payment, are forced to take up their *Oat-meal*, and other Necessaries of Life, at almost double Value; and, consequently, are not able to discharge half their Score; especially under the Scarceness of *Corn*, for two Years past; and the melancholly Disappointment of the present *Crop*.[4]

THE Causes of this, and a Thousand other Evils, are clear and manifest to you, and all thinking Men; although hidden from the Vulgar: These indeed complain of hard Times, the Dearth of Corn, the Want of Money, the Badness of Seasons; that their Goods bear no Price, and the Poor cannot find work; but their weak Reasonings never carry them to the Hatred and Contempt born us by our Neighbours and Brethren,[5] without the least Grounds of Provocation; who rejoyce at our Sufferings, although sometimes to their own Disadvantage. They consider not the dead Weight upon every beneficial Branch of our Trade; that half our Revenues are annually sent to *England;* with many other Grievances peculiar to this unhappy Kingdom; which keep us from enjoying the common Benefits of Mankind; as you and some other Lovers of their Country have so often observed, with such good Inclinations, and so little Effect.

IT is true indeed, that under our Circumstances in general; this Complaint for the Want of *Silver*, may appear as ridiculous, as for a Man to be impatient about a *Cut-Finger*, when he is struck with the *Plague:* And yet a poor Fellow going to the *Gallows*, may be allowed to feel the Smart of *Wasps* while he is

---

[2]As the gold guinea was worth three pence more in Ireland than in England, silver rather than gold was used by Irish businessmen to pay off English debts, producing a severe scarcity of silver coins in Ireland.

[3]Portuguese and Spanish gold coins used in Ireland to make up for its scarcity of specie and its inability to coin its own money. The "double pistole" was worth £1 17 *s* Irish and the Portuguese moidore was worth £1 10 *s* Irish (Woolley).

[4]Circumstances that produced the serious famine that Swift addresses through irony in *A Modest Proposal.*

[5]The English.

upon *Tyburn-Road*. This Misfortune is so urging, and vexatious in every Kind of small Traffick; and so hourly pressing upon all Persons in the Country whatsoever; that a Hundred Inconveniences, of perhaps greater Moment in themselves, have been tamely submitted to, with far less Disquietude and Murmurs. And the Case seems yet the harder, if it be true, what many skilful Men assert, that nothing is more easy than a Remedy; and, that the Want of *Silver*, in Proportion to the little *Gold* remaining among us, is altogether as unnecessary, as it is inconvenient. A Person of Distinction assured me very lately, that, in discoursing with the *Lord Lieutenant*, before his last Return to *England*; his *Excellency* said, *He had pressed the Matter often, in proper Time and Place, and to proper Persons; and could not see any Difficulty of the least Moment, that could prevent us from being made easy upon this Article.*[6]

WHOEVER carries to *England* twenty seven *English* Shillings, and brings back one *Moidore* of full Weight, is a Gainer of Nine Pence *Irish:* In a *Guinea*, the Advantage is Three Pence; and Two Pence in a *Pistole*. The BANKERS, who are generally Masters of all our *Gold* and *Silver*, with this Advantage, have sent over as much of the latter, as came into their Hands. The Value of One Thousand *Moidores* in *Silver*, would thus amount in clear Profit, to 37*l*. 10*s*. The *Shopkeepers*, and other *Traders*, who go to *London* to buy Goods, followed the same Practice; by which we have been driven into this insupportable Distress.

To a common Thinker, it should seem, that nothing would be more easy, than for the *Government* to redress this Evil, at any Time they shall please. When the Value of *Guineas* was lowered in *England* from 21*s*. and 6*d*. to only 21*s*.[7] the Consequences to this Kingdom were obvious, and manifest to us all: And a sober Man may be allowed at least to wonder, although he dare not complain, why a new Regulation of *Coin* among us, was not then made; much more, why it hath never been since. It would surely require no very profound Skill in *Algebra*, to reduce the Difference of *Nine Pence in Thirty Shillings*; or *Three Pence* in a *Guinea* to less than a *Farthing;* and so small a Fraction could be no Temptation, either to *Bankers* to hazard their *Silver* at Sea, or Tradesmen to load themselves with it, in their journeys to *England*. In my humble Opinion it would be no unseasonable Condescension, if the *Government* would graciously please to signify to the *poor loyal Protestant Subjects* of *Ireland*, either that this miserable Want of *Silver*, is not possible to be remedied in any Degree, by the nicest Skill in *Arithmetick;* or else, that it doth not stand with the good Pleasure of *England*, to suffer any *Silver* at all among us. In the former Case, it would be Madness to expect Impossibilities; and in the other, we must submit: For, Lives and Fortunes are always at the Mercy of the CONQUEROR.

---

[6] John, Lord Carteret, Lord-Lieutenant of Ireland from 1724 to 1730, was more sensitive to Ireland's sufferings than his predecessors. The year before, he had unsuccessfully lobbied to get the value of silver raised in Ireland.

[7] In late 1717.

T HE Question hath been often put in *printed Papers*, by the D RAPIER and others, or, perhaps, by the same W RITER, under different Styles; why this Kingdom should not be permitted to have a *Mint* of its own, for the Coinage of *Gold, Silver*, and *Copper*; which is a Power exercised by many *Bishops*, and every petty Prince in *Germany*? But this Question hath never been answered; nor the least Application, that I have heard of, made to the *Crown* from hence, for the Grant of a *Publick Mint*; although it stands upon Record, that several Cities and Corporations here, had the Liberty of *Coining Silver*. I can see no Reasons, why we alone of all Nations, are thus restrained; but such as I dare not mention: Only thus far, I may venture; that *Ireland* is the first Imperial Kingdom, since *Nimrod*,[8] which ever wanted Power, to *Coin* their own *Money*.

I KNOW very well, that in *England*, it is lawful for any Subject to peti- tion either the *Prince* or the *Parliament*, provided it be done in a dutiful and regular Manner: But what is lawful for a Subject of *Ireland*, I profess I cannot determine: Nor will undertake, that your *Printer* shall not be prose- cuted, in a *Court of Justice*, for publishing my *Wishes*, that a poor Shopkeeper might be able to change a *Guinea*, or a *Moidore*, when a Customer comes for a *Crown*'s Worth of Goods. I have known less Crimes punished with the utmost Severity, under the Title of *Disaffection*.[9] And I cannot but approve the Wisdom of the *Antients*, who, after *Astrea* had fled from the Earth, at least took Care to provide *three upright Judges for Hell*.[10] Mens Ears, among us, are indeed grown so nice,[11] that whoever happens to think out of Fashion, in what relates to the Welfare of this Kingdom, dare not so much as complain of the *Toothach*; lest our weak and busy Dablers in Politicks, should be ready to swear against him for *Disaffection*.[12]

T HERE was a Method practised by Sir *Ambrose Crawley*, the great Dealer in *Iron-works*;[13] which I wonder the Gentlemen of our Country, under this great Exigence, have not thought fit to imitate. In the several Towns and Villages where he dealt, and many Miles round; he gave *Notes* instead of

---

[8] A Mesopotamian monarch who appears as a "mighty hunter" in Genesis 10:8–10. In later scriptural commentary, he was portrayed negatively as a tyrant and a hunter of men.

[9] A pointed glance at Swift's printers' (and his own) run-ins with the law over his published writings.

[10] Astrea, daughter of Zeus and Themis, was the goddess of justice who lived on earth with humans during the Golden Age but who departed in disgust, ascending into the heavens to become the constellation Virgo, when corruption ushered in the Bronze Age. Swift is here insinuating the absence of such "upright Judges" in Ireland.

[11] Excessively sensitive or delicate; punctilious; overattentive to matters of reputation or conduct.

[12] The subject of Swift's sermon, *On False Witness*. In *A Letter form Dr. Swift to Mr. Pope* (1721?), Swift castigates "the whole Tribe of Informers, the most accursed, and prostitute, and abandoned race, that God ever permitted to plague mankind."

[13] Sir Ambrose Crowley (1658–1713) was a rich and prominent ironmonger who served as Alderman and Sheriff of London, a director general of the South Sea Company, and an M.P. for Andover during the final year of his life. He was known for business dealings that were both highly successful and enlightened.

Money, from *Two Pence* to *Twenty Shillings*; which passed current in all Shops and Markets, as well as in Houses, where Meat or Drink was sold. I see no Reason, why the like Practice may not be introduced among us, with some Degree of Success; or at least may not serve as a poor Expedient, in this our *blessed Age of Paper*;[14] which, as it dischargeth all our greatest Payments, may be equally useful in the smaller, and may just keep us alive until an *English Act of Parliament shall forbid it.*

I HAVE been told, that among some of our poorest *American* Colonies, upon the Continent, the People enjoy the Liberty of cutting the little *Money* among them into Halves and Quarters, for the Conveniences of small Traffick. How happy should we be, in Comparison of our present Condition, if the like Privilege were granted to us, of employing the Sheers, for want of a *Mint,* upon our *foreign Gold* by clipping it into *Half-Crowns,* and *Shillings,* and even lower Denominations; for Beggars must be content to live upon Scraps; and it would be our Felicity, that these Scraps could never be exported to other Countries, while any Thing better was left.

IF neither of these Projects will avail, I see nothing left us, but to truck and barter our Goods, like the *wild Indians,* with each other; or with our too powerful Neighbours; only with this Disadvantage on our Side, that the *Indians* enjoy the Product of their own Land; whereas the better half of ours is sent away, without so much as a Recompence in *Bugles*[15] or *Glass* in return.

IT must needs be a very comfortable Circumstance, in the present Juncture, that some Thousand Families are gone, or going, or preparing to go from hence, and settle themselves in *America.* The poorer Sort, for want of Work; the Farmers whose beneficial Bargains are now become a Rack-Rent[16] too hard to be born. And those who have any *ready Money,* or can purchase any, by the Sale of their Goods or Leases; because they find their Fortunes hourly decaying, that their Goods will bear no Price, and that few or none have any *Money* to buy the very Necessaries of Life, are hastening to follow their departed Neighbours. It is true, *Corn* among us carries a very high Price; but it is for the same Reason, that *Rats,* and *Cats,* and dead *Horses,* have been often bought for *Gold* in a Town besieged.

THERE is a Person of Quality in my Neighbourhood,[17] who Twenty Years ago, when he was just come to Age, being unexperienced, and of a generous Temper, let his Lands, even as Times went then, at a low Rate to able Tenants; and consequently by the Rise of Land since that Time, looked upon his Estate to be set at half Value: But Numbers of these Tenants, or their Descendants,

---

[14] A mocking epithet used by Augustan satirists to characterize both a newly emergent print culture marked by the proliferation of hack-writing and government-sponsored newspapers; and (as it is meant here) a new world of banking and speculation in which hard currency had been replaced by stocks, bonds, and letters of credit.

[15] Glass beads used for ornamenting apparel.

[16] An exorbitantly high rent almost equal to the full value of the land.

[17] This too is a reference to Sir Arthur Acheson.

are now offering to sell their Leases by Cant,[18] even those which were for Lives, some of them renewable for ever, and some Fee-Farms,[19] which the Landlord himself hath bought in at half the Price they would have yielded seven Years ago. And some Leases let at the same Time for Lives, have been given up to him, without any Consideration at all.

THIS is the most favourable Face of Things at present among us; I say, among us of the *North*, who are esteemed the only thriving People of the Kingdom.[20] And how far, and how soon this Misery and Desolation may spread, is easy to foresee.

THE vast Sums of *Money* daily carried off, by our numerous Adventurers to *America*, have deprived us of our *Gold* in these Parts, almost as much as of our *Silver*.

AND the good Wives who come to our Houses, offer us their Pieces of Linen, upon which their whole Dependence lies, for so little Profit, that it can neither half pay their Rents, not half support their Families.

IT is remarkable, that this Enthusiasm spread among our *Northern* People, of sheltering themselves in the Continent of *America*, hath no other Foundation, than their present insupportable Condition at home.[21] I have made all possible Enquiries, to learn what Encouragement our People have met with, by any Intelligence from those Plantations, sufficient to make them undertake so tedious and hazardous a Voyage, in all Seasons of the Year; and so ill accommodated in their Ships, that many of them have died miserably in their Passage; but could never get one satisfactory Answer. Somebody, they know not who, had written a Letter to his Friend or Cousin from thence, inviting him, by all Means, to come over; that it was a fine fruitful Country, and to be held for ever at a *Penny* an Acre.[22] But the Truth of the Fact is this: The *English* established in those Colonies, are in great Want of Men to inhabit that Tract of Ground, which lies between them and the *wild Indians,* who are not reduced under their Dominion. We read of some barbarous People, whom the *Romans* placed in their Armies, for no other Service than to blunt their Enemies Swords, and afterwards to fill up Trenches with their dead Bodies. And thus our People, who transport themselves, are settled in

---

[18] Offering them to the highest bidder at a public auction.

[19] Land held of another in fee, in consideration solely of an annual rent (i.e., without having to render additional services).

[20] Largely on the strength of the linen trade in the North.

[21] In the year that this tract was written, 4,000 settlers in the North of Ireland had departed for the New World. A combination of rack-renting, crop failures, food shortages, and smallpox epidemics, bolstered by a desire for greater religious freedom, prompted the massive waves of emigration mostly by Ulster Presbyterians, which totaled well over 100,000 in the period between 1700 and 1776. Most of these emigrants settled in New England and in the Delaware River ports in Pennsylvania.

[22] In a tract written in 1729, Swift relates that William Penn himself discredited a pamphlet promoting the attractions of Pennsylvania to prospective Irish emigrants, telling Swift that "his Country wanted the shelter of mountains, which left it open to the Northern winds from Hudson's bay and the frozen sea, which destroyed all Plantations of Trees, and was even pernicious to all common vegetables."

those interjacent Tracts, as a Screen against the Assaults of the *Savages*; and may have as much Land as they can clear from the Woods at a very reasonable Rate, if they can afford to pay about a *Hundred* Years Purchase, by their Labour. Now, besides the *Fox*'s Reasons, which inclines all those who have already ventured thither, to represent every Thing in a false Light, as well for justifying their own Conduct, as for getting Companions in their Misery:[23] The governing People in those Plantations, have also wisely provided, that no Letters shall be suffered to pass from thence hither, without being first viewed by the Council; by which, our People here are wholly deceived, in the Opinions they have of the happy Condition of their Friends gone before them. This was accidentally discovered some Months ago, by an honest Man; who having transported himself and Family thither, and finding all Things directly contrary to his Hope, had the Luck to convey a private Note, by a faithful Hand, to his Relation here; entreating him not to think of such a Voyage, and to discourage all his Friends from attempting it. Yet this, although it be a Truth well known, hath produced very little Effect, which is no Manner of Wonder; for as it is natural to a Man in a *Fever* to turn often, although without any Hope of Ease; or when he is pursued, to leap down a Precipice, to avoid an Enemy just at his Back; so, Men in the extremest Degree of Misery and Want, will naturally fly to the first Appearance of Relief, let it be ever so vain or visionary.

YOU may observe, that I have very superficially touched the Subject I began with, and with the utmost Caution: For I know how criminal the least Complaint hath been thought, however seasonable, or just, or honestly intended; which hath forced me to offer up my daily Prayers, that it may never, at least in my Time, be interpreted by *Inuendo's* as a false, scandalous, seditious and disaffected Action, for a Man to roar under an acute Fit of the *Gout*; which, beside the Loss and the Danger, would be very inconvenient to one of my Age, so severely afflicted with that Distemper.

I WISH you good Success; but I can promise you little, in an ungrateful Office you have taken up, without the least View, either to Reputation or Profit. Perhaps your Comfort is, that none but *Villains* and *Betrayers* of their Country, can be your *Enemies*. Upon which I have little to say, having not the Honour to be acquainted with many of that Sort; and therefore, as you easily may believe, am compelled to lead a very retired Life.

> I am, Sir,
> *Your most obedient,*
> *Humble Servant,*

A. NORTH.

County of *Down*,
Dec. 2, 1728.

---

[23] See Aesop's fable, "The Fox Who Lost His Tail."

AN ANSWER TO A PAPER, called
A Memorial *of the poor* Inhabitants,
Tradesmen, *and* Labourers
of the Kingdom of IRELAND

Here again Swift is responding to John Browne (see headnote to A Short View of the State of Ireland): *this time, to a tract he published anonymously in Dublin, which was specifically addressed to Swift, requesting his support for a proposal to import 100,000 barrels of wheat to alleviate the country's famine conditions, to be financed by an increase in taxes on other imported goods. Swift's reply is significant for the sense of urgency it conveys about the desperate plight of the starving poor (with whom he personally identifies) and for the exasperation it expresses with projectors who formulate absurdly "visionary" solutions to Ireland's problems while ignoring its harsh realities. This pamphlet thus provides important background and context for* A Modest Proposal, *written in the following year (1729). The pamphlet's concluding diatribe against the recently deceased William Whitshed (judicial harasser of Swift's printers) and others of his ilk has interesting implications for Swift's conception of the aims and justification of satire.*

* * *

I Received a *Paper* from you, wherever you are, printed without any Name of Author or Printer; and sent, I suppose, to me among others, without any particular Distinction. It contains a Complaint of the Dearness of Corn; and some Schemes of making it cheaper, which I cannot approve of.

BUT pray permit me, before I go further, to give you a short History of the Steps by which we arrived at this hopeful Situation.

IT was indeed the shameful Practice of too many *Irish* Farmers, to wear out their Ground with Plowing; while, either through Poverty, Laziness, or Ignorance, they neither took Care to manure it as they ought; nor gave Time to any Part of the Land to recover itself. And when their Leases were near expiring, being assured that their Landlords would not renew, they Ploughed even the Meadows, and made such a Havock, that many Landlords were considerable Sufferers by it.

THIS gave Birth to that abominable Race of Graziers, who, upon Expiration of the Farmers Leases, are ready to engross great Quantities of Land;[1] and the Gentlemen having been before, often ill paid, and their Land worn out of Heart, were too easily tempted, when a rich Grazier made him an Offer to take all his Land, and give him Security for Payment. Thus, a vast Tract of Land, where Twenty or Thirty Farmers lived together, with their Cottagers, and Labourers in their several Cabins, became all desolate, and easily managed by one or two Herdsmen, and their Boys; whereby the Master-Grazier, with little Trouble, seized to himself the Livelyhood of a Hundred People.

IT must be confessed, that the Farmers were justly punished for their *Knavery, Brutality,* and *Folly.* But neither are the *'Squires* and *Landlords* to be excused; for to them is owing the depopulating of the *Country,* the vast Number of *Beggars* and the Ruin of those few sorry Improvements we had.

THAT *Farmers* should be limited in Ploughing, is very reasonable, and practiced in *England;* and might have easily been done here, by penal Clauses in their Leases: But to deprive them, in a manner, altogether from Tilling their Lands, was a most stupid Want of Thinking.

HAD the *Farmers* been confined to plough a certain Quantity of Land, with a Penalty of Ten Pounds an Acre, for whatever they exceeded; and farther limited for the Three or Four last Years of their Leases; all this Evil had been prevented; the Nation would have saved *a Million of Money;* and been more populous by above *Two Hundred Thousand Souls.*

FOR a People denied the Benefit of *Trade,* to manage their Lands in such a Manner, as to produce nothing but what they are forbidden to trade with; or, only such Things as they can neither export, nor manufacture, to Advantage; is an Absurdity, that a *wild Indian* would be ashamed of; especially when we add, that we are content to purchase this hopeful Commerce, by sending to foreign Markets for our Daily Bread.

THE *Grazier's* Employment is to feed great Flocks of *Sheep,* or *Black Cattle,*[2] or both. With Regard to *Sheep;* as Folly is usually accompanied with Perverseness, so it is here. There is something so monstrous to deal in a Commodity, (further than for our own Use) which we are not allowed to export manufactured, nor even un-manufactured, but to *one certain Country,* and only to some *few* Ports in that Country;[3] there is, I say, something so sottish, that it wants a Name, in our Language, to express it by: And, the Good of it is, that the more *Sheep* we have, the fewer human Creatures are left to wear the *Wool,* or eat the *Flesh. Ajax* was mad when he mistook a Flock of *Sheep* for his Enemies: But we shall never be sober, until we have the same Way of Thinking.[4]

---

[1]A frequent target of Swift's condemnation; see opening paragraph of *A Proposal for the Universal Use of Irish Manufacture.*

[2]Cattle reared for slaughter, as distinguished from dairy (or "white") cattle.

[3]As stipulated by the Woollen Act of 1699, which limited Ireland's exports to certain ports in England.

[4]During the Trojan War the Greek warrior Ajax, enraged that the slain Achilles' armor was awarded to Odysseus rather than to himself, resolved to kill the Greek kings. However,

THE other Part of the *Grazier's* Business is, what we call *Black-Cattle*; producing *Hides, Tallow*, and *Beef* for Exportation. All which are good and useful Commodities, if rightly managed. But it seems, the greatest Part of the *Hides* are sent out raw, for want of *Bark* to *Tan* them; and that Want will daily grow stronger: For, I doubt,[5] the new Project of *Tanning* without it, is at an End. Our *Beef*, I am afraid, still continues scandalous in foreign Markets, for the old Reasons. But, our *Tallow*, for any Thing I know, may be good. However, to bestow the whole Kingdom on *Beef* and *Mutton*, and thereby drive out half the People who should eat their Share, and force the rest to send sometimes as far as *Egypt*, for Bread to eat with it; is a most peculiar and distinguished Piece of publick Oeconomy; of which I have no Comprehension.

I KNOW very well, that our Ancestors, the *Scythians*, and their Posterity our Kinsmen the *Tartars*, lived upon the Blood and Milk, and raw Flesh of their Cattle; without one Grain of *Corn*; but I confess my self so degenerate, that I am not easy without *Bread* to my Victuals.[6]

WHAT amazed me for a Week or two, was to see, in this prodigious Plenty of *Cattle*, and Dearth of *human Creatures*, and Want of *Bread*, as well as *Money to buy it*; that all Kind of *Flesh-meat* should be monstrously *dear*, beyond what was ever known in this Kingdom. I thought it a Defect in the Laws; that there was not some Regulation in the Price of *Flesh*, as well as *Bread*. But I imagine my self to have guessed out the Reason. In short, I am apt to think, that the whole Kingdom is overstocked with *Cattle*, both *Black and White:* And, as it is observed that the poor *Irish* have a Vanity, to be rather Owners of two lean Cows, than one Fat, although with double the Charge of Grazing, and but half the Quantity of Milk; so I conceive it much more difficult, at present, to find a fat *Bullock*, or *Weather*,[7] than it would be, if half of both were fairly knocked on the Head: For, I am assured, that the District in the several Markets, called *Carrion-Row*, is as reasonable as the Poor can desire; only the Circumstance of *Money to purchase it*; and of *Trade*, or *Labour*, to *purchase that Money*; are, indeed, wholly wanting.

NOW, Sir, to return more particularly to you, and your Memorial.

A HUNDRED thousand Barrels of *Wheat*, you say, should be imported hither; and Ten thousand Pounds, *Præmium*, to the Importers. Have you looked into the Purse of the Nation? I am no Commissioner of the *Treasury*; but am well assured, that the whole running *Cash* would not supply you with a Sum to purchase so much *Corn*; which, only at Twenty Shillings a

---

deceived by Athena into thinking a flock of sheep were the kings, he slew and tortured the animals instead. The story appears in Sophocles' play, *Ajax*.

[5] Think; believe.

[6] The Scythians and Tartars (or Taters) were nomadic tribes from Russia and central Asia, often invoked as symbols of primitive, savage peoples associated with cannibalism. Note that Swift is identifying himself here with the native Irish ("<u>our</u> Ancestors"), as the Scythians were regularly linked to the native Catholic population by their British and Anglo-Irish deriders.

[7] Wether; castrated sheep or goat.

Barrel, will be a Hundred thousand Pounds; and Ten thousand more for the *Præmiums.* But you will traffick for your *Corn* with other Goods: And where are those Goods? If you had them, they are all engaged to pay the Rents of *Absentees,* and other Occasions in *London;* besides a huge Ballance of Trade this Year against us. Will Foreigners take our Bankers Paper? I suppose, they will value it at little more than so much a Quire. Where are these *rich Farmers* and *Ingrossers of Corn,* in so bad a Year, and so little Sowing?

YOU are in Pain of two Shillings *Præmium,* and forget the Twenty Shillings for the Price; find me out the latter, and I will engage for the former.

YOUR Scheme for a *Tax* for raising such a Sum, is all visionary; and owing to a great want of Knowledge in the *miserable State* of this Nation. *Tea, Coffee, Sugar, Spices, Wine,* and *foreign Cloaths,* are the Particulars you mention, upon which this Tax should be raised. I will allow the two first, because they are unwholsome; and the last, because I should be glad if they were all burned; but I beg you will leave us our Wine, to make us a while forget our Misery; or give your Tenants leave to plough for *Barley.*[8] But I will tell you a *Secret,* which I learned many Years ago from the Commissioners of the *Customs* in *London:* They said, when any *Commodity* appeared to be taxed above a *moderate Rate,* the Consequence was to lessen that Branch of the Revenue by one Half; and one of those Gentlemen pleasantly told me, that the Mistake of Parliaments, on such Occasions, was owing to an Error of computing Two and Two to make Four; whereas, in the Business of laying *heavy Impositions,* Two and Two never made more than One; which happens by lessening the Import, and the strong Temptation of running such Goods as paid high Duties. At least in this Kingdom, although the Women are as vain and extravagant as their Lovers, or their Husbands can deserve; and the Men are fond enough of Wine; yet the Number of both, who can afford such Expences, is so small, that the major Part must refuse gratifying themselves; and the Duties will rather be lessened than increased. But, allowing no Force in this Argument; yet so prœternatural a Sum, as one Hundred and ten Thousand Pounds, raised all on a sudden, (for there is no dallying with Hunger) is just in Proportion, with raising a Million and a half in *England;* which, as Things now stand, would probably bring that opulent Kingdom under some Difficulties.

YOU are concerned, how strange and surprising it would be in foreign Parts, to hear that the Poor were starving in a RICH Country, &c. Are you in earnest? Is *Ireland* the *rich Country* you mean? Or are you insulting our *Poverty?* Were you ever out of *Ireland?* Or were you ever in it till of late? You may probably have a good Employment, and are saving all you can, to purchase a good Estate in *England.* But by talking so familiarly of one Hundred

---

[8]Swift strongly opposed a parliamentary bill levying an additional duty on French wine, wryly noting that "there is no nation yet known, in either hemisphere, where the people of all conditions are more in want of some cordial, to keep up their spirits, than in this of ours," and warning that raising the duty would eliminate "the only hold we have of keeping among us the few gentlemen of any tolerable estates" (*A Proposal to the Ladies of Ireland*). The bill was nevertheless passed in December 1729.

and ten Thousand Pounds, by a Tax upon a few *Commodities;* it is plain, you are either naturally or affectedly ignorant of our present Condition; or else you would know and allow, that such a Sum is not to be raised here, without a *general Excise;* since, in Proportion to our Wealth, we pay already in *Taxes* more than *England* ever did, in the Heighth of the War. And when you have brought over your Corn, who will be the Buyers? Most certainly, not the Poor, who will not be *able* to purchase the Twentieth Part of it.

SIR, upon the whole, your Paper is a very crude Piece, liable to more Objections than there are Lines; but, I think, your Meaning is good, and so far you are pardonable.

IF you will propose a general Contribution, in supporting the Poor in *Potatoes* and *Butter-milk*, till the new Corn comes in, perhaps you may succeed better; because the Thing, at least, is possible: And, I think, if our Brethren in *England* would contribute, upon this Emergency, out of the Million they gain from us every Year, they would do a Piece of *Justice* as well as *Charity*. In the mean Time, go and preach to your own Tenants, to fall to the Plough as fast as they can; and prevail with your neighbouring 'Squires to do the same with theirs; or else die with the Guilt of having driven away half the Inhabitants, and starving the rest. For as to your Scheme of raising *one Hundred and ten Thousand Pounds,* it is as vain as that of *Rabelais;* which was to squeeze out Wind from the Posteriors of a dead Ass.[9]

BUT, why all this Concern for the Poor? We want them not, as the Country is now managed; they may follow Thousands of their Leaders, and seek their Bread abroad. Where the Plough has no Work, one Family can do the Business of Fifty, and you may send away the other Forty-nine. An admirable Piece of Husbandry, never known or practised by the wisest Nations; who erroneously thought People to be the Riches of a Country.

IF so wretched a State of Things would allow it, methinks I could have a malicious Pleasure, after all the Warning I have in vain given the Publick, at my own Peril, for several Years past; to see the Consequences and Events answering in every Particular. I pretend to no Sagacity: What I writ was little more than what I had discoursed to several Persons, who were generally of my Opinion: And it was obvious to every common Understanding, that such Effects must needs follow from such Causes. A fair Issue of Things, begun upon Party Rage, while some sacrificed the Publick to Fury, and others to Ambition! While a Spirit of Faction and Oppression reigned in every Part of the Country; where Gentlemen, instead of consulting the Ease of their Tenants, or cultivating their Lands, were worrying one another, upon Points of *Whig* and *Tory*, of *High Church* and *Low Church*; which no more concerned them, than the long and famous Controversy of *Strops for Razors.*[10] While *Agriculture* was wholly discouraged, and consequently half

---

[9]A reference to Rabelais's *Gargantua and Pantagruel*, Book 5, Chapter 5, xxii.

[10]Swift's *Journal to Stella* (Jan. 1711) also mentions this controversy, as does Addison in *The Tatler, No. 224,* in a discussion of polemical advertisements. The controversy is pronounced to be "now happily subsided" by Samuel Johnson in *The Idler, No. 40* (1759).

the Farmers, and Labourers, and poorer Tradesmen, forced to Beggary or Banishment. *Wisdom crieth in the Streets; because I have called and ye refused; I have stretched out my Hand, and no Man regarded. But ye have set at nought all my Counsel, and would none of my Reproof. I also will laugh at your Calamity, and mock when your Fear cometh.*[11]

I HAVE now done with your Memorial, and freely excuse your Mistakes, since you appear to write as a Stranger, and as of a Country which is left at Liberty to enjoy the Benefits of Nature; and to make the best of those Advantages which God hath given it in Soil, Climate, and Situation.

BUT having lately sent out a Paper, entitled, *A Short View of the State of* Ireland; and hearing of an Objection, that some People think I have treated the Memory of the late Lord Chief Justice *Whitshed,* with an Appearance of Severity;[12] since I may not probably have another Opportunity of explaining my self in that Particular, I chuse to do it here. Laying it therefore down for a Postulatum;[13] which, I suppose, will be universally granted; That no *little Creature,* of so *mean* a Birth and Genius, had ever the *Honour* to be a *greater Enemy* to his Country, and to all Kinds of Virtue, than HE, I answer thus: whether there be two different Goddesses called *Fame,* as some Authors contend, or only one Goddess, sounding two different Trumpets;[14] it is certain, that People distinguished for their *Villainy,* have as good a Title for a Blast from the *proper Trumpet,* as those who are most renowned for their *Virtues,* have from the other; and have equal Reason to complain, if it be refused them. And accordingly, the Names of the most *celebrated Profligates,* have been faithfully transmitted down to Posterity. And although the Person here understood, acted his Part in an obscure Corner of the World; yet his Talents might have shone with Lustre enough in the noblest Scene.

As to my naming a Person Dead, the plain honest Reason is the best. He was armed with Power, Guilt, and Will to do Mischief, even where he was not provoked; as appeared by his prosecuting two *Printers,* one to Death, and both to Ruin, who had neither offended God, nor the King, nor Him, nor the Publick.[15]

WHAT an Encouragement to Vice is this? If an ill Man be alive, and in Power, we dare not attack him; and if he be weary of the World, or of his own Villainies, he has nothing to do but die, and then his Reputation is safe. For, these excellent Casuists know just *Latin* enough, to have heard a most foolish

---

[11] Proverbs 1:20–26.

[12] Whitshed had died on August 26, 1727.

[13] Postulate; basic principle.

[14] Refers to the allegorical representation of the goddess Fame with two trumpets, one for good and the other for ill-repute. In Chaucer's *House of Fame,* the goddess tells her assistant Æolus to bring her a golden trumpet for praise and a black trumpet for slander.

[15] The two printers were John Harding and Edward Waters. Harding died on April 19, 1725—probably several months after being released from jail for having printed *Drapier's Letter IV,* though he was depicted in contemporary poems (and implicitly, by Swift here) as a martyr who perished in prison.

Precept, that *de mortuis nil nisi bonum;*[16] so that if *Socrates*, and *Anytus* his Accuser, had happened to die together, the Charity of Survivers must either have obliged them to hold their Peace, or to fix the same Character on both.[17] The only Crime of charging the Dead, is when the least Doubt remains, whether the Accusation be true; but when Men are openly abandoned, and lost to all Shame, they have no Reason to think it hard, if their Memory be reproached. Whoever reports, or otherwise publisheth any Thing, which it is possible may be false, that Man is a Slanderer, *Hic niger est, hunc tu Romane caveto.*[18] Even the least Misrepresentation, or Aggravation of Facts, deserves the same Censure in some Degree: But in this Case I am quite deceived, if my Error hath not been on the Side of Extenuation.

I HAVE now present before me the Idea of some Persons, (I know not in what Part of the World) who spend every Moment of their Lives, and every Turn of their Thoughts while they are awake, (and probably of their Dreams while they sleep) in the most detestable Actions and Designs; who delight in *Mischief, Scandal,* and *Obloquy,* with the *Hatred* and *Contempt* of all Mankind against them; but chiefly of those among their own Party, and their own Family; such, whose *odious Qualities* rival each other for Perfection: *Avarice, Brutality, Faction, Pride, Malice, Treachery, Noise, Impudence, Dulness, Ignorance, Vanity,* and *Revenge,* contending every Moment for Superiority in their Breasts. Such Creatures are not to be reformed; neither is it Prudence, or Safety to attempt a Reformation. Yet, although their Memories will *rot,* there may be some Benefit for their Survivers, to smell it while it is *rotting.*

I am, SIR,

Your humble Servant,

A. B.

Dublin, March
25th, 1728.

---

[16] "Speak only good of the dead." First recorded in Diogenes Laertius, *The Lives and Opinions of the Eminent Philosophers.*

[17] Anytus was the most influential of the three accusers of Socrates; for the relationship between them, see Plato's *Meno.*

[18] "[He who rails against absent friends, or hears them libeled but doesn't defend them; he who cannot keep a secret] Such a man is evil; beware of him, Roman." Horace, *Satire* I.4.85.

MAXIMS CONTROLLED IN IRELAND

The Truth of some Maxims in State and Government, examined with reference to Ireland

Written in 1729 but not published until 1765, this (unfinished) piece empha-sizes a point Swift repeatedly came back to in his writings: namely, that Ireland's semi-colonial situation was so uniquely insupportable and anomalous that it differed from all other countries and thus was not governed by the same gen-eral laws and principles that prevailed everywhere else. This point is reinforced through the enumeration of several maxims judged to be universally applicable but "controlled" (i.e., contradicted) in Ireland. The implication is that Ireland's problems require very special solutions, ones not based on the experiences or prac-tices of other countries. Copy-text: Works, ed. Deane Swift (1765).

*   *   *

THERE are certain Maxims of State, founded upon long observation and experience, drawn from the constant practice of the wisest nations, and from the very principles of government, nor ever controlled by any writer upon politics. Yet all these Maxims do necessarily presuppose a kingdom, or com-monwealth, to have the same natural rights common to the rest of mankind who have entered into civil society. For, if we could conceive a nation where each of the inhabitants had but one eye, one leg, and one hand, it is plain that, before you could institute them into a republic, an allowance must be made for those material defects, wherein they differed from other mortals. Or, imagine a legislator forming a system for the government of Bedlam, and, proceeding upon the maxim that man is a sociable animal, should draw them out of their cells, and form them into corporations or general assem-blies; the consequence might probably be, that they would fall foul on each other, or burn the house over their own heads.

Of the like nature are innumerable errors, committed by crude and short thinkers, who reason upon general topics, without the least allowance for the most important circumstances, which quite alter the nature of the case.

This hath been the fate of those small dealers, who are every day publish-ing their thoughts either on paper or in their assemblies for improving the trade of Ireland, and referring us to the practice and example of England, Holland, France, or other nations.

I shall therefore examine certain Maxims of government, which generally pass for uncontrolled in the world, and consider how far they will suit with the present condition of this kingdom.

First, it is affirmed by wise men, that the dearness of things necessary for life, in a fruitful country, is a certain sign of wealth and great commerce; For, when such necessaries are dear, it must absolutely follow that money is cheap and plentiful.

But this is manifestly false in Ireland, for the following reason. Some years ago, the species of money here, did probably amount to six or seven hundred thousand pounds; and I have good cause to believe, that our remittances then did not much exceed the cash brought in to us. But the prodigious discouragements we have since received in every branch of our trade, by the frequent enforcements, and rigorous execution of the navigation act,[1] the tyranny of under custom-house officers, the yearly addition of absentees, the payments to regiments abroad, to civil and military officers residing in England, the unexpected sudden demands of great sums from the treasury, and some other drains of perhaps as great consequence, we now see ourselves reduced to a state (since we have no friends) of being pitied by our enemies, at least, if our enemies were of such a kind as to be capable of any regards towards us, except of hatred and contempt.

Forty years are now passed since the Revolution, when the contention of the British empire was, most unfortunately for us, and altogether against the usual course of such mighty changes in government, decided in the least important nation, but with such ravages and ruin executed on both sides, as to leave the kingdom a desert, which, in some sort, it still continues.[2] Neither did the long rebellions in 1641 make half such a destruction of houses, plantations, and personal wealth, in both kingdoms, as two years campaigns did in ours, by fighting England's battles.[3]

By slow degrees, and by the gentle treatment we received under two auspicious reigns, we grew able to live without running in debt. Our absentees were but few, we had great indulgence in trade, a considerable share in employments of church and state; and, while the short leases continued,

---

[1] The Navigation Acts of 1663 and 1671 that placed severe restrictions on the exportation of Irish goods in order to eliminate competition with the English export trade.

[2] Refers to the Glorious Revolution of 1688 and the ensuing Williamite Wars in Ireland between the forces of the new monarch William III and the deposed James II, which ended in the former's favor in the summer of 1790. Although technically a sectarian battle between Protestant and Catholic over the throne of England, the larger context (glanced at here) involved the struggle between Britain and France for military and imperial domination.

[3] The Rebellion of 1641 began as an uprising in Ulster of Catholic gentry fearful of the threat posed by the Puritan forces then uniting against King Charles I; the event was blown up and sensationalized by later Protestant commentators. This passage suggests Swift's departure from the conventional Protestant (Whig) view of the "heroic" Williamite Wars as opposed to the execrable 1641 Rebellion. See *Reasons Humbly Offered to the Parliament of Ireland.*

which were let some years after the war ended, tenants paid their rents with ease and chearfulness, to the great regret of their landlords, who had taken up a spirit of oppression that is not easily removed. And although in these short leases, the rent was gradually to encrease after short periods; yet, as soon as the term elapsed, the land was let to the highest bidder, most commonly without the least effectual clause for building or planting. Yet by many advantages, which this island then possessed, and hath since utterly lost, the rents of lands still grew higher upon every lease that expired, until they have arrived at the present exorbitance; when the frog, over-swelling himself, burst at last.[4]

With the price of land, of necessity rose that of corn and cattle, and all other commodities that farmers deal in: Hence likewise, obviously, the rates of all goods and manufactures among shopkeepers, the wages of servants, and hire of labourers. But, although our miseries came on fast with neither trade nor money left, yet neither will the landlord abate in his rent, nor can the tenant abate in the price of what that rent must be paid with, nor any shopkeeper, tradesman, or labourer live at lower expence, for food and clothing, than he did before.

I have been the larger upon this first head, because the same observations will clear up and strengthen a good deal of what I shall affirm upon the rest.

The second Maxim of those who reason upon trade and government, is to assert, that low interest is a certain sign of great plenty of money in a nation, for which, as in many other articles, they produce the examples of Holland and England. But, with relation to Ireland, this Maxim is likewise entirely false.

There are two reasons for the lowness of interest in any country. First, that which is usually alleged, the great plenty of species; and this is obvious. The second is the want of trade, which seldom falls under common observation, although it be equally true. For, where trade is altogether discouraged, there are few borrowers. In those countries where men can employ a large stock, the young merchant, whose fortune may be four or five hundred pounds, will venture to borrow as much more, and can afford a reasonable interest. Neither is it easy at this day to find many of those, whose business reaches to employ even so inconsiderable a sum, except among the importers of wine; who, as they have most part of the present trade in these parts of Ireland in their hands, so they are the most exorbitant, exacting, fraudulent dealers, that ever trafficked in any nation, and are making all possible speed to ruin both themselves and the nation.[5]

From this defect, of gentlemen's not knowing how to dispose of their ready money, ariseth the high purchase of lands, which in all other countries is reckoned a sign of wealth. For, the frugal squires, who live below their

---

[4]A reference to Aesop's fable, "The Frog and the Ox."

[5]A matter of particular concern to Swift, who was a regular wine drinker; see *An Answer to a Paper, called a Memorial*, note 8.

incomes, have no other way to dispose of their savings but by mortgage or
purchase, by which the rates of land must naturally encrease; and, if this
trade continues long under the uncertainty of rents, the landed men of ready
money will find it more for their advantage to send their cash to England,
and place it in the funds;[6] which I myself am determined to do, the first considerable sum I shall be master of.

It hath likewise been a Maxim among politicians, that the great encrease
of buildings in the metropolis argues a flourishing state. But this, I confess,
hath been controlled from the example of London; where, by the long and
annual parliamentary sessions, such a number of senators, with their families, friends, adherents, and expectants, draw such prodigious numbers to
that city, that the old hospitable custom of lords and gentlemen living in
their antient seats, among their tenants, is almost lost in England; is laughed
out of doors; insomuch that, in the middle of summer, a legal House of
Lords and Commons might be brought in a few hours to London from their
country villas within twelve miles round.

The case in Ireland is yet somewhat worse: For the absentees of great
estates, who, if they lived at home, would have many rich retainers in their
neighbourhoods, having learned to rack their lands,[7] and shorten their
leases, as much as any residing squire; and the few remaining of these latter,
having some vain hope of employments for themselves or their children, and
discouraged by the beggarliness and thievery of their own miserable farmers
and cottagers, or seduced by the vanity of their wives, on pretence of their
children's education, (whereof the fruits are so apparent) together with that
most wonderful and yet more unaccountable zeal for a seat in their assembly, though at some years purchase of their whole estates. These and some
other motives better let pass, have drawn such a concourse to this beggarly
city, that the dealers of the several branches of building have found out all
the commodious and inviting places for erecting new houses, while fifteen
hundred of the old ones, which is a seventh part of the whole city, are said
to be left uninhabited, and falling to ruin. Their method is the same with
that which was first introduced by Doctor Barebone at London, who died
a bankrupt.[8] The mason, the bricklayer, the carpenter, the slater, and the
glazier, take a lot of ground, club[9] to build one or more houses, unite their
credit, their stock, and their money, and when their work is finished, sell it
to the best advantage they can. But, as it often happens, and more every day,

---

[6]Public securities (bonds, tradable notes called "annuities," etc.) offered to individuals by
the state for money borrowed of them; also the offerings of public ("monied") companies such
as the East India Company.

[7]Raise rents above a reasonable amount.

[8]Refers to Nicholas Barbon (c. 1640–98), trained as a physician but known primarily as a
financial speculator, real estate developer, and writer of economic tracts, who took advantage
of the Great Fire of London (1666) to launch the first fire insurance business as well as to
rebuild and sell properties throughout the city. He also founded his own land bank, amassing
considerable wealth but incurring enormous debt before he died.

[9]Combine their individual assets into a common stock.

that their fund will not answer half their design, they are forced to undersell it at the first story, and are all reduced to beggary. Insomuch, that I know a certain fanatic brewer,[10] who is reported to have some hundreds of houses in this town, is said to have purchased the greater part of them at half value from ruined undertakers,[11] hath intelligence of all new houses where the finishing is at a stand, takes advantage of the builder's distress, and, by the advantage of ready money, gets fifty *per cent.* at least for his bargain.

It is another undisputed Maxim in government, that people are the riches of a nation; which is so universally granted, that it will be hardly pardonable to bring it in doubt. And I will grant it to be so far true, even in this island, that, if we had the African custom or privilege, of selling our useless bodies for slaves to foreigners, it would be the most useful branch of our trade, by ridding us of a most unsupportable burthen, and bringing us money in the stead. But, in our present situation, at least five children in six who are born lie a dead weight upon us for the want of employment. And a very skilful computer assured me, that above one half of the souls in this kingdom supported themselves by begging and thievery, whereof two thirds would be able to get their bread in any other country upon earth. Trade is the only incitement to labour: where that fails, the poorer native must either beg, steal, or starve, or be forced to quit his country. This hath made me often wish, for some years past, that, instead of discouraging our people from seeking foreign soil, the public would rather pay for transporting all our unnecessary mortals, whether Papists or Protestants, to America, as drawbacks are sometimes allowed for exporting commodities where a nation is over-stocked. I confess myself to be touched with a very sensible pleasure, when I hear of a mortality in any country-parish or village, where the wretches are forced to pay for a filthy cabin and two ridges of potatoes treble the worth, brought up to steal or beg, for want of work, to whom death would be the best thing to be wished for, on account both of themselves and the public.

Among all taxes imposed by the legislature, those upon luxury are universally allowed to be the most equitable and beneficial to the subject; and the commonest reasoner on government might fill a volume with arguments on the subject. Yet here again, by the singular fate of Ireland, this maxim is utterly false; and the putting it in practice may have such a pernicious consequence, as I certainly believe the thoughts of the proposers were not able to reach.

The miseries we suffer by our absentees are of a far more extensive nature than seems to be commonly understood.[12] I must vindicate myself to the

---

[10] The Dissenter ("fanatic") Joseph Leeson, who made a fortune through the profits of his trade as well as through extensive property he acquired in the area between Trinity College, Dublin and St. Stephen's Green.

[11] Refers either to those who undertook to hold Crown lands, or to those who undertook particular business enterprises.

[12] Refers both to absentee landlords and to those holding lucrative sinecures in Ireland while living in England. A partial list of these absentees appears in *Drapier's Letter IV.*

reader so far, as to declare solemnly that what I shall say of those lords and squires, doth not arise from the least regard I have for their understandings, their virtues, or their persons. For, although I have not the honour of the least acquaintance with any one among them, (my ambition not soaring so high) yet I am too good a witness of the situation they have been in for thirty years past, the veneration paid them by the people, the high esteem they are in among the prime nobility and gentry, the particular marks of favour and distinction they receive from the court: The weight and consequence of their interest, added to their great zeal and application for preventing any hardships their country might suffer from England, wisely considering that their own fortunes and honours were embarked in the same bottom.

A MODEST PROPOSAL

FOR Preventing the Children of poor People in Ireland, from being a Burden to their Parents or Country; and for making them beneficial to the Publick

Written in the Year 1729

Perhaps the best-known and most often cited satire in the English language, this work was in part a response to the serious famine, resulting from the failure of the corn crop, that had ravaged the country in the preceding months, which worsened an already dire economic situation and brought questions of food and consumption (or their lack) to the forefront of national consciousness. Reversing the age-old stereotype of the Irish as cannibals fostered in English writings, Swift depicts a situation in which the Irish are the devoured rather than the devourers, though not entirely blameless for their plight. Through his satiric persona he exposes the underlying causes of Ireland's desperate circumstances while parodying the many fatuous and ill-informed "proposals" for a solution to Ireland's ills being circulated at the time, often written by people who had little personal knowledge of the country and no genuine concern for its inhabitants.

* * *

IT is a melancholly Object to those, who walk through this great Town, or travel in the Country; when they see the *Streets,* the *Roads,* and *Cabbindoors* crowded with *Beggars* of the Female Sex, followed by three, four, or six Children, *all in Rags,* and importuning every Passenger for an Alms.[1] These *Mothers,* instead of being able to work for their honest Livelyhood, are forced to employ all their Time in stroling to beg Sustenance for their *helpless Infants;* who, as they grow up, either turn *Thieves* for want of Work;

---

[1] Cf. the opening of Swift's sermon *Causes of the Wretched Condition of Ireland,* which uses similar language to describe Dublin ("this great Town").

or leave their *dear Native Country, to fight for the Pretender in* Spain; or sell themselves to the *Barbadoes*.[2]

I THINK it is agreed by all Parties, that this prodigious Number of Children in the Arms, or on the Backs, or at the *Heels* of their *Mothers,* and frequently of their *Fathers, is in the present deplorable State of the Kingdom,* a very great additional Grievance; and therefore, whoever could find out a fair, cheap, and easy Method of making these Children sound and useful Members of the Commonwealth, would deserve so well of the Publick, as to have his Statue set up for a Preserver of the Nation.

BUT my Intention is very far from being confined to provide only for the Children of *professed Beggars:* It is of a much greater Extent, and shall take in the whole Number of Infants at a certain Age, who are born of Parents, in effect as little able to support them, as those who demand our Charity in the Streets.

As to my own Part, having turned my Thoughts for many Years, upon this important Subject; and maturely weighed the several *Schemes of other Projectors,*[3] I have always found them grosly mistaken in their Computation. It is true, a Child, *just dropt from its Dam,* may be supported by her Milk, for a Solar Year with little other Nourishment; at most not above the Value of two Shillings; which the Mother may certainly get, or the Value in *Scraps,* by her lawful Occupation of *Begging:* And, it is exactly at one Year old, that I propose to provide for them in such a Manner, as, instead of being a Charge upon their *Parents,* or the *Parish,* or *wanting Food and Raiment* for the rest of their Lives; they shall, on the contrary, contribute to the Feeding, and partly to the Cloathing, of many Thousands.

THERE is likewise another great Advantage in my *Scheme,* that it will prevent those *voluntary Abortions,* and that horrid Practice of *Women murdering their Bastard Children;* alas! too frequent among us;[4] sacrificing the *poor innocent Babes,* I doubt, more to avoid the Expence than the Shame; which would move Tears and Pity in the most Savage and inhuman Breast.

THE Number of Souls in *Ireland* being usually reckoned one Million and a half,[5] of these I calculate there may be about Two Hundred Thousand Couple whose Wives are Breeders; from which Number I substract thirty thousand Couples, who are able to maintain their own Children; although I apprehend there cannot be so many, under *the present Distresses of the Kingdom;* but this being granted, there will remain an Hundred and Seventy

---

[2] Refers both to the Catholics who went abroad to fight on behalf of the Pretender, and to the Protestants (mostly Ulster Presbyterians) who went to the American colonies and the West Indies in search of employment and riches.

[3] A term having highly pejorative connotations for Swift; applied to those presenting wild schemes that were fraudulent, impractical, or overly speculative.

[4] A significant social problem at this time. One of the explicit aims of the Dublin Workhouse and Foundling Hospital, established at the beginning of the century, was to prevent "the exposure, death, and actual murder of illegitimate children."

[5] Arthur Dobbs, Surveyor-General of Ireland, put the figure at 2,000,000 in 1730. Both figures have since been thought to be on the low side.

Thousand Breeders. I again substract Fifty Thousand, for those Women who miscarry, or whose Children die by Accident, or Disease, within the Year. There only remain an Hundred and Twenty Thousand Children of poor Parents, annually born: The Question therefore is, How this Number shall be reared, and provided for?[6] Which, as I have already said, under the present Situation of Affairs, is utterly impossible, by all the Methods hitherto proposed: For we can *neither employ them in Handicraft* or *Agriculture;* we neither build Houses, (I mean in the Country) nor cultivate Land: They can very seldom pick up a Livelyhood *by Stealing* until they arrive at six Years old; except where they are of towardly Parts;[7] although, I confess, they learn the Rudiments much earlier; during which Time, they can, however, be properly looked upon only as *Probationers;*[8] as I have been informed by a principal Gentleman in the County of *Cavan,*[9] who protested to me, that he never knew above one or two Instances under the Age of six, even in a Part of the Kingdom *so renowned for the quickest Proficiency in that Art.*

I AM assured by our Merchants, that a Boy or a Girl before twelve Years old, is no saleable Commodity; and even when they come to this Age, they will not yield above Three Pounds, or Three Pounds and half a Crown at most, on the Exchange; which cannot turn to Account either to the Parents or Kingdom; the Charge of Nutriment and Rags, having been at least four Times that Value.

I SHALL now therefore humbly propose my own Thoughts; which I hope will not be liable to the least Objection.

I HAVE been assured by a very knowing *American* of my Acquaintance in *London;* that a young healthy Child, well nursed, is, at a Year old, a most delicious, nourishing, and wholesome Food; whether *Stewed, Roasted, Baked,* or *Boiled;* and, I make no doubt, that it will equally serve in a *Fricasie,* or *Ragoust.*[10]

I DO therefore humbly offer it to *publick Consideration,* that of the Hundred and Twenty thousand Children, already computed, Twenty thousand may be reserved for Breed; whereof only one Fourth Part to be Males; which is more than we allow to *Sheep, black Cattle,* or *Swine;* and my Reason

---

[6]This paragraph is meant to evoke the style and tone of political economists and demographic "scientists" such as Sir William Petty (1623–87), author of *Political Arithmetic* and *Political Anatomy of Ireland.* Petty's county surveys of Ireland during Oliver Cromwell's Irish campaign, his theories for eugenically arranged marriages and for massive forced migrations to bring about the "replantation" of Ireland, and his role as a cofounder of the Royal Society made him an especially fitting target for Swift's satire here.

[7]Promising; quick to learn.

[8]Novices; qualifiers for a position.

[9]No doubt a tongue-in-cheek reference to Thomas Sheridan, whose house in Cavan (Quilca) was often visited by Swift.

[10]Dishes viewed as *haute cuisine* and stigmatized by their association with France. Swift writes in *A Panegyrick on the Dean* (1730) that Gluttony "sent her Priests in Wooden Shoes/ From haughty *Gaul* to make Ragous./Instead of wholsome Bread and Cheese,/To dress their Soupes and Fricassyes" (ll. 263–66).

is, that these Children are seldom the Fruits of Marriage, *a Circumstance not much regarded by our Savages;* therefore, *one Male* will be sufficient to serve *four Females.* That the remaining Hundred thousand, may, at a Year old, be offered in Sale to the *Persons of Quality* and *Fortune,* through the Kingdom; always advising the Mother to let them suck plentifully in the last Month, so as to render them plump, and fat for a good Table. A Child will make two Dishes at an Entertainment for Friends; and when the Family dines alone, the fore or hind Quarter will make a reasonable Dish; and seasoned with a little Pepper or Salt, will be very good Boiled on the fourth Day, especially in *Winter.*

I HAVE reckoned upon a Medium, that a Child just born will weigh Twelve Pounds; and in a solar Year, if tolerably nursed, encreaseth to twenty eight Pounds.

I GRANT this Food will be somewhat dear, and therefore very *proper for Landlords;* who, as they have already devoured most of the Parents, seem to have the best Title to the Children.

INFANTS Flesh will be in Season throughout the Year; but more plentiful in *March,* and a little before and after: For we are told by a grave Author, an eminent *French* Physician, that *Fish being a prolifick Dyet,* there are more Children born in *Roman Catholick Countries* about Nine Months after *Lent,* than at any other Season:[11] Therefore reckoning a Year after *Lent,* the Markets will be more glutted than usual; because the Number of *Popish Infants,* is, at least, three to one in this Kingdom; and therefore it will have one other Collateral Advantage, by lessening the Number of *Papists* among us.

I HAVE already computed the Charge of nursing a Beggar's Child (in which List I reckon all *Cottagers, Labourers,* and Four fifths of the *Farmers)* to be about two Shillings *per Annum,* Rags included; and I believe, no Gentleman would repine to give Ten Shillings for the *Carcase of a good fat Child;* which, as I have said, will make four Dishes of excellent nutritive Meat, when he hath only some particular Friend, or his own Family, to dine with him. Thus the Squire will learn to be a good Landlord, and grow popular among his Tenants; the Mother will have Eight Shillings net Profit, and be fit for Work until she produceth another Child.

THOSE who are more thrifty *(as I must confess the Times require)* may flay the Carcase; the Skin of which, artificially dressed, will make admirable *Gloves for Ladies,* and *Summer Boots for fine Gentlemen.*

As to our City of *Dublin;* Shambles may be appointed for this Purpose, in the most convenient Parts of it; and Butchers we may be assured will not be wanting; although I rather recommend buying the Children alive, and dressing them hot from the Knife, as we do *roasting Pigs.*[12]

---

[11] Refers to Book V, ch. xix of *Pantagruel* by François Rabelais (c. 1494–1553), who was an important influence on Swift's satiric writing.

[12] "Shambles" are places where meat is sold or where animals are slaughtered for food. Part of the irony here is that the majority of butchers in Dublin—such as those of the Ormonde Market in the Liberties—were Catholic.

A VERY worthy Person, *a true Lover of his Country,* and whose Virtues I highly esteem, was lately pleased, in discoursing on this Matter, to offer a Refinement upon my Scheme. He said, that many Gentlemen of this Kingdom, having of late destroyed their Deer; he conceived, that the Want of Venison might be well supplied by the Bodies of young Lads and Maidens, not exceeding fourteen Years of Age, nor under twelve; so great a Number of both Sexes in every County being now ready to starve, for Want of Work and Service: And these to be disposed of by their Parents, if alive, or otherwise by their nearest Relations. But with due Deference to so excellent a Friend, and so deserving a Patriot, I cannot be altogether in his Sentiments. For as to the Males, my *American* Acquaintance assured me from frequent Experience, that their Flesh was generally tough and lean, like that of our School-boys, by continual Exercise; and their Taste disagreeable; and to fatten them would not answer the Charge. Then, as to the Females, it would, I think, with humble Submission, *be a Loss to the Publick,* because they soon would become Breeders themselves: And besides it is not improbable, that some scrupulous People might be apt to censure such a Practice (although indeed very unjustly) as a little bordering upon Cruelty; which, I confess, hath always been with me the strongest Objection against any Project, how well soever intended.

BUT in order to justify my Friend: he confessed, that this Expedient was put into his Head by the famous *Salmanaazor,*[13] a Native of the Island *Formosa,* who came from thence to *London,* above twenty Years ago, and in Conversation told my Friend, that in his Country, when any young Person happened to be put to Death, the Executioner sold the Carcase to *Persons of Quality,* as a prime Dainty; and that, in his Time, the Body of a plump Girl of fifteen, who was crucified for an Attempt to poison the Emperor, was sold to his Imperial *Majesty's prime Minister of State,* and other great *Mandarins* of the Court, *in Joints from the Gibbet,* at Four hundred Crowns. Neither indeed can I deny, that if the same Use were made of several plump young Girls in this Town, who, without one single Groat to their Fortunes, cannot stir Abroad without a Chair,[14] and appear at the *Play-house* and *Assemblies* in foreign Fineries, which they never will pay for; the Kingdom would not be the worse.

SOME Persons of a desponding Spirit are in great Concern about that vast Number of poor People, who are Aged, Diseased, or Maimed; and I have been desired to employ my Thoughts what Course may be taken, to ease the Nation of so grievous an Incumbrance. But I am not in the least Pain upon that Matter; because it is very well known, that they are every Day *dying,* and

---

[13] George Psalmanazar (c. 1679–1763) was a Frenchman who claimed to be from Formosa and published a spurious *Historical and Geographical Description of Formosa* in London in 1704—a famous travel-book hoax that would have been of particular interest to the author of *Gulliver's Travels.*

[14] That is, a sedan–chair; a chair connected on top to a pole and carried by two men, which was a common form of urban transport in the eighteenth century.

rotting, by *Cold* and *Famine,* and *Filth,* and *Vermin,* as fast as can be reasonably expected. And as to the younger Labourers, they are now in almost as hopeful a Condition: They cannot get Work, and consequently pine away for Want of Nourishment, to a Degree, that if at any Time they are accidentally hired to common Labour, they have not Strength to perform it; and thus the Country, and themselves, are in a fair Way of being soon delivered from the Evils to come.

I HAVE too long digressed; and therefore shall return to my Subject. I think the Advantages by the Proposal which I have made, are obvious, and many, as well as of the highest Importance.

FOR, *First,* as I have already observed, it would greatly lessen *the Number of Papists,* with whom we are yearly over-run; being the principal Breeders of the Nation, as well as our most dangerous Enemies; and who stay at home on Purpose, with a Design *to deliver the Kingdom to the Pretender;* hoping to take their Advantage by the Absence *of so many good Protestants,* who have chosen rather to leave their Country, than stay at home, and pay Tithes against their Conscience, to an idolatrous *Episcopal Curate.*[15]

SECONDLY, The poorer Tenants will have something valuable of their own, which, by Law, may be made liable to Distress,[16] and help to pay their Landlord's Rent; their Corn and Cattle being already seized, and *Money a Thing unknown.*

THIRDLY, Whereas the Maintenance of an Hundred Thousand Children, from two Years old, and upwards, cannot be computed at less then ten Shillings a Piece *per Annum,* the Nation's Stock will be thereby encreased Fifty Thousand Pounds *per Annum;* besides the Profit of a new Dish, introduced to the Tables of all *Gentlemen of Fortune* in the Kingdom, who have any Refinement in Taste; and the Money will circulate among our selves, the Goods being entirely of our own Growth and Manufacture.

FOURTHLY, The constant Breeders, besides the Gain of Eight Shillings *Sterling per Annum,* by the Sale of their Children, will be rid of the Charge of maintaining them after the first Year.

FIFTHLY, This Food would likewise bring great *Custom to Taverns,* where the Vintners will certainly be so prudent, as to procure the best Receipts[17] for dressing it to Perfection; and consequently, have their Houses frequented by all the *fine Gentlemen,* who justly value themselves upon their Knowledge in good Eating; and a skilful Cook, who understands how to oblige his Guests, will contrive to make it as expensive as they please.

SIXTHLY, This would be a great Inducement to Marriage, which all wise Nations have either encouraged by Rewards, or enforced by Laws and

---

[15] Refers to the Presbyterians and other Nonconformists who emigrated to America and elsewhere in order to escape having to pay tithes to the Established (Anglican) Church. The reference to Catholics as "our most dangerous Enemies" is ironic; Swift repeatedly dismissed the argument that they were a threat.

[16] Subject to forfeiture for payment of outstanding debts.

[17] Recipes.

Penalties. It would encrease the Care and Tenderness of Mothers towards their Children, when they were sure of a Settlement for Life, to the poor Babes, provided in some Sort by the Publick, to their annual Profit instead of Expence. We should soon see an honest Emulation among the married Women, *which of them could bring the fattest Child to the Market.* Men would become as *fond* of their Wives, during the Time of their Pregnancy, as they are now of their *Mares* in Foal, their *Cows* in Calf, or *Sows* when they are ready to farrow; nor offer to beat or kick them, (as it is too *frequent* a Practice) for fear of a Miscarriage.

MANY other Advantages might be enumerated. For Instance, the Addition of some Thousand Carcasses in our Exportation of barrelled Beef: The Propagation of *Swines Flesh,* and Improvement in the Art of making good *Bacon;* so much wanted among us by the great Destruction of *Pigs,* too frequent at our Tables, and are no way comparable in Taste, or Magnificence, to a well-grown fat yearly Child; which, roasted whole, will make a considerable Figure at a *Lord Mayor's Feast,* or any other publick Entertainment. But this, and many others, I omit; being studious of Brevity.

SUPPOSING that one Thousand Families in this City, would be constant Customers for Infants Flesh; besides others who might have it at *merry Meetings,* particularly at *Weddings* and *Christenings;* I compute that *Dublin* would take off, annually, about Twenty Thousand Carcasses; and the rest of the Kingdom (where probably they will be sold somewhat cheaper) the remaining Eighty Thousand.

I CAN think of no one Objection, that will possibly be raised against this Proposal; unless it should be urged, that the Number of People will be thereby much lessened in the Kingdom. This I freely own; and it was indeed one principal Design in offering it to the World. I desire the Reader will observe, that I calculate my Remedy *for this one individual Kingdom of* IRELAND, *and for no other that ever was, is, or I think ever can be upon Earth.* Therefore, let no Man talk to me of other Expedients:[18] *Of taxing our Absentees at five Shillings a Pound: Of using neither Cloaths, nor Houshold Furniture; except what is of our own Growth and Manufacture: Of utterly rejecting the Materials and Instruments that promote foreign Luxury: Of curing the Expensiveness of Pride, Vanity, Idleness, and Gaming in our Women: Of introducing a Vein of Parsimony, Prudence and Temperance: Of learning to love our Country; wherein we differ even from* LAPLANDERS, *and the Inhabitants of* TOPINAMBOO:[19] *Of quitting our Animosities, and Factions; nor act any longer like the* Jews, *who were murdering one another at the very Moment their City*

---

[18]Actual proposals that Swift had been urging throughout the preceding decade, though to little effect.

[19]The Tupinamba were a tribe of Indians indigenous to coastal Brazil, whose ritual cannibalism was described (somewhat ambivalently) in Jean de Léry's popular and widely read *History of a Voyage to the Land of Brazil* (1578).

was taken.[20] *Of being a little cautious not to sell our Country and Consciences for nothing.*[21] *Of teaching Landlords to have, at least, one Degree of Mercy towards their Tenants.* Lastly, *Of putting a Spirit of Honesty, Industry, and Skill into our Shop-keepers; who, if a Resolution could now be taken to buy only our native Goods, would immediately unite to cheat and exact upon us in the Price, the Measure, and the Goodness; nor could ever yet be brought to make one fair Proposal of just Dealing, though often and earnestly invited to it.*[22]

THEREFORE I repeat; let no Man talk to me of these and the like Expedients; till he hath, at least, a Glimpse of Hope, that there will ever be some hearty and sincere Attempt to put *them in Practice.*

BUT, as to my self; having been wearied out for many Years with offering vain, idle, visionary Thoughts; and at length utterly despairing of Success, I fortunately fell upon this Proposal; which, as it is wholly new, so it hath something *solid* and *real,* of no Expence, and little Trouble, full in our own Power; and whereby we can incur no Danger in *disobliging* ENGLAND: For, this Kind of Commodity will not bear Exportation; the Flesh being of too tender a Consistence, to admit a long Continuance in Salt; *although, perhaps, I could name a Country, which would be glad to eat up our whole Nation without it.*[23]

AFTER all, I am not so violently bent upon my own Opinion, as to reject any Offer proposed by wise Men, which shall be found equally innocent, cheap, easy, and effectual. But before something of that Kind shall be advanced, in Contradiction to my Scheme, and offering a better; I desire the Author, or Authors, will be pleased maturely to consider two Points. *First,* As Things now stand, how they will be able to find Food and Raiment, for a Hundred Thousand useless Mouths and Backs? And *secondly,* There being a round Million of Creatures in human Figure, throughout this Kingdom; whose whole Subsistence, put into a common Stock, would leave them in Debt two Millions of Pounds *Sterling;* adding those, who are Beggars by Profession, to the Bulk of Farmers, Cottagers, and Labourers, with their Wives and Children, who are Beggars in Effect; I desire those Politicians, who dislike my Overture, and may perhaps be so bold to attempt an Answer, that they will first ask the Parents of these Mortals, Whether they would not, at this Day, think it a great Happiness to have been sold for Food at a Year old, in the Manner I prescribe; and thereby have avoided such a perpetual Scene of Misfortunes, as they have since gone through; by the *Oppression of Landlords;* the Impossibility of paying Rent, without Money or Trade; the Want of common Sustenance, with neither House nor Cloaths, to cover

---

[20] Refers to the Emperor Titus's siege of Jerusalem in 70 C.E. and the ensuing destruction of the Temple because of the Jews' failure to unite in their own defense.

[21] A recurring accusation in Swift's writings; cf. his depiction of Ireland as a land "Where every knave & fool is bought/Yet kindly sells himself for nought" (*Irel[an]d*).

[22] A complaint that recurs throughout Swift's tracts; see, e.g., *A Proposal for the Universal Use of Irish Manufacture* and his sermon *Doing Good,* n. 3.

[23] A wry reference to the fact that Irish salt beef had become an important export commodity (to France and the West Indies in particular) in the preceding decades, and used by England (the "*Country*" referred to here) to feed its navy.

them from the Inclemencies of Weather; and the most inevitable Prospect of intailing the like, or greater Miseries upon their Breed for ever.

I PROFESS, in the Sincerity of my Heart, that I have not the least personal Interest, in endeavouring to promote this necessary Work; having no other Motive than the *publick Good of my Country, by advancing our Trade, providing for Infants, relieving the Poor, and giving some Pleasure to the Rich.* I have no Children, by which I can propose to get a single Penny; the youngest being nine Years old, and my Wife past Child-bearing.

SERMON,
CAUSES of the WRETCHED
CONDITION of IRELAND

This sermon of uncertain date (not published until 1762) well demonstrates why Swift termed his sermons "preaching pamphlets." Composed of a litany of complaints directed against what he deemed the causes of Ireland's misery, and throwing a particular spotlight on problems related to the lower classes (beggars and servants) and poorly administered charitable institutions, the sermon combines a deep sense of outrage and despair with a refusal to relinquish the search for solutions to the country's seemingly insoluble social and economic woes. As in other of Swift's Irish tracts, the poor are here treated harshly, without a shred of sentimentality, while the ultimate blame is directed at "those Oppressors, who first stripped them of all their Substance." Copy-text: Works, ed. Faulkner (1762).

*   *   *

Psalm CXLIV. Part of the 13th and 14th Ver.

That there be no Complaining in our Streets. Happy is the People that is in such a Case.

IT is a very melancholy Reflection, that such a Country as ours which is capable of producing all Things necessary, and most Things convenient for Life, sufficient for the Support of four Times the Number of its Inhabitants, should yet lye under the heaviest Load of Misery and Want, our Streets crouded with Beggars, so many of our lower Sort of Tradesmen, Labourers and Artificers, not able to find Cloaths and Food for their Families.[1]

I THINK it may therefore be of some Use, to lay before you the chief Causes of this wretched Condition we are in, and then it will be easier to assign what Remedies are in our Power towards removing, at least, some Part of these Evils.

FOR it is ever to be lamented, that we lie under many Disadvantages, not by our own Faults, which are peculiar to ourselves, and which no other Nation under Heaven hath any Reason to complain of.

---

[1]Note the echoes here of the opening paragraph of *A Modest Proposal*—which may indicate that the two pieces were composed at about the same time.

I SHALL, therefore first mention some Causes of our Miseries, which I doubt[2] are not to be remedied, until God shall put it in the Hearts of those who are the stronger, to allow us the common Rights and Privileges of Brethren, Fellow-Subjects, and even of Mankind.

THE first Cause of our Misery is the intolerable Hardships we lie under in every Branch of our Trade, by which we are become as *Hewers of Wood, and Drawers of Water,*[3] to our rigorous Neighbours.

THE second Cause of our miserable State is the Folly, the Vanity, and Ingratitude of those vast Numbers, who think themselves too good to live in the Country which gave them Birth, and still gives them Bread; and rather chuse to pass their Days, and consume their Wealth, and draw out the very Vitals of their Mother Kingdom, among those who heartily despise them.[4]

THESE I have but lightly touched on, because I fear they are not to be redressed, and, besides, I am very sensible how ready some People are to take Offence at the honest Truth; and, for that Reason, I shall omit several other Grievances, under which we are long likely to groan.

I SHALL therefore go on to relate some other Causes of this Nation's Poverty, by which, if they continue much longer, it must infallibly sink to utter Ruin.

THE first, is that monstrous Pride and Vanity in both Sexes, especially the weaker Sex, who, in the Midst of Poverty, are suffered to run into all Kind of Expence and Extravagance in Dress, and particularly priding themselves to wear nothing but what cometh from Abroad, disdaining the Growth or Manufacture of their own Country, in those Articles where they can be better served at Home with half the Expence; and this is grown to such a Height, that they will carry the whole yearly Rent of a good Estate at once on their Body.[5] And, as there is in that Sex a Spirit of Envy, by which they cannot endure to see others in a better Habit than themselves; so those, whose Fortunes can hardly support their Families in the Necessaries of Life, will needs vye with the Richest and Greatest amongst us, to the Ruin of themselves and their Posterity.

NEITHER are the Men less guilty of this pernicious Folly, who, in Imitation of a Gaudiness and Foppery of Dress, introduced of late Years into our neighbouring Kingdom, (as Fools are apt to imitate only the Defects of their Betters) cannot find Materials in their own Country worthy to adorn their Bodies of Clay, while their Minds are naked of every valuable Quality.

---

[2] Think; believe.

[3] See Joshua 9:21–27. The expression denotes menial servants, or those placed in perpetual bondage (as was the fate of the Gibeonites when they lied to the princes of Israel); often used by the English as a term of contempt for the Irish.

[4] A reference to the absentees, whom Swift repeatedly described in cannibalistic terms; cf. his depiction of "that mongrel breed,/Who from thee [Ireland] spring, yet on thy vitals feed" in his *Verses occasion'd by the Sudden Drying up of St Patrick's Well.*

[5] The main provocation for Swift's urging of a national boycott against imported goods in *A Proposal for the Universal Use of Irish Manufacture* (1720).

THUS our Tradesmen and Shopkeepers, who deal in Home-Goods, are left in a starving Condition, and only those encouraged who ruin the Kingdom by importing among us foreign Vanities.

ANOTHER Cause of our low Condition is our great Luxury,[6] the chief Support of which is the Materials of it brought to the Nation in Exchange for the few valuable Things left us, whereby so many thousand Families want the very Necessaries of Life.

THIRDLY, in most Parts of this Kingdom the Natives are from their Infancy so given up to Idleness and Sloth, that they often chuse to beg or steal, rather than support themselves with their own Labour; they marry without the least View or Thought of being able to make any Provision for their Families; and whereas, in all industrious Nations, Children are looked on as a Help to their Parents, with us, for want of being early trained to work, they are an intolerable Burthen at Home, and a grievous Charge upon the Public, as appeareth from the vast Number of ragged and naked Children in Town and Country, led about by stroling Women,[7] trained up in Ignorance and all Manner of Vice.

LASTLY, A great Cause of this Nation's Misery, is that *Ægyptian* Bondage of cruel, oppressing, covetous Landlords, expecting that all who live under them should *make Bricks without Straw*,[8] who grieve and envy when they see a Tenant of their own in a whole Coat, or able to afford one comfortable Meal in a Month, by which the Spirits of the People are broken, and made for Slavery; the Farmers and Cottagers,[9] almost through the whole Kingdom, being to all Intents and Purposes as real Beggars, as any of those to whom we give our Charity in the Streets. And these cruel Landlords are every Day unpeopling their Kingdom, by forbidding their miserable Tenants to till the Earth, against common Reason and Justice, and contrary to the Practice and Prudence of all other Nations, by which numberless Families have been forced either to leave the Kingdom, or stroll about, and increase the Number of our Thieves and Beggars.

SUCH, and much worse, is our Condition at present, if I had Leisure or Liberty to lay it before you; and, therefore, the next Thing which might be considered is, whether there may be any probable Remedy found, at the least against some Part of these Evils; for most of them are wholly desperate.

BUT this being too large a Subject to be now handled, and the Intent of my Discourse confining me to give some Directions concerning the Poor of this City, I shall keep myself within those Limits. It is indeed in the Power of the Lawgivers to found a School in every Parish of the Kingdom, for teaching the meaner and poorer Sort of Children to speak and read the English

---

[6] Lust; excessive appetite (for material goods, sensual indulgence, etc.); the term for an all-encompassing moral corruption that was a major target of conservative satirists throughout the eighteenth century.

[7] Vagrants; itinerant beggars; prostitutes.

[8] See Exodus 5:7–19.

[9] Peasants or tenant farmers who cultivate a small parcel of land by their own labor.

Tongue, and to provide a reasonable Maintenance for the Teachers. This would, in Time, abolish that Part of Barbarity and Ignorance, for which our Natives are so despised by all Foreigners; this would bring them to think and act according to the Rules of Reason, by which a Spirit of Industry, and Thrift, and Honesty, would be introduced among them. And, indeed, considering how small a Tax would suffice for such a Work, it is a publick Scandal that such a Thing should never have been endeavoured, or, perhaps, so much as thought on.

To supply the Want of such a Law, several pious Persons, in many Parts of this Kingdom, have been prevailed on, by the great Endeavours and good Example set them by the Clergy, to erect Charity-Schools in several Parishes, to which very often the richest Parishioners contribute the least.[10] In these Schools, Children are, or ought to be, trained up to read and write, and cast Accompts;[11] **and these Children should, if possible, be of honest Parents, gone to Decay through Age, Sickness, or other unavoidable Calamity, by the Hand of God; not the Brood of wicked Strolers;** for it is by no means reasonable, that the Charity of well-inclined People should be applied to encourage the Lewdness of those profligate, abandoned Women, who croud our Streets with their borrowed or spurious Issue.

IN those Hospitals[12] which have good Foundations and Rents[13] to support them, whereof, to the Scandal of Christianity, there are very few in this Kingdom; I say, in such Hospitals, the Children maintained, ought to be only of decayed Citizens, and Freemen,[14] and be bred up to good Trades. But in these small Parish Charity Schools which have no Support, but the casual good Will of charitable People, I do altogether disapprove the Custom of putting the Children 'Prentice, except to the very meanest Trades; otherwise the poor honest Citizen who is just able to bring up his Child, and pay a small Sum of Money with him to a good Master, is wholly defeated, and the Bastard Issue, perhaps, of some Beggar, preferred before him. And hence we come to be so over-stocked with 'Prentices and Journeymen,[15] more than our discouraged Country can employ; and, I fear, the greatest Part of our Thieves, Pickpockets, and other Vagabonds are of this Number.

I THINK there is no Complaint more just than what we find in almost every Family, of the Folly and Ignorance, the Fraud and Knavery, the Idleness and

---

[10] A charity-school movement developed and attracted considerable attention in both Britain and Ireland during the first two decades of the eighteenth century. Swift himself promoted and participated in it, especially in his capacity as a member of the Board of the Dublin Workhouse and Foundling Society and of the Blue Coat School, as well as a charter member of the Incorporated Society in Dublin for Promoting English Protestant Schools in Ireland.

[11] Archaic form of "accounts"; money reckoning.

[12] Charitable institutions for the education and maintenance of children.

[13] Sources of revenue or income.

[14] Those who enjoy a certain legal status and privileges within a particular jurisdiction.

[15] Apprentices and those who, having finished their apprenticeship (of seven years' duration in most trades), are qualified to hire themselves out for days' wages.

Viciousness, the wasteful squandering Temper of Servants, who are, indeed, become one of the many publick Grievances of the Kingdom; whereof, I believe, there are few Masters that now hear me, who are not convinced by their own Experience. And I am very confident, that more Families, of all Degrees, have been ruined by the Corruptions of Servants, than by all other Causes put together.[16] Neither is this to be wondered at, when we consider from what Nurseries so many of them are received into our Houses. The first is the Tribe of wicked Boys, wherewith most Corners of this Town are pestered, who haunt publick Doors. These, having been born of Beggars, and bred to pilfer as soon as they can go or speak, as Years come on, are employed in the lowest Offices to get themselves Bread, are practised in all Manner of Villainy, and when they are grown up, if they are not entertained in a Gang of Thieves, are forced to seek for a Service. The other Nursery is the barbarous and desert Part of the Country, from whence such Lads come up hither to seek their Fortunes, who are bred up from the Dunghill in Idleness, Ignorance, Lying, and Thieving.[17] From these two Nurseries, I say, a great Number of our Servants come to us, sufficient to corrupt all the rest. Thus, the whole Race of Servants in this Kingdom have gotten so ill a Reputation, that some Persons from *England,* come over hither into great Stations, are said to have absolutely refused admitting any Servant born among us into their Families. Neither can they be justly blamed; for, although it is not impossible to find an honest Native fit for a good Service, yet the Enquiry is too troublesome, and the Hazard too great for a Stranger to attempt.

IF we consider the many Misfortunes that befal private Families, it will be found that Servants are the Causes and Instruments of them all: Are our Goods embezzled, wasted, and destroyed? Is our House burnt down to the Ground? It is by the Sloth, the Drunkenness or the Villainy of Servants. Are we robbed and murdered in our Beds? It is by Confederacy with our Servants. Are we engaged in Quarrels and Misunderstandings with our Neighbours? These were all begun and inflamed by the false, malicious Tongues of our Servants. Are the Secrets of our Family betrayed, and evil Repute spread of us? Our Servants were the Authors. Do false Accusers rise up against us? (an Evil too frequent in this Country) they have been tampering with our Servants. Do our Children discover Folly, Malice, Pride, Cruelty, Revenge, Undutifulness in their Words and Actions? Are they seduced to Lewdness or scandalous Marriages? It is all by our Servants. Nay, the very Mistakes, Follies, Blunders, and Absurdities of those in our Service, are able to ruffle

---

[16] Swift's unfinished work, *Directions to Servants* (pub. 1745), treats this subject comically, exploiting the satiric potential of servants' morally lax and incompetent behavior. Despite such complaints, a rich oral tradition about "Paddy and the Dane" records Swift's affectionately bantering relationship with members of the servant class; and he honored his own servant, Alexander McGee, with a tablet in St. Patrick's Cathedral.

[17] Interestingly, the language and imagery here are also used in *The Intelligencer, No. IX* (1728) to characterize the offspring of the wealthy country squire, who "bred in Sloth and Idleness...goes out of the World a Beggar, as his Father came in."

and discompose the mildest Nature, and are often of such Consequence, as to put whole Families into Confusion.

SINCE therefore not only our domestick Peace and Quiet, and the Welfare of our Children, but even the very Safety of our Lives, Reputations, and Fortunes have so great a Dependence upon the Choice of our Servants, I think it would well become the Wisdom of the Nation to make some Provision in so important an Affair: But, in the mean Time, and perhaps, to better Purpose, it were to be wished, that the Children of both Sexes, entertained in the Parish Charity-Schools, were bred up in such a Manner as would give them a teachable Disposition, and qualify them to learn whatever is required in any Sort of Service. For Instance, they should be taught to read and write, to know somewhat in casting Accompts, to understand the Principles of Religion, to practise Cleanliness, to get a Spirit of Honesty, Industry, and Thrift, and be severely punished for every Neglect in any of these Particulars. For, it is the Misfortune of Mankind, that if they are not used to be taught in their early Childhood, whereby to acquire what I call a teachable Disposition, they cannot, without great Difficulty, learn the easiest Thing in the Course of their Lives, but are always aukward and unhandy; their Minds, as well as Bodies, for want of early Practice, growing stiff and unmanageable, as we observe in the Sort of Gentlemen, who, kept from School by the Indulgence of their Parents but a few Years, are never able to recover the Time they have lost, and grow up in Ignorance and all Manner of Vice, whereof we have too many Examples all over the Nation.[18] But to return to what I was saying: If these Charity-Children were trained up in the Manner I mentioned, and then bound Apprentices in the Families of Gentlemen and Citizens, (for which a late Law giveth great Encouragement)[19] being accustomed from their first Entrance to be always learning some useful Thing, they would learn in a Month more than another, without those Advantages[,] can do in a Year; and, in the mean Time, be very useful in a Family, as far as their Age and Strength would allow. And when such Children come to Years of Discretion, they will probably be a useful Example to their Fellow Servants, at least they will prove a strong Check upon the rest; for, I suppose, every Body will allow, that one good, honest, diligent Servant in a House may prevent Abundance of Mischief in the Family.

THESE are the Reasons for which I urge this Matter so strongly, and I hope those who listen to me will consider them.

I SHALL now say something about that great Number of Poor, who, under the Name of common Beggars, infest our Streets, and fill our Ears with their continual Cries, and craving Importunity. This I shall venture to call an unnecessary Evil, brought upon us for the gross Neglect, and want of proper Management, in those whose Duty it is to prevent it: But, before I proceed farther, let me humbly presume to vindicate the Justice and Mercy,

---

[18]A point elaborated upon in *The Intelligencer, Number IX*, in the course of countering Locke's argument for private tutors over public schools.

[19]The Servants Act passed in 1715 (2 George I, c. 17).

of God and his Dealings with Mankind. Upon this Particular He hath not dealt so hardly with his Creatures as some would imagine, when they see so many miserable Objects ready to perish for Want: For it would infallibly be found, upon strict Enquiry, that there is hardly one in twenty of those miserable Objects who do not owe their present Poverty to their own Faults; to their present Sloth and Negligence; to their indiscreet Marriage without the least Prospect of supporting a Family, to their foolish Expensiveness, to their Drunkenness, and other Vices, by which they have squandered their Gettings, and contracted Diseases in their old Age. And, to speak freely, is it any Way reasonable or just, that those who have denied themselves many lawful Satisfactions and Conveniencies of Life, from a Principle of Conscience, as well as Prudence, that they might not be a Burthen to the Public, should be charged with supporting Others, who have brought themselves to less than a Morsel of Bread by their Idleness, Extravagance, and Vice? Yet such and no other, are for the Greatest Number not only in those who beg in our Streets, but even of what we call poor decayed House-keepers,[20] whom we are apt to pity, as real Objects of Charity, and distinguish them from common Beggars, although, in Truth, they both owe their Undoing to the same Causes; only the former is either too nicely bred to endure walking half naked in the Streets, or too proud to own their Wants. For the Artificer or other Tradesman, who pleadeth he is grown too old to work or look after Business, and therefore expecteth Assistance as a decayed House-keeper; may we not ask him, why he did not take Care, in his Youth and Strength of Days, to make some Provision against old Age, when he saw so many Examples before him of People undone by their Idleness and vicious Extravagance? And to go a little higher; whence cometh it that so many Citizens and Shopkeepers, of the most creditable Trade, who once made a good Figure, go to Decay by their expensive Pride and Vanity, affecting to educate and dress their Children above their Abilities, or the State of Life they ought to expect?

HOWEVER, since the best of us have too many Infirmities to answer for, we ought not to be severe upon those of others; and, therefore, if our Brother, thro' Grief, or Sickness, or other Incapacity, is not in a Condition to preserve his Being, we ought to support him to the best of our Power, without reflecting over seriously on the Causes that brought him to his Misery. But in order to [do] this, and to turn our Charity into its proper Channel, we ought to consider who and where those Objects are, whom it is chiefly incumbent upon us to support.

BY the antient Law of this Realm, still in Force, every Parish is obliged to maintain its own Poor, which although some may think to be not very equal, because many Parishes are very rich, and have few Poor among them, and others the contrary; yet, I think, may be justly defended: For, as to remote Country Parishes in the desart Parts of the Kingdom, the Necessaries of Life are there so cheap, that the infirm Poor may be provided for with little

---

[20] Heads of a household or family; persons in charge of a house or place of business.

Burden to the Inhabitants. But in what I am going to say, I shall confine myself only to this City, where we are over-run, not only with our own Poor, but with a far greater Number from every Part of the Nation. Now, I say, this Evil of being encumbered with so many foreign Beggars, who have not the least Title to our Charity, and whom it is impossible for us to support, may be easily remedied, if the Government of this City, in Conjunction with the Clergy and Parish Officers, would think it worth their Care; and I am sure few Things deserve it better. For, if every Parish would take a List of those begging Poor which properly belong to it, and compel each of them to wear a Badge, marked and numbered, so as to be seen and known by all they meet, and confine them to beg within the Limits of their own Parish, severely punishing them when they offend, and driving out all Interlopers from other Parishes, we could then make a Computation of their Numbers; and the Strolers from the Country being driven away, the Remainder would not be too many for the Charity of those who pass by, to maintain; neither would any Beggar, although confined to his own Parish, be hindered from receiving the Charity of the whole Town; because in this Case, those well-disposed Persons who walk the Streets, will give their Charity to such whom they think proper Objects, where-ever they meet them, provided they are found in their own Parishes, and wearing their Badges of Distinction.[21] And, as to those Parishes which border upon the Skirts and Suburbs of the Town, where Country Strolers are used to harbour themselves, they must be forced to go back to their Homes, when they find no Body to relieve them, because they want that Mark which only gives them Licence to beg. Upon this Point, it were to be wished, that inferior Parish Officers had better Encouragement given them, to perform their Duty in driving away all Beggars who do not belong to the Parish, instead of conniving at them, as it is said they do for some small Contribution; for the whole City would save much more by ridding themselves of many hundred Beggars, than they would lose by giving Parish Officers a reasonable Support.

IT should seem a strange, unaccountable Thing, that those who have probably been reduced to Want by Riot,[22] Lewdness, and Idleness, although they have Assurance enough to beg Alms publickly from all they meet, should yet be too proud to wear the Parish Badge, which would turn so much to their own Advantage, by ridding them of such great Numbers, who now intercept the greatest Part of what belongeth to them: Yet, it is certain, that there are very many who publickly declare they will never wear those Badges, and many others who either hide or throw them away. But the Remedy for this is very short, easy, and just, by tying them like Vagabonds and sturdy Beggars, and forcibly driving them out of the Town.

[21] Cf. Swift's *Proposal for Giving Badges to the Beggars of Dublin* (1737). Swift himself was known to be one such "well-disposed" person who habitually walked the streets around St. Patrick's Cathedral and gave generously to the poor he met along the way.
[22] Wanton behavior; debauchery.

THEREFORE, as soon as this Expedient of wearing Badges shall be put in Practice, I do earnestly exhort all those who hear me, never to give their Alms to any publick Beggar who doth not fully comply with this Order; by which our Number of Poor will be so reduced, that it will be much easier to provide for the rest. Our Shop-Doors will be no longer crouded with so many Thieves and Pick-pockets, in Beggars Habits, nor our Streets so dangerous to those who are forced to walk in the Night.[23]

THUS I have, with great Freedom delivered my Thoughts upon this Subject, which so nearly concerneth us. It is certainly a bad Scheme, to any Christian Country which God hath blessed with Fruitfulness, and where the People enjoy the just Rights and Privileges of Mankind, that there should be any Beggars at all. But, alas! among us, where the whole Nation itself is almost reduced to Beggary by the Disadvantages we lye under, and the Hardships we are forced to bear; the Laziness, Ignorance, Thoughtlessness, squandering Temper, slavish Nature, and uncleanly Manner of Living in the poor Popish Natives, together with the cruel Oppressions of their Landlords, who delight to see their Vassals in the Dust; I say, that in such a Nation, how can we otherwise expect than to be over-run with Objects of Misery and Want? Therefore, there can be no other Method to free this City from so intolerable a Grievance, than by endeavouring, as far as in us lies, that the Burden may be more equally divided, by contributing to maintain our own Poor, and forcing the Strolers and Vagabonds to return to their several Homes in the Country, there to smite the Conscience of those Oppressors, who first stripped them of all their Substance.

I MIGHT here, if Time would permit, offer many Arguments to persuade to Works of Charity; but you hear them so often from the Pulpit, that I am willing to hope you may not now want[24] them. Besides, my present Design was only to shew where your Alms would be best bestowed, to the Honour of God, your own Ease and Advantage, the Service of your Country, and the Benefit of the Poor. I desire you will all weigh and consider what I have spoken, and, according to your several Stations and Abilities, endeavour to put it in Practice; and God give you good Success, to whom, with the Son and Holy Ghost, be all Honour, &c.

The Grace of God, &c.

---

[23]Street crime was a serious problem in Dublin, especially in the areas surrounding St. Patrick's Cathedral; see *The Last Speech and Dying Words of Ebenezor Elliston*, note 1.
[24]Need.

A PROPOSAL FOR AN ACT of PARLIAMENT to pay off the DEBT of the Nation,

without taxing the Subject, by which the Number of landed Gentry, and substantial Farmers will be considerably encreased, and no Person will be the poorer, or contribute one Farthing to the Charge.

This tract, published in 1732, is one of several pieces on ecclesiastical matters that were written during this period, all critical of the excessive power and wealth of the Irish bishops (see the poem On the Irish Bishops*). In this case, the subject is dealt with through humor and irony. Adopting the persona of an Englishman who has recently obtained a lucrative employment in the country, Swift presents himself as someone eager to make a contribution to his new home by coming up with a way to solve Ireland's high national debt—specifically, through a proposal that bishops help pay off this debt by agreeing to the sale of church lands and by accepting restrictions on their "fines"—that is, the fees they get, equivalent to the increase in rent, each time their tenants' leases are renewed.*

* * *

THE Debts contracted some Years past, for the Service and Safety of the Nation, are grown so great, that under our present distressed Condition, by the Want of Trade, the great Remittances to pay *Absentees*, Regiments serving abroad, and many other Drains of Money, well enough known and felt; the Kingdom seems altogether unable to discharge them by the common Methods of Payment: And either a *Pole* or *Land Tax*, would be too odious to think of, especially the latter; because the Lands which have been let for these Ten or Dozen Years past, were raised so high, that the Owners can, at present, hardly receive any Rent at all. For, it is the usual Practice of an *Irish* Tenant, rather than want Land, to offer more for a Farm than he knows he can be ever able to pay; and in that Case he grows desperate, and pays nothing at all. So that a *Land Tax,* upon a rackt Estate, would be a Burthen wholly insupportable.

THE Question will then be, how these national Debts can be paid; and how I can make good the several Particulars of my Proposal; which I shall now lay open to the Publick.

THE Revenues of their Graces and Lordships, the Archbishops and Bishops of this Kingdom, (excluding the Fines) do amount by a moderate Computation to 36,800 *l. per Ann.* I mean the Rents which the Bishops receive from their Tenants. But the real Value of those Lands, at a full Rent, taking the several Sees one with another, is reckoned to be, at least, three Fourths more; so that multiplying 36,800 *l.* by 4, the full Rent of all the Bishops Lands, will amount to 147200 *l. per Ann.* from which subtracting the present Rent received by their Lordships, that is 36,800 *l.* the Profits of the Lands received by the first and second Tenants (who both have great Bargains) will rise to the Sum of 110400 *l. per Ann.* which Lands, if they were to be sold at Twenty-two Years Purchase, would raise a Sum of 2,428,800 *l.* reserving to the Bishops their present Rents, only excluding Fines.

OF this Sum I propose, that out of the one Half which amounts to 1,214,400 *l.* so much be applied, as will entirely discharge the Debts of the Nation; and the Remainder laid up in the Treasury, to supply Contingencies, as well as to discharge some of our heavy Taxes, until the Kingdom shall be in a better Condition.

BUT, whereas the present Set of Bishops would be great Losers by this Scheme, for want of their Fines; which would be hard Treatment to such *religious, loyal,* and *deserving* Personages; I have therefore set apart the other Half, to supply that Defect; which it will more than sufficiently do.

A BISHOP's Lease for the full Term, is reckoned to be worth Eleven Years Purchase; but if we take the Bishops round, I suppose there may be four Years of each Lease elapsed; and many of the Bishops being well stricken in Years, I cannot think their Lives round to be worth more than seven Years Purchase; so that the Purchasers may very well afford Fifteen Years Purchase for the Reversion;[1] especially by one great additional Advantage, which I shall soon mention.

THIS sum of 2,428,800 *l.* must likewise be sunk very considerably; because the Lands are to be sold only at Fifteen Years Purchase, and this lessens the Sum to about 1,656,000 *l.* of which I propose Twelve Hundred Thousand Pounds, to be applied partly for the Payment of the national Debt, and partly as a Fund for future Exigencies; and the remaining 456,000 *l.* I propose

---

[1]The right of succession to the office (and its perks) after the current holder's death or retirement.

as a Fund for paying the present Set of Bishops their Fines; which it will abundantly do, and a great Part remain as an Addition to the public Stock.

Although the Bishops round do not, in Reality, receive three Fines a Piece, which take up 21 Years, yet I allow it to be so; but then, I will suppose them to take but one Year's Rent, in Recompense of giving them so large a Term of Life; and thus multiplying 36800 *l.* by 3, the Product will be only 110400 *l.* so that above three Fourths will remain, to be applied to public Use.

If I have made wrong Computations, I hope to be excused, as a Stranger to the Kingdom, which I never saw till I was called to an Employment, and yet where I intend to pass the Rest of my Days; but I took Care to get the best Information I could, and from the most proper Persons; however, the Mistakes I may have been guilty of, will very little affect the Main of my Proposal; although they should cause a Difference of one Hundred Thousand Pounds, more or less.

These Fines are only to be paid to the Bishop, during his Incumbency in the same See: If he change it for a better, the Purchasers of the vacant See Lands, are to come immediately into Possession of the See he hath left; and both the Bishop who is removed, and he who comes into his Place, are to have no more Fines; for the removed Bishop will find his Account by a larger Revenue; and the other See will find Candidates enough. For the Law Maxim will here have Place: *Caveat Emptor.*[2] I mean the Persons who succeed, may chuse whether they will accept or no.

As to the Purchasers, they will probably be Tenants to the See, who are already in Possession, and can afford to give more than any other Bidders.

I will further explain myself. If a Person already a Bishop, be removed into a richer See, he must be content with the bare Revenues, without any Fines; and so must he who comes into a Bishopric vacant by Death: And this will bring the Matter sooner to bear; which, if the Crown shall think fit to countenance, will soon change the present Set of Bishops, and consequently encourage Purchasers of their Lands. For Example: If a Primate should die, and the Gradation be wisely made, almost the whole Set of Bishops might be changed in a Month, each to his great Advantage, although no Fines were to be got;[3] and thereby save a great Part of that Sum, which I have appropriated towards supplying the Deficiency of Fines.

I have valued the Bishops Lands two Years Purchase, above the usual computed Rate; because those Lands will have a Sanction from the King and Council in *England,* and be confirmed by an Act of Parliament here: Besides, it is well known, that higher Prices are given every Day for worse Lands, at the remotest Distances, and at Rack Rents,[4] which I take to be

---

[2] "Let the buyer beware."

[3] In other words, if an archbishop ("Primate") dies, all lower bishops could be moved up a step in rank to fill the vacancy above them; the more lucrative pay for these advanced positions would then compensate each cleric for the loss of his "fine."

[4] Exorbitant rents nearly equal to the full value of the land.

occasioned by Want of Trade: When there are few Borrowers, and the little Money in private Hands lying dead, there is no other way to dispose of it, but in buying of Land; which consequently makes the Owners hold it so high.

BESIDES paying the Nation's Debts, the Sale of these Lands would have many other good Effects upon the Nation. It will considerably increase the Number of Gentry, where the Bishops Tenants are not able or willing to purchase; for the Lands will afford an Hundred Gentlemen a good Revenue to each. Several Persons from *England*, will probably be glad to come over hither, and be the Buyers, rather than give Thirty Years Purchase at home, under the Loads of Taxes for the Publick and the Poor, as well as Repairs; by which Means, much Money may be brought among us; and probably some of the Purchasers themselves, may be content to live cheap in a worse Country, rather than be at the Charge of Exchange and Agencies; and perhaps of *Non-solvencies* in Absence, if they lett their Lands too high.

THIS proposal will also multiply Farmers, when the Purchasers will have Lands in their own Power, to give long and easy Leases to industrious Husbandmen.

I HAVE allowed some Bishopricks, of equal Income, to be of more or less Value to the Purchaser, according as they are circumstanced. For Instance: The lands of the Primacy, and some other Sees, are lett so low, that they hardly pay a fifth Penny of the real Value to the Bishop, and there the Fines are the greater. On the contrary, the Sees of *Meath* and *Clonfert*, consisting, as I am told, much of Tythes, those Tythes are annually lett to the Tenants, without any Fines. So the See of *Dublin* is said to have many Fee-Farms,[5] which pay no Fines; and some Leases for Lives, which pay very little, and not so soon nor so duly.

I CANNOT but be confident, that their Graces my Lords the Archbishops, and my Lords the Bishops, will heartily join in this Proposal, out of Gratitude to his late and present Majesty, the best of Kings,[6] who have bestowed on them such high and opulent Stations; as well as in Pity to this Country, which is now become their own; whereby they will be instrumental towards paying the Nation's Debts, without impoverishing themselves; enrich an Hundred Gentlemen, as well as free them from Dependance; and thus remove that Envy which is apt to fall upon their Graces and Lordships, from considerable Persons; whose Birth and Fortunes, rather qualify them to be Lords of Mannors, than servile Dependents upon Churchmen, however dignified or distinguished.

IF I do not flatter my self, there could not be any Law more popular than this. For the immediate Tenants to Bishops, being some of them Persons of Quality, and good Estates; and more of them grown up to be Gentlemen by the Profits of these very Leases, under a Succession of Bishops; think it a Disgrace to be Subject both to Rents and Fines, at the Pleasure of their

---

[5]A type of tenure by which land is held subject to a perpetual fixed rent, without any other services demanded and without limitation to any particular class of heirs.

[6]Georges I and II. The latter ascended to the throne in 1727, upon his father's death.

Landlords. Then, the Bulk of the Tenants, especially the *Dissenters*, who are our *true loyal* Protestant Brethren, look upon it, both as an unnatural and iniquitous Thing, that Bishops should be Owners of Land at all; (wherein I beg to differ from them) being a Point so contrary to the Practice of the Apostles, whose Successors they are deemed to be, and who, although they were contented that Land should be sold, for the common Use of the Brethren; yet would not buy it themselves; but had it laid at their Feet, to be distributed to poor Proselytes.[7]

I WILL add one Word more; that by such a wholesome Law, all the Oppressions felt by under Tenants of Church Leases, which are now laid on by the Bishops; would entirely be prevented, by their Graces and Lordships consenting to have their Lands sold for Payment of the Nation's Debts; reserving only the present Rent for their own plentiful and honourable Support.

I BEG leave to add one Particular; that, when Heads of a Bill (as I find the Style runs in this Kingdom) shall be brought in for forming this Proposal into a Law;[8] I should humbly offer, that there might be a Power given to every Bishop, (except those who reside in *Dublin*) for applying one Hundred acres of profitable Land, that lies nearest to his Palace, as a Demesne for the Conveniency of his Family.

I KNOW very well, that this Scheme hath been much talked of for some Time past, and is in the Thoughts of many Patriots; neither was it properly mine, although I fell readily into it, when it was first communicated to me.

ALTHOUGH I am almost a perfect Stranger in this Kingdom; yet since I have accepted an Employment here, of some Consequence as well as Profit; I cannot but think my self in Duty bound to consult the Interest of a People, among whom I have been so well received. And if I can be any way instrumental, towards contributing to reduce this excellent Proposal into a Law; which, being not in the least injurious to *England*, will, I am confident, meet with no Opposition from that Side; my sincere Endeavours to serve this Church and Kingdom, will be well rewarded.

---

[7] An ironic slap both at the Dissenters, whose professions of Protestant unity masked a hostility toward the Church of Ireland, and at the Irish bishops, whose financial dealings, it is suggested, are a far cry from the altruistic and charitable practices of their forbears.

[8] "Heads of bills" were brief outlines of bills originating in Ireland that were then sent to England for approval or modification before being returned to the Irish Parliament for acceptance or rejection (amendment was not an option).

AN EXAMINATION *of Certain Abuses, Corruptions, and Enormities, in the* City of Dublin

Written in the Year 1732

Printed in 1732 in both Dublin and London (where it appeared under its alternate title, "City Cries, Instrumental and Vocal"), this work makes use of the word-play, mock-allegory, and scatological humor so favored by Swift in order to expose the atmosphere of political harassment and paranoia that he saw permeating Irish society, one that he felt personally victimized by. He achieves his satiric ends by creating as his comically delusional speaker a zealous Whig who equates Tories with the despised Jacobites (those desiring the Stuarts' return to the throne) and who discovers traitorous plots and conspiracies everywhere he looks.

* * *

NOTHING is held more commendable in all great Cities, especially the Metropolis of a Kingdom, than what the *French* call the *Police:* By which Word is meant the Government thereof, to prevent the many Disorders occasioned by great Numbers of People and Carriages, especially through narrow Streets. In this Government our famous City of *Dublin* is said to be very defective; and universally complained of.[1] Many wholesome Laws have been enacted to correct those Abuses, but are ill executed; and many more are wanting; which I hope the united Wisdom of the Nation (whereof so many good Effects have already appeared this Session) will soon take into their profound Consideration.

As I have been always watchful over the Good of mine own Country; and particularly for that of our renowned City; where, *(absit invidia)*[2] I had the Honour to draw my first Breath; I cannot have a Minute's Ease or Patience to forbear enumerating some of the greatest Enormities, Abuses,

---

[1] Unlike Paris with its relatively centralized and well-coordinated policing activities, Dublin had no professional police force at this time and had to rely instead on short-term, unpaid constables and elderly watchmen who got their jobs through parish charity.

[2] "Let ill will be absent."

and Corruptions spread almost through every Part of *Dublin; and* proposing such Remedies, as, I hope, the Legislature will approve of.

THE narrow Compass to which I have confined my self in this Paper, will allow me only to touch the most important Defects; and such as I think, seem to require the most speedy Redress.

AND first: Perhaps there was never known a wiser Institution than that of allowing certain Persons of both Sexes, in large and populous Cities, to cry through the Streets many Necessaries of Life:[3] It would be endless to recount the Conveniences which our City enjoys by this useful Invention; and particularly Strangers, forced hither by Business, who reside here but a short time: For, these having usually but little Money, and being wholly ignorant of the Town, might at an easy Price purchase a tolerable Dinner, if the several Criers would pronounce the Names of the Goods they have to sell, in any tolerable Language. And therefore until our Law-makers shall think it proper to interpose so far as to make those Traders pronounce their Words in such Terms, that a plain Christian Hearer may comprehend what is cryed; I would advise all new Comers to look out at their Garret Windows, and there see whether the Thing that is cryed be *Tripes,* or *Flummery,*[4] *Buttermilk*, or *Cowheels.* For, as Things are now managed, how is it possible for an honest Countryman, just arrived, to find out what is meant, for instance, by the following Words, with which his Ears are constantly stunned twice a Day, *Muggs, Juggs, and Porringers,*[5] *up in the Garret, and down in the Cellar.* I say, how is it possible for any Stranger to understand that this Jargon is meant as an Invitation to buy a Farthing's Worth of Milk for his Breakfast or Supper, unless his Curiosity draws him to the Window, or until his Landlady shall inform him? I produce this only as one Instance, among a Hundred much worse; I mean where the Words make a Sound wholly inarticulate, which give so much Disturbance, and so little Information.

THE Affirmation solemnly made in the Cry of *Herrings,* is directly against all Truth and Probability; *Herrings alive, alive here:* The very Proverb will convince us of this; for what is more frequent in ordinary Speech, than to say of some Neighbour for whom the Passing-Bell rings, that *he is dead as a Herring.*[6] And, pray how is it possible, that a *Herring,* which, as *Philosophers* observe, cannot live longer than One Minute, Three Seconds and a half out of Water, should bear a Voyage in open Boats from *Howth* to *Dublin,* be tossed into twenty Hands, and preserve its Life in Sieves for several Hours? Nay, we have Witnesses ready to produce, that many Thousands of these

---

[3]City "cryers," or hawkers of goods, were a common sight on the streets of eighteenth-century Dublin and London, as well as a frequent subject of broadsides and books of prints. Swift versified several of their cries and recorded ones he heard from his London window in *The Journal to Stella.* Addison devoted *The Spectator, No. 251* to a description of them; like the speaker here, he criticized their habit "of Crying so as not to be understood."

[4]A type of food made by coagulation of wheat flour or oatmeal.

[5]Small metal, earthenware, or wooden vessels used for eating soup and porridge.

[6]A proverb that dates back to around 1600, as first recorded in Shakespeare's *The Merry Wives of Windsor* (II. iii) (*The Wordsworth Dictionary of Proverbs*).

Herrings, so impudently asserted to be alive, have been a Day and a Night upon dry land. But this is not the worst. What can we think of those impious Wretches, who dare in the Face of the Sun, vouch the very same Affirmative of their *Salmon;* and cry, *Salmon alive, alive;* whereas, if you call the Woman who cryes it, she is not ashamed to turn back her Mantle, and shew you this individual Salmon cut into a dozen Pieces. I have given good Advice to these infamous Disgracers of their Sex and Calling, without the least Appearance of Remorse; and fully against the Conviction of their own Consciences. I have mentioned this Grievance to several of our Parish Ministers; but all in vain: So that it must continue until the Government shall think fit to interpose.

THERE is another *Cry,* which, from the strictest Observation I can make, appears to be very modern, and it is that of *Sweet-hearts*; and is plainly intended for a Reflection upon the Female Sex; as if there were at present so great a Dearth of Lovers, that the Women instead of receiving Presents from Men, were now forced to offer Money, to purchase *Sweet-hearts.*[7] Neither am I sure, that this *Cry* doth not glance at some Disaffection against the Government; insinuating, that while so many of our Troops, are engaged in foreign Service; and such a great Number of our gallant Officers constantly reside in *England*; the Ladies are forced to take up with *Parsons* and *Attornies:* But this is a most unjust Reflection; as may soon be proved by any Person who frequents the *Castle,* our public Walks, our Balls and Assemblies; where the Crowds of *Toupees*[8] were never known to swarm as they do at present.

THERE is a *Cry* peculiar to this City, which I do not remember to have been used in *London;* or at least, not in the same Terms that it hath been practised by both Parties, during each of their Power; but, very unjustly by the *Tories.* While these were at the Helm, they grew daily more and more impatient to put all true *Whigs* and *Hanoverians* out of Employments. To effect which, they hired certain ordinary Fellows, with large Baskets on their Shoulders, to call aloud at every House, *Dirt to carry out;* giving that Denomination to our whole Party; as if they would signify, that the Kingdom could never be *cleansed,* until we were *swept* from the Earth like *Rubbish.* But, since that happy Turn of Times, when we were so *miraculously* preserved by just an *Inch,* from *Popery, Slavery, Massacre,* and the *Pretender;*[9] I must own it Prudence in us, still to go on with the same *Cry;* which hath ever since been so effectually observed, that the true *political Dirt* is wholly removed, and thrown on its proper Dunghills, there to corrupt and be no more heard of.

---

[7] *A Sort of Sugar-Cakes in the Shape of Hearts* (Faulkner's note).

[8] *A new Name for a modern Periwig, and for its owner, now in Fashion, Dec. 1, 1733* (Faulkner's note). For Swift's satire on these "toupees," see *The Humble Petition of the Footmen of Dublin* (1732).

[9] James Edward Francis Stuart (1688–1766), son of the deposed James II and the symbolic leader of the Jacobites, who wished to restore the (Catholic) Stuart line. "That happy Turn of Times" refers to the successful suppression of the Jacobite Rebellion of 1715 and glances back to the defeat of James II by the forces of William III in 1691.

BUT, to proceed to other Enormities: Every Person who walks the Streets, must needs observe the immense Number of human Excrements at the Doors and Steps of waste Houses, and at the Sides of every dead Wall; for which the disaffected Party hath assigned a very false and malicious Cause. They would have it that these Heaps were laid there privately by *British Fundaments,*[10] to make the World believe, that our *Irish* Vulgar do daily eat and drink; and consequently, that the Clamour of Poverty among us, must be false; proceeding only from *Jacobites* and *Papists.* They would confirm this, by pretending to observe, that a *British Anus* being more narrowly perforated than one of our own Country; and many of these Excrements, upon a strict View appearing Copple-crowned,[11] with a Point like a Cone or Pyramid, are easily distinguished from the *Hibernian,* which lie much flatter, and with less Continuity. I communicated this Conjecture to an eminent Physician, who is well versed in such profound Speculations; and at my Request was pleased to make Trial with each of his Fingers, by thrusting them into the *Anus* of several Persons of both Nations; and professed he could find no such Difference between them as those ill-disposed People alledge. On the contrary, he assured me, that much the greater Number of narrow Cavities were of *Hibernian* Origin. This I only mention to shew how ready the *Jacobites* are to lay hold of any Handle to express their Malice against the Government. I had almost forgot to add, that my Friend the Physician could, by smelling each Finger, distinguish the *Hibernian* Excrement from the *British;* and was not above twice mistaken in an Hundred Experiments; upon which he intends very soon to publish a learned Dissertation.[12]

THERE is a Diversion in this City, which usually begins among the *Butchers;* but is often continued by a Succession of other People, through many Streets. It is called the COSSING *of a Dog:* And I may justly number it among our Corruptions. The Ceremony is thus: A strange Dog happens to pass through a Flesh-Market: Whereupon an expert *Butcher* immediately cries in a loud Voice, and the proper Tone, *Coss, Coss,* several Times: The same Word is repeated by the People.[13] The Dog, who perfectly understands the Term of Art, and consequently the Danger he is in, immediately flies. The People, and even his own *Brother Animals* pursue: The Pursuit and Cry attend him perhaps half a Mile; he is well worried in his Flight; and sometimes hardly escapes. This, our Ill-wishers of the *Jacobite* Kind, are pleased to call a *Persecution;* and affirm, that it always falls upon *Dogs* of the *Tory* Principle. But, we can well defend our selves, by justly alledging, that, when

---

[10] Buttocks or anuses.

[11] Crested; peaked.

[12] Suggests a kinship with the scientists satirized in *A Tale of a Tub* and *Gulliver's Travels,* though the minute inspection of excrement was a common medical practice of the day.

[13] "Coss" is an Anglo-Indian term, derived from both Hindi and Sanskrit words, which signifies a call made over a specific measure of distance (between 1¼ and 2½ miles), or the distance at which a man's voice can be heard.

they were uppermost, they treated our *Dogs* full as inhumanly: As to my own Part, who have in former Times often attended these *Processions*; although I can very well distinguish between a *Whig* and a *Tory Dog*; yet I never carried my Resentments very far upon a *Party Principle,* except it were against certain malicious *Dogs,* who most discovered their Enmity against us in the *worst of Times.* And, I remember too well, that in the wicked Ministry of the Earl of *Oxford*,[14] a large Mastiff of our Party being unmercifully *cossed*; ran, without Thinking, between my Legs, as I was coming up *Fishamble-street*; and, as I am of low Stature, with very short Legs, bore me riding backwards down the Hill, for above Two Hundred Yards: And, although I made use of his Tail for a Bridle, holding it fast with both my Hands, and clung my Legs as close to his Sides as I could; yet we both came down together into the Middle of the Kennel;[15] where after rowling three or four Times over each other, I got up with much ado, amidst the Shouts and Huzza's[16] of a Thousand malicious *Jacobites*: I cannot, indeed, but gratefully acknowledge, that for this and many other *Services* and *Sufferings,* I have been since more than over-paid.

THIS Adventure, may, perhaps, have put me out of Love with the Diversion of *Cossing*; which I confess myself an Enemy too; unless we could always be sure of distinguishing *Tory Dogs*; whereof great Numbers have since been so prudent, as entirely to change their Principles; and are now justly esteemed the best *Worriers*[17] of their former Friends.

I AM assured, and partly know, that all the Chimney-Sweeper Boys, where Members of Parliament chiefly lodge, are hired by *our Enemies* to sculk in the Tops of Chimneys, with their Heads no higher than will just permit them to look round; and at the usual Hours when Members are going to the House, if they see a Coach stand near the Lodging of any *loyal* Member; they call *Coach, Coach,* as loud as they can bawl, just at the Instant when the Footman begins to give the same Call. And this is chiefly done on those Days, when any Point of Importance is to be debated. This Practice may be of very dangerous Consequence. For, these Boys are all hired by Enemies to the Government: And thus, by the Absence of a few Members for a few Minutes, a Question may be carried against the *true Interest* of the Kingdom; and, very probably, not without an Eye towards the *Pretender.*

I HAVE not observed the Wit and Fancy of this Town, so much employed in any one Article as that of contriving Variety of Signs to hang over Houses, where *Punch* is to be sold.[18] The Bowl is represented full of *Punch*; the Ladle stands erect in the middle; supported sometimes by one, and sometimes by

---

[14] Robert Harley (1661–1724), 1st Earl of Oxford, was Lord-Treasurer of the Tory ministry for which Swift worked during the 1710–14 period.

[15] Gutter.

[16] Cheers uttered by a large group in unison.

[17] Harassers; tormentors.

[18] This beverage was relatively new to the British Isles, having been introduced in the seventeenth century by merchant seamen returning from India.

two Animals, whose Feet rest upon the Edge of the Bowl. These Animals are sometimes one black *Lion,* and sometimes a Couple; sometimes a single *Eagle,* and sometimes a spread One; and we often meet a *Crow,* a *Swan,* a *Bear,* or a *Cock,* in the same Posture.[19]

Now, I cannot find how any of these Animals, either separate, or in Conjunction, are, properly speaking, fit Emblems or Embellishments, to advance the Sale of *Punch.* Besides, it is agreed among *Naturalists,* that no Brute can endure the Taste of strong Liquor; except where he hath been used to it from his Infancy: And, consequently, it is against all the Rules of *Hieroglyph,*[20] to assign those Animals as patrons, or Protectors of *Punch.* For, in that Case, we ought to suppose that the Host keeps always ready the real Bird, or Beast, whereof the Picture hangs over his Door, to entertain his Guests; which, however, to my Knowledge, is not true in Fact: Not one of those Birds being a proper companion for a *Christian,* as to aiding and assisting in making the *Punch.* For, as they are drawn upon the Sign, they are much more likely to mute,[21] or shed their Feathers into the Liquor. Then, as to the *Bear,* he is too terrible, awkward, and slovenly a Companion to converse with; neither are any of them all *handy* enough to fill Liquor to the Company: I do, therefore, vehemently suspect a Plot intended against the Government, by these Devices. For, although the *Spread-Eagle* be the Arms of *Germany,* upon which Account it may possibly be a lawful *Protestant* Sign; yet I, who am very suspicious of fair Outsides, in a Matter which so nearly concerns our Welfare; cannot but call to Mind, that the *Pretender's* Wife is said to be of *German* Birth:[22] And that many *Popish* Princes, in so vast an Extent of Land, are reported to excel both at making and drinking *Punch.* Besides, it is plain, that the *Spread-Eagle* exhibits to us the Figure of a *Cross;* which is a Badge of *Popery.* Then, as to the *Cock,* he is well known to represent the *French* Nation, our old and dangerous Enemy.[23] The *Swan,* who must of Necessity cover the entire Bowl with his Wings, can be no other than the *Spaniard;* who endeavours to engross all the Treasures of the *Indies* to himself.[24] The *Lion* is indeed the common Emblem of Royal Power, as well as the Arms of *England*: But to paint him black, is perfect *Jacobitism;* and a manifest Type of those who *blacken* the Actions of the best Princes. It is not easy to distinguish whether that other Fowl painted over the *Punch-Bowl,* be

---

[19] Many public houses in Dublin during Swift's time were named after animals, including the White Hart, the Bear and Ragged Staff, the Eagle Tavern, and the Bull's Head in Fishamble Street.

[20] The fixed or recognized systems of meaning according to which signs or emblems are interpreted.

[21] Defecate.

[22] Princess Maria Clementina Sobieska, granddaughter of John III, King of Poland, married the Pretender in 1719.

[23] Based on the conflation of the two meanings of the Latin word "gallus," signifying both a rooster and a Gaul.

[24] Refers to Spain's harassment and seizure of British ships attempting to trade with the Spanish colonies in America, a right accorded them by the Treaty of Utrecht (1713).

a *Crow* or *Raven?* It is true, they have both been held ominous Birds: But I rather take it to be the former; because it is the Disposition of a *Crow,* to pick out the Eyes of other Creatures; and often even of *Christians,* after they are dead; and is therefore drawn here, with a Design to put the *Jacobites* in Mind of their old Practice; first to lull us a-sleep, (which is an Emblem of Death) and then to blind our Eyes, that we may not see their dangerous Practices against the State.

To speak my private Opinion; the least offensive Picture in the whole Sett, seems to be the *Bear;* because he represents *Ursa Major,* or the *Great Bear,* who presides over the *North;* where the *Reformation* first began; and which, next to *Britain,* (including *Scotland* and the *North* of *Ireland)* is the great Protector of the *true Protestant* Religion. But, however, in those Signs where I observe the *Bear* to be *chained,* I cannot help surmising a *Jacobite* Contrivance; by which, these Traytors hint an earnest Desire of using all *true Whigs,* as their Predecessors did the primitive Christians: I mean, to represent us as *Bears,* and then halloo their *Tory-Dogs* to bait us to Death.[25]

THUS I have given a fair Account of what I dislike, in all the Signs set over those Houses that invite us to *Punch.* I own it was a Matter that did not need explaining; being so very obvious to common Understanding: Yet, I know not how it happens, but methinks there seems a fatal Blindness, to overspread our corporeal Eyes, as well as our intellectual; and I heartily wish, I may be found a false Prophet. For, these are not bare Suspicions, but manifest Demonstrations.

THEREFORE, away with these *Popish, Jacobite,* and idolatrous Gew-gaws.[26] And I heartily wish a Law were enacted, under severe Penalties, against drinking any *Punch* at all: For, nothing is easier, than to prove it a disaffected Liquor. The chief Ingredients, which are *Brandy, Oranges,* and *Lemons,* are all sent us from *Popish* Countries; and nothing remains of *Protestant* Growth, but *Sugar* and *Water.* For, as to Biscuit, which formerly was held a necessary Ingredient, and is truly *British,* we find it is entirely rejected.

BUT I will put the Truth of my Assertion past all Doubt: I mean, that this Liquor is by one important Innovation, grown of ill Example, and dangerous Consequence to the Publick. It is well known, that, by the true original Institution of making *Punch,* left us by Captain *Ratcliff,* the Sharpness is only occasioned by the Juice of *Lemons;* and so continued until after the happy *Revolution.*[27] *Oranges,* alas! are a meer Innovation, and, in a manner, *but of Yesterday.* It was the Politicks of *Jacobites* to introduce them gradually: And, to what Intent? The Thing speaks it self. It was cunningly to shew their Virulence against his sacred Majesty King *William, of ever glorious and*

---

[25] Bear-baiting was a popular eighteenth-century entertainment in which dogs were set upon chained bears and encouraged to fight to the death; of a piece with cockfighting and other blood sports favored by gamblers of all classes at the time.

[26] Gaudy trifles; playthings; "vanities."

[27] The Glorious Revolution (1688) that brought William and Mary to the throne.

immortal Memory.[28] But of late (to shew how fast Disloyalty increaseth) they came from one to two, and then to three *Oranges;* nay, at present, we often find *Punch* made all with *Oranges;* and not one single *Lemon.* For, the *Jacobites,* before the Death of that immortal Prince, had, by a Superstition, formed a private Prayer; that, as they *squeezed the Orange,* so might that *Protestant* King be *squeezed* to Death:[29] According to the known *Sorcery* described by *Virgil; Limus ut hic durescit, & haec ut cera liquescit,* &c.[30] And, thus the *Romans,* when they sacrificed an Ox, used this Kind of Prayer: *As I knock down this Ox, so may thou, O* Jupiter, *knock down our Enemies.*[31] In like Manner, after King *William*'s Death, whenever a *Jacobite* squeezed an *Orange,* he had a mental Curse upon the *glorious Memory;* and a hearty Wish for Power to *squeeze* all his Majesty's Friends to Death, as he *squeezed* that *Orange,* which bore one of his Titles, as he was Prince of *Orange.* This I do affirm for Truth; many of that Faction having confessed it to me, under an *Oath of Secrecy;* which, however, I thought it my Duty not to keep, when I saw my dear Country in Danger. But, what better can be expected from an *impious* Set of Men, who never scruple to drink CONFUSION to all *true Protestants,* under the Name of *Whigs?* A most unchristian and inhuman Practice; *which, to our great Honour and Comfort, was* never *charged upon us, even by our most malicious Detractors.*[32]

THE Sign of two *Angels,* hovering in the Air, and with their Right Hands supporting a *Crown,* is met with in several Parts of this City; and hath often given me great Offence: For, whether by the Unskilfulness, or dangerous Principles of the Painters, (although I have good Reasons to suspect the latter) those *Angels* are usually drawn with such horrid, or indeed rather diabolical *Countenances,* that they give great Offence to every loyal Eye; and equal Cause of Triumph to the *Jacobites;* being a most infamous Reflection upon our able and excellent Ministry.

I NOW return to that great Enormity of City *Cries;* most of which we have borrowed from *London.* I shall consider them only in a *political* View, as they nearly affect the Peace and Safety of both Kingdoms: And having been originally contrived by wicked *Machiavels,* to bring in *Popery, Slavery,* and *arbitrary Power,* by defeating the *Protestant* Succession, and introducing the *Pretender;* ought, in justice, to be here laid open to the World.

ABOUT two or three Months after the happy *Revolution,* all Persons who possest any Employment, or Office, in Church or State, were obliged by an Act of Parliament, to take the Oaths to King *William* and Queen *Mary.* And a

---

[28] A cant phrase used by Whigs and mocked in several of Swift's works.

[29] With its obvious pun on William of Orange, the term "to squeeze an orange" was a popular Jacobite toast during William's reign. William died in 1702.

[30] "[As by the kindling of the self-same fire], Harder this clay, this wax the softer grows." Virgil, *Eclogue VIII,* 80.

[31] Livy, *The History of Rome,* Book I, ch. 24. Swift substitutes "ox" for Livy's "swine."

[32] In *The Examiner,* No. 20, Swift "charged" the Whigs with precisely this practice; and in the *Journal to Stella* he described the penalty meted out to several Whig army officers for (among other things) "drinking destruction to the present ministry."

great Number of disaffected Persons, refusing to take the said Oaths, from a pretended Scruple of Conscience, but really from a Spirit of *Popery* and Rebellion, they contrived a Plot, to make the swearing to those Princes odious in the Eyes of the People. To this End, they hired certain Women of ill Fame, but loud shrill Voices, under the Pretence of selling Fish, to go through the Streets, with Sieves on their Heads, and cry, *buy my Soul, buy my Soul;* plainly insinuating, that all those who swore to King *William,* were just ready to sell their *Souls* for an Employment. This Cry was revived at the Death of Queen *Anne,* and I hear still continues in *London,* with much Offence to all *true Protestants;* but, to our great Happiness, seems to be almost dropt in *Dublin.*

BUT, because I altogether contemn the Displeasure and Resentment of *High-flyers,*[33] *Tories, and Jacobites,* whom I look upon to be *worse even than profest Papists;* I do here declare, that those Evils which I am going to mention, were all brought upon us in the *worst of Times,*[34] under the late Earl of *Oxford's* Administration, during the four last Years of Queen *Anne's* Reign. *That wicked Minister was universally known to be a Papist in his Heart. He was of a most avaricious Nature, and is said to have died worth four Millions,* sterl. *besides his vast Expences in Building, Statues, Plate, Jewels, and other costly Rarities. He was of a mean obscure Birth, from the very Dregs of the People; and so illiterate, that he could hardly read a Paper at the Council Table. I forbear to touch at his open, prophane, profligate Life; because I desire not to rake into the Ashes of the Dead; and therefore I shall observe this wise Maxim:* De mortuis nil nisi bonum.[35]

THIS flagitious Man, in order to compass his black Designs, employed certain wicked Instruments (which great Statesmen are never without) to adapt several *London* Cries, in such a Manner as would best answer his Ends. And, whereas it was upon good Grounds grievously suspected, that all *Places* at Court were sold to the highest Bidder: Certain Women were employed by his Emissaries, to carry *Fish* in Baskets on their Heads, and bawl through the Streets, *Buy my fresh Places.* I must, indeed, own that other Women used the same Cry, who were innocent of this wicked Design, and really sold their Fish of that Denomination, to get an honest Livelyhood: But the rest, who were in the *Secret,* although they carried *Fish* in their Sieves or Baskets, to save Appearances; yet they had likewise a certain Sign, somewhat resembling that of the *Free-Masons,*[36] which the Purchasers of *Places* knew well enough,

---

[33] High Church proponents; those who supported extreme claims for the authority of the church.

[34] *A Cant-Word used by Whigs for the four last Years of Queen* Anne*'s Reign, during the Earl of* Oxford*'s Ministry; whose Character here is an exact Reverse in every Particular* (Faulkner's note).

[35] "[Speak] nothing but good of the dead." A proverb thought to have originated in Greek with Chilon's *Diogenes Laertes.*

[36] A secret, all-male order founded in London as the Grand Lodge of Masonry in 1717 and brought to Ireland eight years later. It espoused the "mysteries" of antiquity and claimed ancestry among the ancient Egyptians and Greeks.

and were directed by the Women whither they were to resort, and make their Purchase. And, I remember very well, how oddly it lookt, when we observed many Gentlemen finely drest, about the Court-End of the Town, and as far as *York-Buildings,* where the Lord-Treasurer *Oxford* dwelt; calling the Women who cried *Buy my fresh Places,* and talking to them in the Corner of a Street, until they understood each other's Sign. But we never could observe that any Fish was bought.

SOME Years before the Cries last mentioned; the Duke of *Savoy* was reported to have made certain Overtures to the Court of *England,* for admitting his eldest Son, by the Dutchess of *Orleans*'s Daughter, to succeed to the Crown, as next Heir, upon the *Pretender*'s being rejected; and that Son was immediately to turn *Protestant.*[37] It was confidently reported, that great Numbers of People disaffected to the then *Illustrious* but now *Royal* House of *Hanover,* were in those Measures. Whereupon, another Sett of Women were hired by the *Jacobite* Leaders, to cry through the whole Town, *Buy my* Savoys, *dainty* Savoys, *curious* Savoys.[38] But, I cannot directly charge the late Earl of *Oxford* with this *Conspiracy,* because he was not then chief Minister. However, this wicked Cry still continues in *London,* and was brought over hither; where it remains to this Day; and is in my humble Opinion, a very offensive Sound to every true Protestant, who is old enough to remember those *dangerous* Times.

DURING the Ministry of that corrupt and *Jacobite* Earl abovementioned, the secret pernicious Design of those in Power, was to sell *Flanders* to *France:*[39] The Consequence of which, must have been the infallible Ruin of the *States-General,* and would have opened the Way for *France* to obtain that universal Monarchy, they have so long aimed at; to which *the British* Dominions must next, after *Holland,* have been compelled to submit. Whereby the *Protestant* Religion would be rooted out of the World.

A DESIGN of this vast Importance, after long Consultation among the *Jacobite* Grandees,[40] with the Earl of *Oxford* at their Head; was at last determined to be carried on by the same Method with the former: It was therefore again put in Practice; but the Conduct of it was chiefly left to chosen Men, whose Voices were louder and stronger than those of the other Sex. And upon this Occasion, was first instituted in *London,* that famous Cry of FLOUNDERS. But the Cryers were particularly directed to pronounce the Word *Flaunders,* and not *Flounders.* For, the Country which we now by

[37] Victor Amadeus II (1666–1732), Duke of Savoy (a duchy in the western Alps), was a Protestant ally of England in the War of the Spanish Succession; he was married to Anne Marie d'Orleans, maternal grandmother of Louis XV and heiress presumptive to the Jacobite claim to the British throne from 1714 to 1720.

[38] Short for "Savoy cabbages"—a rough-leaved, hearty variety of the common cabbage.

[39] Swift is here mocking a frequent Whig accusation against the Tories for their attempts to bring about peace with France and end the War of the Spanish Succession. Flanders was viewed by the Dutch Republic ("the *States-General*") as an indispensable barrier against (Catholic) France. There is also punning play here on Flanders lace.

[40] Men of high rank or eminence.

Corruption call *Flanders*, is in its true Orthography spelt *Flaunders*, as may
be obvious to all who read old *English* Books. I say, from hence begun that
thundering Cry, which hath ever since stunned the Ears of all *London*, made
so many Children fall into Fits, and Women miscarry; *Come buy my fresh*
Flaunders, *curious* Flaunders, *charming* Flaunders, *alive, alive, ho;* which last
Words can with no Propriety of Speech, be applied to Fish manifestly dead,
(as I observed before in *Herrings* and *Salmon*) but very justly to ten Provinces,
containing many Millions of living *Christians*. But the Application is still
closer, when we consider that all the People were to be taken like *Fishes*
in a Net; and, by Assistance of the *Pope*, who sets up to be the *Universal
Fisher of Men,*[41] the whole innocent Nation was, according to our common
Expression, to be *laid as flat as a* Flounder.

I REMEMBER, my self, a particular Cryer of *Flounders* in *London,* who
arrived at so much Fame for the Loudness of his Voice, as to have the
Honour of being mentioned, upon that Account, in a Comedy. He hath
disturbed me many a Morning, before he came within Fifty Doors of my
Lodging: And although I were not, in those Days, so fully apprized of the
Designs which our common Enemy had then in Agitation; yet, I know not
how, by a secret Impulse, young as I was, I could not forbear conceiving a
strong Dislike against the Fellow; and often said to my self, this Cry seems
to be forged in the *Jesuites* School: *Alas, poor* England! *I am grievously mistaken, if there be not some* Popish *Plot at the Bottom.*[42] I communicated my
Thoughts to an intimate Friend, who reproached me with being too visionary in my Speculations. But it proved afterwards, that I conjectured right.
And I have since reflected, that if the wicked Faction could have procured
only a Thousand Men, of as strong Lungs as the Fellow I mentioned, none
can tell how terrible the Consequences might have been, not only to these
two Kingdoms, but over all *Europe,* by selling *Flanders* to *France.* And yet
these Cries continue unpunished, both in *London* and *Dublin;* although,
I confess, not with equal Vehemency or Loudness; because the Reason for
contriving this desperate Plot, is, to our great Felicity, wholly ceased.

IT is well known, that the Majority of the *British* House of Commons, in
the last Years of Queen *Anne*'s Reign, were in their Hearts directly opposite to the Earl of *Oxford*'s pernicious Measures; which put him under the
Necessity of bribing them with Sallaries. Whereupon he had again Recourse
to his old Politicks. And accordingly, his Emissaries were very busy in
employing certain artful Women, of no good Life or Conversation, (as it was
fully proved before Justice *Peyton*)[43] to cry that Vegetable commonly called
Sollary,[44] through the Town. These Women differed from the common cryers

---

[41] Based on Jesus's words to his disciples in Matthew 4: 18–19.
  [42] A glance at the infamous Popish Plot of 1678, when the fabricated testimony of Titus
Oates was used as evidence of a Catholic conspiracy to murder Charles II and take back the
throne.
  [43] *A famous Whig Justice in those Times* (Faulkner's note).
  [44] A variant spelling of "celery" during this period.

of that Herb, by some private Mark which I could never learn; but the Matter
was notorious enough, and sufficiently talked of; and about the same Period
was the Cry of *Sollary* brought over into this Kingdom. But since there is
not, at this present, the least Occasion to suspect the Loyalty of our Cryers
upon that Article, I am content that it may still be tolerated.

I SHALL mention but one Cry more, which hath any Reference to Politicks;
but is, indeed, of all others, the most insolent, as well as treasonable, under
our present happy Establishment. I mean that of *Turnups*; not of *Turnips*,
according to the best Orthography, but absolutely *Turnups*. Although
this Cry be of an older Date than some of the preceding Enormities; for
it began soon after the Revolution; yet was it never known to arrive at so
great an Height, as during the Earl of *Oxford*'s Power. Some People, (whom
I take to be private Enemies) are, indeed, as ready as my self to profess their
Disapprobation of this Cry, on Pretence that it began by the Contrivance of
certain old Procuresses, who kept Houses of ill Fame, where lewd Women
met to draw young Men into Vice. And this they pretend to prove by some
Words in the Cry; because, after the Cryer had bawled out *Turnups, ho, buy
my dainty Turnups*, he would sometimes add the two following Verses.

> *Turn up the Mistress, and turn up the Maid,*
> *Turn up the Daughter, and be not afraid.*

THIS, say some political Sophists, plainly shews, that there can be nothing
further meant in so infamous a Cry, than an Invitation to Lewdness; which,
indeed, ought to be severely punished in all well regulated Governments; yet
cannot be fairly interpreted as a Crime of State. But, I hope, we are not so
weak and blind to be deluded at this Time of Day, with such poor Evasions.
I could, if it were Proper, demonstrate the very Time when those two Verses
were composed, and name the Author, who was no other than the famous
Mr. *Swan*, so well known for his Talent at Quibbling; and was as virulent a
Jacobite as any in *England*.[45] Neither could he deny the Fact, when he was
taxed for it in my Presence, by Sir *Harry Dutton-Colt*, and Colonel *Davenport*,
at the *Smyrna* Coffee-House, on the 10th of *June*, 1701.[46] Thus it appears
to a Demonstration, that those Verses were only a Blind to conceal the most
dangerous Designs of the Party; who from the first Years after the happy

---

[45] This same Swan appears as "the famous Punnster" (or "quibbler") in *The Spectator, No. 61*
and is described as a better punster than Horace in Dryden's *Discourse concerning the Original
and Progress of Satire*. He refused to take the oath of allegiance to William and Mary, which
reportedly cost him his fellowship at Cambridge.

[46] Sir Henry Dutton Colt was a Whig baronet and court flunkey who was defeated in the
1710 Tory landslide; he is the subject of a satiric verse by Swift. The Smyrna Coffeehouse was
once a favorite meeting place of the Scriblerus Club in London but by this time had become a
Jacobite resort. The 10th of June was the birthday of the Old Pretender and was commemo-
rated by Jacobites with street and public-house celebrations.

Revolution, used a Cant-way of talking[47] in their Clubs, after this Manner: *We hope to see the Cards shuffled once more, and another King* TURNUP *Trump:* And, *When shall we meet over a Dish of* TURNUPS? The same Term of Art was used in their Plots against the Government, and in their treasonable Letters writ in Cyphers, and decyphered by the famous Dr. *Wallis,* as you may read in the Trials of those Times.[48] This I thought fit to set forth at large, and in so clear a Light; because the *Scotch* and *French* Authors have given a very different Account of the Word TURNUP; but whether out of Ignorance or Partiality, I shall not decree; because, I am sure the Reader is convinced by my Discovery. It is to be observed, that this Cry was sung in a particular Manner, by Fellows in Disguise, to give Notice where those Traytors were to meet, in order to concert their villainous Designs.

I HAVE no more to add upon this Article, than an humble Proposal, that those who cry this Root at present in our Streets of *Dublin,* may be compelled by the Justices of the Peace, to pronounce *Turnip,* and not *Turnup;* for, I am afraid, we have still too many Snakes in our Bosom; and it would be well if their Cellars were sometimes searched, when the Owners least expect it; for I am not out of Fear, that *latet anguis in Herba.*[49]

THUS, we are zealous in Matters of small Moment, while we neglect those of the highest Importance. I have already made it manifest, that all these Cries were contrived in the *worst of Times,* under the Ministry of that desperate Statesman, *Robert,* late Earl of *Oxford;* and for that very Reason, ought to be rejected with Horror, as begun in the Reign of *Jacobites,* and may well be numbered among the Rags of *Popery* and *Treason:* Or if it be thought proper, that these Cries must continue, surely they ought to be only trusted in the Hands of *true Protestants* who have given Security to the Government.[50]

---

[47]The secret language or jargon of a particular group (often used in relation to thieves, gypsies, etc.).

[48]John Wallis (1616–1703), Savilian Professor of Geometry at Oxford, was a founding member of the Royal Society; he decoded Royalist ciphers for the Parliamentary side during the English Civil War and was later employed to decipher encoded documents for the royal court.

[49]"A snake lurks in the grass." Virgil, *Eclogue III,* 93; proverbial phrase signifying danger or deception.

[50]The London edition of this work contains a final paragraph that contends that the numerous signs around town of "King George the Second" and the cipher "G.R.II" are meant to insinuate that King George is "only a Kind of second King, or Viceroy, till the Pretender shall come over and seize the Kingdom."

TO the HONOURABLE House of COMMONS, &C.

The humble PETITION of the Footmen in and about the City of DUBLIN

Written in the Year 1732

One of a number of Swift pieces that make use of speakers from the lower classes, this tract is perhaps most reminiscent of his poem, The Humble Petition of Frances Harris *(1701), which likewise exploits the satiric potential in humble members of Irish society appealing to the highest authorities in the land for redress of grievances. The Footmen's Petition takes aim at one of Swift's favorite targets, the changing fashions in society and the fops who follow them. In its play upon the close resemblance between original and imitation, hence the extreme difficulty of distinguishing between the two, it echoes a tactic used by Swift in his comments on* "true" *versus* "false" *astrologers in* "Predictions for the Year 1708" from The Bickerstaff Papers, *and by the Earl of Rochester in* Doctor Bendo's Bill *(c. 1675), which confounds the distinction between the "true" doctor and the mountebank.*

* * *

Humbly Sheweth,

That your *Petitioners* are a great and numerous *Society,* endowed with several Privileges, Time out of Mind.

That certain *lewd, idle,* and *disorderly* Persons, for several Months past, as it is notoriously known, have been daily seen in the publick Walks of this City, habited sometimes in *Green Coats,* and sometimes *laced,* with long *Oaken Cudgels* in their Hands, and without Swords; in hopes to procure Favour, by that Advantage, with a great Number of Ladies who frequent those Walks; pretending and giving themselves out to be true genuine *Irish Footmen.* Whereas they can be proved to be no better than common *Toupees;*[1] as a judicious Eye may soon discover, by their *awkward, clumsy, ungenteel* Gait,

---

[1]A note to *An Examination of Certain Abuses…in Dublin* explains that "Toupees" are "*A new Name for a modern Periwig, and for its owner, now in Fashion.*" Periwigs were wigs formerly worn as fashionable headdresses.

and Behaviour; by their Unskilfulness in Dress, even with the Advantage
of wearing our Habits; by their ill-favoured Countenances; with an Air of
Impudence and *Dullness* peculiar to the rest of their Brethren: Who have
not yet arrived at that transcendent Pitch of Assurance. Although, it may be
justly apprehended, that they will do so in time, if these *Counterfeits* shall
happen to succeed in their evil Design, of passing for *real Footmen*, thereby
to render themselves more amiable to the Ladies.[2]

YOUR *Petitioners* do further alledge; that many of the said *Counterfeits*,
upon a strict Examination, have been found in the very Act of *strutting*,
staring, *swearing*, *swaggering*, in a Manner that plainly shewed their best
Endeavours to imitate us. Wherein, although they did not succeed; yet by
their ignorant and ungainly Way of copying our Graces, the utmost Indignity
was endeavoured to be cast upon our whole Profession.

YOUR *Petitioners* do therefore make it their humble Request, that this
Honourable House (to many of whom your *Petitioners* are nearly *allied*)[3] will
please to take this Grievance into your most serious Consideration: Humbly
submitting, whether it would not be proper, that certain *Officers* might,
at the Publick Charge, be employed to search for, and discover all such
Counterfeit Footmen, and carry them before the next *Justice* of Peace; by
whose Warrant, upon the first Conviction, they should be stripped of their
Coats and *Oaken* Ornaments, and be set two Hours in the Stocks.[4] Upon the
second Conviction, besides stripping, be set six Hours in the Stocks, with a
Paper pinned on their Breast, signifying their Crime, in large Capital Letters,
and in the following Words. *A. B.* commonly called *A. B.* Esq; a *Toupee*, and
a notorious *Impostor*, who presumed to personate a *true Irish Footman*.

AND for any further Offence, the said *Toupee* shall be committed to
Bridewell,[5] whipped three Times, forced to hard Labour for a Month, and
not to be set at Liberty, till he shall have given sufficient Security for his
good Behaviour.

YOUR *Honours* will please to observe, with what Lenity we propose to
treat these enormous Offenders, who have already brought such a Scandal
on our *Honourable Calling*, that several well-meaning People have mistaken
them to be of our *Fraternity*; in Diminution to that Credit and Dignity
wherewith we have supported our Station, as we always did, in the *worst of*

---

[2] In "Directions to the Footman" from *Directions to Servants* (pub. 1745), the Swiftian
persona tells the footman, "you are the fine Gentleman of the Family, with whom all the
Maids are in Love. You are sometimes a Pattern of Dress to your Master, and sometimes he
is to you."

[3] A dig at the low breeding of many members of the House of Commons, consistent with
their portrayal in Swift's verse, *A Character...of the Legion Club*; see, e.g., the depiction of Sir
Thomas Prendergast as "Worthy Offspring of a Shoeboy" and a "Footman" (ll. 68–69).

[4] An instrument of punishment made of two planks framed between posts, set edgewise one
over the other, the upper plank being capable of sliding up and down, with holes at the edges
of the planks that were used to confine the wrists and ankles.

[5] A house of correction, located in James Street, where prostitutes, vagrants, and other lesser
offenders were confined.

Times.[6] And we further beg Leave to remark, that this was manifestly done with a *seditious* Design, to render us less capable of serving the *Publick* in any great Employments, as several of our *Fraternity,* as well as our *Ancestors* have done.

WE do therefore, humbly implore *your Honours* to give necessary Orders for our Relief, in this present Exigency, and your *Petitioners* (as in Duty bound) shall ever pray, *&c.*

Dublin,
1732.

---

[6] A cant phrase used by Whigs to designate the period of the Tory ministry (1710–14). Its use here suggests that this piece is intended as a political satire along the lines of *An Examination of Certain Abuses... in the City of Dublin,* which was written in the same year.

REASONS humbly offered to the PARLIAMENT of *IRELAND,*

for repealing the SACRAMENTAL TEST, in favour of the CATHOLICKS

Written in the Year 1733

A staunch defender of the Sacramental Test Act, which required officeholders to take the sacraments according to the rites of the Anglican Church, Swift was moved to write this piece soon after the Lord-Lieutenant of Ireland, Lionel Sackville, 1st Duke of Dorset, indicated his support for legislation that would repeal the Test Act at the opening of the new session of Parliament in October 1733. This work makes the case for maintaining the Test by emphasizing the need to preserve an established national religion and by reminding readers of the role the Dissenters played during the English Civil Wars, which Swift saw as having continuing relevance for their current views. While primarily an ironic tract, Reasons humbly offered *features a Catholic persona who puts forward serious and plausible arguments for the proposition that it is not the Dissenters but the Roman Catholics who deserve to be the beneficiaries of a repeal of the Test Act, given the Catholics' resistance to the Puritan revolutionaries of the previous century and their demonstrated loyalty (then and now) to the Crown. In the course of making its argument, this tract presents something almost never seen in Protestant texts of the period: an account that acknowledges the Catholic view of Irish history in several important regards, and that convincingly refutes the charges regularly directed against the Catholics in contemporary Protestant histories. Copy-text:* Works, *ed. Faulkner (1746), collated with the edition of 1752.*

* * *

IT is well known, that the first Conquerors of this Kingdom were *English Catholicks,* Subjects to *English Catholick* Kings, from whom, by their Valour and Success, they obtained large Portions of Land given them as a Reward for their many Victories over the *Irish:* To which Merit our *Brethren* the Dissenters of any Denomination whatsoever, have not the least Pretensions.

It is confessed, that the Posterity of those first victorious *Catholicks* were often forced to rise in their own Defence, against new Colonies from *England,* who treated them like mere native *Irish,* with innumerable Oppressions; depriving them of their Lands, and driving them by Force of Arms into the most desolate Parts of the Kingdom; until in the next Generation, the Children of these Tyrants were used in the same Manner by the new *English* Adventurers, which Practice continued for many Centuries. But it is agreed on all Hands, that no Insurrections were ever made, except after great Oppressions by fresh Invaders: Whereas all the Rebellions of *Puritans, Presbyterians, Independents,* and other Sectaries,[1] constantly began before any Provocations were given, except that they were not suffered to change the Government in Church and State, and seize both into their own Hands; which, however, at last they did, with the Murder of their King, and of many thousands of his best Subjects.[2]

The *Catholicks* were always Defenders of Monarchy, as constituted in these Kingdoms; whereas our *Brethren* the *Dissenters* were always Republicans both in Principle and Practice.

It is well known, that all the *Catholicks* of these Kingdoms, both Priests and Laity, are true *Whigs* in the best and most proper Sense of the Word; bearing as well in their Hearts, as in their outward Profession, an entire Loyalty to the Royal House of *Hanover,* in the Person and Posterity of *George* II. against the Pretender, and all his Adherents:[3] To which they think themselves bound in Gratitude as well as Conscience, by the Lenity where-with they have been treated since the Death of Queen *Anne,* so different from what they suffered in the four last Years of that Princess, during the Administration of that *wicked* Minister, the Earl of *Oxford.*[4]

The *Catholicks* of this Kingdom humbly hope, that they have at least as fair a Title as any of their *Brother* Dissenters, to the Appellation of *Protestants.* They have always *protested* against the selling, dethroning, or murdering their Kings; against the Usurpations and Avarice of the *Court of Rome*; against *Deism, Atheism, Socinianism, Quakerism, Muggletonianism, Fanaticism, Brownism,*[5] as well as against all *Jews, Turks, Infidels,* and *Hereticks.* Whereas

---

[1] Members of any schismatic religious sect; in this case all factions of the English Protestant Dissenters.

[2] Refers to the execution of King Charles I by the Puritans on January 30, 1649 and their elimination of many of his supporters to expedite the end of monarchical government.

[3] Against the Catholic James Francis Edward Stuart, son of the deposed James II, and his followers (known as Jacobites).

[4] The characterization here of Robert Harley (1st Earl of Oxford) is ironic, though it is true that the Catholics suffered greatly under the penal statutes enacted in Queen Anne's reign.

[5] Listed here are religious beliefs opposed to the tenets of the Episcopal establishment. Deism is a religion based on reason that rejects all supernatural manifestations such as Christian mysteries and miracles. Socinianism, which stresses the importance of man's reason in interpreting religious matters, rejects the notion of Original Sin and denies both the tenets of the Trinity and the divinity of Christ. Muggletonianism was a small millennial sect, an outgrowth of seventeenth-century Puritanism, which rejected the need for external religious ceremonies, emphasizing instead divine inner visions and the imminent Second Coming of Christ.

the Title of *Protestants,* assumed by the whole Herd of Dissenters, (except our-selves) dependeth entirely upon their *protesting against Archbishops, Bishops, Deans, and Chapters, with their Revenues; and the whole Hierarchy;* which are the very Expressions used in *The Solemn League and Covenant,*[6] where the Word *Popery* is only mentioned *ad invidiam;*[7] because the *Catholicks* agree with the episcopal Church in those Fundamentals.

Although the *Catholicks* cannot deny, that in the great Rebellion against King *Charles* I. more Soldiers of their Religion were in the Parliament Army, than in his Majesty's Troops; and that many Jesuits and Friars went about, in the Disguise of *Presbyterian* and *Independent* Ministers, to preach up Rebellion, as the best Historians of those Times inform us; yet the Bulk of *Catholicks* in both Kingdoms preserved their Loyalty entire.

The *Catholicks* have some Reason to think it a little hard, when their Enemies will not please to distinguish between the Rebellious Riot com-mitted by that brutal Ruffian, Sir *Phelim O Neal,* with his tumultuous Crew of Rabble; and the Forces raised afterwards by the *Catholick* Lords and Gentlemen of the *English* Pale, in Defence of the King, after the *English* Rebellion began.[8] It is well known, that his Majesty's Affairs were in great Distraction some Time before, by an Invasion of the *Covenanting, Scottish, Kirk Rebels,* and by the base Terms the King was forced to accept, that they might be kept in Quiet, at a juncture when he was every Hour threatned at Home by that Fanatick Party, which soon after set all in a Flame.[9] And, if the *Catholick* Army in *Ireland* fought for their King against the Forces sent out by the Parliament, then in actual Rebellion against him, what Person

---

Brownism was a religious sect founded by the Puritan preacher Robert Browne (1550–1633), who (at least during the first half of his life) fiercely opposed episcopacy and articulated beliefs that became the basis of Congregationalism. "Fanaticism" was Swift's usual term for Puritanism, and for the religious zealotry and irrational enthusiasm he associated with it.

[6] An agreement drawn up in 1643 between the Scottish (Presbyterian) Covenanters and the English Parliamentarians, whereby the Scots pledged military support to the latter in their fight against royalist forces (especially newly recruited Irish Catholics), in exchange for the preservation of the reformed religion in Scotland, the reformation of the church in England along Scottish Presbyterian lines, and the extirpation of popery.

[7] *Lit.,* [as an argument directed] to envy; an appeal to base passions and prejudices.

[8] Sir Phelim O'Neill (c. 1603–53) was from an old Gaelic family of landowners and an M.P. for Dungannon when he became leader of the Catholic forces in the North that began an uprising in October 1641 against Ulster Protestant settlers, putatively in support of Charles I and his royalist forces in their struggle against the English Puritan rebels. In later commentar-ies, O'Neill was regularly blamed for the atrocities that occurred against the Protestant set-tlers in the early weeks of the uprising. The speaker here is eager to distance the actions of the Catholic gentry in the English Pale from the brutal behavior of the Gaelic lords in the north, as a way of countering the highly sensationalized and inflammatory descriptions by English and Anglo-Irish writers of what happened to Protestants during the rebellion, which became a staple of anti-Catholic propaganda; see, e.g., Sir John Temple's *History of the Irish Rebellion* (1644).

[9] There were four Scottish invasions of England between 1640 and 1651. In the summer of 1640 Scottish forces defeated Charles's army in the north of England and seized Newcastle and Durham.

of loyal Principles can be so partial to deny, that they did their Duty, by joining with the Marquis of *Ormond,* and other Commanders, who bore their Commissions from the King?[10] For which, great Numbers of them lost their Lives, and forfeited their Estates; a great Part of the latter being now possessed by many Descendants from those very Men who had drawn their Swords in the Service of that rebellious Parliament which cut off his Head, and destroyed Monarchy.[11] And what is more amazing, although the same Persons, when the *Irish* were intirely subdued, continued in Power under the *Rump;*[12] were chief Confidents, and faithful Subjects to *Cromwell,* yet being wise enough to foresee a *Restoration,* they seized the Forts and Castles here, out of the Hands of their *old Brethren in Rebellion,* for the Service of the King; just saving the Tide, and putting in a Stock of Merit, sufficient not only to preserve the Lands which the *Catholicks* lost by their Loyalty; but likewise to preserve their Civil and Military Employments, or be higher advanced.

Those Insurrections wherewith the *Catholicks* are charged, from the Beginning of the Seventeenth Century to the great *English* Rebellion, were occasioned by many Oppressions they lay under. They had no Intention to introduce a *new* Religion, but to enjoy the Liberty of preserving the *old;* the very same which their Ancestors professed from the Time that *Christianity* was first introduced into this Island, which was by *Catholicks;* but whether mingled with Corruptions, as some pretend, doth not belong to the Question. They had no Design to change the Government; they never attempted to fight against, to imprison, to betray, to sell, to bring to a Tryal, or to murder their King. The Schismaticks acted by a Spirit directly contrary; they united in a *Solemn League and Covenant,* to alter the whole System of Spiritual Government, established in all Christian Nations, and of Apostolick Institution; concluding the Tragedy with the Murder of the King in cold Blood, and upon mature Deliberation; at the same Time changing the Monarchy into a Commonwealth.

The *Catholicks* of *Ireland,* in the great Rebellion, lost their Estates for fighting in Defence of their King. The Schismaticks, who cut off the Father's Head, forced the Son to fly for his Life, and overturned the whole ancient Frame of Government, Religious and Civil; obtained Grants of those very Estates which the *Catholicks* lost in Defence of the ancient Constitution, many of which Estates are at this Day possessed by the Posterity of those

---

[10] James Butler, 1st Duke of Ormonde (1610–88) was from an Old English family in Ireland with strong Catholic ties, though he himself was raised a Protestant. Based in Dublin, he commanded the royalist forces in Ireland with a direct commission from the king, eventually becoming Lord-Lieutenant of Ireland.

[11] Refers to the widespread confiscations of Catholic-owned lands during Cromwell's rule and their transfer into Protestant hands, a situation reinforced by subsequent penal laws restricting the property rights of Irish Catholics.

[12] The remnant of Parliament that constituted itself as a high court of justice to try the king. After finding him guilty and ordering his execution, the Rump Parliament ruled England from 1649 to 1653, when Cromwell took over as Lord Protector.

Schismaticks: And thus they gained by the *Rebellion,* what the *Catholicks* lost by their *Loyalty.*

We allow the *Catholicks* to be *Brethren* of the Dissenters; some People, indeed, (which we cannot allow) would have them to be our Children, because *we* both dissent from the Church established, and both agree in abolishing this persecuting Sacramental Test; by which *negative Discouragement* we are both rendered incapable of Civil and Military Employments. However, we cannot but wonder at the bold Familiarity of these Schismaticks, in calling the Members of the National Church their *Brethren* and *Fellow-Protestants.* It is true, that all these Sects (except the *Catholicks*) are *Brethren* to each other in Faction, Ignorance, Iniquity, Perverseness, Pride, and (if we except the *Quakers*) in Rebellion. But, how the Churchmen can be styled their *Fellow Protestants,* we cannot comprehend. Because, when the whole *Babel* of Sectaries joined against the Church, the King, and the Nobility, for twenty Years, in a MATCH AT FOOT-BALL; where the Proverb expressly tells us, that *All are* FELLOWS;[13] while the three Kingdoms were tossed to and fro, the Churches, and Cities, and Royal Palaces, shattered to Pieces, by their *Balls,* their *Buffets,* and their *Kicks;* the Victors would allow no more FELLOWS AT FOOT-BALL; but murdered, sequestered, plundered, deprived, banished to the Plantations, or enslaved all their Opposers who had *lost the Game.*

It is said the World is governed by *Opinion;* and Politicians assure us, that all Power is founded thereupon. Wherefore, as all human Creatures are fond to Distraction of their own Opinions; and so much the more, as those Opinions are absurd, ridiculous, or of little Moment; it must follow, that they are equally fond of Power. But no Opinions are maintained with so much Obstinacy as those in Religion, especially by such Zealots who never bore the least Regard to Religion, Conscience, Honour, Justice, Truth, Mercy, or common Morality, farther than in outward Appearance; under the Mask of Hypocrisy, to promote their diabolical Designs. And, therefore, Bishop *Burnet,* one of their Oracles, tells us honestly, that the *Saints* of those Fanatick Times, pronounced themselves above Morality, which they reckoned among *beggarly Elements;* but the Meaning of those two last Words thus applied, we confess to be above our Understanding.[14]

---

[13] Swift probably has in mind here the Latin proverb (included in Erasmus's *Adages*), "Ne Hercules contra duos": "Not even Hercules can take on two opponents"; which was associated with the maxim, "two to one are odds at football," the point being that not Hercules himself could resist such odds.

[14] Gilbert Burnet (1643–1715), Bishop of Salisbury, was a political writer and author of *History of His Own Times,* whose staunch Whig politics and Low Church sentiments made him an object of Swift's abiding dislike. The quoted phrase is from Galatians 4:9, where St. Paul castigates the Galatians for remaining in bondage to "weak and beggarly elements" even after they have come to know God (i.e., for clinging to Old Testament observances and thus preferring the letter to the spirit of the law). Burnet cites the phrase in this generally accepted way in his *History of the Reformation of the Church of England* and *An Exposition of the Thirty-Nine Articles of the Church of England.* Swift may be misremembering Burnet's exact words

Among those Kingdoms and States which first embraced the Reformation, *England* appeareth to have received it in the most regular Way; where it was introduced in a peaceable Manner, by the supreme Power of a King,[15] and the three Estates in Parliament; to which, as the highest legislative Authority, all Subjects are bound passively to submit. Neither was there much Blood shed on so great a Change of Religion. But a considerable Number of Lords, and other Persons of Quality through the Kingdom still continued in their old Faith, and were, notwithstanding their Difference in Religion, employed in Offices Civil as well as Military, more or less in every Reign, until the Test Act in the Time of King *Charles* II.[16] However, from the Time of the Reformation, the Number of *Catholicks* gradually and considerably lessened: So that in the Reign of King *Charles* I. *England* became, in a great Degree, a Protestant Kingdom, without taking the Sectaries into the Number; the Legality whereof, with respect to human Laws, the *Catholicks* never disputed: But the *Puritans,* and other Schismaticks, without the least Pretence to any such Authority, by an open Rebellion, destroyed that legal Reformation, as we observed before, murdered their King, and changed the Monarchy into a Republick. It is therefore not to be wondered at, if the *Catholicks,* in such a *Babel* of Religions, chose to adhere to their own Faith left them by their Ancestors, rather than seek for a better among a Rabble of hypocritical, rebellious, deluding Knaves, or deluded Enthusiasts.

We repeat once more, that if a national Religion be changed, by the supreme Legislative Power, we cannot dispute the human Legality of such a Change. But we humbly conceive, that if any considerable Party of Men, which differs from an Establishment, either old or new, can deserve Liberty of Conscience, it ought to consist of those, who, for want of Conviction, or of a right Understanding the Merits of each Cause, conceive themselves bound in Conscience to adhere to the Religion of their Ancestors; because they are of all others least likely to be Authors of Innovations, either in Church or State.

On the other Side: If the Reformation of Religion be founded upon Rebellion against the King, without whose Consent, by the Nature of our Constitution, no Law can pass: If this Reformation be introduced by only one of the three Estates, I mean the Commons, and not by one half even of those Commons, and this by the Assistance of a Rebel Army:[17] Again, if this Reformation were carried on by the Exclusion of Nobles, both Lay and Spiritual, (who constitute the two other Parts of the three Estates) by the

---

here or else deliberately misinterpreting them so as to place him (along with the Dissenting sects) in a dubious light.

[15] Henry VIII, in 1534.

[16] The Test Act of 1673 effectively excluded Catholics from public office by requiring all such officeholders to renounce belief in transubstantiation and to take the sacraments according to the rites of the Anglican church.

[17] Refers to the fact that many M.P.s were prevented by the army from entering parliament for the trial of Charles I, leaving only a group of Cromwell loyalists in charge of deciding the fate of the king (and, by extension, of the nation).

Murder of their King, and by abolishing the whole System of Government; the *Catholicks* cannot see why the Successors of those Schismaticks, who are universally accused by all Parties except themselves, and a few infamous Abettors, for still retaining the same Principles in Religion and Government, under which their Predecessors acted, should pretend to a better Share of Civil or Military Trust, Profit and Power, than the *Catholicks,* who, during all that Period of twenty Years, were continually persecuted with the utmost Severity, merely on account of their Loyalty and constant Adherence to Kingly Power.

We now come to those Arguments for repealing the Sacramental Test, which equally affect the *Catholicks,* and their Brethren the Dissenters.

First, We agree with our Fellow-Dissenters; that *Persecution, merely for Conscience Sake, is against the Genius of the Gospel.*[18] And so likewise is *any Law for depriving Men of their natural and civil Rights which they claim as Men.* We are also ready enough to allow, that *the smallest negative Discouragements for Uniformity's Sake are so many Persecutions.* Because, it cannot be denied, that the Scratch of a Pin is in some Degree a real Wound, as much as a Stab through the Heart. In like Manner, an Incapacity by Law for any Man to be made a Judge, a Colonel, or Justice of the Peace, *merely on a Point of Conscience, is a negative Discouragement,* and consequently a real Persecution: For, in this Case, the Author of the Pamphlet quoted in the Margin, puts a very pertinent and powerful Question: That, *If God be the sole Lord of the Conscience, why should the Rights of Conscience be subject to human Jurisdiction?* Now to apply this to the *Catholicks*: The Belief of Transubstantiation *is a Matter purely of Religion and Conscience, which doth not affect the political Interest of Society as such. Therefore, Why should the Rights of Conscience, whereof* GOD *is the sole Lord, be subject to human Jurisdiction?* And why should GOD be deprived of this Right over a *Catholick's* Conscience any more than over that of any other Dissenter?[19]

And whereas another Author among our Brethren the Dissenters, hath very justly complained, that by this persecuting Test Act, great Numbers of *true Protestants* have been forced to leave the Kingdom, and fly to the Plantations, rather than stay here BRANDED with an Incapacity for Civil and Military Employments; we do affirm, that the *Catholicks* can bring many more Instances of the same Kind; some thousands of their Religion having been forced, by the Sacramental Test, to retire into other Countries, rather

---

[18] This statement and the other italicized ones in this paragraph are taken from the pamphlet, *Reasons for the Repeal of the Sacramental Test* (1733), written by the prominent Irish Presbyterian minister, John Abernethy (1680–1740), a liberal thinker known as "the father of non-subscription."

[19] Swift's own view of individual conscience is evident from his sermon, *On the Testimony of Conscience*, which distinguishes between private belief and public proselytizing, and from his tract, *Some Thoughts on Free-Thinking*, which states that if men "keep their thoughts within their own breasts, they can be of no consequence, further than to themselves. If they publish them to the world, they ought to be answerable for the effects their thoughts produce upon others."

than live here under the Incapacity of wearing Swords, sitting in Parliament, and getting that Share of Power and Profit which belongs to them as *Fellow Christians,* whereof they are deprived *merely upon Account of Conscience, which would not allow them to take the Sacrament after the Manner prescribed in the Liturgy.* Hence it clearly follows, in the Words of the same Author, That, *if we* Catholicks *are uncapable of Employments, we are punished for our Dissent,* that is, *for our Conscience, which wholly turns upon political Considerations.*

The *Catholicks* are willing to acknowledge the King's Supremacy, whenever their Brethren the Dissenters shall please to shew them an Example.

Further, the *Catholicks,* whenever their Religion shall come to be the national established Faith, are willing to undergo the same *Test* offered by the Author already quoted. His Words are these: *To end this Debate, by putting it upon a Foot, which, I hope, will appear to every impartial Person a fair and equitable one; we* Catholicks *propose, with Submission to the proper Judges, that effectual Security be taken against Persecution, by obliging all who are admitted into Places of Power and Trust, whatever their religious Profession be, in the most solemn Manner, to disclaim Persecuting Principles.* It is hoped the Publick will take Notice of these Words, *Whatever their religious Profession be;* which plainly includes the *Catholicks;* and for which we return Thanks to *our Dissenting Brethren.*

And, whereas it is objected by those of the established Church, that, if the Schismaticks and Fanaticks were once put into a Capacity of professing Civil and Military Employments; they would never be at Ease, until they had raised their own Way of Worship into the National Religion, through all his Majesty's Dominions, equal with the *true orthodox Scottish Kirk;* which, when they had once brought to pass, they would no more allow Liberty of Conscience to Episcopal Dissenters, than they did in the Time of the great *English* Rebellion, in the succeeding Fanatick Anarchy, until the King was restored. There is another very learned schismatical Pamphleteer, who, in Answer to a malignant Libel, called, *The Presbyterians Plea of Merit, &c.* clearly wipes off this Aspersion; by assuring all Episcopal Protestants of the present Church, upon his own Word, and to his own Knowledge, that our Brethren the Dissenters will never offer at such an Attempt.[20] In like Manner, the *Catholicks,* when legally required, will openly declare, *upon their Words and Honours,* that as soon as their *negative Discouragements* and their *Persecutions* shall be removed by repealing the Sacramental Test, they will leave it entirely to the Merits of the Cause, whether the Kingdom shall think fit to make their Faith the established Religion, or not.

And again, Whereas our *Presbyterian* Brethren, in many of their Pamphlets, take much Offence, that the great Rebellion in *England,* the Murder of the King, with the entire Change of Religion and Government, are perpetually objected against them both in and out of Season, by our common Enemy, the

---

[20] A reference to the pamphlet, *Vindication of the Protestant Dissenters;* the tract it was answering, *The Presbyterians Plea of Merit* (1733), was written by Swift himself.

present Conformists: We do declare, in the Defence of our said Brethren, that the Reproach aforesaid is *an old worn-out threadbare Cant,* which they always disdained to answer: And I very well remember, that, having once told a certain Conformist, how much I wondered to hear him and his Tribe, dwelling perpetually on so beaten a Subject; he was pleased to divert the Discourse with a foolish Story, which I cannot forbear telling to his Disgrace. He said, there was a Clergyman in *Yorkshire,* who, for fifteen Years together, preached every *Sunday* against Drunkenness: Whereat, the Parishioners being much offended, complained to the Archbishop; who, having sent for the Clergyman, and severely reprimanded him, the Minister had no better an Answer, than by confessing the Fact; adding, that all the Parish were Drunkards; that he desired to reclaim them from one Vice, before he would begin upon another; and, since they still continued to be as great Drunkards as before, he resolved to go on, except his Grace would please to forbid him.

We are very sensible, how heavy an Accusation lyeth upon the *Catholicks* of *Ireland;* that some Years before King *Charles* II. was restored, when theirs and the King's Forces were entirely reduced, and the Kingdom declared by the Rump to be settled; after all his Majesty's Generals were forced to fly to *France,* or other Countries, the Heads of the said *Catholicks,* who remained here in an enslaved Condition, joined to send an Invitation to the Duke of *Lorrain;* engaging, upon his appearing here with his Forces, to deliver up the whole Island to his Power, and declare him their Sovereign;[21] which, after the Restoration, was proved against them by Dean *Boyle,* since Primate, who produced the very original Instrument at the Board.[22] The *Catholicks* freely acknowledge the Fact to be true; and, at the same Time, appeal to all the World, whether a wiser, a better, a more honourable, or a more justifiable Project could have been thought of. They were then reduced to Slavery and Beggary by the *English* Rebels, many thousands of them murdered, the rest deprived of their Estates, and driven to live on a small Pittance in the Wilds of *Connaught;*[23] at a Time, when either the *Rump* or *Cromwell* absolutely governed the three Kingdoms. And the Question will turn upon this, Whether the *Catholicks,* deprived of all their Possessions, governed with a Rod of Iron, and in utter Despair of ever seeing the Monarchy restored, for the Preservation of which they had suffered so much, were to be blamed for calling in a foreign Prince of their own Religion, who had a considerable Army to support them; rather than submit to so infamous an Usurper as *Cromwell,*

---

[21] In 1650 a group of Irish prelates offered the protectorate of Ireland to Charles IV (sometimes designated Charles III), Duke of Lorraine (1604–75). For three years thereafter negotiations between Irish Catholics and the Duke were carried on in Brussels, Paris, and Galway, at times under the direction of the Duke of Ormonde. The sole results of these talks were occasional monetary grants by Charles to assist the Irish loyalists in purchasing arms and ammunition.

[22] Michael Boyle (c. 1609–1702) was Archbishop of Dublin and Armagh and Primate of All Ireland; he also served as Lord Chancellor of Ireland.

[23] The (north)western province of Ireland.

or such a bloody and ignominious Conventicle[24] as the *Rump*. And I have often heard, not only our Friends the Dissenters, but even our common Enemy the Conformists, who are conversant in the History of those Times, freely confess, that considering the miserable Situation the *Irish* were then in, they could not have thought of a braver or more virtuous Attempt; by which they might have been Instruments of restoring the lawful Monarch, at least to the Recovery of *England* and *Scotland,* from those Betrayers, and Sellers, and Murderers of his Royal Father.

To conclude, Whereas the last quoted Author complains, very heavily and frequently, of a BRAND that lyes upon them; it is a great Mistake; for the first original BRAND hath long been taken off. Only, we confess, the Scar will probably remain and be visible for ever to those who know the Principles by which they acted, until those Principles shall be openly renounced; else it must continue to all Generations, like the Mark set upon *Cain,* which some Authors say descended to all his Posterity; or, like the *Roman* nose, and *Austrian* Lip, or like the long Bag of Flesh hanging down from the Gills of the People in *Piedmont*.[25] But, as for any *Brands* fixed on Schismaticks for several Years past, they have all been made with *cold Iron;* like Thieves, who, by the BENEFIT OF THE CLERGY, are condemned to be only burned in the Hand; but escape the Pain and the Mark, by being in *Fee* with the JAYLOR. Which Advantage the Schismatical Teachers will never want, who, as we are assured, and of which there is a *very fresh Instance,* have the Souls, and Bodies, and Purses of their People an hundred Times more at their Mercy, than the *Catholick* Priests could ever pretend to.

Therefore, upon the Whole, the *Catholicks* do humbly petition *(without the least Insinuation of Threatening)* that upon this *favourable* Juncture their Incapacity for Civil and Military Employments may be wholly taken off, for the very same Reasons (besides others more cogent) that are now offered by their *Brethren* the *Dissenters.*

And your Petitioners, as in Duty bound, shall ever pray, &c.

Dublin, Nov.
1733.

---

[24]An unauthorized or clandestine meeting, usually for religious purposes; in the sixteenth and seventeenth centuries, the term was used to describe secret assemblies of Protestant Dissenters.

[25]In Piedmont and other northern Italian regions where goiter was common, the villainous characters in religious paintings (as of the Passion) were depicted with a hideous bag of flesh under their chins.

ADVICE TO THE Free-Men of the City of *Dublin* in the Choice of a Member to Represent them in PARLIAMENT

In this 1733 pamphlet, Swift uses the impending election for M.P. between Humphrey French, Mayor of Dublin, and Alderman John Macarell as an occasion to promote the "Irish interest" over the "English interest" in the country, arguing for the inherent incompatibility of holding an elected Irish office while (like Macarell) simultaneously receiving financial rewards from the British Crown. Although the tone of the tract is mild, its message is uncompromising: dependence on Court favor has poisoned the political system in Ireland, producing politicians who routinely betray the interests of their country for personal gain—or even merely for empty promises of future advantage. Swift's strong support of French—which included resurrecting the Drapier on his behalf—was based on his view of the mayor (expressed in a letter to Faulkner) as a "great Patriot" and "an Example to all future Magistrates." French's victory in the election was seen as another political triumph for the Drapier-Dean. Copy-text: Works, ed. Faulkner, 1746.

* * *

Those few Writers, who since the Death of Alderman *Burton,* have employed their Pens in giving Advice to our Citizens how they should proceed in electing a new Representative for the next Sessions, having laid aside their Pens; I have reason to hope, that all true Lovers of their Country in general, and particularly those who have any Regard for the Priviledges and Liberties of this great and ancient City, will think a second and a third time before they come to a final Determination upon what Person they resolve to fix their Choice.

I am told there are only two Persons who set up for Candidates; one is the present Lord Mayor,[1] and the other, a Gentleman, of good Esteem, an Alderman of the City, a Merchant of Reputation, and possess'd of a

---

[1] *Humphry French,* Lord Mayor of *Dublin* for the year 1732–33, was elected to succeed Alderman *Samuel Burton* (Faulkner's note).

considerable Office under the Crown.[2] The Question is, which of these two Persons it will be most for the Advantage of the City to elect? I have but little Acquaintance with either, so that my Inquiries will be very impartial, and drawn only from the general Character and Situation of both.

In order to this, I must offer my Countrymen and Fellow Citizens, some Reasons, why I think they ought to be more than ordinarily careful at this juncture upon whom they bestow their Votes.

To perform this with more Clearness, it may be proper to give you a short State of our unfortunate Country.

We consist of two Parties, I do not mean Popish and Protestant, High and Low Church, Episcopal and Sectarians, Whig and Tory; but of those *English* who happen to be born in this Kingdom (whose Ancestors reduced the whole Nation under the obedience of the *English* Crown,) and the Gentlemen sent from the other Side to possess most of the chief Employments here: This latter Party is very much enlarged and strengthened by the whole Power in the Church, the Law, the Army, the Revenue, and the Civil Administration deposited in their Hands. Although out of political Ends, and to save Appearances, some Employments are still deposited (yet gradually in a smaller Number) to Persons born here: This Proceeding, fortified with good Words and many Promises, is sufficient to flatter and feed the Hopes of Hundreds, who will never be one Farthing the better, as they might easily be convinced, if they were qualifyed to think at all.

Civil Employments of all kinds, have been for several Years past, with great Prudence made precarious, and during Pleasure;[3] by which Means the Possessors are, and must inevitably be, for ever dependent: Yet those very few of any Consequence, which are dealt with so sparing a Hand to Persons born among us, are enough to keep Hope alive in great Numbers who desire to mend their Condition by the Favour of those in Power.

Now, my dear Fellow-Citizens, how is it possible you can conceive, that any Person who holds an Office of some Hundred Pounds a Year, which may be taken from him whenever Power shall think fit, will if he should be chosen a Member for any City, do the least thing when he sits in the House, that he knows or fears may be displeasing to those who gave him or continue him in that Office. Believe me, these are no times to expect such an exalted Degree of Virtue from mortal Men. *Blazing stars* are much more frequently seen than such heroical Worthies. And I could sooner hope to find ten thousand Pounds by digging in my Garden than such a *Phoenix*, by searching among the present Race of Mankind.

I cannot forbear thinking it a very erroneous as well as modern Maxim of Politicks, in the *English* Nation, to take every Opportunity of depressing *Ireland*; whereof an hundred Instances may be produced in Points of the

---

[2] *John Macarrell*, Register to the Barracks, shortly after this date elected to the representation of *Carlingford* (Faulkner's note).

[3] "During Pleasure (of the Crown)"; in other words, dependent on the continued favor of those in power.

highest Importance, and within the Memory of every middle-aged Man; Although many of the greatest Persons among that Party which now prevails, have formerly upon that Article much differed in their Opinion from their present Successors.

But so the Fact stands at present. It is plain, that the Court and Country Party here (I mean in the House of Commons) very seldom agree in any thing but their Loyalty to His present Majesty, their Resolutions to make him and his Viceroy[4] easy in the Government, to the utmost of their Power, under the present Condition of the Kingdom. But the Persons sent from *England*, who (to a Trifle) are possessed of the sole executive Power in all its Branches, with their few Adherents in Possession who were born here, and Hundreds of Expectants, Hopers, and Promissees, put on quite contrary Notions with regard to *Ireland*. They count upon a universal Submission to whatever shall be demanded; wherein they act safely, because none of themselves, except the Candidates, feel the least of our Pressures.

I remember a Person of Distinction some Days ago affirmed in a good deal of mixt Company, and of both Parties; That the Gentry from *England* who now enjoy OUR highest Employments of all kinds, can never be possibly Losers of one Farthing, by the greatest Calamities that can befal this Kingdom, except a Plague that would sweep away a Million of our *Hewers of Wood, and Drawers of Water:*[5] Or an Invasion that would fright our Grandees out of the Kingdom.[6] For this Person argued, that while there was a Penny left in the Treasury, the Civil and Military List must be paid; and that the episcopal Revenues which are usually farmed out at six times below the real Value, could hardly fail. He insisted further, that as Money diminished, the Price of all Necessaries for Life must of Consequence do so too, which would be for the Advantage of all Persons in Employment, as well as of my Lords the Bishops, and to the Ruin of every Body else. Among the Company there wanted not Men in Office, besides one or two Expectants; yet I did not observe any of them disposed to return an Answer: But the Consequences drawn were these; That the great Men in Power sent hither from the other Side, were by no means upon the same Foot with his Majesty's other Subjects of *Ireland*. They had no common Ligament to bind them with us; they suffered not with our Sufferings, and if it were possible for us to have any Cause of Rejoycing, they could not rejoyce with us.

Suppose a Person born in this Kingdom, shall happen by his Services for the *English* Interest, to have an Employment conferred on him worth 400 *l.* a Year; and that he hath likewise an Estate in Land worth 400 *l.* a Year more: Suppose him to sit in Parliament: Then, suppose a Land-Tax to be brought

---

[4] George II and his representative, the Lord-Lieutenant of Ireland.

[5] See Joshua 9:21–27. The phrase was commonly used for the Irish Catholic population, although as a term signifying "slaves" it was at times applied by Swift to Irish Protestants as well.

[6] That is, a Jacobite Rebellion that would cause all persons of high rank or position to flee Ireland.

in of 5*s.* a Pound for ten Years; I tell you how this Gentleman will compute. He has 400 *l.* a Year in Land: The Tax he must pay yearly is 100 *l.* by which in ten Years, he will pay only 1000 *l.* But if he gives his Vote against this Tax, he will lose 4000 *l.* by being turned out of his Employment; together with the Power and Influence he hath, by Virtue or Colour of his Employment; and thus the Ballance will be against him three Thousand Pounds.

I desire, my Fellow-Citizens, you will please to call to mind how many Persons you can vouch for among your Acquaintance, who have so much Virtue and Self-denial, as to lose 400 *l.* a Year for Life; together with the Smiles and Favour of Power, and the Hopes of higher Advancement, meerly out of a generous Love of his Country.

The Contentions of Parties in *England,* are very different from those among us. The Battle there is fought for Power and Riches; and so it is indeed among us: But, whether a great Employment be given to *Tom* or to *Peter,* they were both born in *England,* the Profits are to be spent there. All Employments (except a very few) are bestowed on the Natives: They do not send to *Germany, Holland, Sweden,* or *Denmark,* much less to *Ireland,* for Chancellors, Bishops, Judges, or other Officers. Their Salaries, whether well or ill got, are employed at home; and whatever their Morals or Politicks be, the Nation is not the poorer.

The House of Commons in *England,* have frequently endeavoured to limit the Number of Members who should be allowed to have Employments under the Crown: several Acts have been made to that Purpose, which many wise Men think are not yet effectual enough, and many of them are rendered ineffectual, by leaving the Power of Re-election: Our House of Commons consists, I think, of about three Hundred Members; if one Hundred of these should happen to be made up of Persons already provided for, joined with Expecters, Compliers, easy to be perswaded, such as will give a Vote for a Friend who is in hopes to get something; if they be merry Companions, without Suspicion, of a natural Bashfulness not apt or able to look forwards; if good Words, Smiles, and Caresses, have any Power over them, the larger Part of a second Hundred may be very easily brought in at a most reasonable Rate.

There is an *Englishman* of no long Standing among us, but in an Employment of great Trust, Power, and Profit.[7] This excellent Person did lately publish, at his own Expence, a Pamphlet printed in *England* by Authority, to justify the Bill for a general *Excise,* or Inland Duty, in order to introduce that blessed Scheme among us. What a tender Care must such an *English* Patriot for *Ireland* have of our Interest, if he should condescend to sit in our Parliament. I will bridle my Indignation. However, methinks I long to see that Mortal, who would with Pleasure blow us up all at a Blast: But, he

[7] *Edward Thompson,* Esq., Member of Parliament for *York,* and a Commissioner of the Revenue in *Ireland* (Faulkner's note).

duly receives his Thousand Pounds a Year; makes his Progresses like a King;[8] is received in Pomp at every Town and Village where he travels, and shines in the *English* News-Papers.

I will now apply what I have said to you, my Brethren and Fellow-Citizens. Count upon it, as a Truth next to your Creed, that no one Person in Office, of which he is not Master for Life, whether born here, or in *England,* will ever hazard that Office for the Good of this Country.

One of your Candidates is of this Kind and I believe him to be an honest Gentleman, as the Word *Honest* is generally understood. But he loves his Employment better than he does you, or his Country, or all the Countries upon Earth. Will you contribute and give him City Security, to pay him the Value of his Employment, if it should be taken from him, during his Life, for voting on all Occasions with the honest Country Party in the House; although I much question, whether he would do it, even upon that Condition.

Wherefore, since there are but two Candidates, I intreat you will fix on the present Lord-Mayor. He hath shewn more Virtue, more Activity, more Skill, in one Year's Government of the City, than a Hundred Years can equal. He hath endeavoured, with great Success, to banish Frauds, Corruptions, and all other Abuses from amongst you.[9]

A Dozen such Men in Power, would be able to reform a Kingdom. He hath no Employment under the Crown; nor is likely to get or solicite for any; his Education having not turned him that Way. I will assure for no Man's future Conduct; but he who hath hitherto practised the Rules of Virtue with so much Difficulty, in so great and busy a Station, deserves your Thanks, and the best Returns you can make him; and you, my Brethren, have no other to give him; than that of representing you in Parliament. Tell not me of your Engagements and Promises to another. Your Promises were Sins of Inconsideration at best; and you are bound to repent and annul them. That Gentleman, though with good Reputation, is already engaged on the other Side. He hath 400 *l.* a Year under the Crown, which he is too wise to part with, by sacrificing so good an Establishment to the empty Names of Virtue, and Love of his Country. I can assure you, the *DRAPIER* is in the Interests of the present Lord-Mayor, whatever you may be told to the Contrary. I have lately heard him declare so in publick Company, and offer some of these very Reasons in Defence of his Opinion; although he hath a Regard and Esteem for the other Gentleman, but would not hazard the Good of the City and the Kingdom, for a Compliment.

---

[8] Mr. *Thompson* was presented with his Freedom of several Corporations in *Ireland* (Faulkner's note).

[9] French's reputation for integrity had earned him the appellation of "the Good Lord Mayor" and a formal encomium by the scholars of Trinity College, as well as inspiring a number of poetic tributes including one, "Horace, Book IV, Ode IX. Addressed to Humphry French, Esq.," that was erroneously attributed to Swift.

The Lord-Mayor's Severity to some unfair Dealers, should not turn the honest Men among them against him. Whatever he did, was for the Advantage of those very Trades whose dishonest Members he punished. He hath hitherto been above Temptation to act wrong; and therefore, as Mankind goes, he is the most likely to act right as a Representative of your City, as he constantly did in the Government of it.

A DIALOGUE IN HYBERNIAN STILE BETWEEN A. AND B.; and IRISH ELOQUENCE

The following pieces, which were first printed by Walter Scott in his 1824 edition of Swift's Works, *cannot be dated with any certainty. Because they deal satirically with the practices of spoken language, they are often associated with his* Polite Conversation *(pub. 1738, though written over a period of more than two decades). The* Dialogue *and* Irish Eloquence *take as their object of ridicule the non-standard English of the "planters": those settlers, largely soldiers and adventurers, who "planted" a colony in Ireland out of lands confiscated from the native Catholics as a result of the Cromwellian campaign in Ireland in the mid-seventeenth century. Political, cultural, and class factors would have made this group a particularly fitting target of Swift's satire. We might keep in mind, however, that counterbalancing Swift's censoriousness at violations of linguistic norms was a fascination with the varieties of the spoken and written word—a delight in linguistic diversity evident in his own use of dialectal and colloquial expressions and* jeux d'esprit *composed in Anglo-Latin and Hiberno-English. Full background and contexts for the following pieces are provided in the edition by Alan Bliss; most word definitions can be found in Dolan's* Dictionary of Hiberno-English *(see "Further Reading"). Copytext: Huntington Library Manuscripts HM 14342 and HM 14343. Care has been taken to remain as faithful to the MSS as possible while yet providing a readable text.*

* * *

A. [*Is* not][1] *Them* apples is very good?

B. I am *again* you in that.

A. Lord I was so bodderd[2] tother day with that prating fool Tom!

B. Pray, how does he *get* his health?

A. He's often very *unwell*.

B. [Lord ... He always keeps half a dozen Pet Dogs][3] [I] hear he was a great pet of yours. Where does he live?

---

[1] Crossed out in MS.

[2] Bothered; bewildered or deafened with noise.

[3] Crossed out in MS.

A. Opposite the red Lyon.[4]

B. I think he behaved very ill the last sessions.[5]

A. [Pray, will you give me a *Drink* of your small beer?][6] That's true, but I cannot forbear loving his Father's child: Will you tast a glass of my Ale?

B. No, I thank you; I took a drink of small bear[7] at home before I came here.

A. I always brew with my own Bear:[8] You have a Country-house, are you [a] Planter?

B. Yes, I have planted a great many Oak trees and Ash trees, and some Elm trees round a loough.[9]

A. And a good warrant you have; it is kind Father for you.[10] And what Breakfast do you take in the Country?

B. Why, sometimes Sowins,[11] and sometimes Stirabout,[12] and in summer we have the best Frawhawns[13] in all the County.

A. What kind of Man is your Neighbor, Squire Dolt?

B. Why, a meer Buddogh.[14] He sometimes coshers[15] with me; And once a month I take a Pipe with him, and we shoh it about for an hour together.[16]

A. Well, I'd give a Cow in Connaugh[17] to see you together. I hear he keeps good horses.

B. None but Garrawns,[18] and I have seen him often riding on a Sougawn.[19] In short, he is no better than a Spawlpeen;[20] a perfect Monaghan.[21] When I was there last, we had nothing but a Maddor[22] to drink out of, and the

---

[4] No doubt the name of a tavern.

[5] That is, "sessions of the peace": the periodic sittings of justices of the peace; usually four times a year in a county or borough.

[6] Crossed out in MS.

[7] That is, small beer; beer of a weak or inferior quality.

[8] A type of barley; Swift also uses this term (spelled "Bere") in *Drapier's Letter I.*

[9] "Loch," meaning "lake." There is an obvious pun on the word "planter" here.

[10] That is, "you've got your nature from your father" or "you've inherited that quality from your father"; an Irish idiom.

[11] A type of beer made from husks (produced from milled oats) that ferment after being steeped in water.

[12] Porridge made by stirring oatmeal in boiling water or milk.

[13] Bilberries (from the Irish word *fraochán*).

[14] Peasant; churl.

[15] Dines or feasts; can also mean to take advantage of free room and board or to freely quarter with dependants or kinsmen.

[16] That is, we take turns passing and smoking the pipe; from the Irish *seach*, "a turn or spell, the quantity taken or amount done at a time"; *seach tobac* means "a smoke" (Bliss).

[17] *Lit.*, a cow for sale; *fig.*, the value of a cow.

[18] A small, inferior type of horse indigenous to Ireland and Scotland; a gelding.

[19] A rough saddle made of straw.

[20] A seasonal laborer, hence a low or rough fellow (from the Irish word *spailpín*).

[21] Hiberno-English colloquialism for a clown or fool (*lit.*, a native of County Monaghan).

[22] An English-Irish term designating a square wooden vessel used for drinking (also spelled "mether" or "meadar"). This term also appears in Swift's poem, *A Description of an Irish Feast* (1720).

Devil a Night-gown but a Caddow.[23] Will you go see him when you come into our parts?

A. Not *without* you go with me:

B. Will you lend me your Snuff-box *till* I take a pinch of Snuff?

A. Do you make good Chese and Butter?

B. Yes, when we can get milk; But our Cows will never keep a drop of milk without a Puckawn.[24]

IRISH ELOQUENCE

I hope you will come and take a drink of my Ale. I always brew with my own beare. I was at your Cozen Tom's house in the County of Fermanagh.[25] He has planted a great many oak trees, and elm trees round his lough: And, a good warrent he had; it is kind Father for him. I stayd with him a week. At Breakfast we had sometimes Sowins, and sometimes Stirabout, and sometimes Fraughawns and milk; but his cows [will not][26] would hardly give a drop of milk, for his herd had lost the Puckaun. His neighbor Squire Dolt is a meer Buddough. I'd give a Cow in Canaught you could see him! He keeps none but garrauns, and he rides on a Soogaun, with nothing for his Bridle but Gadd.[27] In short, he is a meer Spawl[p]een. and a perfect Monaghon, and a Munster Crack[28] into the Bargain. Without you saw him on Sunday you would take him for a Brogadeer and a Spaniel.[29] His cook did not know how to draw Butter. We drank Balcan[30] and Whisky out of Maddors. And the Devil a night-goun [we] had but a Caddow. [Pray lend me a lone of your last news paper til I read it over. I could hardly get a drop of milk in the Country for your Cousin Tom's herd had lost the Puckaun.][31] I wonder your Cozen does not learn him better manners. Your cousin desires you will buy him some Cheney Cups.[32] I remember he had a great many; I wonder what is gone with them. I coshered on him for a week [and twice (or) three times a Day we shoh't a Pipe together:][33] He has a fine Haggard of Corn.[34] Miss Molly is his chief Pet. His Lady has been very Unwell. I was sorry that

---

[23] A rough woolen covering such as a blanket or a cloak.

[24] Hiberno-English term for a billy goat.

[25] A county in Ulster.

[26] Crossed out in MS.

[27] A rope made of twisted fibers of tough twigs.

[28] A term that can mean braggart, liar, or crazy person (as in "crack-brain"); Munster is the southwestern province of Ireland.

[29] Possibly "broganeer," or one who speaks with a brogue (i.e., a native Irishman). A "spaniel" is a submissive, cringing, or obsequious person.

[30] Spirits distilled from black oats.

[31] Crossed out in MS.

[32] That is, cups made of China.

[33] Crossed out in MS.

[34] "Haggard" is a term for a stackyard in Ireland and the Isle of Man.

any thing should ayl her Father's child. Pray lend me a loan of your last news-paper, till I read it over. Firing[35] is very dear thereabout. The Turf is drawn two miles in kishes.[36] And they send new rounds from the Mines, nothing comes in the Cleeves but Slack.[37] [We had once a foreroan of Bief, and once a Rump for Dinner][38]

---

[35] The feeding and tending of a fire for cooking.
[36] Large wickerwork baskets, used in Ireland for carrying turf.
[37] "Cleeves" are cliffs; "Slack" is a term for small or refuse coal.
[38] Crossed out in MS.

PART 2

POEMS

The Humble Petition of
Frances Harris

*This poem was written while Swift was in Ireland in 1701 as chaplain to the
2nd Earl of Berkeley, one of the Lords Justices appointed by the government to
substitute in the absence of the Lord-Lieutenant. Chaplaincies to powerful or
aspiring politicians were sought by ambitious clergymen to improve their own
chances for advancement in the church; obviously, then, Swift as Berkeley's chaplain would not be inclined to court anyone as humble as Frances Harris, who
was employed as a waiting woman to Lord Berkeley's daughter, Lady Elizabeth
(the poem's "Lady Betty"). The humor of the poem, thus, rolls out at Harris's
expense, yet Swift's simultaneous empathy toward her is evident in his sensitive
use of this ordinary woman's style of speech.*

* * *

To their Excellencies the LORDS JUSTICES of *IRELAND*.[1]

*The humble Petition of Frances Harris,
Who must starve, and die a Maid if it miscarries.*

Humbly sheweth,[2]
> That I went to warm myself in Lady *Betty*'s Chamber, because I was cold;
> And I had in a Purse Seven Pounds, Four Shillings and Six Pence (besides
>   Farthings) in Money and Gold;[3]
> So, because I had been buying Things for my *Lady* last Night,
> I was resolv'd to tell[4] my Money, to see if it was right.
> Now you must know, because my Trunk has a very bad Lock,
> Therefore all the Money I have, (which, God knows, is a very small Stock,)
> I keep in my Pocket, ty'd about my Middle, next my Smock.

---

[1] "Earl of *Berkeley*, and the Earl of *Galway*" (Faulkner's note). Two or three Lords Justices,
appointed by the Lord-Lieutenant and confirmed by the ministry in London, headed the Irish
administration in Dublin Castle in the absence of the Lord-Lieutenant, who generally resided
in Ireland only during parliamentary sessions.

[2] Mimicking the opening formula of petitions to high authority.

[3] A pound sterling was made up of 20 shillings, the shilling of 12 pennies (pence), and the
penny of 2 half-pence or 4 farthings. At the beginning of the eighteenth century an amount of
the sort mentioned here could be composed of gold coins, both English and continental, for
amounts of 5 shillings and above, silver coins for amounts of 3 pence to 5 shillings, and copper
coins for pence and fractions. Copper was "money" but not legal tender, a point Swift used to
good effect in the Wood's half-pence controversy (see *The Drapier's Letters*).

[4] Count.

So, when I went to put up my Purse, as God would have it, my Smock was
    unript;
And instead of putting it into my Pocket, down it slipt:[5]
10   Then the Bell rung, and I went down to put my *Lady* to Bed;
And, God knows, I thought my Money was as safe as my Maidenhead.
So, when I came up again, I found my Pocket feel very light,
But when I search'd, and miss'd my Purse, *Lord!* I thought I should have
    sunk outright:
Lord! Madam, says *Mary,*[6] how d'ye do? Indeed, said I, never worse:
But pray, *Mary,* can you tell what I have done with my Purse?
Lord help me, said *Mary,* I never stirr'd out of this Place:
Nay, said I, I had it in Lady *Betty*'s chamber, that's a plain Case.
So *Mary* got me to Bed, and cover'd me up warm;
However, she stole away my Garters, that I might do myself no Harm.
20   So, I tumbl'd and toss'd all Night, as you may very well think;
But hardly ever set my Eyes together, or slept a Wink.
So, I was a-dream'd, methought, that we went and searched the Folks round:
And in a corner of Mrs. *Duke*'s Box,[7] ty'd in a Rag, the Money was found.
So, next Morning we told *Whittle,*[8] and he fell a swearing;
Then my Dame *Wadgar*[9] came, and she, you know, is thick of Hearing:
Dame, said I, as loud as I could bawl, do you know what a loss I have had?
Nay, said she, my Lord *Collway*'s[10] folks are all very sad,
For my Lord *Dromedary*[11] comes a *Tuesday* without fail;
Pugh! said I, but that's not the Business that I ail.
30   Says *Cary,*[12] says he, I have been a Servant this five and twenty years, come
    Spring,
And in all the places I lived, I never heard of such a Thing.
Yes, says the Steward, I remember when I was at my Lady *Shrewsbury*'s,
Such a Thing as this happen'd, just about the time of *Gooseberries.*[13]
So I went to the Party suspected, and I found her full of Grief;
(Now you must know, of all Things in the world, I hate a Thief.)
However, I was resolv'd to bring the Discourse slily about;
Mrs. *Dukes,* said I, here's an ugly Accident has happen'd out;

---

[5] In the eighteenth century a "pocket" was a small bag or pouch usually worn inside a garment. Thus to put her purse into her pocket Harris would have to slip it through a slit or rip
in her smock, which she was unable to do if the smock was "unript," so that the purse would
have slid to the floor of the room.

[6] A subordinate servant.

[7] Mrs. Dukes is identified in a subsequent Faulkner note as "A servant, one of the Footmen's
Wives."

[8] "Earl of *Berkeley*'s Valet" (Faulkner's note).

[9] "The old deaf Housekeeper" (Faulkner's note).

[10] "*Galway*" (Faulkner's note). Henri de Massue de Ruvigny, 1st Earl of Galway (1648–1720),
was a French-born military commander who fought under William III in Ireland.

[11] "*Drogheda,* who with the Primate were to succeed the two Earls" (as lords justices)
(Faulkner's note). The references are to Henry Hamilton Moore, 3rd Earl of Drogheda
(c. 1650–1714) and Narcissus March (1638–1713).

[12] "Clerk of the Kitchen" (Faulkner's note).

[13] In gooseberry season, mid-May to about mid-August in Ireland and Britain.

'Tis not that I value the Money three Skips of a Louse;[14]
But the Thing I stand upon, is the Credit of the House;
40   'Tis true, Seven Pounds, Four Shillings, and Six Pence, makes a great Hole in
            my Wages;
Besides, as they say, Service is no Inheritance in these Ages.
Now, Mrs. *Dukes*, you know, and every Body understands,
That tho' 'tis hard to judge, yet Money can't go without Hands.[15]
The *Devil* take me, said she (blessing her self), if ever I saw't!
So she roared like a *Bedlam*,[16] as tho' I had call'd her all to naught:[17]
So you know, what could I say to her any more:
I e'en left her, and came away as wise as I was before.
Well: But then they would have had me gone to the *Cunning-Man*:[18]
No, said I, 'tis the same Thing, the *Chaplain* will be here anon.[19]
50   So the *Chaplain* came in. Now the Servants say he is my Sweet-heart,
Because he's always in my Chamber, and I always take his Part;
So, as the *Devil* would have it, before I was aware, out I blunder'd,
Parson, said I, can you cast a *Nativity*,[20] when a Body's plunder'd?
(Now you must know, he hates to be call'd *Parson* like the *Devil*.)
Truly, says he, Mrs. *Nab*, it might become you to be more civil:
If your Money be gone, as a learned *Divine* says, d'ye see,
You are no *Text* for my handling, so take that from me:
I was never taken for a *Conjuror* before, I'd have you to know:
Lord, said I, don't be angry, I am sure I never thought you so:
60   You know, I honour the Cloth; I design to be a *Parson*'s Wife;
I never took one in *your Coat*[21] for a *Conjuror* in all my Life.
With that, he twisted his *Girdle*[22] at me like a Rope, as who should say,
Now you may go hang yourself for me; and so went away.
Well; I thought I should have swoon'd: *Lord*, said I, what shall I do?
I have lost my *Money*; and I shall lose my *True-love* too.
So, my *Lord* call'd me; *Harry*,[23] said my *Lord*, don't cry,
I'll give something towards thy Loss; and says my *Lady*, so will I.
Oh! but, said I, what if after all, the Chaplain won't *come to?*[24]
For that, he said (an't please your *Excellencies*) I must petition You.

70   The Premisses tenderly considered, I desire your *Excellencies* Protection:
And that I may have a share in next *Sunday*'s Collection:

---

[14] "An usual saying of hers" (Faulkner's note). Also a proverbial saying that appears elsewhere in Swift's poetry.
[15] Playing upon the proverb, "Nothing is stolen without hands."
[16] That is, like a Bedlamite, or an inmate of Bethlehem Hospital in London, an insane asylum.
[17] "As though I had treated her unjustly."
[18] Fortune teller.
[19] Swift, here being equated with a conjurer.
[20] Make a horoscope prediction.
[21] Clerical costume; "cloth."
[22] A belt worn around the waist to secure garments—in this case, the clerical robe.
[23] "A Cant Word [i.e., nickname] of my Lord and Lady to Mrs. *Harris*" (Faulkner's note).
[24] Come around; relent toward her.

And over and above, that I may have your *Excellencies* Letter,
With an Order for the *Chaplain* aforesaid; or instead of him a better.
And then your poor *Petitioner,* both Night and Day,
Or the *Chaplain* (for 'tis his *Trade*) as in Duty bound, shall ever *pray.*[25]

---

[25] Official petitions to the authorities ended with this formula. See *The Humble Petition of the Footmen of Dublin*.

MARY the Cook-Maid's Letter to
Dr. SHERIDAN

*Written in 1718 as part of a series of humorous verses addressed to the Rev.
Thomas Sheridan, with whom Swift maintained a close but bantering (and on
occasion querulous) friendship, this poem has Swift speaking through the con-
versational cadences of his cook Mary to chastise Sheridan for going beyond the
bounds of propriety in his raillery of Swift in an earlier verse. As with* Frances
Harris's Petition, *the impersonation of his cook suggests at once Swift's enjoy-
ment of his superior social status—"mocking" this servant in both senses of that
word—and his fundamental appreciation of her loyalty to him, along with his
obvious relish in being able to inhabit her social and linguistic worlds.*

* * *

WELL, if ever I saw such another Man since my Mother bound my Head,[1]
You a Gentleman! marry come up,[2] I wonder where you were bred?
I am sure such Words does not become a Man of your Cloth,
I would not give such Language to a Dog, faith and troth.
Yes; you call'd my Master a Knave: Fie, Mr. *Sheridan*, 'tis a Shame
For a Parson, who should know better Things, to come out with such a
    Name.
Knave in your Teeth, Mr. *Sheridan*, 'tis both a Shame and a Sin,
And the Dean, my Master, is an honester Man than you and all your Kin:
He has more Goodness in his little Finger, than you have in your whole
    Body,
10 My Master is a parsonable[3] Man, and not a spindle-shank'd Hoddy-doddy.[4]
And now whereby I find you would fain make an Excuse,
Because my Master one day, in Anger, call'd you Goose.
Which, and I am sure I have been his Servant four Years since *October*,
And he never call'd me worse than *Sweet-heart*,[5] drunk or sober:
Not that I know his Reverence was ever concern'd[6] to my Knowledge,

---

[1] Since infancy, when mothers commonly bound the heads of babies.

[2] An exclamation, originally invoking the Virgin Mary, to express exaggeration.

[3] Personable, spelled as pronounced in the common eighteenth-century English fashion,
to pun on the fact that Swift was, like Sheridan, a parson, though in Mary's eyes a better-
bred one.

[4] A general term of abuse, though more particularly a short chubby man (with thin legs in
this case, however); Rogers suggests the term is also used of a cuckold.

[5] Swift's common term for his large, loud, pockmarked cook.

[6] Drunk.

Tho' you and your Come-rogues[7] keep him out so late in your wicked
    College.[8]
You say you will eat Grass on his Grave; a Christian eat Grass!
Whereby you now confess your self to be a Goose or an Ass:[9]
But that's as much as to say, that my Master should die before ye;

20   Well, well, that's as God pleases, and I don't believe that's a true Story,
And so say I told you so, and you may go tell my Master; what care I?
And I don't care who knows it, 'tis all one to *Mary.*
Every Body knows that I love to tell Truth, and shame the Devil;
I am but a poor Servant, but I think Gentle-folks should be civil.[10]
Besides, you found Fault with our Vittels[11] one day that you was here;
I remember it was upon a *Tuesday,* of all Days in the Year.
And *Saunders* the Man[12] says, you are always jesting and mocking,
Mary, said he, (one Day, as I was mending my Master's Stocking,)
My Master is so fond of that Minister that keeps the School;[13]

30   I thought my Master a wise Man, but that Man makes him a Fool.
Saunders, said I, I would rather than a Quart of Ale,
He would come into our Kitchin, and I would pin a Dish-clout to his Tail.[14]
And now I must go, and get *Saunders* to direct this Letter,[15]
For I write but a sad Scrawl, but my Sister *Marget* she writes better.
Well, but I must run and make the Bed before my Master comes from
    Pray'rs,
And see now, it strikes Ten, and I hear him coming up Stairs:
Whereof I cou'd say more to your Verses, if I could write written Hand,[16]
And so I remain in a civil Way, your Servant to command,

MARY

---

[7] Playing upon "comrades" and "rogues" to mean "drinking buddies."

[8] Sheridan was a Fellow of Trinity College, Dublin.

[9] Refers to the final lines of Sheridan's poem, *A Highlander once fought,* written as a retort to Swift's verse, *Sheridan, A Goose*: "Tho' you call me a goose, you pitiful slave, / I'll feed on the grass that grows on your grave."

[10] A favorite rhyme of Swift's; see *The Humble Petition of Frances Harris,* 54–55 and *Stella at Woodpark,* 21–22.

[11] A spelling of "victuals" (food, meal) to reflect its actual pronunciation.

[12] Swift's name for Alexander McGee, the servant he liked best, who died at 29 in 1722. Remarkably, Swift gave him a gentleman's funeral and placed a tablet in St. Patrick's Cathedral commemorating his "discretion, fidelity and diligence."

[13] Sheridan operated a school at the time in Capel Street, Dublin.

[14] "A punishment often threatened by the female servants in a kitchen, to a man who pries too minutely into the secrets of that place" (Grose's *Dictionary of the Vulgar Tongue,* 1811); a "Dish-clout" is a dishcloth.

[15] Address it.

[16] If my handwriting were legible.

The Description of an Irish-Feast,
translated almost literally out of the
Original Irish

Translated in the Year 1720

This verse is a translation from the Irish Pléaráca na Ruarcach, a contemporary poem by Aodh Mac Gabhráin (Hugh MacGauran) celebrating an O'Rourke chieftain of the sixteenth century who rebelled against the English overlords. Swift no doubt worked from a literal translation in prose, perhaps supplied by MacGauran himself. A manuscript of the Irish text is preserved in Trinity College Library, Dublin, followed by Swift's poem (TCD MS 1325). The poem in Irish was set to music by the famous blind harper Turlough O'Carolan (or Carolan), the most "classical" of Irish composers in his time, and folk anecdotes link him with Swift, even asserting that they met—a distinct possibility since Swift's friend, the Rev. Patrick Delany, was a patron of O'Carolan.

*   *   *

    O'ROURK's noble Fare
      Will ne'er be forgot,
    By those who were there,
      Or those who were not.
    His Revels to keep,
      We sup and we dine,
    On seven Score Sheep,
      Fat Bullocks and Swine.
    Usquebagh[1] to our Feast
10   In Pails was brought up,
    An Hundred at least,
      And a Madder[2] our Cup.
    O there is the Sport,
      We rise with the Light,
    In disorderly Sort,
      From snoring all Night.
    O how was I trick't,
      My Pipe it was broke,
    My Pocket was pick't,

---

[1] Whiskey, from the Irish original *uisge bheatha,* "water of life."
[2] "Wooden Vessel" (Faulkner's note); usually a deep, square-sided carved mug.

20   I lost my new Cloak[3]
          I'm rifled,[4] quoth *Nell*,
            Of Mantle and Kercher,[5]
          Why then fare them well,
            The De'el take the Searcher.[6]
          Come, Harper, strike up,
            But first by your Favour,
          Boy, give us a Cup;
            Ay, this has some Savour:
          O *Rourk*'s jolly Boys
30   Ne'er dreamt of the Matter,
          Till rowz'd by the Noise,
            And musical Clatter,
          They bounce from their Nest,
            No longer will tarry,
          They rise ready drest,
            Without one *Ave Mary*.[7]
          They dance in a Round,
            Cutting Capers and Ramping,[8]
          A Mercy the Ground
40   Did not burst with their Stamping,
          The Floor is all wet
            With Leaps and with Jumps,
          While the Water and Sweat,
            Splish, splash in their Pumps.[9]
          Bless you late and early,
            Laughlin O Enagin,[10]
          By my hand, you dance rarely,
            Margery Grinagin.[11]
          Bring Straw for our Bed,
50   Shake it down to the Feet,
          Then over us spread,
            The winnowing Sheet.[12]
          To show, I don't flinch,
            Fill the Bowl up again,
          Then give us a Pinch

---

[3] It is evident from the Irish original that each of the complaints is voiced by a different participant in the revels.

[4] Robbed.

[5] "Handkerchief" (Faulkner's note); though actually a garment for covering the head.

[6] Rather an expression like "who cares" than an actual reference to somebody searching for the missing garments, since the mood is of continued insouciance.

[7] The common Catholic prayer "Hail Mary," or *Ave Maria* in Latin.

[8] Dialectal form of "romping."

[9] Shoes, particularly those designed for dancing. The story goes that O'Carolan was quite taken with the onomatopoeic effects here.

[10] Probably a reference to an actual person, whose identity is otherwise unknown; in the Irish the name is given as "Mhaolsheachluinn Uí Ionagáin," which is fairly closely anglicized.

[11] "The Name of an *Irish* Woman" (Faulkner's note). The original Irish is "Mhairsill ni Ghniodagáin," again anglicized accurately.

[12] The sheet with which grain would have been winnowed of its chaff.

Of your Sneezing;[13] *a Yean*.[14]
Good Lord, what a Sight,
    After all their good Cheer,
For People to fight
60   In the Midst of their Beer:
They rise from their Feast,
    And hot are their Brains,
A Cubit at least
    The length of their Skeans.[15]
What Stabs and what Cuts,
    What clatt'ring of Sticks,
What Strokes on the Guts,
    What Bastings and Kicks!
With Cudgels of Oak,
70   Well harden'd in Flame,
An hundred Heads broke,
    An hundred struck lame.
You Churle,[16] I'll maintain
    My Father built *Lusk*,[17]
The Castle of *Slain*,[18]
    And Carrickdrumrusk:[19]
The Earl of *Kildare*,[20]
    And *Moynalta*,[21] his Brother,
As great as they are,
80   I was nurs'd by their Mother.[22]
Ask that of old *Madam*,[23]
    She'll tell you who's who,
As far up as *Adam*,
    She knows it is true,
Come down with that Beam,
    If Cudgels are scarce,
A Blow on the Weam,[24]
    Or a Kick on the A[r]se.

---

[13] Snuff, which would impel sneezing and was very popular in the eighteenth century.

[14] "Another *Irish* Name for a Woman" (Faulkner's note); almost certainly a rendering of "Áine" (Anne) in the original Irish. The Irish name is pronounced "awn-ya," though a variation such as "aw-yeen-ya" would account for Swift's version.

[15] "Daggers, or short Swords" (Faulkner's note); from the original Irish "sgiain."

[16] Churl; rascal; rude low-bred fellow.

[17] A village near the coast of the Irish Sea, north of Dublin.

[18] Slane Castle, overlooking the River Boyne in Co. Meath.

[19] Transliteration of "Carruig Druim Rúsga" in the original Irish, *anglice* Carrick-on-Shannon, Co. Leitrim.

[20] Exactly which such nobleman is meant here has not been determined, though the family reference is to the FitzGeralds, in the first rank of Irish nobility.

[21] Transliteration of "Mhuige Nealta" in the original Irish, *anglice* Moynalty, Co. Meath.

[22] That is, they had the same wet-nurse, colloquially termed "mother" in Ireland. As Rogers notes, this passage is marked by a comic braggadocio common to this type of Irish poem.

[23] Whether the actual nurse is meant here, or simply a knowledgeable old woman nearby, is unclear; the reference is not present in the original Irish.

[24] Belly.

An Excellent New Song on a Seditious Pamphlet

To the Tune of Packington's Pound

Written in the Year 1720

This poem was accompanied in Faulkner's edition with the following preamble: "The Author [Swift] having wrote a Treatise, advising the People of Ireland *to wear their own Manufactures, a Prosecution was set on foot against Waters the Printer thereof, which was carried on with so much Violence, that one Whitshed, then Chief Justice, thought proper, in a Manner the most extraordinary, to keep the Grand-Jury above twelve Hours, and to send them eleven times out of Court, until he had wearied them into a special Verdict." In other words, the poem must be read in conjunction with Swift's pamphlet,* A Proposal for the Universal Use of Irish Manufacture, *and the judicial controversy it provoked. A fine example of Swift's links to a popular satiric tradition, this work demonstrates the way he used ballads and verse to reach a wider audience for the ideas espoused in his polemical tracts: in this case, by ironically reaffirming the argument of the* Proposal *via a speaker who expressly (and perversely) rejects it. The poem was set to "Packington's Pound," which was perhaps the most popular of all contemporary ballad tunes, dating from the Renaissance (it was also used by John Gay in* The Beggar's Opera*).*

*   *   *

BROCADO's, and Damasks, and Tabbies, and Gawses,[1]
   Are by *Robert Ballentine* lately brought over;
With Forty Things more: Now hear what the Law says,
   Whoe'er will not were[2] them, is not the King's Lover.
      Tho' a Printer and Dean
      Seditiously mean
   Our true *Irish* hearts from old *England* to wean;

---

[1] Finely woven fabrics used mainly for fashionable women's clothing. Brocades were adorned with a pattern of raised figures; damasks were of shiny silk; "tabbies" was the term for silk taffeta, or for the dresses made of that material.
[2] Wear.

We'll buy *English* silks for our Wives and our Daughters,
In Spight of his Deanship and Journeyman *Waters*.[3]

II.

10   In *England* the Dead in Woollen are clad,[4]
        The Dean and his Printer then let us cry Fye[5] on;
    To be cloth'd like a Carcass would make a Teague[6] mad,
        Since a living Dog better is than a dead Lyon,
            Our Wives they grow sullen
            At wearing of Woollen,
        And all we poor Shopkeepers must our Horns pull in.[7]
    Then we'll buy *English* Silks, *&c.*

III.

    Whoever our Trading with *England* would hinder,
        To *inflame* both the Nations do plainly conspire;
20 Because *Irish* Linen will soon turn to Tinder;
        And Wool it is greasy, and quickly takes Fire.
            Therefore I assure ye,
            Our noble Grand Jury,
        When they saw the Dean's Book[8] they were in a great Fury:
    They would buy *English* silks for their Wives, &c.

IV.

    This wicked Rogue *Waters*, who always is sinning,
        And before *Corum Nobus*[9] so oft has been call'd,
    Henceforward shall print neither Pamphlets nor Linnen,
        And, if Swearing can do't, shall be swingingly[10] mawl'd:
30   And as for the *Dean*,
            You know whom I mean,
        If the Printer will peach[11] him, he'll scarce come off clean.
    Then we'll buy *English* Silks for our Wives and our Daughters,
    In Spight of his Deanship and Journeyman *Waters*.

---

[3] The printer Edward Waters was a "journeyman" in the sense that he could ply his trade for pay after having served his apprenticeship; but the speaker (given his bias) is probably using the term pejoratively, to paint Waters as Swift's mere hireling or drudge.

[4] By a statute enacted in 1667 and not repealed until 1815, the dead in England had to be buried clothed in wool; this was a boon, of course, to the domestic wool trade.

[5] As in "fie on you," a term of disgust.

[6] A generic term for an Irishman, from *Tadhg*, Timothy. See Swift's comment to a correspondent, "I am a Teague, or an Irishman, or what people please"; also see *My Lady's Lamentation and Complaint against the Dean*, ll. 161–62.

[7] Curb our desire to buy.

[8] *A Proposal for the Universal Use of Irish Manufacture.*

[9] Correctly, *coram nobis*, "to our presence," a term used in a legal summons. Waters had previous to his current difficulties been summoned to the bar of the Irish House of Commons to hear reprimands and make apologies.

[10] Immensely or severely; punningly evokes the image of hanging.

[11] Impeach; implicate.

An Epilogue to a Play for the Benefit of the Weavers in Ireland

Written in the Year 1721

In the early 1720s Ireland was suffering a severe recession, which hit the weavers especially hard since their trade was already hampered by English legislation prohibiting the export of woolen cloth from Ireland into Great Britain (and elsewhere). To assist the weavers, a charity production of Hamlet *was performed on April 1, 1721, at the Theatre Royal in Dublin's Smock Alley, with a prologue by Swift's friend the Rev. Thomas Sheridan, and this recitation by Swift at its end.*

* * *

WHO dares affirm this is no pious Age,
When Charity begins to tread the Stage?
When Actors, who at best are hardly Savers,[1]
Will give a Night of Benefit to Weavers?[2]
Stay, —— let me see, how finely will it sound!
Imprimis,[3] from his Grace[4] an Hundred Pound.
Peers, Clergy, Gentry, all are Benefactors;
And then comes in the *Item* of the Actors.
Item, the Actors freely gave a Day,—
10   The Poet had no more, who made the Play.[5]
    BUT whence this wond'rous Charity in Play'rs?
They learnt it not at Sermons, or at Pray'rs:
Under the Rose,[6] since here are none but Friends,

---

[1] Alluding to the financial insecurity of acting as a profession.

[2] Commonly, the run of a play would have occasional "benefit" performances in which the profits would be devoted to an advertised cause; for these performances, however, even the actors evidently gave up their pay to help the weavers—in this line pronounced "Wavers" to rhyme with "Savers": a distinctively Irish rhyme looked down upon by English standards of pronunciation.

[3] "To begin," as for a schedule of accounts or "items."

[4] The Archbishop of Dublin, William King, who likewise took up the weavers' cause.

[5] That is, in receiving nothing for their labors in this performance, the actors received the same as Shakespeare, the author of the play. A living author would normally get the profits from every third performance.

[6] *Sub rosa*; confidentially.

(To own the Truth) we have some private Ends.[7]
Since Waiting-Women, like exacting Jades,
Hold up the Prices of their old *Brocades;*
We'll dress in *Manufactures* made at home;[8]
Equip our *Kings* and *Generals* at the *Comb;*[9]
We'll rig in *Meath-street*[10] *Ægypt*'s haughty *Queen;*[11]
20   And *Anthony* shall court her in *Ratteen.*[12]
In *blew Shalloon*[13] shall *Hannibal* be clad,
And *Scipio* trail an *Irish purple Plad.*[14]
In Drugget[15] drest, of Thirteen Pence a Yard,
See *Philip*'s Son amidst his *Persian* Guard;
And proud *Roxana* fir'd with jealous Rage,[16]
With fifty Yards of Crape,[17] shall sweep the Stage.
In short, our Kings and Princesses within,
Are all resolv'd the Project to begin;
And you, our Subjects, when you here resort,
30   Must imitate the Fashion of the Court.

OH! cou'd I see this Audience clad in *Stuff*,[18]
Tho' Money's scarce, we should have Trade enough:
But *Chints*,[19] *Brocades*, and *Lace*, take all away,
And scarce a Crown[20] is left to see a Play:
Perhaps you wonder whence this Friendship springs
Between the Weavers and us Play-House Kings:
But Wit and Weaving had the same Beginning;
Pallas[21] first taught us Poetry and Spinning:
And next observe how this Alliance fits,

---

[7] Personal reasons (i.e., to promote the use of Irish-made fabrics).

[8] Just as the old fancy dresses of great ladies can be sold for high prices by the women the ladies employ, we will benefit the weavers by advertising their products.

[9] The Coombe, "a Street in *Dublin* famous for Woollen Manufactures" (Faulkner's note); one of the principal streets of the Liberties of St. Patrick's Cathedral, Swift's own neighborhood in Dublin.

[10] Another important street in the Liberties, adjoining The Coombe.

[11] Cleopatra, probably as presented in John Dryden's *All for Love* (1677).

[12] A thick twill.

[13] Wool used commonly for lining garments.

[14] Hannibal and Scipio are both characters in Nathaniel Lee's *Sophonisba* (1676).

[15] Cheap cloth.

[16] Alexander 'the Great' ("*Philip*'s Son") and Roxana are both characters in *The Rival Queens* (1677), Nathaniel Lee's most popular drama, frequently revived on the eighteenth-century stage.

[17] Crepe; thinly woven cloth, usually black.

[18] Heavy woolen fabric.

[19] Chintz, printed cotton cloth, imported like brocades and lace and more expensive than the coarser fabrics produced by the Dublin weavers.

[20] A coin worth five shillings (each equal to twelve pence, so sixty pence in total); one-quarter of the pound sterling.

[21] Pallas Athene, the Greek goddess of wisdom, and patron of weaving as well as learning; known as Minerva in Roman mythology.

40   For *Weavers* now are just as poor as *Wits*:
       Their Brother Quill-Men, Workers for the Stage,[22]
       For sorry Stuff[23] can get a Crown a Page;
       But *Weavers* will be kinder to the *Players*,
       And sell for Twenty Pence a Yard of theirs.[24]
       And, to your Knowledge, there is often less in
       The *Poet*'s Wit, than in the *Player*'s Dressing.

---

[22] Playwrights (writers' pens would be made of goose or turkey quills).

[23] Very poor writing, with a play on the word to which note 18 refers, above.

[24] That is, a yard of fabric will sell for a third of what a page of writing would cost, but in Swift's estimation would be worth more.

The Part of a Summer, at the House of George Rochfort, Esq.

Swift made a long visit to Gaulstown House, the Co. Meath home of his friend George Rochfort, from mid-June until early October 1721. He was part of a group including various Rochforts, among them the father of the family, a retired Lord Chief Baron of the Exchequer of Ireland (an ancient title for the supervisory judge of Ireland's highest court) and his own clergymen friends Thomas Sheridan, Patrick Delany, and Daniel Jackson. His abrupt, unceremonious departure from the house, and his biting satire on one of the other guests in the first version of this poem, produced controversy and published innuendoes about Swift's breach of the laws of hospitality. The poem's alternate title, The Journal *(used by Harold Williams in his edition), underscores the lively detailed account it offers of the daily activities at Gaulstown House.*

* * *

THALIA,[1] tell in sober Lays,
How *George, Nim, Dan, Dean,*[2] pass their Days.

BEGIN, my Muse. First, from our Bow'rs
We sally forth at diff'rent Hours;
At Seven, the *Dean* in Night-gown drest,
Goes round the House to wake the rest:
At Nine, grave *Nim* and *George* facetious,
Go to the *Dean* to read *Lucretius:*[3]
At Ten, my Lady[4] comes and hectors,
10   And kisses *George,* and ends our Lectures;
And when she has him by the Neck fast,
Hauls him, and scolds us, down to Breakfast.
We squander there an Hour or more;
And then all Hands, Boys, to the Oar;
All, heteroclite[5] *Dan* except,

---

[1] Muse of comedy and pastoral poetry.

[2] George Rochfort, John Rochfort (who loved to hunt, hence called "Nim"—short for Nimrod, a great hunter in the Bible), Daniel Jackson, and Dean Swift.

[3] First-century B.C.E. Roman poet and philosopher, author of *De rerum natura* (*On the Nature of Things*); frequently referred to in Swift's writings.

[4] George Rochfort's wife, Lady Elizabeth (Betty) Rochfort ("Lady," because she was the daughter of the Earl of Drogheda).

[5] Different by nature, eccentric.

Who never Time, nor Order kept,
But by peculiar Whimsies drawn,
Peeps in the Ponds to look for Spawn;
O'ersees the Work, or *Dragon*[6] rows,
20   Or mars a Text, or mends his Hose;[7]
Or —— but proceed we in our Journal ——
At Two, or after, we return all.
From the four Elements assembling,[8]
Warn'd by the Bell, all Folks come trembling;
From airy Garrets some descend,
Some from the Lake's remotest End:
My Lord[9] and *Dean* the Fire forsake;
Dan leaves the earthly Spade and Rake:
The Loit'rers quake, no Corner hides them,
30   And Lady *Betty* soundly chides them,
Now Water's brought, and Dinner's done;
With Church and King the Lady's gone:[10]
(Not reck'ning half an Hour we pass
In talking o'er a moderate Glass.)
Dan, growing drowsy, like a Thief,
Steals off to dose[11] away his Beef;
And this must pass for reading *Hammond* ——[12]
While *George* and *Dean* go to Back-Gammon.
George, Nim and *Dean* set out at Four,
40   And then again, Boys, to the Oar.
But when the Sun goes to the Deep,
(Not to disturb him in his Sleep,
Or make a Rumbling o'er his Head,
His Candle out, and He a-bed)
We watch his Motions to a Minute
And leave the Flood, when he goes in it.[13]
Now Stinted in the short'ning Day,
We go to Pray'rs, and then to Play:
Till Supper comes, and after that,
50   We sit an Hour to drink and chat.
'Tis late —— the old and younger Pairs,
By *Adam*[14] lighted, walk up Stairs.

---

[6] "My Lord Chief Baron's smaller Boat" (Faulkner's note).

[7] Stocking(s). Men wore stockings reaching above the knee, secured with garters or the ends of their breeches, which conventionally reached just below the knee.

[8] From air, water, fire, and earth; Swift is parodying the Last Judgment.

[9] Lord Chief Baron Rochfort.

[10] Women would frequently leave the table when dinner was done, after toasts of loyalty were offered to the Church of Ireland and the King, while the men would continue drinking.

[11] Doze.

[12] Henry Hammond, an Anglican devotional writer of the seventeenth century, particularly favored by those inclined to High Church principles.

[13] That is, they set out upon the lake (or simply a canal?), but go back to the shore at sunset.

[14] "The Butler" (Faulkner's note).

The weary *Dean* goes to his Chamber,
And *Nim* and *Dan* to Garret clamber.
So when this Circle we have run,
The Curtain falls, and all is done.

  I MIGHT have mention'd sev'ral Facts,
Like Episodes between the Acts;
And tell who loses, and who wins,
60 Who gets a Cold, who breaks his Shins;
How *Dan* caught nothing in his Net,
And how the Boat was overset.
For Brevity I have retrench'd
How in the Lake the *Dean* was drench'd.
It would be an Exploit to brag on,
How valiant *George* rode o'er the *Dragon*;
How steady in the Storm he sat,
And sav'd his Oar, but lost his Hat.
How *Nim* (no Hunter e'er could match him,)
70 Still brings us Hares, when he can catch 'em:
How skilfully *Dan* mends his Nets;
How Fortune fails him, when he sets.
Or how the *Dean* delights to vex
The Ladies, and lampoon the Sex.
Or how our Neighbour[15] lifts his Nose,
To tell what ev'ry School-Boy knows,
And, with his Finger on his Thumb
Explaining, strikes opposers dumb:
Or how his Wife, that Female Pedant,
80 (But now there need no more be said on't,)
Shews all her Secrets of House-keeping;
For Candles how she trucks her Dripping;[16]
Was forc'd to send three Miles for Yest,
To brew her Ale, and raise her Paste;[17]
Tells ev'ry Thing that you can think of:
How she cur'd *Tommy* of the Chin-cough;[18]
What gave her Brats and Pigs the Meazles,
And how her Doves were kill'd by Weezles;
How *Jowler*[19] howl'd, and what a Fright
90 She had with Dreams the other Night.

---

[15] Initially the text here contained a negative reference to another guest, the Rev. William Percival, Archdeacon of Cashel, a High-Flying Tory extremist whom Swift disliked (see headnote). It was removed for the Faulkner *Works*, and the reference to the "Neighbour" substituted.

[16] The fat collected from cooking meat; lard. Candles made from dripping would retain the odors of cooking, suggesting that those who used such candles were poor or very stingy.

[17] Dough; "yest" was a variant spelling of "yeast."

[18] Whooping-cough; the name "Tommy" is meant to be generic; originally the name given was "Charley," which had Percival connections.

[19] A generic name for a large dog.

BUT now, since I have gone so far on,
A Word or two of Lord Chief Baron;
And tell how little Weight he sets
On all *Whig* Papers, and *Gazetts*;[20]
But for the Politicks of *Pue*[21]
Thinks every Syllable is true.
And since he owns the King of *Sweden*[22]
Is dead at last, without evading;
Now all his Hopes are on the *Czar*;[23]
100 "Why, *Muscovy*[24] is not so far;
Down the *Black-Sea*, and up the *Streights*,[25]
And in a Month he's at your Gates:
Perhaps from what the Packet[26] brings
By *Christmas* we shall see strange Things."

WHY should I tell of Ponds and Drains,
What Carps we met with for our Pains;
Of Sparrows tam'd, and Nuts innumerable,
To choak the Girls, and to consume a Rabble?
But you, who are a Scholar, know
110 How transient all Things are below;
How prone to Change is human Life;
Last Night arriv'd *Clem* and his Wife ——[27]
This grand Event hath broke our Measures;
Their Reign began with cruel Seizures:
The *Dean* must with his Quilt supply
The Bed in which these Tyrants lie:
Nim lost his Wig-Block, *Dan* his *Jordan*;[28]
(My Lady says she can't afford one)
George is half scar'd out of his Wits,

---

[20] *The London Gazette* was the official journal of record of the British government and Britain's oldest continuously published newspaper, first appearing in 1666.

[21] "A Tory News-Writer" (Faulkner's note). *Pue's Occurrences* was begun by Richard Pue of Dublin early in the eighteenth century and promoted the Tory line; it remained a Tory paper, but with a moderated tone, after Pue died in 1722 and was succeeded by his son, also Richard.

[22] Charles XII of Sweden, who died in battle in 1718, was thought to favor the Tories in Britain, and perhaps even the Jacobite cause. He was admired by Swift, who thought about dedicating his *Abstract of the History of England* to him.

[23] Peter I, "the Great." Peter's Russia and Charles's Sweden were at war; Swift is satirizing the often absurd hopefulness of British Jacobites.

[24] Russia.

[25] The Bosphorus and Dardanelles, between the Black and the Aegean Seas.

[26] A ship bringing letters, hence news, from various ports. Eighteenth-century British and Irish newspapers took much of their content from such sources.

[27] 'Mr. Clement Barry' (Faulkner's note). Clement Barry, from Saggart, near Dublin, was a popular figure in the neighborhood of Gaulstown.

[28] A "Wig-Block" is a wig-stand; a "*Jordan*" is a chamber-pot.

120   For *Clem* gets all the tiny[29] Bits.

Henceforth expect a different Survey;
This House will soon turn Topsy-turvey.
They talk of further Alterations,
Which *causes many Speculations.*[30]

---

[29]"Dainty" in the early versions of the text. Barry would appear to have been fond of delicacies, which George, as host, would have to give up in favor of his guest.

[30]A phrase common in newspapers of the period, when discussing political shifts and changes.

STELLA *at Wood-Park*

A House of CHARLES FORD, Esq; eight Miles from *Dublin*

——*Cuicunq; nocere volebat*
Vestimenta dabat pretiosa.

Written in the Year 1723

Swift's dear friend Esther Johnson, nicknamed "Stella" in his poetry, left Dublin for a lengthy visit to Charles Ford's house at Woodpark—eight Irish miles (or a bit more than 10 English or U.S. miles) from Dublin, in Co. Meath—in the summer of 1723, while Swift himself was travelling through the southwestern parts of Ireland. He wrote the poem at the end of his summer travels, gently mocking Stella for having acquired a taste for the finer things while in the company of Ford, known for his love of London's culture and ambience. The epigraph, from Horace, Epistles I, *xviii, 31–32, sets this theme: "to somebody he wished to injure, he gave expensive clothes."*

*   *   *

DON *Carlos*[1] in a merry Spight,[2]
Did *Stella* to his House invite:
He entertain'd her half a Year
With gen'rous Wines and costly Chear.
Don *Carlos* made her chief Director,
That she might o'er the Servants hector.[3]
In half a Week the Dame grew nice,[4]
Got all things at the highest Price.
Now at the Table-Head she sits,
10   Presented with the nicest[5] Bits:
She look'd on Partridges with Scorn,

---

[1] Swift's nickname for Ford.
[2] A mood or humor.
[3] Lord it over.
[4] Overparticular.
[5] Choicest.

Except they tasted of the Corn:
A Haunch of Ven'son made her sweat,
Unless it had the right *Fumette*.[6]
Don *Carlos* earnestly would beg,
Dear Madam, try this Pigeon's Leg;
Was happy when he could prevail
To make her only touch a Quail.
Through Candle-Light she viewed the Wine,
20   To see that ev'ry Glass was fine.
At last grown prouder than the D[evi]l,
With feeding high, and Treatment civil,
Don *Carlos* now began to find
His Malice work as he design'd:
The Winter-Sky began to frown,
Poor *Stella* must pack off to Town.
From purling Streams[7] and Fountains bubbling,
To *Liffy*'s[8] stinking tide in *Dublin*:
From wholesome Exercise and Air
30   To sossing[9] in an easy Chair;
From Stomach sharp and hearty feeding,
To piddle like a Lady breeding:[10]
From ruling there the Houshold singly,
To be directed here by *Dingly*:[11]
From ev'ry Day a lordly Banquet,
To half a Joint, and God be thank it:
From ev'ry meal *Pontack*[12] in plenty,
To half a Pint one Day in twenty.
From *Ford* attending at her Call,
40   To Visits of [Archdeacon Wall.][13]
From *Ford*, who thinks of nothing mean,
To the poor Doings of the D[ea]n.
From growing Riche[r] with good Chear,
To running out by starving here.

BUT now arrives the dismal Day:
She must return to *Ormond-Key*:[14]
The Coachman stopt, she lookt, and swore

---

[6]The odor of game.

[7]A satirical reference to conventional pastoral description.

[8] "The River that runs through Dublin" (Faulkner's note).

[9]Lounging lazily.

[10]To pick at her food like a pregnant woman. "Stella" was known for having a poor appetite, which was linked to her declining health throughout the 1720s (she died in January 1728).

[11]Stella's much older companion, Rebecca Dingley, whom she first met when she was a child at Moor Park (Sir William Temple's estate); the two left England for Ireland in 1701 and lodged together until Stella's death.

[12]A sweet French wine.

[13]Rev. Thomas Walls, Archdeacon of Achonry and a master at St. Patrick's Cathedral School, a loyal and useful friend to Swift whose wife was close to Stella and Mrs. Dingley.

[14]Ormond Quay, "Where both the ladies lodged" (Faulkner's note).

The Rascal had mistook the Door:
At coming in you saw her stoop;
50   The Entry[15] brushed against her Hoop:
Each Moment rising in her Airs,
She curst the narrow winding Stairs:
Began a Thousand Faults to spy;
The Ceiling hardly six Foot high;
The smutty Wainscot[16] full of cracks,
And half the Chairs with broken Backs:
Her Quarter's out at *Lady-Day*;[17]
She vows she will no longer stay,
In Lodgings, like a poor *Grizette*,[18]
60   While there are [Houses] to be lett.

    HOWE'ER, to keep her Spirits up,
She sent for Company to sup;
When all the while you might remark,
She strove in vain to ape *Wood-Park*.
Two Bottles call'd for, (half her Store;
The Cupboard could contain but four;)
A Supper worthy of her self,
Five *Nothings* in five plates of *Delph*.[19]

    THUS, for a Week the Farce went on;
70   When all her Country-Savings gone,
She fell into her former Scene.
Small Beer,[20] a Herring, and the D[ea]n.

  THUS far in jest. Though now I fear
You think my Jesting too severe:
But Poets when a Hint is new
Regard not whether false or true:
Yet Raillery gives no Offence,
Where Truth has not the least Pretence;
Nor can be more securely plac't
80   Than on a Nymph of *Stella*'s Taste.
I must confess, your Wine and Vittle[21]
I was too hard upon *a little;*
Your Table neat, your Linnen fine;
And, though in Miniature, you shine.

---

[15] Entryway or vestibule.

[16] The wood paneling on the walls.

[17] Houses were normally leased for three-month periods; this "quarter's" lease would be expiring on Lady-Day, March 25.

[18] Grisette, a skilled female worker, e.g., a seamstress. See Swift's poem, *To Betty the Grizette* (1730).

[19] Crockery from Delft, in Holland; the terminal "t" was rarely sounded in colloquial speech.

[20] Weak ale, cheaper than any other alcoholic beverage.

[21] Victual(s); food.

Yet, when you sigh to leave *Wood-Park*,
The Scene, the Welcome, and the Spark,[22]
To languish in this odious Town,
And pull your haughty Stomach[23] down;
We think you quite mistake the Case;
90 The Virtue lies not in the Place:
For though my Raillery were true,
A Cottage is *Wood-Park* with you.

---

[22] Beau; dandy.
[23] Temper.

Prometheus

On Wood the Patentee's Irish Half-pence

This popular broadside of 1724 works as a double parody, foreshadowed by its first line: William Wood styled himself "William Wood, Esq." to imply a higher social standing than he would have as the owner of an iron works; hence he was "Squire," though as a dealer in metals, an ironmonger, he is belittled by the term "tinker," which denotes a worker in tin (hence one who might solder pieces of metal together), and in Ireland describes an itinerant metal worker. The term is very degrading in modern Ireland and was equally so in Swift's day, when it connoted a gypsy or tramp. In analogy with this double play on Wood's occupation, the poem mixes a story from classical mythology—that of the Titan Prometheus, who steals fire from Zeus to give to mortals and is punished by being bound to a rock, an eagle continually eating his liver—with the current controversy over Wood's patent for minting small coins for Ireland. See The Drapier's Letters *for the historical context of this verse.*

*   *   *

I.

As, when the 'Squire and Tinker, *Wood,*
Gravely consulting *Ireland*'s Good,
Together mingl'd in a Mass
Smith's Dust,[1] and Copper, Lead and Brass;
The Mixture thus by Chymick[2] Art
United close in ev'ry Part,
In Fillets[3] roll'd, or cut in Pieces,
Appear'd like one continued Species;
And by the forming Engine struck,
10   On all the same *Impression* stuck.

    So, to confound this *hated Coin,*
All *Parties* and *Religions* join;
Whigs, Tories, Trimmers,[4] *Hanoverians,*
Quakers, Conformists,[5] *Presbyterians.*

---

[1] Metal filings, most commonly of iron.
[2] Chemic; alchemical; implies counterfeit.
[3] Strips of metal from which coins were stamped out.
[4] Those who tend to compromise in politics.
[5] Those belonging to the established church, the Church of Ireland.

Scotch, Irish, English, French,[6] unite
With *equal Int'rest, equal Spight;*
Together mingled in a Lump,
Do all in *one Opinion* jump;[7]
And ev'ry one begins to find
20   The same *Impression* on his Mind.

A STRANGE Event! Whom *Gold* incites,
To Blood and Quarrels, *Brass* Unites:
So Goldsmiths say, the coarsest Stuff
Will serve for *Solder* well enough:
So, by the *Kettle's*[8] loud Alarm,
The *Bees* are gather'd to a *Swarm:*
So, by the *Brazen* Trumpet's Bluster,[9]
Troops of all Tongues and Nations muster:
And so the *Harp* of *Ireland* brings
30   Whole Crowds about its *Brazen* Strings.

II.

THERE is a Chain let down from *Jove,*
But fastened to his Throne above;
So strong, that from the lower End,
They say, all human Things depend:
This Chain, as antient Poets hold,
When *Jove* was young, was made of *Gold.*
Prometheus once this Chain purloin'd,
Dissolv'd, and into *Money* coin'd;
Then whips me[10] on a Chain of *Brass,*
40   (*Venus* was brib'd to let it pass.)[11]

Now, while this brazen Chain prevail'd,
Jove saw that all Devotion fail'd;
No Temple to his Godship rais'd;
No Sacrifice on Altars blaz'd;
In short, such dire Confusion follow'd,
Earth must have been in Chaos swallow'd.
Jove stood amaz'd, but looking round,
With much ado the Cheat he found;

---

[6] Huguenots, many of whom took refuge in Ireland after their virtual expulsion from France when the Edict of Nantes was revoked by Louis XIV in 1685. A number of them, weavers by trade, settled in the Liberties near St. Patrick's Cathedral.

[7] Move together; agree.

[8] Kettledrum, often used in martial music.

[9] The trumpet, most commonly of brass, is also martial; Wood's "brass" coins call all the Irish together in opposition, as a trumpet arouses an army.

[10] An example of the ethical dative case in (mostly Latin) grammar; signifies that the person or thing spoken of is regarded with particular interest by the speaker.

[11] "A great Lady was reported to have been bribed by Wood" (Faulkner's note); the Duchess of Kendal, King George I's mistress, was commonly thought to have been bribed by Wood to the tune of £10,000 for the royal patent allowing him to mint copper coins for Ireland.

'Twas plain he could no longer hold
50   The world in any Chain but *Gold*;
And to the God of Wealth, his Brother,[12]
Sent *Mercury* to get another.

III.

Prometheus on a Rock was laid,
Ty'd with the Chain himself had made;
On Icy *Caucasus* to shiver,
While Vultures eat his growing Liver.

IV.

YE Pow'rs of *Grub-street*,[13] make me able,
Discreetly to apply this Fable,
Say, who is to be understood
60   By that old Thief *Prometheus?* WOOD.
For *Jove*, it is not hard to guess him,
I mean His M[ajest]y, *God bless Him.*
This Thief and Blacksmith was so bold,
He strove to steal that Chain of Gold,
Which links the Subject to the King;
And change it for a *Brazen* String.
But sure, if nothing else must pass,
Between the King and us but *Brass,*
Although the Chain will never crack,
Yet our Devotion may grow slack.[14]

70   BUT *Jove* will soon convert, I hope,
This brazen Chain into a Rope;
With which *Prometheus* shall be ty'd,
And high in Air for ever ride;
Where, if we find his Liver grows,
For want of Vultures we have Crows.[15]

---

[12]Swift is confusing Plutus, the god of wealth but not Jove's brother, with Pluto, who was Jove's brother. Mercury was the messenger of the gods, and especially Jove's.

[13]Those middle- and lower-class professional writers who produced pamphlets, miscellanies, occasional pieces, etc. for pay, and who were generally denigrated as "hacks" by the Tory satirists. But Swift's invocation here is perhaps slyly winking at his own affinities with them as an occasional writer himself and a producer of popular broadsides (of which this poem is one).

[14]That is, Wood's "brass" will weaken the link between monarch and subject, and hence the latter's devotion.

[15]Swift is likening the end he wishes for Wood to the practice in certain historical periods, following an execution, of leaving the bodies of criminals, bound in chains or rope, hanging along roadways, where crows would eat the carrion, just as vultures ate the liver of Prometheus. The idea of hanging Wood is the central conceit of Swift's prose broadside, *A Full and True Account of...the Execution of William Wood,* and also appears in his verse, *A Serious Poem Upon William Wood* (ll. 109–33). A Dublin mob actually hung Wood in effigy in September 1724.

Whitshed's Motto on his Coach

Libertas & natale Solum

Liberty and my native Country

Written in the Year 1724

William Whitshed, whose family motto was "Libertas et natale solum," *was in Faulkner's words* "That infamous Chief Justice, who twice prosecuted the Drapier, and dissolved the Grand Jury for not finding the Bill against him." *He was in office as Lord Chief Justice of the Common Pleas in 1724, when the government tried to prosecute the anonymous author of the* Fourth Drapier's Letter *(whom all knew to be Swift) and John Harding, the printer. But two successive grand juries refused to present any indictment against either, despite Whitshed's strenuous urging, and chose instead to return a presentment against* "all such persons as have attempted . . . to impose the halfpence on us." *See head-note to* An Excellent New Song on a Seditious Pamphlet *and* A Short View of the State of Ireland, *note 7.*

*   *   *

LIBERTAS & natale Solum;
Fine Words; I wonder where you stole 'um.
Could nothing but thy chief Reproach,
Serve for a Motto on thy Coach?
But, let me now the Words translate:
Natale Solum: My Estate:[1]
My dear Estate, how well I love it;
My Tenants, if you doubt, will prove it;
They swear I am so kind and good,
10   I hug them till I squeeze their Blood.

   LIBERTAS bears a large Import;[2]
First; how to swagger in a Court;
And, secondly, to shew my Fury

---

[1] Swift is torturing the Latin idiom for "my native land" to mean "my estate."
[2] Has a wide range of meanings.

Against an uncomplying Jury:[3]
And, Thirdly; 'tis a new Invention
To favour *Wood* and keep my Pension:
And, Fourthly; 'tis to play an odd Trick,
Get the Great Seal, and turn out *Brod'rick*.[4]
And, Fifthly; you know whom I mean,
20   To humble that vexatious Dean.[5]
And, Sixthly; for my Soul, to barter it
For Fifty Times its Worth, to *Carteret*.[6]

    Now, since your Motto thus you construe,
I must confess you've spoken once true.
Libertas & natale Solum;
You had good Reason when you stole 'um.

---

[3]The grand jury that would not cooperate in the prosecution of Swift's printer.

[4]Whitshed had hoped to succeed Alan Brodrick, 1st Viscount Midleton, as Lord Chancellor of Ireland (the keeper of the "Great Seal"). The *Sixth Drapier's Letter* is addressed to Midleton, who unlike Whitshed had not favored Wood's half-pence.

[5]Swift himself.

[6]The Lord-Lieutenant; Swift is implying that Whitshed was selling out Ireland's freedom to England, represented by the English Lord-Lieutenant, Lord Carteret.

On *WOOD* the Iron-monger

Written in the Year 1725

*This is another example of Swift's playfulness with classical myth to produce
an analogue for a current issue. Here, the Drapier is compared to Jove in
the myth of Salmoneus (see Virgil's* Aeneid, *vi, 585–94), and* The Drapier's
Letters, *to the thunderbolts of the Almighty. The title is again playing upon
Wood's status as a dealer in iron and other metals. The poem was written
after it became clear that the anti-Wood forces would soon prevail—hence the
exultant tone of the work.*

*   *   *

SALMONEUS,[1] as the *Grecian* Tale is,
Was a mad Copper-Smith of *Elis:*
Up at his Forge by Morning-peep,
No Creature in the Lane could sleep.
Among a Crew of royst'ring Fellows
Would sit whole Ev'nings at the Ale-House:
His Wife and Children wanted[2] Bread,
While he went always drunk to Bed.
This vap'ring Scab[3] must needs devise
10   To ape the Thunder of the Skies;
With *Brass* two fiery Steeds he shod,
To make a Clatt'ring as they trod.
Of polish't *Brass*, his flaming Car,[4]
Like Light'ning dazzled from a-far:
And up he mounts into the Box,[5]
And HE must thunder, with a Pox.[6]
Then, furious he begins his March;
Drives rattling o'er a brazen Arch:
With Squibs and Crackers[7] arm'd, to throw

---

[1] Swift alters somewhat the story of Salmoneus in Greek myth; there, he is a king of Elis, so
conceited that he wanted to be worshipped as a god, and imitated the divine chariot with one
of brass (so sounding like thunder), from which torches blazed (to resemble lightning). For his
blasphemy, Zeus cast him into hell with a real thunderbolt.

[2] Went without; lacked.

[3] Pretentious, boastful but worthless fellow.

[4] Chariot.

[5] Front of the chariot, where the driver sits or stands.

[6] With oaths and curses like the then-common "pox on it."

[7] Flaming cloths and sticks, and firecrackers.

20   Among the trembling Croud below.
      All ran to Pray'rs, both Priests and Laity,
      To pacify this angry Deity;
      When *Jove*, in Pity to the Town,
      With real Thunder knock't him down.
      Then what a huge Delight were all in,
      To see the wicked Varlet[8] sprawling;
      They search't his Pockets on the Place,
      And found his Copper all was base;
      They laught at such an *Irish* Blunder,[9]
30   To take the Noise of Brass for Thunder!

      THE Moral of this Tale is proper,
      Apply'd to *Wood*'s adult'rate Copper;
      Which, as he scatter'd, we like Dolts,
      Mistook at first for Thunder-Bolts;
      Before the *Drapier* shot a Letter,
      (Nor *Jove* himself could do it better)
      Which lighting on th' Impostor's Crown,
      Like real Thunder knock't him down.

---

[8] Villain.
[9] That is, "Irish" used as it sometimes is in Britain, to mean silly or gullible.

To Quilca, *a Country House in no very good Repair, where the supposed Author, and some of his Friends, spent a Summer, in the Year 1725.*

Swift's friend, the Rev. Thomas Sheridan, owned a modest country residence in the village of Quilca, near Virginia, Co. Cavan, to which Swift made a number of visits between 1722 and 1725. He exhibits here the spirit of mild mockery common in his dealings with a number of his friends (especially those, like Sheridan, with whom he regularly exchanged rhymed raillery and assorted jeux d'esprit*), though much more than annoyance breaks through in the concluding image of a presiding deity of insufficiency attended by laziness, filth, and crime. Nevertheless, Quilca and (in his words) the "very wild country" surrounding it occupied an important place in Swift's imagination, becoming a significant part of his literary and psychological landscape. It is not coincidental that he chose to retire to Quilca in order to finish writing* Gulliver's Travels.

* * *

LET me my Properties explain,
A rotten Cabbin, dropping Rain;
Chimnies with Scorn rejecting Smoak;[1]
Stools, Tables, Chairs, and Bed-steds broke:[2]
Here Elements have lost their Uses,
Air ripens not, nor Earth produces:
In vain we make poor *Sheelah*[3] toil
Fire will not roast, nor Water boil.

---

[1] The chimney will not draw.

[2] Cf. Swift's prose piece, *The Blunders, Deficiencies, Distresses, and Misfortunes of Quilca:* "The Dean's Bed threatening every Night to fall under him. The little Table loose and broken in the Joints.... The large Table in a very tottering Condition. But one Chair in the House fit for sitting on, and that in a very ill State of Health."

[3] The name "Sile" (more often anglicized as "Sheila" in the nineteenth and twentieth centuries) here used generically for an Irish female servant.

Thro' all the Vallies, Hills and Plains,
The Goddess *Want*[4] in Triumph reigns;
And her chief Officers of State,
Sloth, *Dirt* and *Theft* around her wait.

---

[4] Used in the sense of privation, which produces lassitude and erodes any concern for good health as well as respect for private property.

Horace, Book I. Ode XIV

O navis, referent, &c.
Paraphrased and Inscribed to IRELAND

Written in the Year 1726

An uncompromising expression of Swift's anger at the wantonness of Britain's treatment of Ireland, this poem reflects on the fact that even "Protestant" Ireland, with its sense of roots in and kinship with England, has been made to suffer terribly because of the repressive policies of the British government toward its perceived "colony." Swift turns Horace's ode into both a lament for the sad condition of his country and a call to independent action ("Look to thy self") based on a genuinely patriotic ethic, though a sense of pessimism, even despair, pervades the work as a whole. Faulkner includes footnotes, followed here, simply quoting Horace's Latin, to demonstrate Swift's fidelity to the original, and hence the aptness of its contemporary application.

* * *

The INSCRIPTION.

Poor floating Isle, tost on ill Fortune's Waves,
Ordain'd by Fate to be the Land of Slaves:
Shall moving Delos[1] now deep-rooted stand,
Thou, fixt of old, be now the moving Land?
Altho' the Metaphor be worn and stale,
Betwixt a State, and Vessel under Sail;
Let me suppose thee for a Ship a while,
And thus address thee in the Sailor Stile.

UNHAPPY Ship, thou art return'd in vain:[2]
New Waves shall drive thee to the Deep again.
Look to thy self, and be no more the Sport
Of giddy Winds, but make some friendly Port.[3]
Lost are thy Oars that us'd thy Course to guide,[4]
Like faithful Counsellors on either Side.

---

[1] A floating island in the Aegean Sea, created by the god Neptune, where Apollo and his sister Artemis (Diana) were born.

[2] *O navis, referent in mare te novi / Fluctus* [Faulkner] ll. 1–2.

[3] ——*Fortiter occupa / Portum* [Faulkner] ll. 2–3.

[4] *Nudum remigio latus* [Faulkner] l. 4.

    Thy Mast, which like some aged Patriot stood
    The single Pillar for his Country's Good,
    To lead thee, as a Staff directs the Blind,
10 Behold, it cracks by yon rough *Eastern* Wind.[5]
    Your Cables burst, and you must quickly feel[6]
    The Waves impetuous entring at your Keel.
    Thus, Commonwealths receive a foreign Yoke,
    When the strong Cords of Union once are Broke.
    Torn by a sudden Tempest is thy Sail,[7]
    Expanded to invite a milder Gale.

    As when some Writer in a publick Cause,
    His Pen to save a sinking Nation draws,
    While all is Calm, his Arguments prevail,
20 The People's Voice expand his Paper Sail;
    'Till Pow'r discharging all her stormy Bags,
    Flutters the feeble Pamphlet into Rags.
    The Nation scar'd, the Author doom'd to Death,
    Who fondly put his Trust in pop'lar Breath.[8]

    A LARGER Sacrifice in vain you vow;
    There's not a Pow'r above will help you now:[9]
    A Nation thus, who oft Heav'ns Call neglects,
    In vain from injur'd Heaven Relief expects.

    'TWILL not avail, when strong Sides are broke,[10]
30 That thy Descent is from the *British* Oak:[11]
    Or when your Name and Family you boast,
    From Fleets triumphant o'er the *Gallick*[12] Coast.
    Such was *Ierne's*[13] Claim, as just as thine,
    Her Sons descended from the *British* Line;
    Her matchless Sons; whose Valour still remains
    On *French* Records, for Twenty long Campains;
    Yet from an Empress, now a Captive grown,

---

[5] ——*Malus celeri saucius* Africo [Faulkner] l. 5. This ill wind represents repressive actions or policy pronouncements from England. A number of patriots steadfast in Ireland's cause—hence resistant to that wind—had died in the 1720s.

[6] —— *Ac sine funibus / Vix durare carinae / Possint imperiosius / Æquor?* [Faulkner] ll. 6–9.

[7] *Non tibi sunt integra lintea* [Faulkner] l. 9.

[8] It is difficult not to see an autobiographical dimension to these lines: a reflection of Swift's sufferings at the hands of those in power and of his bitterness at the fickleness of his sometime followers.

[9] *Non Di, quos iterum pressa voces malo* [Faulkner] l. 10

[10] *Quamvis Pontica pinus / Silvæ filia nobilis* [Faulkner] ll. 11–12.

[11] The usual timber for British ships, hence connoting strength. The "ship" of Ireland is here being conceived of mainly in terms of those who have descended from English and Scottish settlers.

[12] French.

[13] Ireland's.

She sav'd *Britannia*'s Rights, and lost her own.[14]

    IN Ships decay'd no Mariner confides,[15]
40   Lur'd by the gilded Stern, and painted Sides.
Yet, at a Ball, unthinking Fools delight
In the gay Trappings of a Birth-Day Night:[16]
They on the Gold Brocades and Satins rav'd,
And quite forgot their Country was enslav'd.[17]

    DEAR Vessel, still be to thy Steerage just,[18]
Nor change thy Course with ev'ry sudden Gust:
Like supple Patriots of the modern Sort,
Who turn with ev'ry Gale that blows from Court.

    WEARY and Sea-sick when in thee confin'd,[19]
50   Now, for thy Safety, Cares distract the Mind.
As those who long have stood the Storms of State,
Retire, yet still bemoan their Country's Fate.[20]
Beware, and when you hear the Surges roar
Avoid the Rocks on *Britain*'s angry Shore:
They lye, alas! too easy to be found,
For thee alone they lye the Island round.

---

[14] Though the "Revolution" of 1688–89 is regarded as bloodless in Britain, it was accompanied in Ireland by considerable warfare between Williamites and Jacobites (see *Maxims Controlled in Ireland*, notes 2 & 3). Having sacrificed for the Williamite victory, Irish Protestants have seen their interests neglected by (ungrateful) Britons since. The Declaratory Act (1720), e.g., displaced the notion of Ireland's "Imperial" crown (an "Empress," as the country is emblematized as female), i.e., an independent kingdom, with that of the country as a dependency ("Captive") of the British Parliament.

[15] *Nil pictis timidus navita puppibus* [Faulkner] l. 14. "Confides" here has the meaning of "trusts in."

[16] A royal birthday evening celebration.

[17] An unmistakable echo of Swift's protests elsewhere against the ruin facing Ireland because of its addiction to rich fabrics and fashionable clothing imported from abroad.

[18] *Fidit tu, nisi ventis / Debes ludibrium cave.* [Faulkner] ll. 15–16. The line means, "Always be faithful to your course."

[19] *Nuper sollicitum quæ mihi tædium, / Nunc desiderium, curaque non levis / Interfusa nitentes / Vites æquora Cycladas* [Faulkner] ll. 17–20.

[20] Rogers notes that this is a reference to Midleton's having been forced to resign his Lord Chancellorship of Ireland in 1725.

Irel[an]d

This poem was written in September, 1727 in Holyhead, Wales, while Swift impatiently awaited passage back to Ireland and an ailing "Stella" after an extended visit to England (his last). The prose record he kept of this enforced stay in Wales has come to be known as The Holyhead Journal; *it was accompanied by several verses, this one among them. The poem below satirically exposes the political corruption eating away at the core of Irish society, caused by British misgovernance of the island and by the gutlessness and self-delusion of Irish politicians who are only too eager to do England's bidding despite the fact that they get nothing for it (thus "selling themselves for nought"). Copy-text: MS book, "Holyhead Journal," in the Foster Collection, Victoria and Albert Museum, London (first published in 1882 in the* Gentleman's Magazine).

* * *

Remove me from this land of slaves
Where all are fools and all are knaves
Where every knave & fool is bought
Yet kindly sells himself for nought
Where Whig and Tory fiercely fight
Who's in the wrong, who in the right
And when their country lyse at stake
They only fight for fighting sake,
While English sharpers[1] take the pay,
10 And then stand by to see fair play,
Mean time the whig is always winner
And for his courage gets ——a dinner.
His Excellency[2] too perhaps
Spits in his mouth and stroaks his Chaps[.][3]
The humble whelp[4] gives ev'ry vote[,]
To put the question strains his throat.[5]
His Excellency's condescension[6]
Will serve instead of place or pension[.]

---

[1] Cheats; fraudulent gamesters.
[2] The Lord-Lieutenant of Ireland, Lord Carteret.
[3] Jaw.
[4] "Unlicked cub" or puppy; here, the ordinary member of parliament.
[5] To make a motion in parliament is too much effort (especially a motion opposed to government policy).
[6] Attentiveness.

When to the window he's trepan'd[7]
20   When my L^d shakes him by the hand
Or in the presence of beholders
His arms upon the booby's[8] shoulders
You quickly see the gudgeon[9] bite,
He tells his broth^r fools at night
How well the Governor's inclind.
So just, so gentle and so kind[.]
He heard I kept a pack of hounds,
And longd to hunt upon my grounds[;]
He sd our Ladyes were so fair,
30   The land had nothing to compair.
But that indeed which pleasd me most
He calld my Dol a perfect toast.[10]
He whisprd publick things at last,
Askt me how our elections past.
Some augmentation[11] Sr You know
Would make at least a handsom show[.]
New Kings a compliment expect[12]
I shall not offer to direct[;]
There are some prating folks in town,
40   But S^r we must support the Crown.
Our Letters say a Jesuite boasts
Of some Invasion on your coasts[;]
The King is ready when you will
To pass another Pop-ry bill[,][13]
And for dissenters he intends
To use them as his truest friends[;]
I think they justly ought to share
In all employm^ts we can spare.[14]
Next for encouragm^t of spinning,

---

[7] Drawn in; attracted under false pretenses.

[8] Contemporary colloquial term for a country gentleman, especially someone comparatively uncouth; since most members of parliament were country gentlemen, this is meant generally, referring to the same member as the "humble whelp" in line 15.

[9] Fool or gull; one who readily swallows any bait. This word replaces "coxcomb" in the manuscript.

[10] "He called my lady a woman worthy of a fine gentleman's homage."

[11] Increase (to the government's revenue), hence a raising of taxes, excise, or fees on the part of parliament.

[12] In Ireland parliaments lasted the full reign of the monarch, so the accession of George II (two months earlier) would mean that a new parliament would have been elected and might be expected to show their respect for the new king by voting an increase in revenue.

[13] Capitalizing on fears of an invasion from continental Catholic countries was a frequent way for Irish administrations to convince members to vote their way; country members were often happy to support anti-Catholic legislation (a "Popery" bill).

[14] Support for Dissenters was often Whig policy in Ireland since Dissenters generally voted in favor of Whig candidates (non-Anglican Protestants could vote in elections for Parliament but could not be seated as members in their own right, a situation the Whigs wished to change but that Swift strongly defended).

50 A duty might be layd on linnen
    An act for laying down the Plough,
    England will send you corn enough.
    Anoth^r act that absentees
    For licences shall pay no fees.
    If Englands friendship you would keep
    Feed nothing in your lands but sheep[;]¹⁵
    But make an act secure and full
    To hang up all who smuggle wool.¹⁶
    And then he kindly give[s] me hints
60 That all our wives should go in Chints.¹⁷
    To morrow I shall tell you more,
    For I'm to dine with him at four.
        This was the Speech, and here's the jest[:]
    His arguments convinc't the rest.
    Away he runs with zealous hotness
    Exceeding all the fools of Totness.¹⁸
    To move that all the Nation round
    Should pay a guinnea in the pound[;]¹⁹
    Yet should this Blockhead beg a Place
70 Either from Excellence or [G]race[,]
    Tis pre-eng[a]ged and in his room
    Townshends cast page or Walpole's groom[.]²⁰

---

¹⁵ The measures referred to here—promoting linen production at the expense of woolen manufacture, converting farmland from tillage to livestock, encouraging absentee ownership of Irish estates—were ones that Swift strongly opposed, and that he regarded the Irish administration as supporting. For the final two lines, see *A Proposal for the Universal Use of Irish Manufacture*, note 1.

¹⁶ Since the export of Irish woollen goods was made illegal by the terms of the Woollen Act of 1699, to engage in that activity would be tantamount to smuggling.

¹⁷ Chintz, an imported fabric fashionable for women's dresses; the implication is that the government liked to maintain the contradictions that kept Ireland a poor nation.

¹⁸ Totness, in Devon, had proclaimed its allegiance to the new George II in tones of unusual and often mocked effusiveness.

¹⁹ A guinea was 21 shillings, a pound only 20; to pay a guinea to the pound was to submit, or be fooled, into absurd overpayment, or here, excessive taxation.

²⁰ In other words, the position has already been promised to another, such as a dismissed ("cast") servant of Lord Townsend, brother-in-law and chief lieutenant of the Whig Prime Minister, Sir Robert Walpole, or a servant of Walpole himself.

My Lady's Lamentation and Complaint against the Dean

July 28, 1728

Swift made three prolonged visits in the period 1728–1730 to the estate of Sir Arthur and Lady Acheson at Market Hill, between Armagh and Newry, Co. Down. He may have come into their acquaintance as a friend of Lady Acheson's father, Philip Savage, a former chancellor of the exchequer for Ireland. The friendship ended on a somewhat sour note when the Achesons separated, but not before Swift had written more than a dozen poems about his time at Market Hill. Many, such as the one below (which would appear to be the first of this group), engage in extensive banter and mock-insult. But though Lady Acheson is the main target of the latter, she gives back as much as she receives, and despite her (comically dramatized) complaints about Swift's extended visits, it was she rather than her husband who seems to have been the main draw for Swift and whom he remained friends with the longest. Copy-text: Works, ed. Deane Swift, 1765.

* * *

SURE never did man see
A wretch like poor Nancy,[1]
So teaz'd day and night
By a Dean and a Knight;
To punish my sins,
Sir Arthur begins,
And gives me a wipe[2]
With Skinny and Snipe:[3]
His malice is plain,
10   Hallooing the Dean.[4]
The Dean never stops
When he opens his chops;
I'm quite over-run
With rebus and pun.

Before he came here

---

[1] Lady Acheson's name was Anne.
[2] Jibe.
[3] "The Dean used to call her by those names" (Deane Swift's note).
[4] Swift is here using the common Irish pronunciation, "dane"; a recurring feature of Swift's later poetry.

To spunge[5] for good cheer,
I sat with delight,
From morning till night,
With two bony thumbs
20   Could rub my own gums,
Or scratching my nose,
And jogging my toes;
But at present, forsooth,
I must not rub a tooth:
When my elbows he sees
Held up by my knees,
My arms, like two props,
Supporting my chops,
And just as I handle 'em
30   Moving all like a pendulum;
He trips up my props,
And down my chin drops,
From my head to my heels,
Like a clock without wheels;
I sink in the spleen,[6]
An useless machine.

   If he had his will,
I should never sit still:
He comes with his whims,
40   I must move my limbs;
I cannot be sweet
Without using my feet;
To lengthen my breath
He tires me to death.
By the worst of all Squires
Thro' bogs and thro' briers,
Where a cow would be startled,
I'm in spite of my heart led:
And, say what I will,
50   Haul'd up ev'ry hill;
'Till, daggled[7] and tatter'd,
My spirit's quite shatter'd,
I return home at night,
And fast out of spite:
For I'd rather be dead,
Than it e'er should be said
I was better for him,
In stomach or limb.[8]

   But now, to my diet,

---

[5] To obtain maintenance (food, drink, shelter) from another in a mean or parasitic way.
[6] Plunge into depression.
[7] Bespattered.
[8] In appetite or physical condition.

60　No eating in quiet,
　　He's still finding fault,
　　Too sour or too salt:
　　The wing of a chick
　　I hardly can pick,
　　But trash without measure
　　I swallow with pleasure.

　　　　Next, for his diversion,
　　He rails at my person:
　　What court-breeding this is?
70　He takes me to pieces.
　　From shoulder to flank
　　I'm lean and am lank;
　　My nose, long and thin,
　　Grows down to my chin;
　　My chin will not stay,
　　But meets it half way:
　　My fingers, prolix,[9]
　　Are ten crooked sticks:
　　He swears my el---bows
80　Are two iron crows,[10]
　　Or sharp pointed rocks,
　　And wear out my smocks:
　　To 'scape them, Sir Arthur
　　Is forc'd to lie farther,
　　Or his sides they would gore
　　Like the tusk of a boar.

　　　　Now, changing the scene,
　　But still to the Dean:
　　He loves to be bitter at
90　A lady illiterate;
　　If he sees her but once,
　　He'll swear she's a dunce;
　　Can tell by her looks
　　A hater of books:
　　Thro' each line of her face
　　Her folly can trace;
　　Which spoils ev'ry feature
　　Bestow'd her by nature,
　　But sense gives a grace
100　To the homeliest face:
　　Wise books and reflexion
　　Will mend the complexion:
　　(A civil Divine!
　　I suppose meaning mine.)

---

[9] Long.
[10] Crowbars.

No Lady who wants[11] them
Can ever be handsome.

   I guess well enough
What he means by this stuff:
He haws and he hums,
110   At last out it comes.

   What, Madam? No walking,
No reading, nor talking?
You're now in your prime,
Make use of your time.
Consider, before
You come to threescore,
How the hussies will fleer[12]
Where'er you appear:
That silly old puss
120   Would fain be like us,
What a figure she made
In her tarnish'd brocade![13]

   And then he grows mild:
Come, be a good child:
If you are inclin'd
To polish your mind,
Be ador'd by the men
'Till threescore and ten,
And kill with the spleen
130   The jades of sixteen,
I'll shew you the way:
Read six hours a-day.
The wits will frequent ye,
And think you but twenty.

   Thus was I drawn in,
Forgive me my sin.
At breakfast he'll ask
An account of my task.
Put a word out of joint,
140   Or miss but a point,
He rages and frets,
His manners forgets;
And, as I am serious,
Is very imperious.
No book for delight
Must come in my sight;
But, instead of new plays,

---

[11] Lacks.
[12] Mock; sneer.
[13] Expensive but worn-out attire.

Dull Bacon's Essays,[14]
And pore ev'ry day on
150 That nasty Pantheon.[15]
If I be a drudge,
Let all the world judge.
'Twere better be blind,
Than thus be confin'd.

But, while in an ill tone,
I murder poor Milton,[16]
The Dean, you will swear,
Is at study or pray'r.
He's all the day sauntering,
160 With labourers bant'ring,
Among his colleagues,
A parcel of Teagues,[17]
(Whom he brings in among us
And bribes with mundungus.)[18]
Hail fellow, well met,
All dirty and wet:
Find out, if you can,
Who's master, who's man;
Who makes the best figure,
170 The Dean or the digger;
And which is the best
At cracking a jest.
How proudly he talks
Of zigzacks[19] and walks;
And all the day raves
Of cradles[20] and caves;
And boasts of his feats,
His grottos and seats;
Shews all his gew-gaws,[21]
180 And gapes for applause?
A fine occupation
For one in his station!
A hole where a rabbit
Would scorn to inhabit,
Dug out in an hour,

---

[14] Sir Francis Bacon (1561–1626), whose *Essays* (1597) are referred to elsewhere in Swift's writings.

[15] A popular contemporary compendium of classical mythology, translated out of the French by Andrew Tooke in 1698.

[16] John Milton, author of *Paradise Lost* (1667).

[17] Common folk: from the name Tadg (*anglice* Timothy), used exclusively of Catholics, comparable to the latterly more popular "Paddies." See *An Excellent New Song on a Seditious Pamphlet*, l. 12 and note.

[18] Strong, cheap tobacco.

[19] Zigzag paths up steep heights.

[20] Trellises.

[21] Flashy but worthless ornamentation.

He calls it a bow'r.

    But, Oh, how we laugh,
To see a wild calf
Come, driven by heat,
190 And foul the green seat;
Or run helter-skelter
To his arbor for shelter,
Where all goes to ruin
The Dean has been doing.
The girls of the village
Come flocking for pillage,
Pull down the fine briers,
And thorns, to make fires;
But yet are so kind
200 To leave something behind:
No more need be said on't
I smell when I tread on't.

    Dear friend, Doctor Jenny,
If I could but win ye,
Or Walmsley or Whaley,[22]
To come hither daily,
Since Fortune, my foe,
Will needs have it so,
That I'm, by her frowns,
210 Condemn'd to black gowns;[23]
No 'Squire to be found
The neighbourhood round,
(For, under the rose,[24]
I would rather chuse those:)
If your wives will permit ye,
Come here out of pity,
To ease a poor Lady,
And beg her a play-day.[25]
So may you be seen
220 No more in the spleen:
May Walmsley give wine,
Like a hearty divine;
May Whaley disgrace
Dull Daniel's whey-face;[26]
And may your three spouses
Let you lie at friends houses.

----

[22] Rev. Henry Jenney, D.D., Archdeacon of Armagh, Rev. John Walmsley, and Rev. Nathaniel Whaley, all of them at the time fairly local. Whaley's title to the rectory of Armagh was at the time under litigation, and strongly supported by Swift for political reasons.

[23] Clergymen.

[24] *Sub rosa*; in secret.

[25] A holiday; a day given over to recreation or festivities.

[26] Richard Daniel, Dean of Armagh and poetaster, strongly disliked by Swift for both personal and political reasons; Daniel was opposing Whaley's title to the rectory of Armagh.

Verses Occasioned by the Sudden Drying Up of ST. PATRICK'S WELL near Trinity College, Dublin, in 1726 [1729?]

St. Patrick's Well in Dublin was popularly ascribed to the saint's miraculous powers and was regarded as restoring health to the sick. Despite the "1726" in the title of the first printed edition of the work, the well actually ran dry in 1729 (and was repaired two years later, having perhaps only become clogged by debris requiring clearance). The year 1726 may have seemed suitable for its greater proximity to the Wood's halfpence controversy, in which the triumph of Irish interests was hard won and short-lived. Swift's elaborate antiquarian footnotes to the poem (provided here as they appear in Faulkner's 1762 edition) have seemed to some a parody on pedantic scholarly apparatus in the vein of his earlier Scriblerian satire. But whatever their intention, the poem as a whole presents a picture of Irish history that stands as a forceful condemnation of England's abusive and ungrateful treatment of Ireland and its hypocritical stance of superiority toward its "colony," though the verse ends on a note of disgust for all parties concerned. Copy-text: Works, *ed. Faulkner, 1762 (cited as F '62 in notes).*

* * *

BY holy Zeal inspir'd, and led by Fame,[1]
To thee, once fav'rite Isle, with Joy I came;
What Time the *Goth*, the *Vandal*, and the *Hun*,
Had my own native *Italy*[2] o'er-run.
Ierne, to the world's remotest Parts,
Renowned for Valour,[3] Policy and Arts.

---

[1] *Festus Avienus* flourished in 370. See his Poem *De oris Maritimus*, where he uses this expression concerning Ireland, *Insula sacra et sic Insulam dixere Prisci; eamque late Gens Hibernorum colit* (Note in F '62).

[2] *Italy* was not properly the native Place of St. *Patrick*, but the Place of his Education, and whence he received his Mission; and because he had his new Birth there, hence, by poetical Licence, and by Scripture-Figure, our Author calls that Country his native *Italy* (Note in F '62).

[3] *Julius Solinus*, who lived about the Time of *Tacitus*, in the Year 80, Chap. 21, speaking of the Irish as a warlike Nation, says, that the Wives in Ireland, when delivered of a Son, give the Child its first Food off the Point of their Husband's Sword. *Puerpera, si quando marem edidit,*

HITHER from *Colchos*,[4] with the fleecy Ore,
Jason arrived two thousand Years before.
Thee, happy Island, *Pallas* call'd her own,[5]
10   When haughty *Britain* was a Land unknown.
From thee, with Pride, the *Caledonians*[6] trace
The glorious Founder of their kingly Race:
Thy martial Sons, whom now they dare despise,
Did once their Land subdue and civilize:
Their Dress, their Language, and the *Scottish* Name,
Confess[7] the Soil from whence the Victors came.
Well may they boast that antient Blood, which runs
Within their Veins, who are thy younger Sons,
A Conquest and a Colony from thee,
20   The Mother-Kingdom left her Children free;
From thee no Mark of Slavery they felt,
Not so with thee thy base Invaders dealt,

---

primos Cibos Gladio imponit mariti, inque os Parvuli summo mucrone auspicium alimentorum leviter infert et Gentilibus votis optat, non aliter quam in Bello et inter Arma mortem oppetat. Again, *Præcipua viris Gloria est in Armorum tutela.*

Polydore Virgil says, they were distinguished for their Skill in Music. *Hiberni sunt Musicæ peritissimi.* So *Giraldus Cambrensis*, who was Preceptor to King John, in his *Topographia Hiberniæ*, Chap. 11. *In Musicis solum præ omni Natione, quam vidimus incomparabiliter est instructa Gens hæc* (Note in F '62).

[4] *Orpheus*, or the antient Author of the *Greek* Poem on the *Argonautic* Expedition, whoever he be, says, that *Jason*, who manned the Ship *Argos* at *Thessaly*, sailed to *Ireland*. And *Adrianus Junius* says the same Thing in these Lines

    Illa ego sum Graiis, olim glacialis Ierne
    Dicta, et Jasoniæ Puppis bene cognita Nautis. (Note in F '62)

[5] *Tacitus*, in the Life of *Julius Agricola* says, that the Harbours of *Ireland*, on Account of their Commerce, were better known to the trading Part of the World, than those of *Britain*. *Solum, cælumque, & ingenia cultusque Hominum, haud multum a Britannia differunt; melius aditus, Portusque per Commercia et Negotiatores cogniti* (Note in F '62). The reference to Pallas (Athena) denotes, however, Ireland's ancient reputation for scholarship.

[6] *Fordon*, in his *Scoti-Chronicon*, *Hector Boethius*, *Buchanan*, and all the *Scotch* Historians agree, that *Fergus*, Son of *Ferquard* King of *Ireland*, was the first King of *Scotland*, which Country he subdued. That he began to reign 330 Years before the Christian Æra, and in returning to his native Country, was shipwrecked on those Rocks in the County of *Antrim*, which from that Accident have been since named *Carrickfergus*. His descendants reigned after him in *Scotland*; for the Crown was settled on him and his lineal Successors. See the List of the Kings of *Scotland* in *Hector Boethius* and *George Buchanan*, which begins thus: I. *Fergusius primus Scotorum Rex, filius Ferquardi Regis Hiberniæ, regnare incepit anno ante Christi Servatoris in carnem adventem trecentesimo trigesimo. Regnavit annis* xxv *et naufragio periit ad Scopulum Fergusis (Cragffergus vernacule) in mari Hiberniæ.*
The *Irish* Language and Habit are still retained in the Northern Parts of *Scotland*, where the *Highlanders* speak the *Irish* Tongue and use their antient Dress. As to the Name *Scotland*, *Camden de Hibernia* mentions it from the Authority of *Isidore* and *Beda*, that they called *Ireland*, *Scotia*, and that *Scotland* was termed *Scotia a Scotis Incolis, et inde Scotiæ nomen cum Scotis in Britanniam nostrum commigrasse*. Bede, Lib. I. cap. I, says, *Hibernia propria Scotorum Patria* (Note in F '62).

[7] Manifest; attest.

Invited here to 'vengeful *Morrough*'s aid,[8]
Those whom they could not conquer, they betray'd.
Britain, by thee we fell, ungrateful Isle!
Not by thy Valour, but superior Guile:
Britain, with Shame confess, this Land of mine[9]
First taught thee human Knowledge and divine;
My Prelates and my Students, sent from hence,
30   Made your Sons Converts both to God and Sense:
Not like the Pastors of thy rav'nous Breed,
Who come to fleece the Flocks, and not to feed.[10]

WRETCHED *Ierne*! with what Grief I see
The fatal Changes Time hath made in thee.
The Christian Rites I introduc'd in vain:
Lo! Infidelity return'd again.
Freedom and Virtue in thy Sons I found,
Who now in Vice and Slavery are drown'd.

BY Faith and Prayer, this Crosier in my hand,
40   I drove the venom'd Serpent from thy Land;
The Shepherd in his Bower might sleep or sing,[11]
Nor dread the Adder's Tooth, nor Scorpion's Sting.

---

[8] In the Reign of King *Henry* II. *Dermot M'Morough* King of *Leinster*, being deprived of his Kingdom by *Roderick O'Connor* King of *Connaught*, he invited the *English* over as Auxiliaries, and promised *Richard Strangbow*, Earl of *Pembroke*, his Daughter, and all his Dominions as a Portion. By this Assistance *M'Morough* recovered his Crown, and *Strangbow* became possessed of all *Leinster*. After this, more Forces being sent into *Ireland*, the *English* became powerful here; and when *Henry* II. arrived, the *Irish* Princes submitted to his Government, and began to use the *English* Laws (Note in F '62).

[9] *St. Patrick* arrived in *Ireland* in the Year 431, and compleated the Conversion of the Natives, which had been begun by *Palladius* and others. And as Bishop *Nicholson* observes, (who was better acquainted with all the Contents of all the antient Histories of both Kingdoms than any Man of the Age) *Ireland* soon became the Fountain of Learning, to which all the Western Christians, as well as the *English*, had Recourse, not only for Instruction in the Principles of Religion, but in all Sorts of Literature; *viz. Legendi & Scholasticæ Eruditionis gratia*. For within a Century after the Death of *St. Patrick*, the *Irish* Seminaries of Learning increased to such a Degree, that most Parts of *Europe* sent hither their Children to be educated, and had from hence both their Bishops and Doctors. See venerable *Bede*, an *English* Historian of undoubted Credit, *Hist. Eccles*. Lib. 3, cap. 4, 7, 10, 11, 27. Among other *Irish* Apostles, he says, Saint *Columb* converted all the *Picts*, and many other *Britons*; and that Saint *Aidan* was the Instructor of King *Oswald*'s *Saxon* Subjects in Christianity. *Camden de Hibernia* writes: *Subsequente ætate Scoticis Monarchis nihil Sanctius, nihil Eruditius fuerit, et in universam Europam sanctissimorum virorum Examina emiserint*. He says farther, that they not only repaired to *Ireland*, as to the Mart of Learning, but also brought from thence even the Form of their Letters: *Anglosaxones etiam nostri illa ætate in Hiberniam tanquam ad bonarum Literarum Mercaturam undique confluxerunt; unde de Viris Sanctis sæpissime in nostris Scriptoribus legitur; Amandatus est ad disciplinam in Hiberniam. Indeque nostrates Saxones rationem formandi Literas accepisse videantur, quum eodem plane Charactere usi fuerint, qui hodie Hibernicis est in usu* (Note in F '62).

[10] See Ezekiel 34:2–8.

[11] There are no Snakes, Vipers or Toads in *Ireland*; and even Frogs were not known there until about the Year 1700. The Magpyes came a short Time before, and the *Norway* Rats since

WITH Omens oft I strove to warn thy Swains,
Omens, the Types of thy impending Chains.
I sent the Magpye from the *British* Soil,
With restless Beak thy blooming Fruit to spoil,
To din thine Ears with unharmonious Clack,
And haunt thy holy Walls in white and black.
What else are those thou seest in Bishop's Geer,
50   Who crop the Nurseries of Learning here?
Aspiring, greedy, full of senseless Prate,
Devour the Church, and chatter to the State.

   As you grew more degenerate and base,
I sent you Millions of the croaking Race;[12]
Emblems of Insects vile, who spread their Spawn
Through all thy Land, in Armour, Fur and Lawn:
A nauseous Brood, that fills your Senate Walls,
And in the Chambers of your Viceroy crawls.

   SEE, where the new-devouring Vermin runs,
60   Sent in my anger from the Land of *Huns*;
With harpy Claws it undermines the Ground,
And sudden spreads a numerous Offspring round;
Th' amphibious Tyrant, with his rav'nous Band,
Drains all thy Lakes of Fish, of Fruits thy Land.

   WHERE is the sacred Well, that bore my Name?
Fled to the Fountain back, from whence it came!
Fair Freedom's Emblem once, which smoothly flows,
And Blessings equally on all bestows.
Here, from the neighbouring Nursery of Arts,[13]
70   The Students drinking, rais'd their Wit and Parts;
Here, for an Age and more, improved their Vein,
Their *Phoebus* I, my spring their *Hippocrene*.[14]
Discourag'd Youths, now all their Hopes must fail,
Condemn'd to Country Cottages and Ale;
To foreign[15] Prelates make a slavish Court,
And by their Sweat procure a mean Support;

(Note in F '62). The imagery in lines 40 and 42 contains biblical echoes; see e.g., Psalms 58:4 and 140:8, and Proverbs 23:32.

[12] Frogs; as magpies specifically denote bishops appointed from England, frogs represent those English immigrants who, if we take literally the date in n. 11, above, have overtaken Ireland since the Williamite victories of the early 1690s, and have proliferated in the military, the judiciary and the bench of bishops ("Armour, Fur and Lawn").

[13] The University of *Dublin*, called *Trinity College*, was founded by Queen *Elizabeth* in 1591 (Note in F '62).

[14] The fountain of the Muses on Mount Helicon; hence the source of poetic inspiration. "*Phoebus*" ("the Radiant One") was another name and epithet for Apollo, the Greek Sun-God.

[15] English.

Or, for the Classicks read th' Attorney's Guide;
Collect Excise, or wait upon the Tide.[16]

    O! had I been Apostle to the *Swiss*,
80   Or hardy *Scot*,[17] or any Land but this;
Combined in Arms, they had their Foes defy'd,
And kept their Liberty, or bravely dy'd.
Thou still with Tyrants in Succession curst,
The last Invaders trampling on the first:
Nor fondly hope for some Reverse of Fate,
Virtue herself would now return too late.
Not half thy Course of Misery is run,
Thy greatest Evils yet are scarce begun.
Soon shall thy Sons, the Time is just at Hand,
90   Be all made Captives in their native Land;
When, for the use of no *Hibernian* born,
Shall rise one Blade of Grass, one Ear of Corn;
When Shells and Leather shall for Money pass,
Nor thy oppressing Lords afford thee Brass.[18]
But all turn Leasers to that mongril Breed,[19]
Who from thee sprung, yet on thy Vitals feed;
Who to yon rav'nous Isle thy treasures bear,
And waste in Luxury thy Harvests there;
For Pride and Ignorance a Proverb grown,
100 The Jest of Wits, and to the Court unknown.

    I SCORN thy spurious and degenerate Line,
And from this Hour my Patronage resign.

---

[16] Become a customs officer (also known as a "tide-waiter"); a position usually given to political supporters of the government of the day.

[17] Symbols of national resistance and independence—though unlike the Swiss, the Scots eventually lost theirs (in the Union of 1707).

[18] *Wood*'s ruinous Project against the People of *Ireland*, was supported by Sir *Robert Walpole* in 1724 (Note in F '62).

[19] The Absentees, who spend the Income of their *Irish* Estates, Places and Pensions in *England* (Note in F '62).

DRAPIER'S HILL

Another of the "Market Hill" poems, this one describes Swift's purchase of a plot of land belonging to Sir Arthur Acheson at Drumlack, near Portadown, just north of Sir Arthur's estate, in the summer of 1729. Swift's plans for developing the property came to nothing—in a subsequent poem, The Dean's Reasons for Not Building at Drapier's Hill, *he expresses his realization that "I differ from the Knight / In every point, like black and white" (ll. 71–72) and asks himself, "How could I form so wild a vision, / To seek, in deserts, Fields Elysian?" (ll. 15–16). But the poem* Drapier's Hill *is noteworthy for Swift's explicit reference to himself as an Irish patriot, and for its sardonic glance at how quickly fame fades.*

* * *

    WE give the World to understand,
    Our thriving D[ea]n has purchas'd Land;
    A Purchase which will bring him clear,
    Above his Rent four Pounds a Year;[1]
    Provided, to improve the Ground,
    He will but add two Hundred Pound,
    And from his endless hoarded Store,
    To build a House five Hundred more.
    Sir *Arthur* too shall have his Will,
10   And call the Mansion *Drapier*'s Hill;
    That when a Nation long enslav'd,
    Forgets by whom it once was sav'd;
    When none the DRAPIER'S Praise shall sing;
    His Signs aloft no longer swing;
    His Medals and his Prints forgotten,
    And all his Handkerchiefs are rotten;[2]

---

[1] That is, if funds are spent for building and other improvements and the property is leased out, it would bring in four pounds a year above Swift's previous income from rentals. See the opening of Swift's *Horace, Lib. 2, Sat. 6*, "Part of it Imitated": "I often wish'd, that I had clear / For Life, six hundred Pounds a Year" (1714).

[2] "Medals were cast; many Signs hung up; and Handkerchiefs made with Devices in honour of the Author, under the Name of *M. B. Drapier*" (Faulkner's note).

His famous LETTERS³ made waste Paper;
This Hill may keep the name of DRAPIER:
In Spight of Envy flourish still,
20   And DRAPIER'S vye with COOPER'S Hill.⁴

---

³ *The Drapier's Letters.*

⁴ The famous loco-descriptive poem of 1642, *Cooper's Hill*, by Sir John Denham, set outside London and weighing the contentions between King and Parliament in light of the concept of *concordia discors* (harmony springing from discord), which was often imitated well into the eighteenth century. In *Windsor-Forest* (1713), Pope pays tribute to "majestic *Denham*" and declares, "(On *Cooper*'s Hill eternal Wreaths shall grow, / While lasts the Mountain, or while *Thames* shall flow)" (ll. 265–66); but see the satiric send-up of "apeing Lines from *Cooper's Hill*" in Swift's and Mary Barber's verse, *Apollo's Edict*, ll. 46–49.

A Pastoral Dialogue

Dialogue poems in the pastoral tradition often use either classical names (Phoebe, Meliboeus) or vernacular names drawn from common rural life—sometimes drawn from quite a remove, like Spenser's "Hobbinol," but more often genuine names, like Spenser's "Colin." The names "Diarmuid" and "Sile" were and are common in Ireland, and Swift's anglicized version of the latter name ("Sheelah"), though this spelling is rare nowadays, would have replicated the sound of the Irish accurately. Written in the fall of 1729 (probably at Market Hill), this work mocks the poetic pastoral tradition, demythologizing the romantic language and conventions typically used to paint an idyllic picture of country living, and thus reflecting Swift's general disdain for all attempts to idealize Ireland's harsh or ludicrous realities. The coarse physicality in this poem goes beyond the "realism" of Gay's The Shepherd's Week *(1714) and (though not as lewd) calls to mind the mock-pastoral verses of the Earl of Rochester written in the 1670s.*

*   *   *

DERMOT, SHEELAH

A NYMPH and Swain, *Sheelah* and *Dermot* hight,[1]
Who *wont* to weed the court of *Gosford Knight*,[2]
While each with stubbed[3] Knife remov'd the Roots
That rais'd between the Stones their daily Shoots;
As at their Work they sat in counterview,[4]
With mutual Beauty smit, their Passion grew.
Sing heavenly Muse in sweetly flowing Strain,
The soft endearments of the Nymph and Swain.

DERMOT.

MY love to *Sheelah* is more firmly fixt,
10   Than strongest Weeds that grow these Stones betwixt:
My *Spud*[5] these Nettles from the Stones can part;
No Knife so keen to weed thee from my Heart.

---

[1] Called; an archaism meant at once to invoke and to ridicule the pastoral tradition.
[2] "Sir *Arthur Acheson*, whose Great Grand-Father was Sir *Archibald* of *Gosford* in *Scotland*" (Faulkner's note).
[3] Stubby; short.
[4] Facing one another.
[5] A short weeding-knife.

SHEELAH.

MY Love for gentle *Dermot* faster grows,
Than yon tall Dock[6] that rises to thy Nose.
Cut down the Dock, 'twill sprout again; but O!
Love rooted out, again will never grow.

DERMOT.

No more that Bry'r thy tender Leg shall rake:
(I spare the Thistle for Sir *Arthur*'s sake.)[7]
Sharp are the Stones, take thou this rushy Mat;
20   The hardest Bum will bruise with sitting squat.

SHEELAH.

THY Breeches torn behind, stand gaping wide;
This Petticoat shall save thy dear Back-side;
Nor need I blush, although you feel it wet;
Dermot, I vow, 'tis nothing else but Sweat.

DERMOT.

AT an old stubborn Root I chanc'd to tug,
When the Dean threw me this Tobacco-plug:[8]
A longer Half-p'orth[9] never did I see;
This, dearest *Sheelah*, thou shalt share with me.

SHEELAH.

IN at the Pantry-door this Morn I slipt,
30   And from the Shelf a charming Crust I whipt:
Dennis[10] was out, and I got hither safe;
And thou, my Dear, shalt have the bigger Half.

DERMOT.

WHEN you saw *Tady* at Long-bullets[11] play,
You sat and lous'd[12] him all a Sun-shine Day.
How could you, *Sheelah*, listen to his Tales,
Or crack such Lice as his betwixt your Nails?

---

[6] A broad-leaved weed.

[7] "Who is a great Lover of *Scotland*" (Faulkner's note). The thistle is the national symbol of Scotland, whence the Acheson family originated.

[8] Compressed wad of tobacco for chewing. The "Dean" is Swift himself.

[9] An item valued at a half-penny, hence not very big or significant.

[10] "Sir *Arthur*'s Butler" (Faulkner's note).

[11] A form of bowling still played in Ireland, mainly on country roads, with an iron ball or "bullet" (since a bullet would have been a round ball in the era before cartridges were invented). "*Tady*" is an anglicized version of the Irish name "Tadhg"; other versions are "Teague" and "Thady."

[12] Deloused.

SHEELAH.

WHEN you with *Oonagh*[13] stood behind a Ditch,
I peept, and saw you kiss the dirty Bitch.
Dermot, how could you touch those nasty Sluts!
40   I almost wish this *Spud* were in your Guts.

DERMOT.

IF *Oonah* once I kiss'd, forbear to chide;
Her Aunt's my Gossip[14] by my Father's Side:
But, if I ever touch her Lips again,
May I be doom'd for Life to weed in Rain.

SHEELAH.

DERMOT, I swear, tho' *Tady*'s Locks could hold
Ten Thousand Lice, and ev'ry Louse was Gold.
Him on my Lap you never more should see;
Or may I lose my Weeding-Knife—— and thee.

DERMOT.

O, COULD I earn for thee, my lovely Lass,
50   A Pair of Brogues[15] to bear thee dry to Mass!
But see, where *Norah* with the Sowins[16] comes——
Then let us rise, and rest our weary Bums.

---

[13] An anglicized version of the Irish name Una.
[14] Godmother.
[15] Thick shoes, generally of untanned hide, worn by the poor in the wilder parts of western and northern Ireland.
[16] A porridge of oatmeal that includes the oat-bran or shells, which was at that time common in Scotland and in the north of Ireland. Again a common Irish name (*Norah*) is used for the kitchen maid.

On the Irish-Club

This poem was occasioned by the arrest of news-criers in February 1730 for hawking Swift's Libel on the Reverend Dr. Delany, *an uncompromising attack on* Walpole *("He comes to tye our chains on faster, / And shew us,* England *is our* Master"[125–26]) *and other contemporary politicians, delivered by one "who, from my Soul, sincerely hate / Both* Kings *and* Ministers of State" *(173–74), which provoked considerable controversy as well as the attempted prosecution of the printer by Lord Joshua Allen.* On the Irish Club *attacks censorship of the press as "unpatriotic" and generally lashes out against the kind of political spinelessness and corruptibility that Swift saw destroying all hopes of good governance in Ireland. Here the focus of his wrath is the House of Lords; a later poem makes the House of Commons his satiric target (see* A Character ... of the Legion Club). *Copy-text:* Works, ed. Deane Swift, 1765.

* * *

      YE paultry underlings of state,
      Ye s[enator]s, who love to prate;
      Ye r[ascal]s of inferior note,
      Who, for a dinner, sell a vote;
      Ye pack of pensionary P[ee]rs,[1]
      Whose fingers itch for poets ears;[2]
      Ye bishops far remov'd from saints,
      Why all this rage? Why these complaints?
      Why against Printers all this noise?
10   This summoning of blackguard boys?[3]
      Why so sagacious in your guesses?
      Your *effs* and *tees*, and *arrs*, and *esses*?[4]
      Take my advice; to make you safe,

---

[1] Often the government kept Members and Lords on its side by awarding them with regular payments, or "pensions."

[2] To inflict a punishment on the ears by "boxing" (blows) or cutting, usually for insolence, here more particularly for expressing offensive sentiments; evokes associations with the highly repressive policies of Bishop William Laud in the seventeenth century, who had the ears of Puritans cut off for publishing materials deemed heterodox.

[3] Street 'arabs'; urchins hired to perform menial errands—in this case, to hawk Swift's poem through the streets of Dublin.

[4] The letters are chosen to mock the notion of "sniffing" out a meaning. See *Gulliver's Travels*, Part III, ch. 6, where those dedicated to discovering secret plots "can decypher all initial Letters into political Meanings."

I know a shorter way by half.
The point is plain: Remove the cause;
Defend your liberties and laws.
Be sometimes to your country true,
Have once the public good in view:
Bravely despise Champagne at Court,
20   And chuse to dine at home with Port:⁵
Let Pr[elate]s, by their good behaviour,
Convince us they believe a Saviour;
Nor sell what they so dearly bought,
This country, now their own, for nought.
Ne'er did a true satyric muse
Virtue or innocence abuse;
And 'tis against poetic rules
To rail at men by nature fools:
But * * * * * * * *
* * * * * * * * * *⁶

---

⁵ Port would have been considered at the time a plainer, less fashionable and expensive drink, hence a less likely means of political persuasion or bribery.

⁶ The poem deliberately ends without ending, seemingly to suggest that the Bishops and the other Irish lords *are* by nature fools—a disclosure that cannot be expressly stated because it would violate the "rules" of poetic decorum (not that that had ever deterred Swift before). Yet the asterisks could as readily be substituting for a perhaps even more damning revelation—that these figures are *not* fools but something worse: knaves, or those whose destructive actions emanate from malice aforethought or ruthless calculation rather than mere ignorance or stupidity. Either way, Irish bishops and politicians are caught firmly in Swift's satiric crosshairs, condemned even in the absence of explicit accusation. Swift often used asterisks to good satiric effect in his early writings; see *The Battel of the Books* and *A Tale of a Tub*.

An Excellent New Ballad; or the True English Dean to be Hanged for a Rape

Written in the Year 1730

The Dean of the title here is "——Sawbridge, Dean of Fernes, lately deceased"
(Faulkner's note). Dr. Thomas Sawbridge, who had been appointed Dean of
Ferns in 1728, was accused in June 1730 of the rape of Susanna Runcard, and
acquitted of the crime after a trial later that same month—according to Swift,
because "he bought her off." He died in 1733, without any official effect upon
his deanship. There is an obvious and intended contrast here with Swift, whose
appointment as Dean of St. Patrick's was controversial in 1713 and who was
viewed with suspicion by the Whig government in power after 1714. Darker is
the insinuation that England has, with Sawbridge and by other means, "raped"
Ireland. That Sawbridge had previously served as chaplain for the East India
Company in Bombay made him an especially apt figure to represent Britain's
imperial reach and sense of impunity.

* * *

I.

Our Brethren of *England*, who love us so dear,
   And in all they do for us so kindly do mean,
A Blessing upon them, have sent us this Year,
   For the Good of our Church a true *English* Dean.
A holier Priest ne'er was wrapt up in Crape,[1]
The worst you can say, he committed a Rape.

II.

In his Journey to *Dublin*, he lighted at *Chester*,[2]
   And there he grew fond of another Man's Wife;
Burst into her Chamber, and wou'd have carest her,
10   But she valu'd her Honour much more than her Life.

---

[1] Crepe; cloth traditionally associated with clergy.
[2] An ancient walled city on the River Dee, near the border between England and Wales, which at this time served as an important coaching center on the route from London to Holyhead, from where one could get a boat across the Channel to Ireland. Swift himself was familiar with this route.

She bustled and struggled, and made her Escape,
To a Room full of Guests for fear of a Rape.

III.

THE *Dean* he pursu'd to recover his Game:
  And now to attack her again he prepares;
But the Company stood in Defence of the Dame,
  They cudgel'd, and cuft him, and kick'd him down Stairs.
His Deanship was now in a damnable Scrape,
And this was no Time for committing a Rape.

IV.

To *Dublin* he comes, to the *Bagnio*[3] he goes,
20   And orders the Landlord to bring him a Whore;
No Scruple came on him his Gown to expose,
  'Twas what all his Life he had practis'd before.
He had made himself drunk with the Juice of the Grape,
And got a good *Clap*,[4] but committed no Rape.

V.

THE *Dean*, and his Landlord, a jolly Comrade,
  Resolv'd for a Fortnight to swim in Delight;
For why, they had both been brought up to the Trade
  Of drinking all Day, and of whoring all Night.
His Landlord was ready his Deanship to ape
30 In ev'ry Debauch, but committing a Rape.

VI.

THIS *Protestant* Zealot, this *English* Divine,
  In Church and in State was of Principles sound;
Was truer than *Steele*[5] to the *Hanover* Line,
  And griev'd that a *Tory* should live above Ground.
Shall a Subject so loyal be hang'd by the Nape,
For no other Crime but committing a Rape?

VII.

BY old *Popish* Canons, as wise Men have penn'd 'em,
  Each Priest had a Concubine, *jure Ecclesiæ*;[6]
Who'd be Dean of *Ferns* without a *Commendam*?[7]

---

[3] Literally a bath or bath-house (from the Italian), but generally used to mean a brothel.

[4] Sexually transmitted disease, usually gonorrhea.

[5] Punning play upon the aphorism, "true as steel," and the vocal Whiggish Protestantism of Swift's countryman Sir Richard Steele, with whom he had fallen out during the Harley ministry and who had died in 1729.

[6] Literally, though incorrectly, "by the law of the church," or Canon Law.

[7] Figuratively (from "*in commendam*," "in trust"), the emoluments of an ecclesiastical office, entrusted to someone other than the person normally designated; most commonly therefore used as a supplement to a dignitary's stipend. The revenues of the Church of Ireland cathedral in Ferns, for instance, a village in Co. Wexford, were very low, and the dean's salary thus

40   And Precedents we can produce, if it please ye:
          Then, why should the Dean, when Whores are so cheap,
          Be put to the Peril, and Toyl of a Rape?

VIII.

IF Fortune should please but to take such a Crotchet,[8]
     (To thee I apply great *Smedley*'s Successor)[9]
To give thee *Lawn-Sleeves*, a *Mitre* and *Rotchet*,[10]
     Whom would'st thou resemble? I leave thee a Guesser;
But I only behold thee in *Atherton*'s Shape
For *Sodomy* hang'd, as thou for a Rape.[11]

IX.

AH! dost thou not envy the brave Colonel *Chartres*,[12]
50   Condemn'd for thy Crime, at three Score and Ten?
          To hang him all *England* would lend him their Garters;
            Yet he lives, and is ready to ravish agen.
          Then throttle thy self with an Ell[13] of strong Tape,
          For thou hast not a Groat to attone for a Rape.

X.

THE Dean he was vext that his Whores were so willing:
     He long'd for a Girl that would struggle and squal;
He ravish'd her fairly, and sav'd a good Shilling;
     But, here was to pay the Devil and all.
His Trouble and Sorrows now come in a Heap,
60   And hang'd he must be for committing a Rape.

---

was increased by attaching *commendams*—here being expansively defined to include sexual favors.

    [8] An idiosyncratic opinion or notion, especially one at great variance with common wisdom, like the idea of Sawbridge's becoming a bishop.

    [9] Jonathan Smedley was a nemesis of Swift's, a violent Low Church Whig and author of *Gulliveriana*. He (briefly) preceded Sawbridge as Dean of Ferns before following in Sawbridge's footsteps by taking up a post with the East India Company. The implication here is that the two "resemble" one another in other ways as well.

    [10] Items of episcopal costume: "*Lawn*" and "*Rotchet*" ("rochet") refer to the linen of a bishop's sleeves and surplice, respectively, and a "*Mitre*" is the double-peaked bishop's headgear. In a letter to the 2nd Earl of Oxford in August, 1730, Swift wrote, "I name [Sawbridge] to your Lordship, because I am confident you will hear of his being a Bishop."

    [11] John Atherton, "A Bishop of *Waterford*, sent from *England* a hundred years ago" (Faulkner's note). Appointed Bishop of Waterford and Lismore in 1636, he was hanged in Dublin in 1640 following his conviction for an "unnatural crime" (i.e., buggery with his steward and tithe protector, John Childe).

    [12] Francis Charteris (pron. "charters"), at various times a soldier, a gambler, and a moneylender, of strong Whig sympathies, was convicted of raping his maid-servant, Anne Bond, in 1730 (at the age of 55, not 70) and sentenced to death, but quickly obtained a royal pardon, probably through Walpole's influence. Known as the "Rapemaster General of Great Britain" for a long history of similar incidents, he appears as the sinister figure in the doorway in Plate 1 of Hogarth's *The Harlot's Progress* (1732).

    [13] Length, generally of about a yard.

XI.

IF Maidens are ravish't, it is their own Choice;
  Why are they so wilful to struggle with Men?
If they would but lye quiet, and stifle their Voice,
  No Devil nor Dean could ravish 'em then.
Nor would there be need of a strong Hempen Cape,[14]
Ty'd round the Dean's Neck, for committing a Rape.

XII.

OUR Church and our State dear *England* maintains,
  For which all true Protestant Hearts should be glad;
She sends us our B[ishop]s and J[udge]s and D[ean]s;[15]
70   And better would give us, if better she had;
But, Lord how the Rabble will stare and will gape,
When the good *English* Dean is hang'd up for a Rape.

---

[14] That is, a rope made of hemp.

[15] Note the Irish rhyme here (following upon others, on ll. 41–42 and 59–60), which under-scores the point that this (anonymous) broadside is being written by an *Irishman* protesting the ravishment of his country by the *English* establishment in his native idiom. Since, as a "Ballad," this piece is conceived as a work of oral as much as written literature, the pronuncia-tion of words and general sound of the language is of utmost importance to the poem's power and meaning.

On the Irish Bishops

This poem, which appeared untitled in Faulkner's edition, was occasioned by two bills (a Bill of Residence and a Bill of Division) sponsored by the bishops of the Church of Ireland and passed by the House of Lords in February 1732, which would have compelled most of the lower clergy to reside in their parishes and build on the land allotted to them, and which would have enabled the bishop of the diocese to divide a parish valued at more than £100 per year without the consent of the incumbent parish minister. Since both bills would have had the effect of reducing the income of the inferior clergy while expanding the authority of the bishops, Swift fiercely opposed their passage, accusing their episcopal supporters of acting out of "the spirit of ambition and love of power, to make the whole body of the clergy their slaves and vassals until the day of judgment, under the load of poverty and contempt." Partly on the strength of his high-profile pamphlet campaign against the bills, both were defeated in the House of Commons at the end of February.

*   *   *

We found the following Poem printed in *Fog's* Journal of the 17th of Sept. 1733. It was written in the last Session, and many Copies were taken, but never printed here. The Subject of it is now over; but our Author's known Zeal against that Project made him generally supposed to be the Author. We reprint it just as it lyes in *Fog's* Journal.[1]

The following Poem is the Product of Ireland; *it was occasioned by the B[ishop]s of that Kingdom endeavouring to get an Act to divide the Church Livings, which Bill was rejected by the* Irish *House of Commons. It is said to be written by an honest Curate; the Reader of Taste perhaps, may guess who the Curate could be, that was capable of writing it.*[2]

> OLD *Latimer*[3] preaching did fairly describe
> A B[ishop] who rul'd all the rest of his Tribe;
> And who is this B[ishop]? And where does he dwell?

---

[1] Faulkner's headnote, 1735.

[2] Original headnote in *Fog's Journal*, as given in Faulkner; the date of the issue was actually September 15, 1733.

[3] Hugh Latimer, Bishop of Worcester, a major figure in the English Reformation for his famous preaching and a prominent victim of Queen Mary's persecution of the Protestants; in his sermon "Of the Plough" (1548), he identifies the devil as the most active bishop in England.

Why truly 'tis *Satan*, Arch-b[ishop] of Hell:
And HE was a Primate, and HE wore a Mitre,
Surrounded with Jewels of Sulphur and Nitre.[4]
How nearly this B[ishop] our B[ishop][5] resembles!
But his has the Odds, who *believes and who trembles.*[6]
Cou'd you see his grim *Grace*, for a Pound to a Penny,
10   You'd swear it must be the *Baboon* of K[*ilkenn*]*y*:
Poor *Satan* will think the Comparison odious;
I wish I could find him one more commodious.
But this I am sure, the *Most Rev'rend old Dragon,*[7]
Has got on the Bench many B[ishop]s suffragan:[8]
And all Men believe he presides there *incog.*[9]
To give them by Turns an invisible Jog.

OUR B[ishop]s puft up with Wealth and with Pride,
To Hell on the Backs of the Clergy wou'd ride;
They mounted, and labour'd with Whip and with Spur,
20   In vain ——for the Devil a Parson wou'd stir.
So the *Commons* unhors'd them, and this was their Doom,
On their Crosiers[10] to ride, like a Witch on a Broom.
Tho' they gallop so fast; on the Road you may find 'em,
And have left us but Three out of Twenty behind 'em.
Lord *B[olton]*'s good Grace, Lord *C[arr]*, and Lord *H[oward]*,[11]
In spight of the Devil would still be untoward.[12]
They came of good Kindred and cou'd not endure,
Their former Companions should beg at their Door.

WHEN *CHRIST* was betray'd to *Pilate*, the Prætor,[13]
30   In a Dozen Apostles but one prov'd a Traytor!
One Traytor alone, and faithful Eleven;
But we can afford you Six Traytors in Seven.

---

[4] Both elements associated with hell.

[5] Edward Tenison, at the time Bishop of Ossory, whose seat was in Kilkenny (hence the epithet in line 10). Apart from his strong Whig ties (he served as First Chaplain to the Lord-Lieutenant of Ireland, the 1st Duke of Dorset), Tenison provoked Swift's wrath by introducing heads to the Bill of Residence in the House of Lords in early December, 1731.

[6] 2 James 19: "the devils also believe, and tremble."

[7] Satan.

[8] Associate bishops.

[9] Incognito; in disguise. This is one of the abbreviated words ridiculed as reflective of "the present polite way of writing" in Swift's *The Tatler, No. 230* (1710).

[10] The hook-ended staffs carried by bishops.

[11] Theophilus Bolton, Archbishop of Cashel; Charles Carr, Bishop of Killaloe; and Robert Howard, Bishop of Elphin. The only bishops to have voted against the bills, all three were Irish-born clerics who had attended Trinity College, Dublin and who were sympathetic to the "Irish interest" in the country.

[12] Disinclined (to do something); intractable; stubborn.

[13] Magistrate in ancient Rome. The word was also used in Swift's time for a person holding high civic or administrative office (hence could apply to officials in parliament).

WHAT a Clutter with Clippings, Dividings, and Cleavings!
And the Clergy, forsooth, must take up with their Leavings.
If making *Divisions* was all their Intent,
They've done it, we thank 'em, but not as they meant;
And so may such B[ishop]s for ever *divide*,
That no honest Heathen would be on their Side.
How shou'd we rejoice, if, like *Judas* the first,
40   Those Splitters of Parsons in sunder shou'd burst?[14]

NOW hear an Allusion![15] —— A Mitre, you know,
Is divided above, but united below.
If this you consider, our Emblem is right;
The B[ishop]s *divide*, but the Clergy *unite*.
Should the Bottom be split, our B[ishop]s wou'd dread
That the Mitre wou'd never stick fast on their Head,
And yet they have learnt the chief Art of a Sov'reign,
As *Machiavel* taught 'em; *divide and ye govern*.[16]
But, Courage, my L[or]ds, tho' it cannot be said
50   That one *cloven Tongue*,[17] ever sat on your Head;
I'll hold you a Groat,[18] and I wish I cou'd see 't,
If your Stockings were off, you cou'd show *cloven Feet*.[19]

BUT hold, cry the B[ishop]s; and give us fair Play;
Before you condemn us, hear what we can say.
What truer Affection cou'd ever be shown,
Than saving your Souls, by damning our own?
And have we not practis'd all Methods to gain you;
With the Tyth of the Tyth of the Tyth[20] to maintain you;
Provided a Fund for building you Spittles;[21]
60   You are only to live four Years without Vittles![22]
Content, my good L[or]ds; but let us change Hands;

---

[14] Cf. Swift's poem *Judas* (1731): "As antient *Judas by Trangression fell*, / And *burst asunder* e'er he went to Hell; / ... Each modern *Judas* perish like the first; / Drop from the Tree with all his Bowels burst" (17–18; 21–22). Here too, Judas represents the Irish bishopric.

[15] Explanatory image; parable.

[16] A maxim proverbially attributed to Niccolò Machiavelli (1469–1527), the Italian philosopher and politician whose best-known work, *The Prince*, became synonymous with "realpolitik."

[17] As in the tongues of fire visited upon the apostles at Pentecost.

[18] "I'll wager you a small coin"; Swift also uses this phrase in *A Serious Poem on William Wood* (1724).

[19] The split hooves of the devil.

[20] Tithes, a levy of 10 percent of the income of each member of the parish, were traditionally designed to support all clergymen in the Church of Ireland. The suggestion here is that the bishops have appropriated most of the funds for their own benefit, leaving only a tiny proportion for the maintenance of the lower clergy.

[21] Residences. Where a parish lacked a house for its clergyman, a central fund could be applied to for the money to build one. This would reduce the income of the clergyman for four years, however.

[22] Phonetic spelling of "victuals" (food).

First take you our Tyths, and give us your Lands.[23]

So GOD bless the Church, and three of our Mitres;
And GOD bless the *Commons* for *Biting* the *Biters*.[24]

---

[23] See Swift's ironic tract, *A Proposal to Pay off the Debt of the Nation*, written in the same year as this poem.
[24] "For tricking the tricksters" or "outsmarting the cheats"; for turning the tables on those (the bishops) who would play a (destructive) hoax on others (the inferior clergy). The phrase "the biter bit" was proverbial; the word "bite" was a favorite of Swift's and appears often in his writings.

The Yahoo's Overthrow:
or, The Kevan Bayl's New Ballad, upon Serjeant Kite's insulting the Dean

To the Tune of *Derry down*[1]

This lively broadside peppered with lower-class street slang takes aim at Richard Bettesworth, M.P. for Midleton, Co. Cork, who strongly supported a bill put forward in Parliament in late 1733 that would significantly lower the amount of tithes paid to the Anglican church. Swift, viewing this support as an expression of Bettesworth's general anti-clericalism and promotion of the Presbyterian cause, wrote a poem viciously ridiculing "Booby Bettesworth." The latter's response was to confront Swift menacingly and (according to widespread report) threaten to stab or maim him—which in turn prompted a group of Swift's neighbors to sign a document pledging to defend the Dean against all "ruffians and murderers." In the following poem, Swift figures Bettesworth as "Serjeant Kite," an allusion to a character in George Farquhar's play, The Recruiting Officer *(1706). The word "kite" means a cunning scoundrel, but was a term also used for a junior counsel, hence to Swift appropriate for Bettesworth, who was a prominent barrister and one of three "serjeants at law." A "bayl," or bailey, is a vicinity or neighborhood (cf. "bailiwick"); here it refers to the one belonging to St. Kevin, patron of the parish within which St. Patrick's Cathedral stands. Copy-text:* Works, *ed. Deane Swift, 1765.*

* * *

JOLLY boys of St. Kevans. St. Patrick's, Donore,
And Smithfield,[2] I'll tell you, if not told before,
How B[etteswor]th, that booby, and S[coundre]l in grain,[3]
Hath insulted us all by insulting the Dean.
    Knock him down, down, down, knock him down.

---

[1] "Derry Down," a traditional Renaissance ballad, was a very popular tune in the early eighteenth century, used also by Gay in *The Beggar's Opera.*

[2] Donore is a neighborhood near St. Patrick's; Smithfield, the area around a livestock mart some distance away, across the River Liffey: hence this ballad is presented as popular beyond the immediate environs of Swift's cathedral. The term "JOLLY boys" suggests the youthful street gangs that fought one another (and defended their own) in the Liberties.

[3] An ingrained scoundrel.

The Dean and his merits we ev'ry one know,
But this skip[4] of a Lawyer, where the De'el did he grow?
How greater's his merit at four Courts or House,[5]
Than the barking of Towzer, or leap of a louse?
10   *Knock him down, &c.*

That he came from the Temple, his morals do show,
But where his deep law is, few mortals yet know:
His rhet'ric, bombast, silly jests, are by far
More like to lampooning than pleading at bar.
      Knock him down, &c.

This pedlar,[6] at speaking and making of laws,
Hath met with returns of all sorts but applause;
Has, with noise and odd gestures, been prating some years,
What honester folks never durst for their ears.
20   *Knock him down, &c.*

Of all sizes and sorts, the Fanatical crew[7]
Are his Brother Protestants, good men and true;
Red hat, and blue bonnet, and turbant's the same,[8]
What the De'el is't to him whence the Devil they came!
      Knock him down, &c.

Hobbes, Tindal, and Woolston, and Collins, and Nayler,
And Muggleton, Toland, and Bradley the taylor,[9]
Are Christians alike; and it may be averr'd,
He's a Christian as good as the rest of the herd.
30   *Knock him down, &c.*

He only the rights of the clergy debates,

---

[4] Negligible person; perhaps short for "skipkennel," a footman or lackey.

[5] The Four Courts was a complex of courthouses near Christ Church cathedral (since moved to the north bank of the Liffey); the "House" is the Irish House of Commons.

[6] A dabbler or trifler; a person who acts ineffectually.

[7] Religious Dissenters, especially Presbyterians.

[8] A Catholic Cardinal's red hat, a Scots bonnet (or "tam") in the blue of the seventeenth-century Covenanters, and an Islamic turban: all are to Swift types of religious zealots, in contrast to the moderation of Anglicanism. Bettesworth's religious promiscuity and opportunism are similarly satirized in the poem, *On the Words—Brother Protestants and Fellow Christians* (1733).

[9] This is a list of free-thinkers and others whom Swift regarded as irreligious, balancing the preceding references to zealots: the seventeenth-century philosopher Thomas Hobbes, identified with materialist interpretations of the world and of Christian doctrine in *Leviathan* (1651) and other works; the Deist William Tindal, author of *The Rights of the Christian Church* (1706) opposing the High Church party; the heterodox theologian Thomas Woolston, whose allegorical interpretations of biblical miracles brought him a prison sentence for blasphemy in 1729; the Deist Anthony Collins, whose *Discourse of Freethinking* (1713) prompted a satirical response from Swift; the Quaker James Nayler, a soldier in the parliamentary army during the English Civil War who was convicted of blasphemy (1656); the seventeenth-century transcendentalist and anti-Trinitarian Lodowicke Muggleton, imprisoned for blasphemy in 1653; and the Irish Deist John Toland, author of *Christianity Not Mysterious* (1696), which denied the existence of miracles and all aspects of religion contrary to reason.

Their rights! their importance! We'll set on new rates
On their tythes at half-nothing, their priesthood at less:[10]
What's next to be voted with ease you may guess.[11]
    Knock him down, &c.

At length his Old Master (I need not him name)[12]
To this damnable Speaker had long ow'd a shame;
When his speech came abroad, he paid him off clean,
By leaving him under the pen of the Dean.
40   *Knock him down, &c.*

He kindled, as if the whole Satire had been
The oppression of Virtue, not wages of Sin:
He began as he bragg'd, with a rant and a roar;
He bragg'd how he bounc'd,[13] and he swore how he swore.
    Knock him down, &c.

Tho' he cringed to his Deanship in very low strains,
To others he boasted of knocking out brains,
And slitting of noses, and cropping of ears,
While his own ass's Zaggs[14] were more fit for the shears.
50   *Knock him down, &c.*

On this Worrier of Deans whene'er we can hit,
We'll shew him the way how to crop and to slit;
We'll teach him some better address to afford
To the Dean of all Deans, tho' he wears not a sword.
    Knock him down, &c.

We'll colt[15] him thro' Kevan, St. Patrick's, Donore,
And Smithfield, as Rap[16] was ne'er colted before;
We'll oil him with kennel, and powd'r him with grains[17]
A modus[18] right fit for insulters of Deans.
60   *Knock him down, &c.*

---

[10] Refers to the measure brought before the Irish House of Commons, which would have exempted from tithes land devoted to growing flax. While reducing the income of the Anglican clergy, the measure would have increased the income of those involved in the linen industry, who were concentrated in Ulster, where most Dissenting Protestants lived.

[11] The possibility of disestablishing the Church of Ireland, which Swift constantly feared would result from easing restrictions on non-Anglican Protestants.

[12] God, whose name should not be used lightly.

[13] Blustered; swaggered.

[14] Pointed ears?

[15] Beat with the end of a rope.

[16] A rascal; a good-for-nothing; taken from the Irish-English term for a counterfeit coin. Perhaps also short for "rapparee," signifying an Irish bandit or plunderer, which comes from the Irish word ("rápaire") for a half-pike and hence can also mean a thruster or stabber: a fitting term given the imagery of the poem.

[17] We will smear him with the filth of the gutter, and throw refuse all over him.

[18] Punning on "modus," meaning method or manner of operation, and "modus," referring to a provision in the parliamentary bill that would have required the tithe to be fixed by a cash equivalent.

And when this is over, we'll make him amends,
To the Dean he shall go; they shall kiss, and be friends:
But how? Why, the Dean shall to him disclose
A face for to kiss, without eyes, ears, or nose.[19]
  Knock him down, &c.

If you say this is hard, on a man that is reckon'd
That serjeant at law, whom we call Kite the Second,
You mistake; for a Slave, who will coax his superiors,
70 May be proud to be licking a great man's posteriors.
  Knock him down, &c.

What care we how high runs his passion or pride?
Tho' his soul he despises, he values his hide;
Then fear not his tongue, or his sword, or his knife;
He'll take his revenge on his innocent wife.[20]
  Knock him down, down, down, ——keep him down.

---

[19] That is, his buttocks.

[20] There is no record of Bettesworth's having abused his wife. Swift may here be conflating Bettesworth with the equally detested Richard Tighe, who according to the *Journal to Stella* used to beat his wife in public and who is described as "thrashing *Babby* in her new Stays" in *Dick's Variety*, l. 30 (1728?). See *A Character...of the Legion Club*, l. 149 and note.

On a Printer's being sent to Newgate, by ——

Swift's usual Dublin printer in the 1730s, George Faulkner, was arrested in 1736 for having published the satirical New Proposal for the . . . Improvement of Quadrille *by the Bishop of Kilmore, Josiah Hort, which Swift had revised in advance of publication. The arrest was instigated by Richard Bettesworth, the lawyer and politician whom Swift despised, and upon whom Hort had made a satirical reflection (see* The Yahoo's Overthrow*). Faulkner was jailed in Newgate Prison in Dublin and forced to apologize for a breach of parliamentary privilege (since Bettesworth was a member of parliament); another printer associated with Swift, Edward Waters, who had reprinted Bishop Hort's satire, was also imprisoned briefly. Copy-text:* Works, *ed. Faulkner, 1746.*

* * *

BETTER we all were in our Graves
Than live in Slavery to Slaves,
Worse than the Anarchy at Sea,
Where Fishes on each other prey;[1]
Where ev'ry Trout can make as high Rants
O'er his Inferiors as our Tyrants;
And swagger while the Coast is clear:
But should a lordly Pike appear,
Away you see the Varlet scud,[2]
Or hide his coward Snout in Mud.
Thus, if a Gudgeon meet a Roach[3]
He dare not venture to approach;
Yet still has Impudence to rise,
And, like *Domitian*, leap at Flyes.[4]

---

[1] See Swift's poem *The Bubble* (aka *Upon the South Sea Project*) (1720), ll. 69–72: "As Fishes on each other prey / The great ones swall'wing up the small / So fares it in the *Southern* Sea / But Whale *Directors* eat up all."

[2] See the scoundrel flee; also playing upon the obsolete meaning of "varlet" as "sergeant" (which evokes association with Bettesworth, satirized as "Serjeant Kite" in *The Yahoo's Overthrow*).

[3] Both of these are small fresh-water fish. A "Gudgeon" is often used for bait and invoked as a contemptuous term for a foolish or gullible person.

[4] The Roman emperor Domitian, who ruled from 81 to 96 C.E., was often invoked to represent tyranny; in Suetonius, *Lives of the Caesars*, he is described as impaling flies upon his stylus.

A Character, Panegyric, and Description of the Legion Club

Written in the Year, 1736

In Luke 8:30, Jesus asks a man possessed by devils for his name, and the demons within him answer "Legion," because there were so many of them. The Irish Parliament, Swift's subject here, becomes the "Legion Club" because it was dominated by landowners who only reluctantly gave financial support to the Church of Ireland, though it was the legally established church and the institution that ensured their own privileged position in society, and who continually schemed to reduce that support—in the case occasioning this poem, via a House of Commons bill to remove the tithes on pasturage. Not that it required much to trigger Swift's antagonism toward the Irish Parliament, which he saw as an institution made up of spineless beings who kowtowed to English interests and obsequiously accepted their drastically diminished powers under the Declaratory Act of 1720. Copy-text: Works, ed. Faulkner, 1762.

* * *

AS I strole the City, oft I
Spy a Building large and lofty,[1]
Not a Bow-shot from the College,[2]
Half the Globe from Sense and Knowledge.
By the prudent Architect
Plac'd against the Church[3] direct;
Making good my Grandames Jest,
Near the Church — you know the rest.[4]

TELL us, what this Pile[5] contains?
10   Many a Head that holds no Brains.
These Demoniacs[6] let me dub

---

[1] The Irish Parliament building in College Green, Dublin, an imposing classical structure designed by Sir Edward Lovett Pearce and built between 1728 and 1739.

[2] Trinity College, facing the Parliament across College Green.

[3] St. Andrew's Church, which is not actually next to the Parliament building, as "against" would imply, but separated from it by two streets; "against" has more to do with the anti-Church of Ireland character Swift perceived in the Irish Parliament.

[4] Referring to the proverb, "Near the Church, and far from God."

[5] Building.

[6] The word combines "demons" and "maniacs" to suggest devilish madmen. Rogers notes that there was an actual sect of Anabaptists that went by this name.

With the name of *Legion Club.*
Such Assemblies, you might swear,
Meet when Butchers bait a Bear;[7]
Such a Noise, and such haranguing,
When a Brother Thief is hanging.
Such a Rout and such a Rabble
Run to hear Jackpudding gabble;
Such a Croud their Ordure throws
20   On a far less Villain's Nose.[8]

    C OULD I from the Building's Top
Hear the rattling Thunder drop,
While the Devil upon the Roof,
If the Devil be Thunder Proof,
Should with Poker fiery-red
Crack the Stones, and melt the Lead;
Drive them down on every Scull,
While the Den of Thieves[9] is full;
Quite destroy that Harpies[10] nest,
30   How might then our Isle be blest?
For Divines allow, that God
Sometimes makes the Devil his Rod:
And the Gospel will inform us,
He can punish Sins enormous.

    Y ET should *Swift* endow the Schools
For his Lunatics and Fools,
With a Rood[11] or two of Land,
I allow the Pile may stand.[12]
You perhaps will ask me, why so?
40   But it is with this Proviso,
Since the House is like to last,
Let a royal Grant be pass'd,
That the Club have Right to dwell
Each within his proper Cell;
With a Passage left to creep in,
And a Hole above for peeping.[13]

---

[7]Bear-baiting, in which butchers took a customary part, drew noisy crowds, as did public executions (see line 16), or performances by a clown ("Jackpudding," line 18), which are here likened to the often raucous Irish House of Commons.

[8]Rubbish and filth ("Ordure") were commonly thrown at the criminals in the pillory, whom Swift regards as typically less villainous than Irish M.P.s.

[9]Likening Parliament to Christ's description of the Temple as desecrated by money-changers and vendors of sacrificial animals; see Matthew 21:13.

[10]In classical mythology, filthy and rapacious monsters, part woman, part bird.

[11]A measure of land, equal to one-quarter of an acre.

[12]Referring to Swift's intention to leave a bequest to found an asylum, which had already gained popular attention in the decade before his death; the notion is that members of parliament would each have a space reserved to them there.

[13]To allow them to be observed, especially by visitors. Observing the insane within an asylum was a popular amusement in eighteenth-century London.

LET them, when they once get in,
Sell the Nation for a Pin;
While they sit a picking Straws,
50   Let them rave of making Laws;
While they never hold their Tongue,
Let them dabble in their Dung;[14]
Let them form a grand Committee,
How to plague and starve the City;
Let them stare, and storm, and frown,
When they see a Clergy-Gown.
Let them, 'ere they crack a Louse,
Call for th' Orders of the House;[15]
Let them with their gosling Quills,
60   Scribble senseless Heads of Bills;[16]
We may, while they strain their Throats,
Wipe our A[rse]s with their V[ote]s.[17]

LET Sir T[om], that rampant Ass,[18]
Stuff his Guts with Flax and Grass;
But before the Priest he fleeces,
Tear the Bible all to Pieces.
At the Parsons, Tom, Halloo Boy,[19]
Worthy Offspring of a Shoeboy,
Footman, Traytor, vile Seducer,
70   Perjur'd Rebel, brib'd Accuser;
Lay thy paltry Priviledge aside,
Sprung from Papists and a Regicide;[20]
Fall a Working like a Mole,
Raise the Dirt about your Hole.

---

[14] Cf. Swift's description of Bedlam in *A Tale of a Tub* ("Digression concerning Madness"), where one inmate is "tearing his Straw in piece-meal, Swearing and Blaspheming,...and emptying his Pispot in the Spectator's Faces" while another is "raking in his own Dung, and dabling in his Urine."

[15] The projected schedule of the day, which were available to members at the beginning of each day's session.

[16] Drafts of proposed bills, for submission to the Privy-Council, which could amend or ignore them. The Irish Parliament could only vote for or against the bills as received back from the Privy Council. As goose-quills were normally used for pens, "senseless" bills might appropriately be written with the quills of young geese ("goslings"), suggesting inexperience or silliness.

[17] Records of parliamentary votes were regularly published, unlike most other parliamentary proceedings at this time.

[18] Sir Thomas Prendergast championed the parliamentary opposition to levying tithes on land used for pasturing livestock or for flax yards, which were necessary to produce linen. Both were more profitable uses for land than growing crops; thus the bill would exempt from tithes precisely those who could most afford to pay them.

[19] Likening Prendergast's "attack" on the Church of Ireland ("the Parsons") to a fox-hunt.

[20] Prendergast's father was a Jacobite Catholic, involved in a plot to assassinate King William, who informed on his comrades and was rewarded with a baronetcy, yet died in the service of France, hence the string of epithets. The younger Prendergast had converted to the Church of Ireland, and so could sit in parliament.

COME, assist me, Muse obedient,
Let us try some new Expedient;
Shift the Scene for half an Hour,
Time and Place are in thy Power.
Thither, gentle Muse, conduct me,
80   I shall ask, and thou instruct me.

    SEE, the Muse unbars the Gate;
Hark, the Monkeys, how they prate!

    ALL ye Gods, who rule the Soul;[21]
Styx, through Hell whose Waters roll!
Let me be allow'd to tell
What I heard in yonder Hell.

    NEAR the Door an Entrance gapes,[22]
Crouded round with antic[23] Shapes;
Poverty, and *Grief*, and *Care*,
90   Causeless *Joy*, and true *Despair*;
Discord periwigg'd with Snakes,[24]
See the dreadful Strides she takes.

    BY this odious Crew beset,[25]
I began to rage and fret,
And resolv'd to break their Pates,
'Ere we enter'd at the Gates;
Had not *Clio*, in the Nick,[26]
Whisper'd me, let down your Stick;
What, said I, is this the Mad-House?
100   These, she answer'd, are but Shadows,
Phantoms, bodiless and vain,
Empty Visions of the Brain.

    IN the Porch *Briareus* stands,[27]
Shews a Bribe in all his Hands:

---

[21] Alluding directly to the description of the underworld in Vergil's *Aeneid*, here the muse is invoked to guide an exploration of the madness of the members of Parliament. Faulkner's note quotes *Aeneid* vi, 264–66: *Dii, quibus imperium est animarum, &c. / Sit mihi fas audita loqui, &c.* ("You gods, who rule souls...Allow me to be heard"), which Swift translates literally.

[22] Faulkner quotes *Aeneid* vi, 273–74: *Vestibulum ante ipsum primisq[ue]; in faucibus Orci / Luctus et ultrices, &c.* ("Just before the entrance, in the jaws of hell / Grief and vengeful [cares]").

[23] Grotesque; bizarre.

[24] Faulkner quotes *Aeneid* vi, 280–81: *Discordia demens, / Vipereum crinem vittis innexa cruentis.* ("Mad strife [binds] her snaky hair with a bloody ribbon").

[25] Faulkner quotes *Aeneid* vi, 290–91: *Corripit hic subita trepidus formidine ferrum / Aeneas, strictamq[ue] aciem venientibus offert.* ("Suddenly fearful, he drew the shining blade against those coming").

[26] Faulkner quotes *Aeneid* vi, 292: ——*ni docta comes tenues sine corpore vitas.* ("The wise guide [told him that these were] shapes without bodies"). Clio is the muse of history.

[27] Faulkner quotes *Aeneid* vi, 287: *Et centum geminus Briareus* ("Briareus clutching with his hundred [hands]"). The bountifully bribing Briareus here is Walter Cary, who as secretary to the Lord-Lieutenant of Ireland was influential in dispensing patronage and pensions.

Briareus the Secretary,
But we Mortals call him *Cary*.
When the Rogues their Country fleece,
They may hope for Pence a Piece.

    CLIO, who had been so wise
110   To put on a Fool's Disguise,
To bespeak some Approbation,
And be thought a near Relation;
When she saw three hundred Brutes,[28]
All involv'd in wild Disputes;
Roaring till their Lungs were spent,
P[rivi]l[e]ge of P[ar]l[ia]m[e]nt,
Now a new Misfortune feels,
Dreading to be laid by th' Heels.[29]
Never durst a Muse before
120   Enter that Infernal Door;
Clio stifled with the Smell,
Into Spleen and Vapours[30] fell;
By the *Stygian*[31] Steams that flew,
From the dire infectious Crew.
Not the stench of Lake *Avernus*,[32]
Could have more offended her Nose:
Had she flown but o'er the Top,
She would feel her Pinions drop,
And by Exhalations dire,
130   Though a Goddess[,] must expire.
In a Fright she crept away,
Bravely I resolved to stay.

    WHEN I saw the Keeper frown,
Tipping him with Half a Crown;[33]
Now, said I, we are alone,
Name your Heroes[,] one by one.'

    WHO is that Hell-featured Brawler,
Is it Satan? No, 'tis W[aller].
In what Figure can a Bard dress
140   *Jack*, the Grandson of Sir *Hardress*?[34]
Honest Keeper, drive him further,
In his Looks are Hell and Murther;

---

[28]The Irish House of Commons had 300 members.

[29]Clio fears she might be arrested ("laid by th' Heels"), a punishment from which the (mad) members are immune for whatever they might say in parliament.

[30]Into irritable temper and hysteria.

[31]Referring to the River Styx.

[32]The lake, notorious for its offensive odor, through which the underworld is entered.

[33]A silver coin worth two shillings and six pence.

[34]John Waller, an Irish M.P. whose grandfather, Sir Hardress Waller, was one of the judges at the trial of Charles I in 1649.

See the Scowling Visage drop,
Just as when he murther'd *T[hrop]*.[35]

    KEEPER, shew me where to fix
On the Puppy Pair of *Dicks*;
By their lanthorn Jaws and Leathern,
You might swear they both are Brethren:
Dick Fitz-Baker, Dick the Player,[36]
150 Old Acquaintance, are you there?
Dear Companions hug and kiss,
Toast *old Glorious* in your Piss.[37]
Tye them Keeper in a Tether,
Let them stare and stink together;
Both are apt to be unruly,
Lash them daily, lash them duly,
Though 'tis hopeless to reclaim them,
Scorpion Rods perhaps may tame them.

    KEEPER, yon old dotard smoke,[38]
160 Sweetly snoring in his Cloak
Who is he? 'Tis hum-drum *W[ynne]*,[39]
Half encompass'd by his Kin:
There observe the tribe of *B[yngha]m*,[40]
For he never fails to bring 'em;
While he sleeps the whole Debate,
They submissive round him wait;
Yet would gladly see the Hunks[41]
In his Grave, and search his Trunks:
See they gently twitch his Coat,
170 Just to yawn, and give his Vote;
Always firm in his Vocation,
For the Court against the Nation.

---

[35] John Waller was the patron of Roger Throp, a clergyman with whom he had feuded, and who had died early in 1736. The accusation of murder is meant to emphasize Waller's familial affinities with his grandfather, who signed the King's death warrant and helped arrange his execution.

[36] Richard Tighe, descended from a baker who supplied Cromwell's troops (hence "*Fitz-Baker*"), and Richard Bettesworth, ridiculed as "the Player" for his oratorical pomposity, were both M.P.s. For Bettesworth, see *The Yahoo's Overthrow*. Tighe became a particular target of Swift's satiric vitriol after he reported Swift's friend Rev. Thomas Sheridan to Dublin Castle authorities for a sermon he preached whose text was open to misinterpretation.

[37] It was a mark of their loyalty for Irish Protestants to toast the "glorious" memory of William III, whose victory over King James II preserved their superior position in Ireland. Swift mocks such loyalism inasmuch as it meant in practice the subordination of Irish interests to English.

[38] Reveal; identify.

[39] One of the three Wynnes in the House of Commons from the West of Ireland, two of them (both named Owen Wynne) from Sligo, one (John Wynne) from Castlebar, Co. Mayo. Which of them had a reputation for sleeping during debates has not been determined.

[40] Sir John Bingham, M.P. for County Mayo, and his brother Henry, M.P. for Castlebar (hence the colleague of John Wynne, above).

[41] A surly, crusty old person; a "bear."

THOSE are A[llen]s, Jack and Bob,[42]
First in every wicked Jobb,[43]
Son and Brother to a Queer,
Brainsick Brute, they call a Peer.
We must give them better Quarter,
For their Ancestor trod Mortar;
And at *Hoath* to boast his Fame,
180 On a Chimney cut his Name.

THERE sit C[lement]s, D[ilkes], and H[arrison],[44]
How they swagger from their Garrison.
Such a Triplet could you tell
Where to find on this Side Hell?
H[arrison], and D[ilkes], and C[lements],
Souse them in their own Ex-crements.[45]
Every Mischief in their Hearts,
If they fail 'tis Want of Parts.

BLESS us, *Morgan!* Art thou there Man?[46]
190 Bless mine Eyes! Art thou the Chairman?
Chairman to yon damn'd Committee!
Yet I look on thee with Pity.
Dreadful Sight! What, learned *Morgan*,
Metamorphos'd to a Gorgon!
For thy horrid Looks, I own,
Half convert me to a Stone.
Hast thou been so long at School,
Now to turn a factious Tool!
Alma Mater was thy Mother,
200 Every young Divine thy Brother.
Thou a disobedient Varlet,[47]
Treat thy Mother like a Harlot!
Thou, ungrateful to thy Teachers,
Who are all grown reverend Preachers!
Morgan! Would it not surprise one?

---

[42] John Allen, M.P. for Carysfort, Co. Dublin, was the son, and Robert Allen, M.P. for Co. Wicklow, the brother, of Lord Allen, the "Queer, / Brainsick Brute" of ll. 175–76; all were related to John Allen, an architect (hence "trod Mortar") of Howth Castle in north Co. Dublin. In his poem *Traulus: The Second Part* (1730), Swift ascribes to Lord Allen a "Butcher's Guile" (l. 37) and says that "he draws his daily Food, / From his Tenants vital Blood" (ll. 41–42).

[43] A public office turned to personal gain or private political advantage.

[44] Most likely the M.P.s Henry or Nathaniel Clements, as well as Michael Dilkes and William Harrison.

[45] The hyphen shifts the accent to the second syllable, to Clements's detriment.

[46] Marcus Antonius Morgan, M.P., chaired a committee of the House of Commons charged with reporting on a petition in March 1736 by a number of freeholders protesting against the tithe on pasturage; the committee reported favorably, and the House (much to Swift's disgust) supported the freeholders.

[47] Knave or rascal. Morgan had been educated at Trinity College, where most of the professors and tutors were clergymen; hence the portrayal of him as having betrayed the church as well as his old school.

Turn thy Nourishment to Poison!
When you walk among your Books,
They reproach you with their Looks;
Bind them fast, or from the Shelves
210   They'll come down to right themselves:
Homer, Plutarch, Virgil, Flaccus,
All in Arms prepare to back us:[48]
Soon repent, or put to Slaughter
Every *Greek* and *Roman* Author.
While you in your Faction's Phrase
Send the Clergy all to graze;
And to make your Project pass,
Leave them not a Blade of Grass.[49]

How I want thee, humorous *Hogart?*[50]
220   Thou, I hear, a pleasant Rogue art;
Were but you and I acquainted,
Every Monster should be painted;
You should try your graving Tools
On this odious Group of Fools;
Draw the Beasts as I describe 'em,
Form their Features, while I gibe them;
Draw them like, for I assure you,
You will need no *Car'catura;*[51]
Draw them so that we may trace
230   All the Soul in every Face.
Keeper, I must now retire,
You have done what I desire:
But I feel my Spirits spent,
With the Noise, the Sight, the Scent.

PRAY be patient, you shall find
Half the best are still behind:
You have hardly seen a Score,
I can shew two hundred more.
Keeper, I have seen enough,
240   Taking then a Pinch of Snuff;
I concluded, looking round 'em,
May their God, the Devil confound 'em.

---

[48]The imagery here calls to mind Swift's early satire, *The Battel of the Books* (pub. 1704).
"*Flaccus*" was the family name of the poet Horace: "Quintus Horatius Flaccus."

[49]A recurring image of Ireland's ruin in Swift's writings; see *Verses...[on] St Patrick's Well,*
ll. 91–92 and Gulliver's description of the devastated landscape in Balnibarbi in Part III of
Gulliver's Travels.

[50]William Hogarth, "*A very famous Designer, Painter, and Engraver. See his* Rake's *and*
Harlot's Progress; Marriage Alamode, *and many other humorous Prints*" (Faulkner's note).

[51]Caricature. See, e.g., Hogarth's illustrations for Butler's *Hudibras* (1725), his etching
Characters and Caricatures (1743), and Plate 2 of his *Analysis of Beauty* (1753).

Ay and No, A Tale from Dublin

Written in 1737

In 1737 Swift attended a banquet for the Lord Mayor of Dublin with the Archbishop of Armagh and Primate of All Ireland, Hugh Boulter (the top official in the Church of Ireland). Boulter was a major supporter of the Whig government and a spokesman for the "English interest" in Ireland who had backed Wood's halfpence against the popular Dean Swift, hence he was a prime target for satiric attack. This was even more the case now, since he had recently championed measures to import £2000 of copper halfpence from England, and to reduce the value of gold coins slightly in Ireland. Although this was an appropriate position to take under the circumstances, it initially excited popular opposition in which Swift quickly joined, apparently eager to reprise his role as the Drapier in his successful battle against Wood's copper halfpence a dozen years earlier. Copy-text: Supplement to Swift's Works, *ed. John Nichols, 1776.*

* * *

AT *Dublin's* high feast sat Primate and Dean,
Both dress'd like divines, with band[1] and face clean,
Quoth *Hugh* of *Armagh,* "The mob is grown bold,"
"Ay, ay," quoth the Dean, "the cause is old gold."
"No, no," quoth the Primate, "if causes we sift,
This mischief arises from witty Dean *Swift.*"[2]
The smart one replied, "There's no wit in the case;
And nothing of that ever troubled your Grace.
Though with your state-sieve your own notions you split,
10   A *Boulter* by name is no *bolter* of wit.[3]
It's matter of weight, and a mere money-job;
But the lower the coin, the higher the mob.[4]
Go tell your friend *Bob* and the other great folk,[5]

---

[1] The white clerical collar, with two vertical bands in front.

[2] Refers to Swift's reputation for arousing popular opinion; in this case he had written one of the few pamphlets in which his authorship was proclaimed, *The Rev. Dean Swift's Reasons against Lowering the Gold and Silver Coin.*

[3] A pun upon "bolter" as a sieve, on the one hand, and on the other hand as the impetus of "bolts" (e.g., of wit), to signify that while Boulter's two measures might be distinguished from each other ("split"), he was not a witty man.

[4] That is, the mob could be provoked by the notion of lowering the value of gold.

[5] Sir Robert Walpole, the Prime Minister, who was influential in having Boulter appointed to the primatial see in Ireland, and his powerful Whig allies at Court.

That sinking the coin is a dangerous joke.
The *Irish* dear joys[6] have enough common sense,
To treat gold reduced like *Wood's* copper pence.
It's a pity a Prelate should die without law;
But if I say the word —— take care of *Armagh!*"[7]

---

[6]A term for common people in Ireland.

[7]Williams cites a contemporary account according to which Swift told Boulter at the banquet that "had it not been for him he (Boulter) would have been torn to pieces by the mob, and that if he held up his finger he could make them do it that instant." One is reminded of Swift's description of himself (recorded in Mrs. Pilkington's *Memoirs*) as "absolute monarch in the *Liberties*, and King of the Mob."

FURTHER READING

N.B. This list includes only works specifically dealing with, or providing important background and context for, Swift in relation to Ireland and/or colonialism.

Editions

The Prose Writings of Jonathan Swift, 13 vols., ed. Herbert Davis. Oxford: Blackwell, 1939–68; vols. 9, 10, and 12 in particular.

The Drapier's Letters, ed. Herbert Davis. Oxford: Clarendon Press, 1935.

Swift's Irish Pamphlets: An Introductory Selection, ed. Joseph McMinn. Gerrards Cross: Colin Smyth, 1991.

The Intelligencer, ed. James Woolley. Oxford: Clarendon Press, 1992.

A Dialogue in Hybernian Stile between A & B & Irish Eloquence, ed. Alan Bliss. Dublin: Cadenus Press, 1977.

The Poems of Jonathan Swift, 3 vols., ed. Harold Williams. Oxford: Clarendon Press, 1937; revised ed., 1958.

Jonathan Swift: The Complete Poems, ed. Pat Rogers. Harmondsworth: Penguin, 1983.

Political, Historical, and Biographical Backgrounds/Contexts

Barnard, Toby, *A New Anatomy of Ireland: The Irish Protestants, 1649–1770*. New Haven, CT: Yale University Press, 2003.

Bartlett, Thomas, "Ireland, Empire, and Union, 1690–1801," in *Ireland and the British Empire*, ed. Kevin Kenny. London: Oxford University Press, 2006, 61–89.

Beckett, J.C., "Swift and the Anglo-Irish Tradition," in *The Character of Swift's Satire: A Revised Focus*, ed. Claude Rawson. Newark: University of Delaware Press, 1983, 151–65.

Boyce, D. George, *Nationalism in Ireland*, 3rd ed., London: Routledge, 1995.

Canny, Nicholas, "Identity Formation in Ireland: The Emergence of the Anglo-Irish," in *Colonial Identity in the Atlantic World, 1500–1800*, ed. Nicholas Canny and Anthony Pagden. Princeton, NJ: Princeton University Press, 1989, 159–212.

———, "The Marginal Kingdom: Ireland as a Problem in the First British Empire," in *Strangers Within the Realm: Cultural Margins of the First British Empire*, ed. Bernard Bailyn and Philip D. Morgan. Chapel Hill: University of North Carolina Press, 1991, 35–66.

Connolly, S.J., *Religion, Law, and Power: The Making of Protestant Ireland 1660–1760*. London: Oxford University Press, 1992.

———, "Swift and Protestant Ireland: Images and Reality," in *Locating Swift: Essays from Dublin on the 250th Anniversary of the Death of Jonathan Swift*, ed. Aileen Douglas, Patrick Kelly, and Ian Campbell Ross. Dublin: Four Courts Press, 1998, 28–46.

Craig, Maurice, *Dublin 1660–1860: A Social and Architectural History*. Dublin: Figgis, 1969.

Cullen, L.M., *An Economic History of Ireland since 1660*. London: Batsford, 1972.

Dickson, David, *New Foundations: Ireland 1660–1800*, 2nd ed. Dublin: Irish Academic Press, 2000.

Ehrenpreis, Irvin, *Swift: The Man, His Works, and the Age*, 3 vols. Cambridge, MA: Harvard University Press, 1962–83.

Fauske, Christopher J., *Jonathan Swift and the Church of Ireland 1710–1724*. Dublin: Irish Academic Press, 2002.

Ferguson, Oliver W., *Jonathan Swift and Ireland*. Urbana: University of Illinois Press, 1962.

Foster, R.F., *Modern Ireland 1600–1972*. London and New York: Penguin, 1989, esp. chs. 6–8 (117–94).

Gilbert, John T., *A History of Dublin*. Dublin: Duffy, 1861.

Hayton, David, "Anglo-Irish Attitudes: Changing Perceptions of National Identity among the Protestant Ascendancy in Ireland, ca. 1690–1750," *Studies in Eighteenth-Century Culture* 17 (1987): 145–57.

Johnston, Denis, "Swift of Dublin," *Éire-Ireland* 3 (Fall 1968): 38–50.

Johnston, Edith Mary, *Ireland in the Eighteenth Century*. Dublin: Gill and Macmillan, 1974.

Kelly, James, "Harvests and Hardships: Famine and Scarcity in Ireland in the Late 1720s," *Studia Hibernica* 26 (1991–92): 65–105.

———, "Jonathan Swift and the Irish Economy in the 1720s," *Eighteenth-Century Ireland* 6 (1991): 7–36.

Kidd, Colin, *British Identities before Nationalism: Ethnicity and Nationhood in the Atlantic World 1600–1800*. Cambridge: Cambridge University Press, 1999, esp. ch. 7, "The Weave of Irish Identities, 1600–1790" (146–81).

Landa, Louis, *Swift and the Church of Ireland*. Oxford: Clarendon Press, 1954.

Leerssen, Joep, "Anglo-Irish Patriotism and Its European Context: Notes towards a Reassessment," *Eighteenth-Century Ireland* 3 (1988): 7–24.

———, *Mere Irish and Fíor Ghael: Studies in the Idea of Irish Nationality, Its Development and Literary Expression prior to the Nineteenth Century*, 2nd Edition. Notre Dame: University of Notre Dame Press in association with Field Day, 1997.

Lein, Clayton, "Jonathan Swift and the Population of Ireland," *Eighteenth-Century Studies* 8.4 (1975): 431–53.

Mahony, Robert, *Jonathan Swift: The Irish Identity*. New Haven, CT: Yale University Press, 1995.

McLoughlin, Thomas, *Contesting Ireland: Irish Voices against England in the Eighteenth Century*. Dublin: Four Courts Press, 1999, ch. 3 (65–87).

McMinn, Joseph, *Jonathan's Travels: Swift and Ireland*. Belfast: Appletree Press, 1994.

Moody, T.W. and Vaughan, W.E. (eds.), *A New History of Ireland: Vol. IV, Eighteenth Century Ireland 1691–1800*. Oxford: Clarendon Press, 1986.

Robbins, Caroline, *The Eighteenth-Century Commonwealthman*. New York: Atheneum, 1968 [1959], chs. 3–5 (56–176).

Simms, J.G., *Colonial Nationalism, 1698–1776: Molyneux's The Case of Ireland ... Stated*. Cork: Mercier Press, 1976.

———, "Ireland in the Age of Swift," in *Jonathan Swift 1667–1967: A Dublin Tercentenary Tribute*, ed. Roger McHugh and Philip Edwards. Dublin: Dolmen Press, 1967, 157–75.

Literary, Generic, and Linguistic Backgrounds/Contexts

Carpenter, Andrew, "A School for a Satirist: Swift's Exposure to the War of Words in Dublin in the 1680s," in *Reading Swift: Papers from the Fourth Münster Symposium on Jonathan Swift*, ed. Hermann J. Real and Helgard Stöver-Leidig. Munich: Fink, 2003, 161–76.

———, *Verse in English from Eighteenth-Century Ireland*. Cork: University Press, 1998.

Coleborne, Bryan, "Jonathan Swift and the Literary World of Dublin," *Englisch Amerikanische Studien* (1988): 6–28.

Deane, Seamus, ed., *The Field Day Anthology of Irish Writing*, 3 vols., Derry: Field Day Publications, 1991; rptd. W. W. Norton, 1992, Vol. 1.

Dolan, T. P., *A Dictionary of Hiberno-English*. Dublin: Gill and Macmillan, 2000.

Douglas, Aileen, "The Novel before 1800," in *The Cambridge Companion to the Irish Novel*, ed. John Wilson Foster. Cambridge: Cambridge University Press, 2006, 1–21.

Fogarty, Anne, "Literature in English, 1550–1690: From the Elizabethan Settlement to the Battle of the Boyne," in *The Cambridge History of Irish Literature*, 2 vols., ed. Margaret Kelleher and Philip O'Leary. Cambridge: Cambridge University Press, 2006, 1: 140–90.

Harrison, Alan, *The Dean's Friend: Anthony Raymond 1675–1726, Jonathan Swift and the Irish Language*. Dublin: Éamonn de Búrca (for Edmund Burke Publisher), 1999.

Jarrell, Mackie L., "'Jack and the Dane': Swift Traditions in Ireland," in *Fair Liberty Was All His Cry: A Tercentenary Tribute to Jonathan Swift 1667–1745*, ed. A. Norman Jeffares. London: Macmillan, 1967, 311–41.

Mercier, Vivian, *The Irish Comic Tradition*. Oxford: Clarendon Press, 1962, esp. ch. 7 (182–209).

———, "Swift and the Gaelic Tradition," in *Fair Liberty Was All His Cry*, ed. Jeffares, 279–89.

Pritchard, Jonathan, "Swift's Irish Rhymes," *Studies in Philology* 104.1 (Winter 2007): 123–58.

Ross, Ian Campbell, "Prose in English, 1690–1800: From the Williamite Wars to the Act of Union," in *The Cambridge History of Irish Literature*, ed. Kelleher and O'Leary, 1: 232–81.

———, "The Scriblerians and Swift in Ireland," in *Reading Swift: Papers from the Second Münster Symposium on Jonathan Swift*, ed. Richard Rodino and Hermann Real. Munich: Fink, 1993, 81–90.

Critical Studies

Aravamudan, Srinivas, *Tropicopolitans: Colonialism and Agency, 1688–1804*. Durham, NC and London: Duke University Press, 1999, 135–56.

Baltes, Sabine, *The Pamphlet Controversy about Wood's Halfpence (1722–25) and the Tradition of Irish Constitutional Nationalism*. Frankfurt: Lang, 2003.

Brown, Laura, "Imperial Disclosures: Jonathan Swift," in *Ends of Empire: Women and Ideology in Early Eighteenth-Century English Literature*. Ithaca, NY and London: Cornell University Press, 1993, 170–200.

Canning, Rick G., "'Ignorant, Illiterate Creatures': Gender and Colonial Justification in Swift's *Injured Lady* and *Answer to the Injured Lady*," *ELH* 64 (1997): 77–98.

Carpenter, Andrew, *The Irish Perspective of Jonathan Swift*. Wuppertal: Hammer, 1978.

———, ed., "Jonathan Swift," in *The Field Day Anthology of Irish Writing*, 1: 327–94.

———, "'A Tale of a Tub' as an Irish Text," *Swift Studies* 20 (2005): 30–40.

Deane, Seamus, "Swift and the Anglo-Irish Intellect," *Eighteenth-Century Ireland* 1 (1986): 9–22.

Deeming, David, "The 'Tale,' Temple, and Swift's Irish Aesthetic," in *Representations of Swift*, ed. Brian A. Connery. Newark: University of Delaware Press, 2002, 25–40.

Eagleton, Terry, *Heathcliff and the Great Hunger: Studies in Irish Culture*. London and New York: Verso, 1995, ch. 5 (145–225).

Ehrenpreis, Irvin, "Dr. S***t and the Hibernian Patriot," in *Jonathan Swift 1667–1967*, ed. McHugh and Edwards, 24–37.

Fabricant, Carole, "Jonathan Swift as Irish Historian," in *Walking Naboth's Vineyard: New Studies of Swift*, ed. Christopher Fox and Brenda Tooley. Notre Dame: University of Notre Dame Press, 1995, 40–72.

———, "Speaking for the Irish Nation: The Drapier, the Bishop, and the Problems of Colonial Representation," *ELH* 66 (1999): 337–72.

———, "Swift the Irishman," in *The Cambridge Companion to Jonathan Swift*, ed. Christopher Fox. Cambridge: Cambridge University Press, 2003, 48–72.

———, *Swift's Landscape*, Baltimore: Johns Hopkins University Press, 1982; Notre Dame: University of Notre Dame Press, 1995.

Firth, C.H., "The Political Significance of 'Gulliver's Travels,'" *Proceedings of the British Academy* 9 (1919–20): 237–59.

Fox, Christopher, "Swift and the Rabble Reformation: *A Tale of a Tub* and the State of the Church in the 1690s," in *Swift as Priest and Satirist*, ed. Todd C. Parker. Newark: University of Delaware Press, 2009, 102–22.

Hawes, Clement, *The British Eighteenth Century and Global Critique*. New York: Palgrave Macmillan, 2005, ch. 6 (139–68).

———, "Three Times Round the Globe: Gulliver and Colonial Discourse," *Cultural Critique* 18 (1991): 187–214.

Kelly, Ann Cline, "Swift's Exploration of Slavery in Houyhnhnmland and Ireland," *PMLA* 91 (1976): 846–55.

Kelly, Patrick, "'Conclusions by No Means Calculated for the Circumstances and Condition of *Ireland*': Swift, Berkeley and the Solution to Ireland's Economic Problems," in *Locating Swift*, ed. Douglas, Kelly, and Ross, 47–59.

Kiberd, Declan, *Irish Classics*. London: Granta, 2000, chs. 6 & 7 (71–106).

Mahony, Robert, "The Irish Colonial Experience and Swift's Rhetorics of Perception in the 1720s," *Eighteenth-Century Life* 22.1 (1998): 63–75.

———, "Protestant Dependence and Consumption in Swift's Irish Writings," in *Political Ideas in Eighteenth-Century Ireland*, ed. S. J. Connolly. Dublin: Four Courts Press, 2000, 83–104.

———, "Swift, Postcolonialism and Irish Studies," in *Representations of Swift*, ed. Connery, 219–35.

McHugh, Roger, "The Woven Figure: Swift's Irish Context," *University Review* (Dublin) 4.1 (Spring 1967): 35–52.

McMinn, Joseph, "A Weary Patriot: Jonathan Swift and the Formation of an Anglo-Irish Identity," *Eighteenth-Century Ireland* 2 (1987): 103–13.

Moore, Sean, "Devouring Posterity: 'A Modest Proposal,' Empire, and the 'Debt of the Nation,'" *PMLA* 122 (2007): 679–95.

_____, "'Our Irish Copper-Farthen Dean': Swift's 'Drapier's Letters,' the Forging of a Modernist Anglo-Irish Literature, and the Atlantic World of Paper Credit," *Atlantic Studies* 2.1 (April 2005): 65–91.

Nolan, Emer, "Swift: The Patriot Game," *British Journal for Eighteenth-Century Studies* 21 (1998): 39–53.

Rawson, Claude, *God, Gulliver, and Genocide: Barbarism and the European Imagination, 1492–1945.* London: Oxford University Press, 2001, esp. pp. 183–255.

_____, "The Injured Lady and the Drapier: A Reading of Swift's Irish Tracts," *Prose Studies* 3 (1980): 15–43.

——, "A Reading of *A Modest Proposal*," in *Augustan Worlds: Essays in Honour of A. R. Humphreys*, ed. J.C. Hilson, M.M.B. Jones, and J.R. Watson. Leicester: Leicester University Press, 1978, 29–50.

Reilly, Patrick, "The Displaced Person: Swift and Ireland," *Swift Studies* 8 (1993): 68–83.

Reilly, Susan P., "'A Soil so Unhappily Cultivated': Balnibarbi and Swift's Georgic Vision of Ireland," *Swift Studies* 16 (2001): 114–26.

Ross, Angus, "The Hibernian Patriot's Apprenticeship," in *The Art of Jonathan Swift*, ed. Clive T. Probyn. London: Vision Press, 1978, 83–107.

Torchiana, Donald T., "Jonathan Swift, the Irish and the Yahoos: The Case Reconsidered," *Philological Quarterly* 54 (1975): 195–212.

Treadwell, J.M., "Swift, William Wood, and the Factual Basis of Satire," *Journal of British Studies* 15 (1976): 76–91.

Zach, Wolfgang, "Jonathan Swift and Colonialism," in *Reading Swift: Papers from the Second Münster Symposium on Jonathan Swift*, ed. Rodino and Real, 91–99.